Recent Advances in Computer-Assisted Learning

Recent Advances in Computer-Assisted Learning

Guest Editor

Ananda Maiti

MDPI

Basel • Beijing • Wuhan • Barcelona • Belgrade • Novi Sad • Cluj • Manchester

Guest Editor
Ananda Maiti
School of Information Technology
Deakin University
Waurn Ponds
Australia

Editorial Office
MDPI AG
Grosspeteranlage 5
4052 Basel, Switzerland

This is a reprint of the Special Issue, published open access by the journal *Computers* (ISSN 2073-431X), freely accessible at: https://www.mdpi.com/journal/computers/special_issues/MP33I5WBP3.

For citation purposes, cite each article independently as indicated on the article page online and as indicated below:

Lastname, A.A.; Lastname, B.B. Article Title. *Journal Name* **Year**, *Volume Number*, Page Range.

ISBN 978-3-7258-7254-1 (Hbk)
ISBN 978-3-7258-7255-8 (PDF)
https://doi.org/10.3390/books978-3-7258-7255-8

Contents

About the Editor

Ananda Maiti

Ananda Maiti obtained his PhD from the School of Engineering at the University of Southern Queensland in 2016. He was a Lecturer at the School of ICT, University of Tasmania, Launceston from 2019 to 2024. He is currently a Lecturer at the School of IT, Deakin University, Waurn Ponds, Australia. His current research interests include the Internet-of-Things and Embedded Systems; Cloud Computing; and AI tools, such as Large Language Models, and their various applications, such as agriculture, regulatory technologies, supply chains, and environmental monitoring.

Preface

This Reprint brings together a curated selection of recent scientific studies that reflect the changing landscape of educational technology. Its subject is the transformation of teaching and learning through artificial intelligence; immersive and game-based pedagogies; and digital platforms that support large-scale, collaborative, and sustainable education. The scope of this Reprint spans higher education, school education, and lifelong learning and includes both conceptual and empirical work that addresses learning design, assessment, learner engagement, platform architecture, and the evolving role of educators in technology-rich environments.

The aim of this collection is to provide a coherent view of how educational technology is moving from isolated digital tools toward integrated learning ecosystems. Rather than treating technology as a simple delivery mechanism, the studies collected here examine how intelligent systems, immersive environments, and smart platforms reshape how learning is designed, experienced, and evaluated. The purpose is not to promote technology for its own sake but to explore how digital innovation can support meaningful learning, the responsible use of data, and sustainable educational practice.

The motivation for preparing this Reprint comes from the rapid pace of change in both technology and education. Developments in artificial intelligence, generative systems, virtual and augmented reality, and cloud platforms are advancing faster than educational institutions can easily adapt. This has created a need for carefully selected, peer-reviewed research that helps educators, researchers, and policymakers understand not only what is technically possible but also what is pedagogically sound, ethically responsible, and socially valuable.

This edition is addressed to researchers in educational technology, learning sciences, and computer science, as well as to educators, instructional designers, school leaders, and policy makers who are engaged in shaping the future of education. It is also intended for postgraduate students and early-career researchers seeking a structured entry point into current debates on AI in learning, immersive pedagogy, and smart education systems. By bringing these works together, this Reprint aims to support informed discussion, critical reflection, and future research on how technology can genuinely enhance education.

Ananda Maiti
Guest Editor

computers

MDPI

Editorial

Editorial: Recent Advances in Computer-Assisted Learning †

Ananda Maiti

School of IT, Deakin University, Waurn Ponds, Geelong, VIC 3216, Australia; anandamaiti@ieee.org

† This Editorial is for the special issue: "Recent Advances in Computer-Assisted Learning (1st Edition)." Link to the Special Issue: https://www.mdpi.com/journal/computers/special_issues/MP33I5WBP3.

1. Introduction

Educational Technology (EdTech) is undergoing a profound transformation through three converging forces: the rapid maturation of artificial intelligence, the rise in immersive and game-based learning environments, and the large-scale phantomization of education through cloud computing, smart systems, and sustainable digital infrastructures. EdTech is no longer limited to digitizing textbooks or delivering content online; it increasingly seeks to personalize learning, anticipate learner needs, support educators with intelligent tools, and design engaging environments that address motivational and cognitive challenges. This shift reflects a broader move from treating technology as an add-on to pedagogy toward treating it as an integral component of how learning is designed, experienced, assessed, and governed.

Across contemporary research, three dominant themes stand out. First, AI and machine learning are being used to analyze learner behavior, automate feedback, generate learning content, and support decision-making. Second, game-based and immersive pedagogies aim to address declining engagement by embedding learning in interactive, experiential, and motivational environments. Third, education is increasingly organized around platforms and smart systems that integrate collaboration, mentoring, scalability, and sustainability. Together, these trends suggest that EdTech is evolving into an ecosystem of intelligent, immersive, and scalable learning infrastructures rather than isolated digital tools.

2. AI/ML in Learning

Artificial intelligence has become the most transformative force in contemporary EdTech, particularly in learning analytics, intelligent tutoring, automated assessment, and generative systems. One major strand of AI focuses on predicting learning outcomes and supporting early intervention. Contribution 1, by Canale et al., demonstrates that machine learning models trained on version control system data can predict student exam performance well before the end of a course, while also emphasizing the importance of explainable AI to enable teachers to understand and trust predictions. Similarly, Contribution 2, by Psathas et al., uses classic machine learning models to predict dropout in MOOCs, showing that behavioral traces combined with self-reported self-regulated learning data provide strong early indicators of risk. These studies position AI as an early warning and decision-support system for educators rather than as a replacement for pedagogical judgment.

Another major area is intelligent tutoring and conversational agents. Contribution 3, by Pérez-Marín et al., explores the use of pedagogic conversational agents designed to teach programming to children and shows that involving pre-service teachers in co-design significantly increases acceptance and classroom integration. This work highlights that technological sophistication alone is insufficient; social and professional acceptance by educators is critical for real impact. Therefore, conversational agents not only emerge as technical systems, but also as socio-technical artifacts that must align with teacher identity and practice.

Automated assessment is another rapidly growing domain. Contribution 4, by Nakamoto et al., addresses the problem of scoring mathematical self-explanations and proposes a semi-supervised approach that uses large language models to generate synthetic training data. Their results show that carefully integrated LLM-generated data can significantly improve scoring accuracy, although excessive synthetic data can degrade performance. This work illustrates how generative AI can act as a data amplifier in educational contexts where high-quality labeled data is scarce.

Generative AI has also become a subject of critical reflection in its own right. Contribution 5, by Montenegro-Rueda et al., conducted a systematic review of the existing research on the use of ChatGPT in education, showing its overall positive impacts on personalization, feedback, writing support, and collaboration, but also identifying major challenges such as a lack of teacher training, ethical risks, hallucinations, and misuse. Their analysis reveals three major research clusters: the changing role of teachers, the impact of chatbots on students, and the socio-technical context of adoption. This not only positions generative AI as a technical innovation, but also as a force that can reshape educational roles, assessment practices, and academic integrity.

AI also has relevance at the infrastructure level. Contribution 6, by Govea et al., shows that integrating AI with cloud computing significantly improves scalability, reduces administrative errors, and enables personalized content delivery in educational platforms. This demonstrates that AI is not only being increasingly embedded in learning activities, but also in the operational backbone of education.

Together, these studies portray the use of AI/ML in learning as moving from experimentation toward systemic integration. AI supports prediction, feedback, content generation, assessment, and platform management. However, across these works, a consistent message emerges: the success of AI in education depends less on algorithmic sophistication than on transparency, teacher training, ethical governance, and thoughtful pedagogical integration.

3. Game-Based and Immersive Pedagogy

Parallel to the rise of AI is a strong focus on engagement, motivation, and experiential learning through games and immersive technologies. Contribution 7, by Nadeem et al., shows that digital game-based learning significantly improves student engagement and motivation compared to traditional online activities, although features such as leaderboards can motivate some students while demotivating others. This highlights that gamification is not universally beneficial; its effects are mediated by learner differences and design choices.

Contribution 8, by Karavidas et al., directly compared the use of serious games for self-assessment in web technologies with the use of online quizzes, finding that while serious games increase engagement and the number of questions attempted, they do not necessarily improve learning outcomes compared to quizzes. This challenges the assumption that more engaging formats automatically yield better learning outcomes and underscores the need to carefully align game mechanics with learning objectives.

Immersive technologies extend this engagement agenda further. Contribution 9, by Esteves et al., provides a systematic review of immersive virtual reality applications for English learning, identifying several categories of design recommendations related to learning, interaction, and sensory experience. Their work shows that immersion and presence can

https://doi.org/10.3390/computers15020080

support vocabulary retention, motivation, and contextual learning, but their effectiveness depend heavily on the quality of the designs and their alignment with pedagogical goals.

These game-based and immersive approaches also intersect with other EdTech domains. Contribution 5, by Montenegro-Rueda et al., notes that ChatGPT and similar tools are sometimes used to support creative, interactive, and collaborative activities that can be integrated into game-like learning designs. Likewise, the use of immersive VR for language learning often incorporates gamified elements such as exploration, tasks, and narrative progression, as shown in Contribution 9.

Across these studies, game-based and immersive pedagogy emerges less as a single method and more as a design philosophy focused on experience, motivation, and participation. However, evidence also shows that engagement alone is insufficient. Effective learning requires careful alignment between game mechanics, immersive features, and cognitive learning goals. The challenge for EdTech is therefore not simply to make learning fun, but to make engagement pedagogically meaningful.

4. Education Platforms and Smart Systems

The third major theme concerns the infrastructure that supports learning: platforms, smart environments, and sustainable systems. Contribution 10, by Nguyen et al., proposes a smart education system that integrates collaborative learning and e-mentoring and demonstrates, through empirical evaluation, that such systems can support diverse learners by combining peer interaction with professional guidance. Their model frames smart education around three elements—smart learners, smart pedagogy, and smart environments—with technology acting as an enabler of flexible learning pathways.

Govea et al.'s work on AI and cloud computing demonstrates how platforms can scale to large user bases while maintaining personalization and reducing administrative burden, as shown in Contribution 6. This reflects a broader shift toward platform-based education in which learning is delivered through integrated ecosystems rather than isolated tools.

Sustainability is also becoming a central concern. Contribution 11, by Mikroyannidis et al., describes the OpenLang Network, a sustainable online platform for language learning across Europe that combines open educational resources, community participation, and long-term governance strategies. Their evaluation shows that sustainability is not only technical, but also social, and depends on openness, community engagement, and institutional support.

In addition, AI intersects with platform design. Predictive analytics from Canale et al. and Psathas et al. in Contribution 1 and 2 can be embedded in platforms to monitor progress and flag risks. Generative tools such as ChatGPT are increasingly being integrated into platforms as learning companions or content generators, as discussed by Montenegro-Rueda et al. in Contribution 5. Thus, platforms are becoming intelligent environments that combine analytics, interaction, automation, and collaboration.

These studies show that the future of EdTech is not just about better tools, but also about better systems: scalable, intelligent, collaborative, and sustainable environments that support diverse learners and long-term educational goals.

5. Conclusions: Toward Intelligent, Immersive, and Scalable Education

Taken together, the eleven papers in this Special Issue depict EdTech as a field moving rapidly toward integrated learning ecosystems. AI and machine learning are reshaping assessment, feedback, prediction, and content generation. Game-based and immersive pedagogies address engagement and experience, but require careful pedagogical design. Platforms and smart systems provide the infrastructure that enables large-scale, personalized, and sustainable education.

https://doi.org/10.3390/computers15020080

Across all themes, a common thread emerges: technology alone does not improve education. Impact depends on design quality, teacher training, ethical governance, and alignment with pedagogy. Whether through AI models predicting dropout, VR environments teaching languages, serious games assessing knowledge, or smart platforms supporting collaboration, the future of EdTech lies in the thoughtful integration of intelligence, immersion, and infrastructure. This Special Issue not only maps the current practices, but also the conceptual foundations for the next generation of educational systems—systems that are adaptive, engaging, and socially responsible.

Funding: This research received no external funding.

Conflicts of Interest: The author declares no conflicts of interest.

List of Contributions:

1. Canale, L.; Cagliero, L.; Farinetti, L.; Torchiano, M. On Predicting Exam Performance Using Version Control Systems' Features. *Computers* **2024**, *13*, 150. https://doi.org/10.3390/computers13060150.
2. Psathas, G.; Chatzidaki, T.K.; Demetriadis, S.N. Predictive Modeling of Student Dropout in MOOCs and Self-Regulated Learning. *Computers* **2023**, *12*, 194. https://doi.org/10.3390/computers12100194.
3. Pérez-Marín, D.; Hijón-Neira, R.; Pizarro, C. A First Approach to Co-Design a Multimodal Pedagogic Conversational Agent with Pre-Service Teachers to Teach Programming in Primary Education. *Computers* **2024**, *13*, 65. https://doi.org/10.3390/computers13030065.
4. Nakamoto, R.; Flanagan, B.; Yamauchi, T.; Dai, Y.; Takami, K.; Ogata, H. Enhancing Automated Scoring of Math Self-Explanation Quality Using LLM-Generated Datasets: A Semi-Supervised Approach. *Computers* **2023**, *12*, 217. https://doi.org/10.3390/computers12110217.
5. Montenegro-Rueda, M.; Fernández-Cerero, J.; Fernández-Batanero, J.M.; López-Meneses, E. Impact of the Implementation of ChatGPT in Education: A Systematic Review. *Computers* **2023**, *12*, 153. https://doi.org/10.3390/computers12080153.
6. Govea, J.; Ocampo Edye, E.; Revelo-Tapia, S.; Villegas-Ch, W. Optimization and Scalability of Educational Platforms: Integration of Artificial Intelligence and Cloud Computing. *Computers* **2023**, *12*, 223. https://doi.org/10.3390/computers12110223.
7. Nadeem, M.; Oroszlanyova, M.; Farag, W. Effect of Digital Game-Based Learning on Student Engagement and Motivation. *Computers* **2023**, *12*, 177. https://doi.org/10.3390/computers12090177.
8. Karavidas, L.; Skraparli, G.; Tsiatsos, T. A Comparison between Online Quizzes and Serious Games: The Case of Friend Me. *Computers* **2024**, *13*, 58. https://doi.org/10.3390/computers13030058.
9. Esteves, J.R.; Cardoso, J.C.S.; Gonçalves, B.S. Design Recommendations for Immersive Virtual Reality Application for English Learning: A Systematic Review. *Computers* **2023**, *12*, 236.https://doi.org/10.3390/computers12110236.
10. Nguyen, L.; Tomy, S.; Pardede, E. Enhancing Collaborative Learning and E-Mentoring in a Smart Education System in Higher Education. *Computers* **2024**, *13*, 28. https://doi.org/10.3390/computers13010028.
11. Mikroyannidis, A.; Perifanou, M.; Economides, A.A. Developing a Sustainable Online Platform for Language Learning across Europe. *Computers* **2023**, *12*, 140. https://doi.org/10.3390/computers12070140.

https://doi.org/10.3390/computers15020080

computers

MDPI

Article

On Predicting Exam Performance Using Version Control Systems' Features

Lorenzo Canale [1,2,†], Luca Cagliero [1,*,†], Laura Farinetti [1,†] and Marco Torchiano [1,†]

1 Dipartimento di Automatica e Informatica, Politecnico di Torino, Corso Duca degli Abruzzi, 24, 10129 Torino, Italy; laura.farinetti@polito.it (L.F.)
2 Centre for Research and Technological Innovation, Radiotelevisione Italiana (RAI), Via Giovanni Carlo Cavalli 6, 10129 Torino, Italy
* Correspondence: luca.cagliero@polito.it; Tel.: +39-011-090-7179
† These authors contributed equally to this work.

Abstract: The advent of Version Control Systems (VCS) in computer science education has significantly improved the learning experience. The Learning Analytics community has started to analyze the interactions between students and VCSs to evaluate the behavioral and cognitive aspects of the learning process. Within the aforesaid scope, a promising research direction is the use of Artificial Intelligence (AI) to predict students' exam outcomes early based on VCS usage data. Previous AI-based solutions have two main drawbacks: (i) They rely on static models, which disregard temporal changes in the student–VCS interactions. (ii) AI reasoning is not transparent to end-users. This paper proposes a time-dependent approach to early predict student performance from VCS data. It applies and compares different classification models trained at various course stages. To gain insights into exam performance predictions it combines classification with explainable AI techniques. It visualizes the explanations of the time-varying performance predictors. The results of a real case study show that the effect of VCS-based features on the exam success rate is relevant much earlier than the end of the course, whereas the timely submission of the first lab assignment is a reliable predictor of the exam grade.

Keywords: version control systems; machine learning; explainable AI; learning analytics

1. Introduction

Version control systems (VCS) are tools aimed at helping teams of software developers to manage code changes. In computer science education, the use of VCSs is established. For example, the GitHub collaborative platform has shown to enhance the learning experience under multiple aspects [1]. In university-level computer science courses, VCSs have gained importance as collaboration platforms in the development of application software projects: they not only support the learning and evaluation processes but also foster students' participation and ease the collaboration between team members [2,3].

Statistical analyses of the interactions between students and VCSs have shown that VCS-based data are effective in characterizing the relationship between the utilization of VCSs and the exam grades. In this regard, various VCS-based features have already been considered, e.g., the selection proposed by [4]. They incorporate information relevant to both behavioral and cognitive engagement levels of the student [5].

This paper analyzes the activities of the students of a university-level Object-Oriented Programming course by monitoring their interactions with a VCS. The purpose is to predict various exam performance indicators early such as the exam success rate, the exam grade, the lab dropout rate (when a student stops attending the laboratory activities from a certain point on), and the number of exam attempts prior to passing the exam. The purpose is to allow timely interventions focused on at-risk situations [6].

Previous works on early prediction of students' performance based on VCS usage data presented by [7,8] have two main drawbacks:

- *Time invariance.* Existing ML models are commonly trained once on the complete set of VCS usage statistics. However, since VCS data are time-evolving, there is a need for time-dependent model analyses and comparisons to allow early prediction of the students' exam performance well before the end of the course.
- *Limited explainability.* AI often produces non-transparent outcomes, which cannot be explained to the teacher. This can lead to trust issues when predictions fail. To overcome this issue, there is a need to involve human experts in the decision-making process.

To address the aforesaid challenges, the present work presents the following contributions.

- *Time-dependent ML model training.* Computer science courses typically entail a sequence of assignments and tests. VCSs continuously trace students' activities on log files throughout the course. The VCS usage data collected in the first part of the course is likely to be correlated with the students' performance. Hence, we investigate the suitability of intermediate VCS usage data to perform early student performance prediction. To this end, we re-train the classifiers on the available statistics to dynamically update the predictive models depending on the availability of up-to-date information.
- *Visual classifier explanation.* We compare the classification models by exploiting a state-of-the-art explainable AI method, namely Shapley Additive explanations (SHAP) [9]. SHAP provides teachers with a visual interpretation of the time-dependent impact of the VCS-based feature values taken by a student on the exam performance predictions.

We carried out an empirical analysis of the presented methodology on real VCS usage data collected during an Object-Oriented Programming course. The main results are summarized below:

- *Predictive power of early VCS-based models.* The VCS usage patterns identified at the very preliminary course stages are, to a good approximation, accurate predictors of the students' exam performance.
- *Negative impact of lab dropout.* The dropout of a student from the course laboratories can be detected by monitoring the VCS commits. The attendance of laboratory activities has shown to be highly discriminating of both exam success rate and grade. Stopping laboratory attendance in the first part of the course has shown to negatively affect exam performance.
- *Positive impact of exam attempt.* The a priori knowledge of the outcomes of past exam sessions has shown to enhance the quality of classifier predictions provided that VCS-based features are considered in the ML model as well.
- *Correlation between exam grades and laboratory attendance.* To obtain high grades, students usually need to attend most of the course laboratories. The attendance to the laboratories at the beginning of the course has shown to be not sufficient to achieve high grades.

The source code of our methodology is available at https://github.com/Loricanal/VESPE (accessed on 1 June 2024). The source data are available for research purposes upon request to the authors.

A paper outline follows. Section 2 provides a literature review. Section 3 introduces the research context. Section 4 presents the proposed architecture. Section 5 discusses the main results. Finally, Section 6 concludes the work and discusses the future research agenda.

2. Literature Review

The learning analytics community has already explored the use of Version Control Systems in education. For example, Refs. [2,3] studied the role of GitHub (https://github.com/ (latest access: 1 May 2024)) as a collaborative resource in large software engineering classes. Thanks to the functionalities provided by the VCS, the majority of the learners have shown to actively contribute to the project through code changes, reviews, and comments. Refs. [10,11] studied the learners' adherence to the iterative software development model as well as the extent to which students interact with each other even in the absence of specific commitments. They show the benefits of using VCSs for individual learning activities.

The correlation between the utilization of VCSs and the exam grades was studied by [4,7,12,13]. They carried out statistical analyses to verify the dependence between a selection of VCS-based features and learners' outcomes. For example, the number and frequency of GitHub commits have shown to be correlated with the exam outcomes.

Parallel attempts to use Machine Learning techniques on top of VCS-based features have been made. For example, Refs. [8,14–16] extracted from the VCS log files a subset of features summarizing the most relevant students' interactions with VCS, collected them into a training dataset, and trained a classification model. The classifier is exploited to predict students' performance. The main limitations of the existing ML-based solutions are (i) the time-invariance of the trained models, which disregard the temporal evolution of the learner's interactions with the VCS, and (ii) the limited interpretability of the trained models, which hinders an in-depth analysis of the ML reasoning.

Position of the present work. We address the limitations of the previous works as follows: (i) We study how the impact of VCS-based features on ML model performance changes over time as a result of the temporal changes in the student–VCS interactions. (ii) We generate visual explanations of the classifiers using an established explainable AI method [9]. The provided visualizations allow for a detailed comparison between the models trained at different course stages.

3. Context of Research

The research presented in this paper draws its data from an object-oriented (OOP) programming course in the second year of the Computer Engineering B.Sc. degree. held every year in spring. The course consists of 70 taught hours and 20 h of laboratory activities devoted to the development of programming assignments. The language of choice for the course is Java (currently, version 8 is used). While previous programming courses in the curriculum adopted paper-based exams, in this one, the teachers opted for a computer-based exam to improve students' practice. All the exercises and submissions are conducted in the laboratory under the teacher's supervision.

Laboratory practices are meant to develop software testing and software configuration skills in compliance with SWECOM 1.0 [17]. Moreover, automated testing appears particularly suited to respond to the Millennials' need for frequent feedback [18]. The tests are performed using the JUnit 5 automated testing framework. Test cases are written as methods within Java classes. Such methods include statements that exercise the code under tests and assertions that check the actual return values vs. the expected ones. The JUnit framework executes all test cases, and for each one, it collects the outcome, i.e., Success (correct execution and all assertions verified), Failure (correct execution but at least one assertion not verified), or Error (incorrect execution). A detailed description of the key practices used in laboratory is given in [19].

4. The Presented Methodology

We present here the Visual Explainable Student performance PrEdictor (VESPE), a machine learning-based method aimed at predicting students' exam performance based on VCS-based features. VESPE allows end-users to apply ML models trained at different course stages and compare them by exploiting ad hoc visual explanations. VESPE end-users are teachers/educators, mainly from the Computer Science area because a minimum level of data and computational literacy are required.

VESPE supports the integration of an arbitrary set of student-related features. They include both time-dependent VCS-based features (e.g., the number of commits) and time-invariant ones (e.g., year of enrollment). Furthermore, it integrates a variety of prediction targets related to the students' exam performance (e.g., exam success, exam grade). Our purpose is to study the impact of VCS-based features on exam performance. Hence, hereafter we will disregard the time-invariant features as their analysis is out of the scope of the present work.

Figure 1 shows the architecture of the proposed methodology where the end-user can feed VCS data, specify prediction targets and related options and then the system produces the time-varying predictions and visualizes the model explanations. A more detailed description of each block follows.

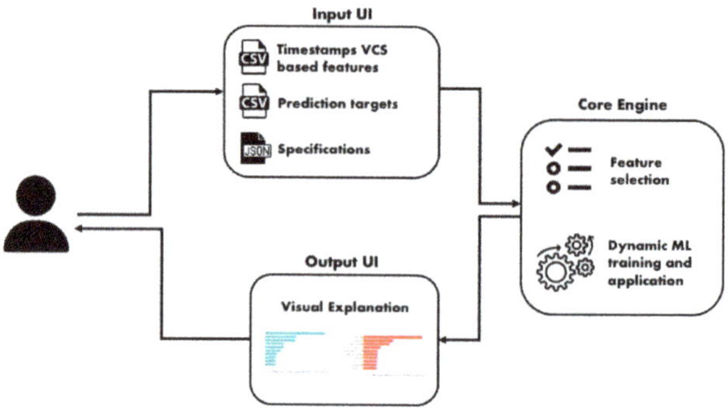

Figure 1. The VESPE architecture.

4.1. Input UI

4.1.1. VCS Usage Data

The input VCS usage data are stored in a relational dataset [20]. Each record corresponds to a different student whereas each attribute is associated with a distinct feature. Analogously, the target dataset stores the values of the target classes for each student in separate attributes. Hence, the target of the prediction could be dynamically set up according to the end-user goals.

4.1.2. Feature Engineering

We focus on the activities carried out by the students on the VCS and related to the course laboratories. The considered features and the corresponding categorizations are reported in Tables 1 and 2. They include both VCS-based feature categories considered in the previous works and newly proposed ones. Specifically, the features related to assignment submissions and commits have already been considered in past research studies. For instance, Ref. [8] carried out an in-depth feature analysis. Conversely, to the best of our knowledge, categories Lab dropout and Exam attempts are new. A complementary goal of our research work is to understand whether the newly proposed VCS-based feature categories are correlated with students' exam performance.

Lab dropout indicates whether a student stops attending the laboratory (Dropout N indicates that the student stopped attending the course after the N-th laboratory). It is an indicator of students' engagement level and, in particular, it is related to both persistence and completion. Notice that stopping lab attendance does not necessarily imply course dropout [21].

Exam attempts indicate the number of exam attempts made by a student. We recall that a student could attend the official exam of a course up to four times per year. Repeated exam attempts can be due to either exam failures or to the rejection of the exam grade.

Table 1. Description of the VCS features extracted from [22].

Feature	Description
Commit numbers ($D = 6$)	
CommitCount#Lab {1,2,3,4,5}	Number of commits for each lab
CommitCount#Total	Total number of commits
Commit quality ($D = 18$)	
Passed#Lab{1,2,3,4,5}	Number of tests passed for each lab
Passed#Total	Total number of passed test
Error#Lab{1,2,3,4,5}	Number of tests that raised errors for each lab
Error#Total	Total number of tests that raised errors
Failed#Lab{1,2,3,4,5}	Number of tests failed for each lab
Failed#Total	Total number of failed tests
Commit frequency ($D = 6$)	
CommitsPerDay#Lab{1,2,3,4,5}	Average number of commits per day for each lab
CommitsPerDay#Total	Average number of commits per day
Active days ($D = 6$)	
ActiveDays#Lab{1,2,3,4,5}	Number of days in which at least 1 commit was carried out for each lab
ActiveDays#Total	Total number of days in which at least 1 commit was carried out
Submitted labs ($D = 6$)	
Done#Lab{1,2,3,4,5}	Lab were submitted or not
DoneLab#Total	Total number of submitted lab
Dropout ($D = 4$)	
Dropout#Lab{2,3,4,5}	Dropout#LabN: the student submitted labs 1 … N − 1

Table 2. Description of Exam attempts features extracted from [22].

Feature	Description
PreviousAttempt	The feature indicates whether the examination was already attempted by the student in the first session; it takes the value 1 if it was attempted (regardless of the outcome) and takes the value 0 if it was not attempted.
PreviousAttemptPass	The feature indicates whether the examination had already been attempted by the student in the first session and passed (0 if it was not attempted or failed, 1 if it was attempted and passed). In practice, this indicates the students who refused the grade.
PreviousAttemptFail	The feature indicates whether the examination had already been attempted by the student in the first session and failed (0 if not attempted or attempted and passed, 1 if attempted and failed).

4.1.3. Model Training

We train multiple ML models at different time points. Specifically, we train a separate model after each laboratory session (which requires tight student–VCS interactions). Notice that the available feature set changes over time because the values of some of the VCS-based features in Tables 1 and 2 are missing or need updates.

The data used to train the ML algorithms at time t_n contains only the features f_x whose time stamp $t_x \leq t_n$. For instance, let us suppose that lab 1 and lab 2 terminated at times t_1 and t_2, respectively. Then, at time t_x $[t_1 \geq t_x \geq t_2]$, ML training can be run on a dataset describing the activities carried out in lab 1, whereas the features related to lab 2 are not available.

In the performed experiments we considered as reference time stamps $t_1, t_2, \ldots, t_n$ the end of each lab of the course. Hence, at the end of an arbitrary lab x, we re-train the ML model by using only the features describing the labs from 1 to x.

4.1.4. Prediction Targets

A student who passes the exam receives a grade. Grades are discretized into bins as follows: grade A is a fairly high grade, grade B accounts for students who obtained an intermediate grade, whereas grade C is relative to the students who passed the exam but with a low grade.

According to the exam statistics, almost all students passed the exam. Students who received a high grade (A) are quite numerous in the first two exam session attempts, whereas getting high grades was less likely in Exams 3 and 4. For the latter exam sessions, the number of students giving the exam is too small to have enough data samples to make accurate predictions.

According to the aforesaid statistics, in our experiments we will focus on a subset of prediction targets for which a sufficiently large set of training samples is available:

Specifically, target Success takes values (1) Pass if the student passed the exam, (2) Fail if the student fails all the attempts, or (3) Dropout if the student performs a course dropout. Similarly, targets Success Exam 1 and Success Exam 2, respectively, indicate whether the student passed the exam at the first/second call or not. Target Grade indicates the exam grade A, B, or C (valid only for the students who passed the exam).

4.1.5. Configuration Settings

The system allows end-users to specify the desired configuration settings. The specifications include: (i) a *target type*, which discriminates between different ML model types (i.e., regression for continuous targets, classification for binary/categorical ones); (ii) a *feature categorization*, which partitions the feature set in the VCS usage dataset into homogeneous groups according to their semantic meaning; (iii) a *timeline*, which indicates for each feature the time stamp at which it takes value in the dataset records; and (iv) the algorithm parameters.

4.2. Feature Selection

The VCS-based features are automatically evaluated and filtered prior to ML training according to their correlation with the selected target.

VESPE integrates a variety of feature selection algorithms available in the the Scikit-Learn library [23], including (i) the unsupervised methods based on the Pearson's correlation (Prs) and Spearman's rank coefficient (Spr) and (ii) the supervised approaches based on statistical methods, i.e., ANOVA correlation coefficient (Anv), Chi-Squared (Chi^2), Mutual Information (MI), and recursive feature elimination, i.e., RFE, RFECV.

4.3. Classification Algorithms

We train classification models representative of various families of algorithms such as ensemble methods, decision tree classifiers, SVM classifiers, and Bayesian models. VESPE integrates the implementations provided by the Scikit-Learn library [23]. A detailed descriptions of the VESPE architecture is given in [22].

4.4. Model Explanation

VESPE adopts the SHAP library to visualize the global explanations [9]. The graphical interface allows end-users to quickly access a summarized view of results. A detailed description of the interface can be found in [22].

5. Experimental Results

All experiments were run on a machine with 1.8 GHz Intel® (Santa Clara, CA, USA) Core® i5, 8 GB of RAM and running macOS High Sierra. We aim to explore the following research directions:

1. Estimate when the exam success rate becomes predictable and identify the most discriminating VCS-based features.
2. Assess the predictability of class dropouts.
3. Analyze the impact of laboratory attendance on exam grades.
4. Study the correlation between exam success and previous exam attempts.

5.1. Evaluation Metrics

We evaluate the performance of the classification algorithms using the standard precision, recall, and F1-Score metrics [20]. Since we are mainly interested in evaluating classifiers' performance on the minority classes (e.g., course dropouts or exam failures), we also consider the Balanced Accuracy, defined by the percentage of correctly classified students weighted by per-class frequencies [24].

5.2. When Does the Exam Success Rate Become Predictable?

Figure 2 shows the variation in the performance metrics over time. Notably, the quality of the predictions is fairly high even at the early course stages. This indicates that the attendance to the first laboratories is already discriminating for predicting exam success.

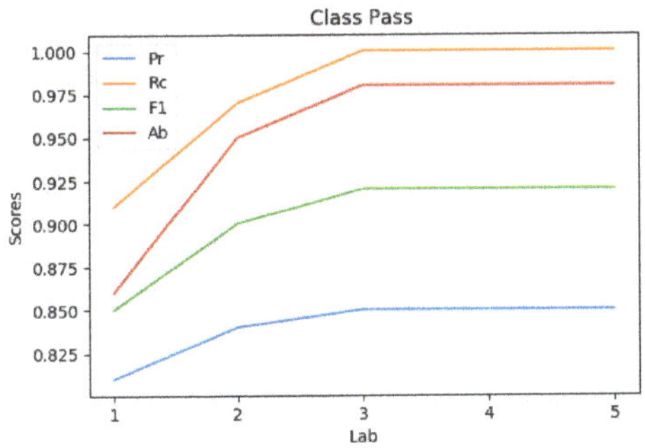

Figure 2. Time dependence of the early predictions for class Pass.

Figure 3 graphically shows the contribution of each Lab feature to the classifier predictions. Feature Done#Lab1 turns out to be the most discriminating one. It indicates that students who attended the first laboratory are likely pass the exam (see Figure 3a). Similar results hold for the target Success Exam 1 (see Figure 3b).

The second most important feature is Done#Lab2, indicating that the attendance to the second laboratory is beneficial as well. Dropout#Lab2 has also an important role. The reason is that Dropout#Lab2 is implicitly related to the student participation in Lab1, which appeared to be the most discriminating feature (Done#Lab1).

Since most of the previous findings pointed out that the first labs were the most significant and the results had shown that the prediction quality was good already after the second lab, we chose to analyze the impact of the features at this time point as well (Figure 4a). The most significant features are related to the commit quality: the higher the number of passed tests (especially in the first lab), the higher the likelihood of passing the exam. The feature types Submitted labs, Commit frequency, and Commit count still have a positive impact on the prediction.

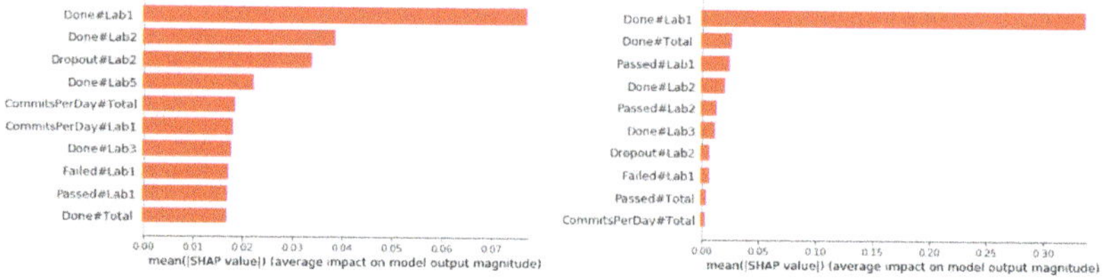

(**a**) Class Pass (**b**) Class Pass Exam 1

Figure 3. Explanations for class Pass and Pass Exam 1.

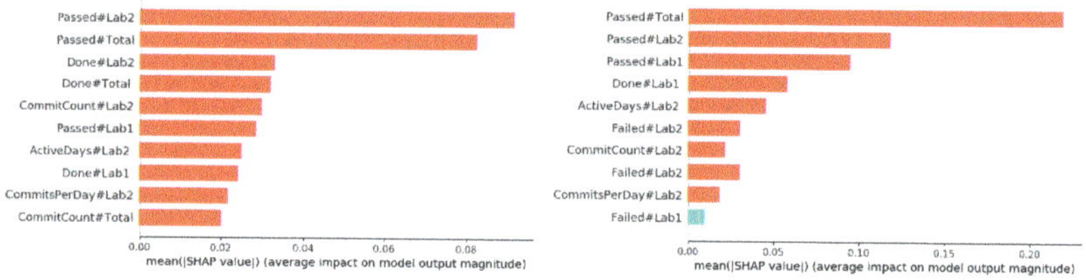

(**a**) Class Pass (**b**) Class Pass Exam 1

Figure 4. Explanations of Pass and Pass Exam 1. Models trained after the second laboratory.

We can conclude that in the instant of time after the second lab, when only features derivable from the first two labs are used, ML predictions mainly rely on the quality of the student's work. Hence, by identifying students who completed the first two labs and passed the tests, we can accurately identify the students who are likely to pass the exam. Conversely, at the end of all labs, doing the first labs remains significant but it seems also important to add activity on some of the remaining labs.

Figure 5 compares two examples of students after laboratory 2, i.e., an at-risk student and an highly engaged one. The former one submitted just the solution of the first laboratory and failed to pass several tests, whereas the latter passed most of the tests related to the first two laboratories. The teacher can early detect the risky situations and actively involve at-risk students accordingly.

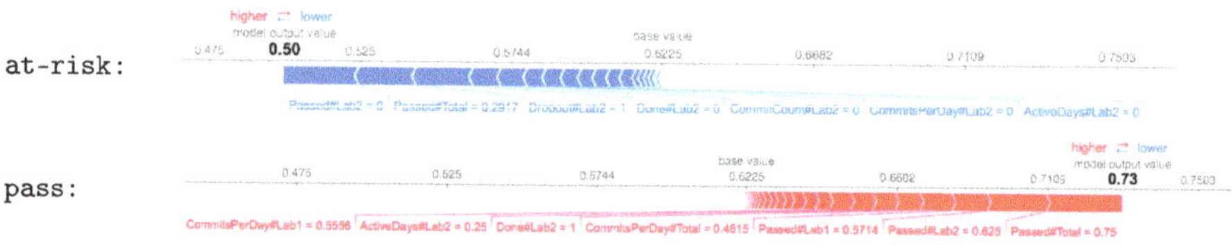

Figure 5. Force plot after lab 2 for two representative students, at-risk and pass, respectively. GNB classifier.

5.3. Predictability of Class Dropout

A Dropout student is deemed as critical because she/he has never attended any course exam. The early identification of these students is particularly useful for optimizing a critical parameter for universities, i.e., the on-time graduation rate.

Figure 6 shows that classifier performance is good well before the end of the course. It increases over time while reaching a steady state after the third course laboratory (when class dropouts become very unlikely).

Figure 7 reports the visual explanations associated with the aforesaid ML models. The main VCS-based features turned out to be negatively correlated with the classifier outcomes. A dropout at labs 2 and 3 (Dropout#Lab2, Dropout#Lab3) negatively affected the prediction. The student has completed at least one lab and it is a sufficient condition to not be marked as Dropout student in this case study. We can conclude that a student is primarily marked as a dropout when either she/he has not attended any laboratory or she/he attended only the first laboratory with little effort. Figure 8 shows an example of a student classified as Dropout because she/he did not attend the first two laboratories.

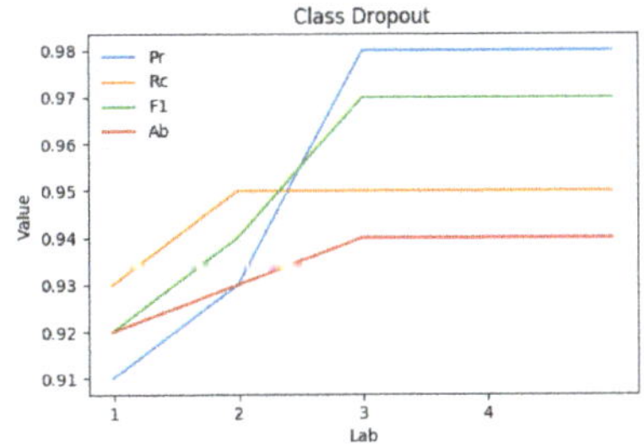

Figure 6. Early prediction of class Dropout based on incomplete feature sets (Dynamic ML). MLP classifier.

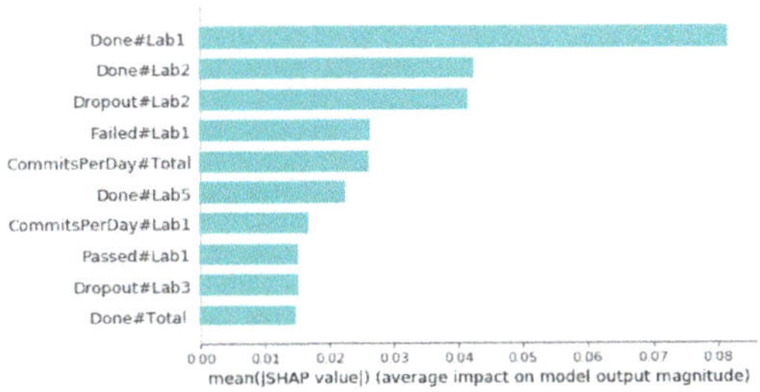

Figure 7. Summary bar plot for class Dropout. MLP classifier.

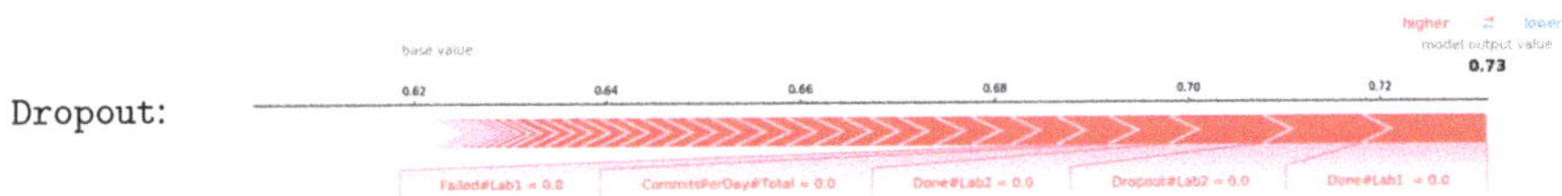

Figure 8. Force plot of a dropout student after laboratory 3. MLP classifier.

5.4. *Correlation between Exam Success and Previous Exam Attempts*

Classifier performance on classes Grade and Grade Exam 1 was fairly low (see Table 3). Unlike exam success and course dropout, VCS-based features have shown to be not very discriminating for the aforesaid targets.

Table 3. Classification performance for class Grade Exam 1.

Features	Alg.	Class Grade C				Class Grade B				Class Grade A				Avg Scores	
		Pr	Rc	F1	Ab	Pr	Rc	F1	Ab	Pr	Rc	F1	Ab	F1	Ab
Commit count	GP	1.00	0.40	0.56	0.70	0.95	0.34	0.49	0.66	0.56	0.98	0.72	0.67	0.59	0.68
Commit quality	SVM	1.00	0.42	0.59	0.71	0.74	0.54	0.59	0.69	0.62	0.86	0.72	0.71	0.63	0.70
Commit frequency	LGR	1.00	0.45	0.61	0.72	0.63	0.54	0.58	0.66	0.62	0.80	0.70	0.69	0.63	0.69
Active days	DT	0.54	0.57	0.55	0.74	0.61	0.60	0.60	0.67	0.63	0.62	0.63	0.66	0.53	0.69
Submitted labs	GP	1.00	0.50	0.66	0.75	0.75	0.35	0.47	0.63	0.57	0.91	0.70	0.67	0.61	0.68
Dropout labs	KN	0.76	0.62	0.59	0.75	0.63	0.69	0.58	0.66	0.83	0.46	0.53	0.65	0.57	0.69
Lab	MLP	0.78	0.48	0.57	0.72	0.63	0.59	0.60	0.67	0.63	0.73	0.67	0.68	0.61	0.69
Lab with feature selection	MLP	0.78	0.48	0.57	0.72	0.63	0.59	0.60	0.67	0.63	0.73	0.67	0.68	0.61	0.69

Figure 9 shows the visual explanations related to the Grade class. Grade explanations are quite diversified. Class Grade A consists of highly engaged students in terms not only of attendance (e.g., of laboratory 3) but also of notified errors (e.g., in laboratory 4). In fact, learning by doing (i.e., trial and error) is known to be beneficial for beginner programmers.

Class Grade B encompass students who either completed at least the first three laboratory or completed all the activities of the last laboratories but with a limited number of commits. Finally, class Grade C includes students who neither completed the first nor the last laboratories. Importantly, submissions to lab 5 only are not sufficient to achieve a better grade.

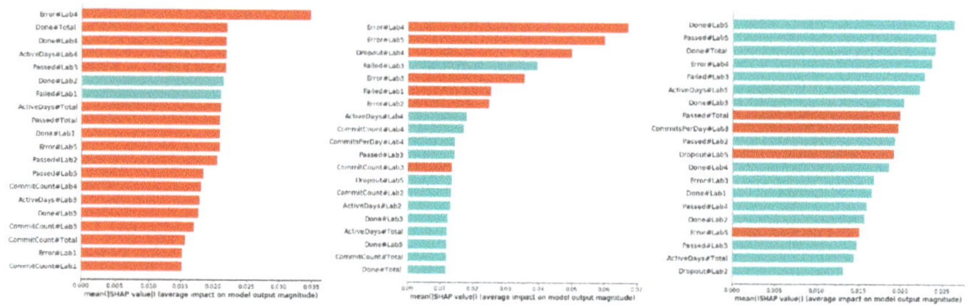

(**a**) Grade A (**b**) Grade B (**c**) Grade C

Figure 9. Explanations for class Grade. GNB classifier.

Figure 10 shows the visual explanations for the Grade Exam 1 class. Class Grade A Exam 1 is composed of students who have been active for most of the laboratories, especially those who have completed labs 1, 3, and 4 (Done#Lab1, Done#Lab3, Done#Lab4 have a positive impact); this class includes also the students who have been active for a significant number of days in labs 1 and 5 (ActiveDays#Lab1, ActiveDays#Lab5). Although Done#Lab2 is not present among the most significant features, students in this class have completed a significant activity in this lab (number of errors before the correct solution —Error#Lab1— has a positive impact, and number of failed tests —Passed#Lab2— also has a positive impact). Hence, we can conclude that having completed lab 2 is not a sufficient condition to obtain a high grade, but putting a strong effort into it is likely paying off.

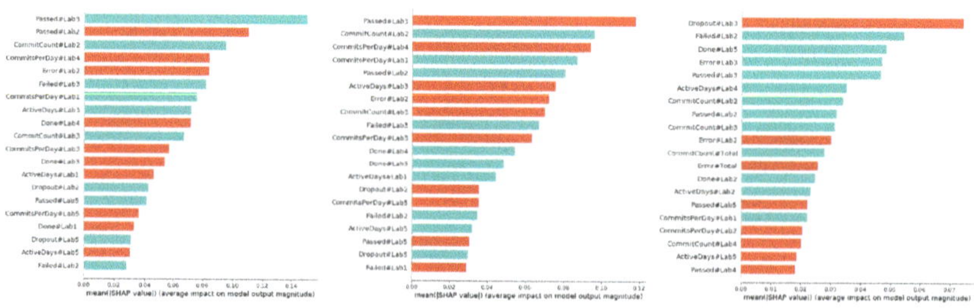

(**a**) Grade A Exam 1 (**b**) Grade B Exam 1 (**c**) Grade C Exam 1

Figure 10. Explanations for class Grade in Exam 1. MLP classifier.

The main behavioral difference between the students who belong to class Grade A Exam 1 and those who belong to class Grade B Exam 1 is that the latter puts more effort into lab 3 activities (Passed#Lab3, tActiveDays#Lab3, CommitCount#Lab3, CommitsPerDay#Lab3 has a positive impact), put less effort in lab 2 and did not do lab 4 (Done#Lab4 has a negative impact). Conversely, for class Grade A, the effort seems more constant during all labs.

Finally, the most significant feature associated with the class Grade C Exam 1 is the dropout from the third laboratory onward (Dropout-#Lab3). Coherently, the features

Done#Lab5, Error#Lab3 and Passed#Lab3 indicate that the activities carried out in the third and fifth lab have a negative impact. Students who were not or less active from the second half of the course onward were therefore classified as Grade C Exam 1.

5.5. *Correlation between Exam Success and Previous Exam Attempts*

We also study the predictability of the exam performance from the second attempt on. Exam success has shown to be not correlated with the number of previous attempts. Conversely, the combination of previous exam attempts and laboratory attendance is discriminating, confirming the significance of the previously results.

6. Conclusions and Future Works

In this work, we explored the time-dependent interactions between the students of an Object-Oriented Programming course and the Version Control Systems used to accomplish lab activities. It applied Machine Learning models on a dataset collecting various behavioral and cognitive descriptors of the students' activities in order to forecast students' performance.

According to the results, we recommend the following actions:

- To early prevent exam failures, teachers are recommended to alert the students who are not active in the first two/three laboratories.
- To prevent student dropout, teachers can encourage student attendance to the very first laboratories in order to learn the necessary fundamentals.
- Students who achieved medium or low grades are likely to have attended only part of the scheduled laboratories. Hence, teachers should push students to attend all the laboratories with a view to the upcoming exam.
- To obtain the highest grade (A), it is necessary to persist in the activities on the VCS for the entire course duration to obtain a high grade. Hence, teachers should encourage students who pursue higher grades to complete all the assignments.
- Including in the ML model the knowledge about the previous exam attempts can be beneficial, but only in combination with other VCS-based features.

As future work, we plan to extend our study firstly to other courses in the area of computer science and then to other disciplines. Furthermore, we aim to tightly integrate the AI technologies described in this paper in the official platforms used in our university in order to simplify the technology and allow teachers to perform deeper analysis.

Author Contributions: Conceptualization, L.C. (Lorenzo Canale), L.C. (Luca Cagliero), L.F., and M.T.; methodology, L.C. (Lorenzo Canale), L.C. (Luca Cagliero), L.F., and M.T.; software, L.C. (Lorenzo Canale), and L.C. (Luca Cagliero); validation, L.C. (Lorenzo Canale), L.C. (Luca Cagliero), and L.F.; formal analysis, L.C. (Lorenzo Canale), L.C. (Luca Cagliero), and L.F.; investigation, L.C. (Lorenzo Canale), L.C. (Luca Cagliero), and L.F; resources, L.C. (Lorenzo Canale), L.C. (Luca Cagliero), and L.F.; data curation, L.C. (Lorenzo Canale), L.C. (Luca Cagliero), and L.F.; writing—original draft preparation, L.C. (Lorenzo Canale), L.C. (Luca Cagliero), and L.F.; writing—review and editing, L.C. (Lorenzo Canale), L.C. (Luca Cagliero), and L.F.; visualization, L.C. (Lorenzo Canale), L.C. (Luca Cagliero), and L.F.; supervision, L.C. (Luca Cagliero), L.F., and M.T. All authors have read and agreed to the published version of the manuscript.

Funding: This research received no external funding.

Institutional Review Board Statement: Not applicable.

Informed Consent Statement: Not applicable.

Data Availability Statement: The research uses publicly available data released by third parties.

Conflicts of Interest: The authors declare no conflicts of interest.

References

1. Zagalsky, A.; Feliciano, J.; Storey, M.A.; Zhao, Y.; Wang, W. The Emergence of GitHub as a Collaborative Platform for Education. In Proceedings of the 18th ACM Conference on Computer Supported Cooperative Work & Social Computing (CSCW '15), Vancouver, BC, Canada, 14–18 March 2015; pp. 1906–1917. [CrossRef]
2. Zakiah, A.; Fauzan, M. Collaborative Learning Model of Software Engineering using Github for informatics student. In Proceedings of the 2016 4th International Conference on Cyber and IT Service Management, Bandung, Indonesia, 26–27 April 2016; pp. 1–5. [CrossRef]
3. Feliciano, J.; Storey, M.; Zagalsky, A. Student Experiences Using GitHub in Software Engineering Courses: A Case Study. In Proceedings of the 2016 IEEE/ACM 38th International Conference on Software Engineering Companion (ICSE-C), Austin, TX, USA, 14–22 May 2016; pp. 422–431.
4. Hsing, C.; Gennarelli, V. Using GitHub in the Classroom Predicts Student Learning Outcomes and Classroom Experiences: Findings from a Survey of Students and Teachers. In Proceedings of the 50th ACM Technical Symposium on Computer Science Education (SIGCSE '19), Minneapolis, MN, USA, 27 February–2 March 2019; pp. 672–678. [CrossRef]
5. Bond, M.; Buntins, K.; Bedenlier, S.; Zawacki-Richter, O.; Kerres, M. Mapping research in student engagement and educational technology in higher education: A systematic evidence map. *Int. J. Educ. Technol. High. Educ.* **2020**, *17*, 2. [CrossRef]
6. Conijn, R.; Snijders, C.; Kleingeld, A.; Matzat, U. Predicting Student Performance from LMS Data: A Comparison of 17 Blended Courses Using Moodle LMS. *IEEE Trans. Learn. Technol.* **2017**, *10*, 17–29. [CrossRef]
7. Isacson, J.; Lindblom, E. Correlation of User Behaviour Patterns and Assignment Supplements in KTH-GitHub Repositories. Bachelor's Thesis, KTH, Stockholm, Sweden, 2017.
8. Guerrero-Higueras, A.; Llamas, C.; Sánchez, L.; Fernández, A.; Costales, G.; Conde-González, M. Academic Success Assessment through Version Control Systems. *Appl. Sci.* **2020**, *10*, 1492. [CrossRef]
9. Lundberg, S.M.; Erion, G.; Chen, H.; DeGrave, A.; Prutkin, J.M.; Nair, B.; Katz, R.; Himmelfarb, J.; Bansal, N.; Lee, S.I. From local explanations to global understanding with explainable AI for trees. *Nat. Mach. Intell.* **2020**, *2*, 2522–5839. [CrossRef]
10. Griffin, T.; Seals, S. GitHub in the classroom: Not just for group projects. *J. Comput. Sci. Coll.* **2013**, *28*, 74.
11. Baumstark, L.; Orsega, M. Quantifying Introductory CS Students' Iterative Software Process by Mining Version Control System Repositories. *J. Comput. Sci. Coll.* **2016**, *31*, 97–104.
12. Tushev, M.; Williams, G.; Mahmoud, A. Using GitHub in large software engineering classes. An exploratory case study. *Comput. Sci. Educ.* **2020**, *30*, 155–186. [CrossRef]
13. Sprint, G.; Conci, J. Mining GitHub Classroom Commit Behavior in Elective and Introductory Computer Science Courses. *J. Comput. Sci. Coll.* **2019**, *35*, 76–84.
14. Guerrero-Higueras, A.M.; DeCastro-García, N.; Matellán, V.; Conde, M.A. Predictive Models of Academic Success: A Case Study with Version Control Systems. In Proceedings of the Sixth International Conference on Technological Ecosystems for Enhancing Multiculturality (TEEM'18), Salamanca, Spain, 24–26 October 2018; pp. 306–312. [CrossRef]
15. Guerrero-Higueras, Á.M.; DeCastroGarcía, N.; RodriguezLera, F.J.; Matellán, V.; Ángel Conde, M. Predicting academic success through students' interaction with Version Control Systems. *Open Comput. Sci.* **2019**, *9*, 243–251. [CrossRef]
16. Mierle, K.; Laven, K.; Roweis, S.; Wilson, G. Mining Student CVS Repositories for Performance Indicators. *SIGSOFT Softw. Eng. Notes* **2005**, *30*, 1–5. [CrossRef]
17. IEEE-CS. *Software Engineering Competency Model*; Technical Report; IEEE Computer Society Press: Washington, DC, USA, 2014.
18. Myers, K.K.; Sadaghiani, K. Millennials in the Workplace: A Communication Perspective on Millennials' Organizational Relationships and Performance. *J. Bus. Psychol.* **2010**, *25*, 225–238. [CrossRef]
19. Torchiano, M.; Bruno, G. Integrating software engineering key practices into an OOP massive in-classroom course: An experience report. In Proceedings of the 2nd International Workshop on Software Engineering Education for Millennials (SEEM '18), Gothenburg, Sweden, 2 June 2018; pp. 64–71. [CrossRef]
20. Zaki, M.J.; Meira, W., Jr. *Data Mining and Machine Learning: Fundamental Concepts and Algorithms*, 2nd ed.; Cambridge University Press: Cambridge, UK, 2020. [CrossRef]
21. Xavier, M.; Meneses, J. A Literature Review on the Definitions of Dropout in Online Higher Education. In Proceedings of the EDEN 2020 Annual Conference, Virtual, 22–24 June 2020. [CrossRef]
22. Canale, L. *Artificial Intelligence Methodologies to Early Predict Student Outcome and Enrich Learning Material*; Politecnico di Torino: Torino, Italy, 2022.
23. Pedregosa, F.; Varoquaux, G.; Gramfort, A.; Michel, V.; Thirion, B.; Grisel, O.; Blondel, M.; Prettenhofer, P.; Weiss, R.; Dubourg, V.; et al. Scikit-learn: Machine Learning in Python. *J. Mach. Learn. Res.* **2011**, *12*, 2825–2830.
24. Brodersen, K.H.; Ong, C.S.; Stephan, K.E.; Buhmann, J.M. The Balanced Accuracy and Its Posterior Distribution. In Proceedings of the 20th International Conference on Pattern Recognition, ICPR 2010, Istanbul, Turkey, 23–26 August 2010; IEEE Computer Society: Washington, DC, USA, 2010; pp. 3121–3124. [CrossRef]

computers

MDPI

Article

A First Approach to Co-Design a Multimodal Pedagogic Conversational Agent with Pre-Service Teachers to Teach Programming in Primary Education

Diana Pérez-Marín [1,*], Raquel Hijón-Neira [1] and Celeste Pizarro [2]

1 Computer Science Department, ETSII, Universidad Rey Juan Carlos, 28032 Madrid, Spain; raquel.hijon@urjc.es
2 Applied Mathematics, Materials Science and Engineering and Electronic Technology, ESCET, Universidad Rey Juan Carlos, 28032 Madrid, Spain; celeste.pizarro@urjc.es
* Correspondence: diana.perez@urjc.es

Abstract: Pedagogic Conversational Agents (PCAs) are interactive systems that engage the student in a dialogue to teach some domain. They can have the roles of a teacher, student, or companion, and adopt several shapes. In our previous work, a significant increase of students' performance when learning programming was found when using PCAs in the teacher role. However, it is not common to find PCAs used in classrooms. In this paper, it is explored whether pre-service teachers would accept PCAs to teach programming better if they were co-designed with them. Pre-service teachers are chosen because they are still in training, so they can be taught what PCAs are and how this technology could be helpful. Moreover, pre-service teachers can choose whether they integrate PCAs in the teaching activities that they carry out as part of their degree's course. An experiment with 35 pre-service primary education teachers was carried out during the 2021/2022 academic year to co-design a robotic PCA to teach programming. The experience validates the idea that involving pre-service teachers in the design of a PCA facilitates their involvement to integrate this technology in their classrooms. In total, 97% of the pre-service teachers that stated in a survey that they believed robot PCA could help children to learn programming, and 80% answered that they would like to use them in their classrooms.

Keywords: basic education; computer programming; higher education; scientific information; online systems

1. Introduction

Pedagogic Conversational Agents (PCAs) can be defined as "lifelike autonomous characters that cohabite the learning environment creating a rich interface face-to-face with student" [1]. Agents can ask students via voice, chat, gestures, or with touch panel screens [2], and students can answer using any of these communication modes. Moreover, agents can be software and cohabitate an educational application, or they can be autonomous robots (hardware) to create communication experiences with the student as close to natural as possible.

Agents, both software and hardware, can have multiple shapes, such as having a human body, being animals, characters, or robots. They can also have several roles in their interaction with the students [3]: teachers, who are the source of knowledge; students, who need to be taught by the students, called Teachable Agents; and, companions, who serve as peer students for emotional support, called Pedagogic Agent as Learning Companions (PALs).

Some benefits that have been published regarding the use of PCAs are the following: the Persona effect [4], according to which the presence of the agent has a positive influence in the students' perception of their learning experience; the Proteus effect [5], according to which students want to become like their agents and this is a source of motivation to interact more with them; and, the Protégé effect [6] (only for Teachable Agents), according to which students make greater efforts to teach their agents than to learn themselves.

A recent systematic review on the topic can be found in [7]. According to this review, and despite the multiple benefits of using PCAs for education that have been published, agents are still not able to communicate fluently in our natural way of communicating. We believe that this problem could be overcome by taking advantage of non-verbal communication by using gestures, in the case of PCAs, focusing on a certain domain instead of trying a general dialogue. Moreover, to take advantage of the Persona and Proteus Effect, Ocaña et al. [8] devised a companion agent, called Alcody.

Alcody's domain was knowing how to program with basic concepts such as inputs/outputs, conditionals, and loops in p-code with the agent. Learning how to program at an early age seems to have multiple benefits such as the development of computational thinking [9,10] and other cognitive skills [11,12]. However, it is still a young research topic that needs more studies to find out which methodologies and technologies could be used, given the lack of children's abstract thinking abilities and the complexity of the concepts to be taught [13,14].

To the best of our knowledge, Alcody was the first PCA that was used to teach programming to children as a learning companion. Having a learning companion seems to help children to make the learning more tangible and adaptable to their needs as a significant increase of their learning was registered as well as high satisfaction levels [15]. However, the use of PCAs to teach programming in primary education has not been integrated in classrooms. It is our research questions that will investigate whether teachers would like to use PCAs to teach programming in their primary education classrooms and find it useful if they were involved in the creation of such technology, and how pre-service teachers would like the PCA to function. Working teachers seem to ignore what PCAs are; thus, upon the experience of Alcody and teaching programming to children, in this paper, we present a co-design experience with pre-service teachers to create a PCA to teach programming to children with them as they are preparing to become teachers and are eager to have more teaching resources. Pre-service teachers were asked to fill in a questionnaire to find out whether they would use PCAs in their classroom once they know what PCAs are and have been involved in their creation. In total, 97% of these pre-service teachers answered that they believed that the PCA could help children to learn programming, and 80% answered that they would like to use them in their classrooms. The resulting prototype of a PCA to teach programming in primary education is shared in this paper for any other pre-service teacher that would like to use it.

This paper is organized into six sections: Section 2 reviews the related work including PCAs, teaching programming in primary education, and outlines the training of pre-service teachers. Section 3 describes the materials and methods of the experiment carried out. Section 4 provides the results. Section 5 discusses the answers to our research questions. Finally, Section 6 ends this paper with the main conclusions and lines of future work.

2. Related Work

2.1. Pedagogic Conversational Agents

Pedagogic Conversational Agents (PCAs) can be defined as a software that can interact with a student in a natural language (Johnson et al., 2000). Some simple examples are Alexa of Amazon, Siri of Apple, or ChatGPT regarding the AI for education [16].

PCAs in the educational domain have been investigated since 2000 [17], including certain intelligence in the dialogue and social support [18]. Some samples include Doroty, for teaching Computer Science [19]; AutoTutor, for teaching Operating Systems [20]; or Betty, for teaching Natural Science [21]. The results achieved have been promising in these school domains. More samples can be found in [3].

Autotutor is a sample of a PCA in the role of a teacher. It has been studied for decades. Originally, spoken and written dialogue to teach Computer Science at the university level has been combined with gestures and even a simulation of breathing to make it more real.

In some cases, the dialogue is guided by the PCA, which makes the questions and awaits the student's answer. In case it is correct, the agent congratulates the student and moves to the next question. But, if the answer is incorrect, the agent explains to the student why, and it teaches the concept until the student understands the correct answer.

AutoTutor is one of the most complex and sophisticated PCAs that exists in the literature that adopts the role of the teacher, i.e., the holder of the knowledge who transmits it to the student. However, it is not the only role for PCAs, as it has been proposed that learning could be more successful if the PCA might play the role of a student. In this case, the agent does not have any information. Thus, it does not ask questions to check whether the student can answer correctly and provides feedback in accordance. On the other hand, the agent asks questions to learn, as in the case of Betty [21].

Given that the agents that serve as students lack any knowledge, it is necessary to introduce another agent that checks whether the information provided by the student is correct. In this case, this agent is called Mr. Davis.

It is also possible that the goal of the PCA is neither to teach nor to learn from the student, but to serve as an emotional companion. In this case, the dialogue of the PCA does not start with a question such in the case of AutoTutor to check the student's knowledge. The dialogue of the PCA does not include quizzes to check whether the agent is learning from the student, such in the case of Betty. The dialogue starts with some kind of emotional sentence to support the student. For instance, the PCA could ask the student how s/he is and, depending on the answer, provide some recommendation. If the student is tired or sad, the PCA might recommend listening to a song before starting the study session so that it is more productive. The emotional PCA could also be helpful in the case that, after experiencing problems, the student declares that s/he is unable to solve the exercises, and it seems advisable to offer some support to make the student understand that, sometimes, problems look very difficult at first sight, but it is possible to improve with practice [3].

However, despite the good results reported in the literature, it is uncommon to find PCAs in use in classrooms. The reason for this has been investigated and it was found that the root is the lack of knowledge of this technology by the teachers or that the teachers dislike it because it does not follow the design principles which they are fond of (even in the case that they know the technology). A survey of 82 teachers (52.4% male; 47.6% female) with 24 questions regarding their knowledge of PCAs, how they would like PCAs in terms of friendliness, gestures with face/body, how to motivate and give advice to students, how to indicate that the student has made a mistake, and if the agent should remember the students' previous choices, and the most advisable frequency of use of the agent by the students [22].

The results of the survey revealed that no teacher knew about PCAs, although 78% of them used a computer as a support for their work by looking for information. This lack of knowledge required to show them several images of PCAs so that they could complete the survey. Once they understood the educational technology, they highlighted that using a PCA should be friendly, able to provide advice to the students, encourage the students to keep studying, and indicate whether the students had made mistakes. The combination of these features would motivate teachers to use PCAs in classrooms, once they were familiar with this educational technology [22].

However, to our knowledge, no survey has been carried out to explore if these features were the same teachers would expect in the specific case of a PCA aimed to teach programming in their primary education classrooms.

2.2. Teaching Programming in Primary Education

The idea of teaching programming in primary education is not new. In fact, it dates back to the 1980s, with Papert's work with LOGO [23]. Papert believed that, in order to teach programming to children, children need to build an object to think, following a constructionism pedagogy [24]. In the LOGO environment, the student interacted with a turtle, which responded to her/his commands as if they were talking. Children must also learn that there is more than one correct solution, but they should test different possibilities until one of them works (i.e., the expected output of the program) [25].

Since then, there have been times when the research of teaching programming has been stopped by the lack of training of teachers and the complexity of the domain. However, in recent decades, the research has resurged from different approaches, such as using multimedia software to program using blocks with the Scratch language with worldwide interest [26]; the use of robots [12]; and the unplugged exercises without using technology [27].

According to the survey carried out by [12], it was commonly agreed upon that primary education students should learn programming skills with a program such as Scratch. It combines the construction idea to learn by creating a program, with gamification, as the program is usually a game which motivates the users [28].

The idea is to imagine the program, create it, and share it with other people. The goal of the program can be to create a story, or to animate a character or a game, among other possibilities. The instructions are blocks that must be dragged and plugged together like a puzzle. Executing the program controls the movements, or other actions, of (for example) a cat, as shown in Figure 1, which illustrates a basic program to say Hello. Once the "say hello" instruction is executed, the cat in the right window outputs the sentence "Hello".

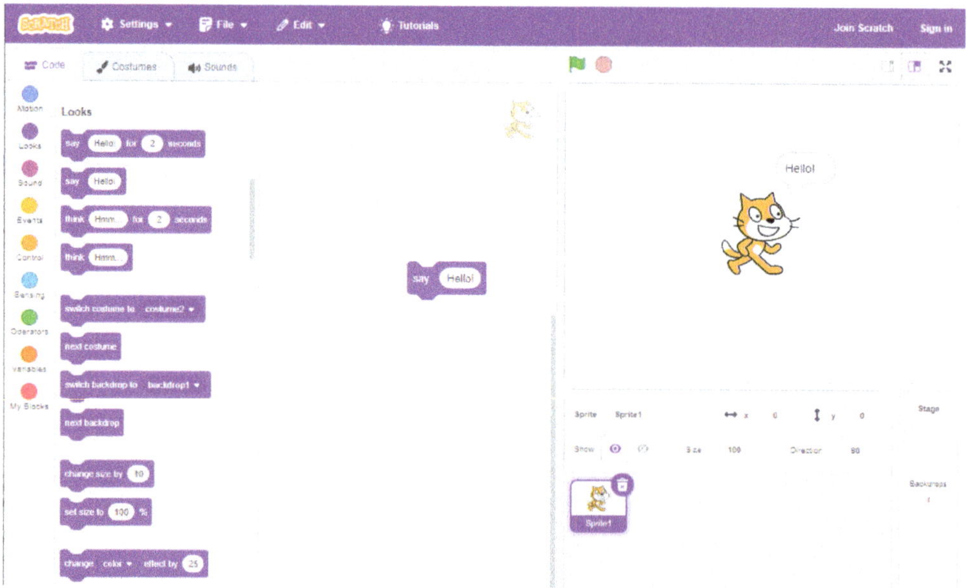

Figure 1. A basic program in Scratch to say "Hello".

Scratch has many tutorials to guide students and teachers. A debugging project was also carried out to help students when the program does not work [29]. However, it has limitations as students are required to have some device to run Scratch, and the execution of the program is always on the device. Therefore, other alternatives have been devised, such as using visual programming languages control robots like LEGO Mindstorms [30] or unplugged approaches [27] with games such as moving the students or objects around the class according to the execution of the program or writing programs on paper. Recently, the use of Pedagogic Conversational Agents to teach programming to primary education students with the companion role [15] and emotional support [31] has also been explored.

Jeppy [32] and Alcody [8] are a few of the PCAs that have been reviewed in the literature to teach programming. Jeppy is an emotional PCA shaped as a dog that gestures to help to correct syntax mistakes. Jeppy gives advice and affective messages to guide students to solve the exercises following a constructivist approach. Figure 2 shows several of Jeppy's gestures.

Figure 2. Some gestures of the PCA Jeppy to teach programming.

In an experiment carried out with novice programming students, it was found out that 66.7% of the students used Jeppy's advice to find the solution and 41.5% found the messages given by Jeppy clear and useful.

Alcody is an emotional learning companion to teach p-code to children following both a constructionism approach [23] and gamification [33]. It is an emotional learning companion because its goal is not to teach, unlike AutoTutor (see Section 2.1), or to learn from the student unlike Betty (see Section 2.2). Instead, the goal is to stay on the screen accompanying the learning scenario. It follows the idea of being a support to the student by talking to the student and providing emotional recommendations to reach the optimum mental state to program. Moreover, Alcody has some games to motivate students to keep programming and to win medals. Figure 3 shows an image of the Alcody agent.

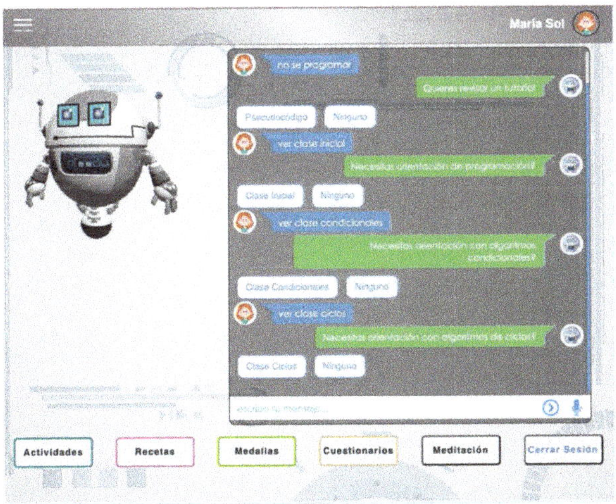

Figure 3. A snapshot of the Alcody emotional learning companion to teach p-code.

As shown in Figure 3 Alcody includes several tutorials to teach students how to program inputs/outputs, conditionals, and loops concepts. Moreover, it offers activities in which students must solve programming exercises such as calculating the factorial of a number given, recipes to play cooking as programming, and medals as students keep completing activities with Alcody [8,31].

2.3. Training of Pre-Service Teachers

How to integrate technology into pre-service science teachers' pedagogical content knowledge is a relevant issue in the literature [34]. Pre-service teachers need to learn both the didactics of the topic and the resources available to teach it, including technological resources that, in some cases, are seen as more complex to implement, even when teachers believe they are important for an effective teaching [35]. To find out what impedes the integration of technology in their teaching is essential for pre-service teachers, particularly as they will become the future teachers [36]. Moreover, pre-service teachers should graduate with the skills to seamlessly integrate technology to advance student learning [37], and they should be asked for their opinions [38–41].

Some researchers have identified several types of barriers into the adoption of technology, both by pre-service and in-service teachers. They can be classified according to the origin of the problem to impede the adoption of the technology as follows [42]:

- First-order barriers: they are related to external causes such as lack of devices, Internet connectivity, or software. Teachers may wonder whether they have enough computers, tablets, if the Internet connection is stable, and if the software is going to work without failures.
- Second-order barriers: they are related to internal fears such as lack of knowledge, digital competence, organizational, or pedagogical concerns. Teachers may wonder how they can have enough confidence to try something new, how the software works, where or when they should use technology, and how to ensure that students obtain adequate computer time without missing other important content and attending to their curricular demands.

Although not all teachers may face all of these barriers, the literature suggests that any one of these barriers alone can impede the integration of technology in their classrooms [43–45]. A solution for pre-service teachers would be to focus on acquiring technical skills during their training to address first-order barriers, as well as acquiring strategies and following recommendations to address second-order barriers [42].

3. Materials and Methods

This research has been approved by the URJC Ethical Committee with ID 19012022202722.

3.1. Research Questions

RQ1. Would pre-service teachers use PCAs to teach programming in their primary education classrooms if they were personally involved in creating such technology?

RQ2. How would pre-service teachers like the PCA to teach programming in primary education?

3.2. Sample

In total, 44 pre-service teachers from the Universidad Rey Juan Carlos were recruited with the motivation of helping in the co-design of a technology to teach programming in primary education (18 to 25 years of age, 70% female, 30% male). Participation in this study was voluntary and anonymous. Pre-service teachers were chosen because they are training to become future teachers, they are trained in didactics and PCA and the profile of primary education students, and are interested in learning new resources and technologies to improve their future teaching. These pre-service teachers also had experience in school contexts, as a part of their training is to assist working teachers in schools. As reviewed in Section 2.3, research with pre-service teachers is highly relevant in the literature.

Moreover, 43.2% of these pre-service teachers indicated that their digital competence ranged between medium and high, as they are used to working with smartphones, computers, and tablets (98% used their smartphones daily, 70% used their computers daily, 63.6% used their tablets daily).

Furthermore, 70% of them claimed to have used applications to learn programming before the course, as the teaching Scratch is common in secondary education in Spain before entering university. However, 91% of these pre-service teachers pointed out that they have never used an educational PCA before. This is why it was necessary to explain the concept of an educational PCA to them before asking about how they would like to design such educational technology to teach programming and the possible features of it that could be customized.

3.3. Materials and Procedure

To answer the research questions, two questionnaires were created for a sample of pre-service teachers.

The initial questionnaire can be found on-line at the following link: http://tinyurl.com/369v3zu2 (last accessed date 23 February 2024). It starts with some general demographic questions, such as age, gender, occupation, level of experience with technology, which technologies they use, and the frequency and purpose of use, to focus on which applications and apps they know for learning programming, and their knowledge of PCAs. Given that it was expected, the questioned pre-service teachers did not have any previous knowledge of PCAs for teaching programming; they watched a video of a sample PCA for familiarization, and were then able to answer the questions. Participants filled in the questionnaire anonymously and voluntarily in February.

After that introduction, they learnt how to teach programming to children for two months. Meanwhile, the prototype was being implemented as requested in the initial questionnaire. In April, pre-service teachers were shown the second final prototype, and they were asked to fill in a final questionnaire to find out their opinions of the resulting PCAs and whether they would like to use it to teach programming. Moreover, they were asked to evaluate the final prototype with questions regarding each screen and the navigation between screens. Pre-service teachers were given the opportunity to express any comment they would like to share with the researchers in a final open-ended Q&A session.

4. Results

4.1. Initial Questionnaire

The analysis of the data gathered in the initial questionnaire reveals a lack of clear consensus among pre-service teachers regarding which device would be the most adequate for using a PCA, as shown in Figure 4. Tablets emerged as the most voted option.

In total, 75% of the pre-service teachers asked for a how-to guide to learn how to use a PCA. Moreover, 63.6% of these pre-service teachers requested to be able to manage several classes and 59.1% indicated that primary education students usually work in teams of two to four kids; 70.5% of these pre-service teachers claimed that it would be of great help to have some students' tracking progress, including at least some information about the number of correct and wrong answers, and the time needed per question.

Figure 5 shows the elements that are considered helpful when creating activities for the PCA to teach programming.

Figure 6 shows the elements that should be customizable.

Regarding the language, most of the participants answered that the PCA should use simple, short, and direct sentences in the students' mother language with an informal, kind, and friendly tone. The vocabulary should be easy for the students to understand. Also, 65.9% of the participants asked for the use of metaphors to teach programming, as can be seen in Figure 7, and 63.6% of the participants considered that images should be presented with descriptive text.

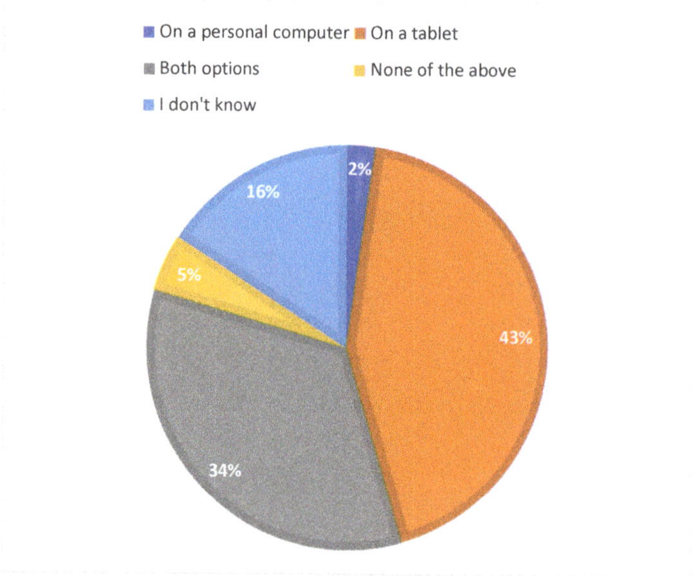

Figure 4. Technology to run the PCA aimed to teach programming.

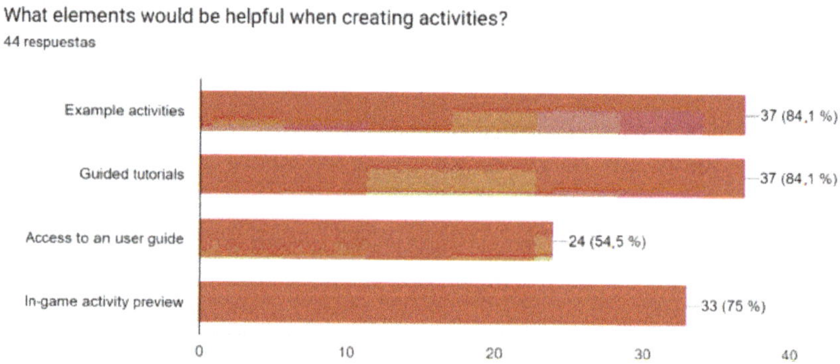

Figure 5. Useful elements to create activities in the PCA.

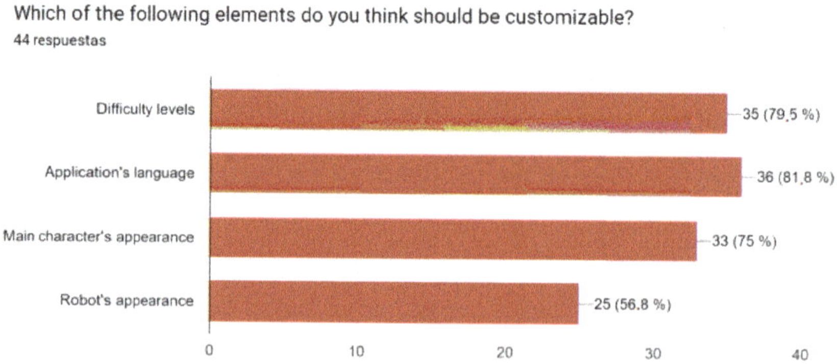

Figure 6. Customizable elements.

Additionally, 45.5% of the participants considered that children who make mistakes should be redirected towards the correct solution through clues, as shown in Figure 8.

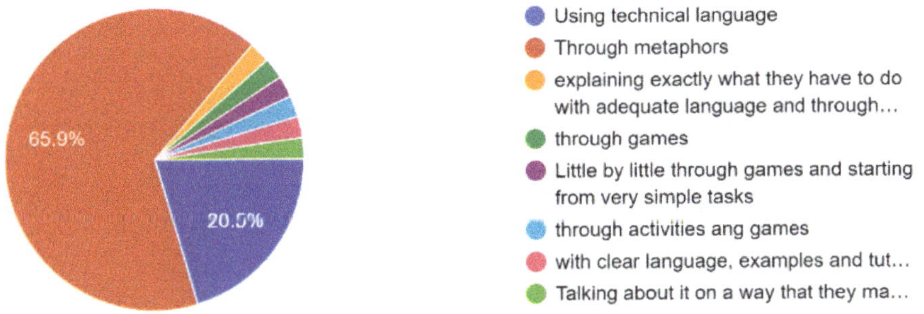

Figure 7. How to introduce children to programming.

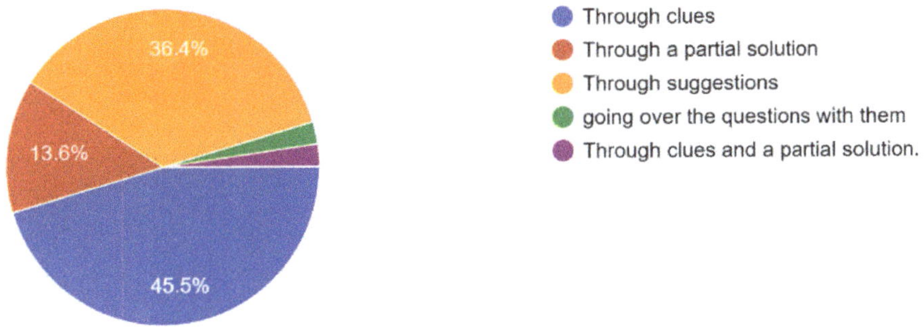

Figure 8. How to guide children towards the solution.

4.2. Prototype

The scenario indicated to the participants was a primary education classroom with 25 children paired in 2–4 groups. Each row of the classrooms had one PCA, as shown in Figure 9. The PCA can work in "teacher mode" to create new activities or in "student mode" to show the activities, so that students can start learning how to program. The teacher can have either a tablet or a digital whiteboard to create the activities and see the progress of the students. The advantage of a digital whiteboard is that teachers could show how to solve an activity to all the students in case all, or a significant part, of them have doubts and do not know how to continue interacting with the PCA.

On the other hand, using a tablet could be beneficial if the teacher would like to track the progress of a given group, out of the sight of the rest of the class, given that the teacher is the only one looking at the tablet.

Figure 10 shows the how-to guide to give to the teacher. It helps the teacher to follow the steps to set up PCAs. For both modes (creating activities or doing activities, Figure 11), the first step is to turn the digital whiteboard on and to open the digital PCA. Next, if the teacher wants to create activities, the creation mode should be chosen to access the authoring tool. In contrast, if the goal is to perform activities, one student per row is responsible to turn their shared PCA robot on as well. The PCA robot has a Bluetooth connection to the digital PCA in the whiteboard.

The first step for teachers is to create groups of students by pressing the "Groups" key, as shown in Figure 12. Additionally, teachers can add, modify, and remove students to the groups and also change each student's info. Secondly, once the groups have been created, teachers can create a variety of activities, as shown in Figure 13.

Figure 9. Scenario to use the robot PCA in the classroom.

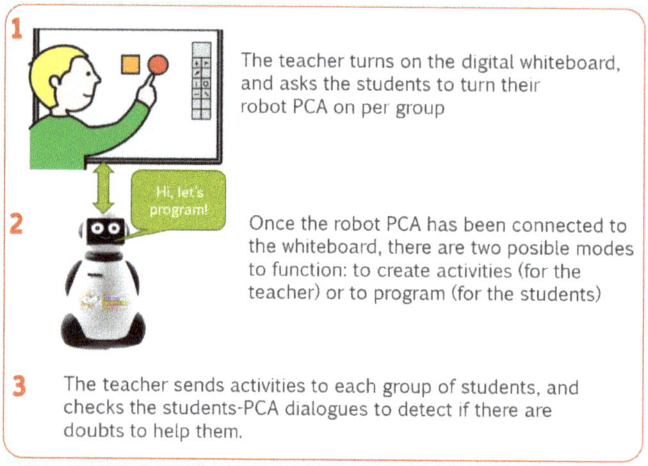

Figure 10. How-to guide for the teacher.

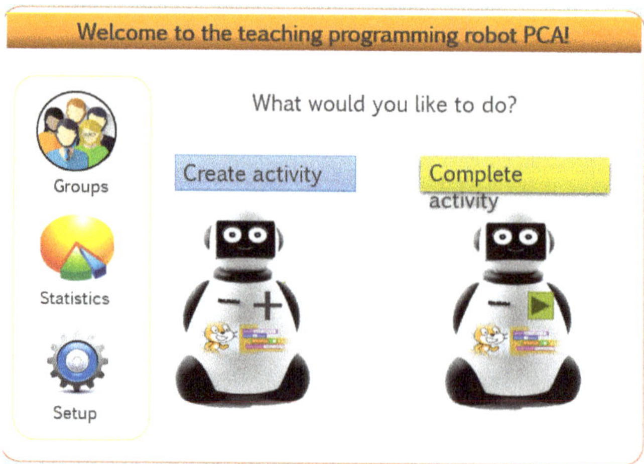

Figure 11. Main menu.

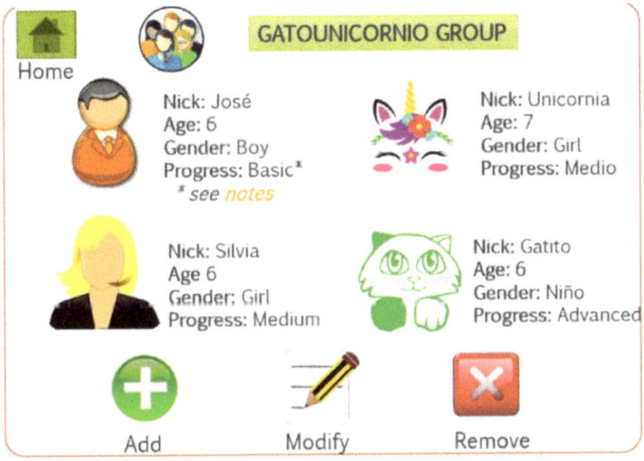

Figure 12. Menu to manage students' groups (the * indicates that the student has some info that the teacher should read).

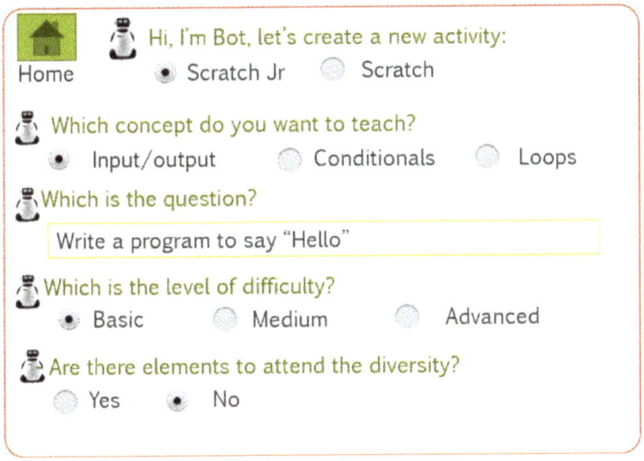

Figure 13. Creating activities with a PCA.

For each activity, teachers must choose the programming language (Scratch Jr or Scratch) according to the age of the students. Then, they must indicate the concepts to be learned: inputs/outputs, conditionals, or loops; the statement of the question, and some possible solution (Figure 14); the level of the difficulty; and if there is any element to deal with diversity. Once the teacher fills in the activity, any team can interact with the bot, as shown in Figure 15. In this case, the team does not know how to program the activity, and thus the PCA provides them with a sample which allows them to perform and solve the activity.

Teachers can also see how many exercises students have passed in global view (all the class) or per team. They can also set up the difficulty level of the activities; the language of the PCA; the shape, both digital and physical; and whether the PCA will be displayed as a teddy bear or robot.

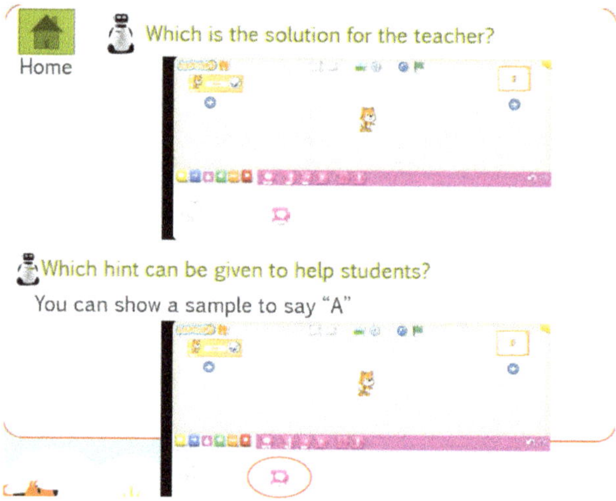

Figure 14. Possible solution for an activity.

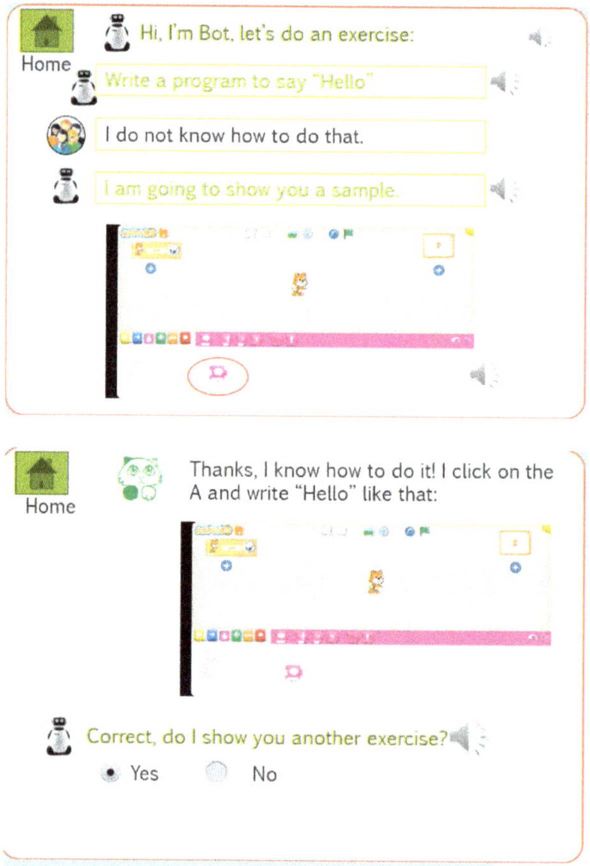

Figure 15. Sample interaction between a team and a PCA.

4.3. Validation Questionnaire

In total, 35 participants completed the questionnaire with 2 yes/no questions to find out whether pre-service teachers believed that the PCA could help children to learn programming and whether they would like to use it in their classrooms. In sum, 97% of them believed that the robot PCA could help children to learn programming (Figure 16), and 80% of the participants would like to use them in the classrooms (Figure 17).

Figure 16. Answers to the question if a PCA robot, like the one shown, can be used to teach programming (NS/NC are the students who have not answered).

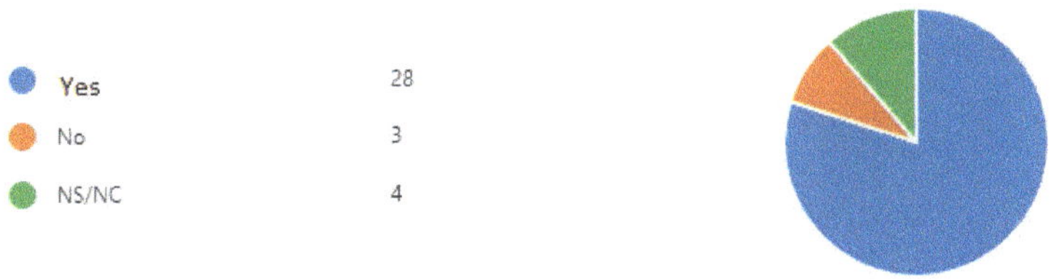

Figure 17. Answers to the question if the future teachers will have enough robots and if they would use them in their lessons (NS/NC are the students who have not answered).

The questionnaire provided some more data:

- In total, 89% appreciated the how-to guide provided for the teacher (Figure 8).
- In total, 71% considered that the sample interaction between the PCA and the team (Figure 16) fulfills their expectations. They also considered that the navigation between screens is adequate.

Table 1 shows the evaluation of the screens on a scale from 1 (dislike) to 5 (like).

Table 1. Evaluation of the prototype screens on the Likert scale (from 1 (dislike) to 5 (like)).

Screen	Figure(s)	Value
Main menu	13	3.4
Groups	12	3.7
Activity creation	13	3.6
Students' activities	15	4.2
Attending to diversity	11–15	4.2
Use of language	11–15	3.7
Intuitiveness	11–15	3.8
Friendliness	11–15	3.7
Ease of use	11–15	3.6

The questionnaire also contained the twelve Likert questions shown in Figure 18. Figure 19 shows the set of bar diagrams for questions Q1 to Q12, indicating the frequency of the answers given on a Likert scale (from 1 (dislike) to 5 (like)) for each of them. In addition, the results obtained through the one-sample Wilcoxon signed-rank test comparing the median of each individual item to the midpoint, 3.00, are marked with vertical marks. All test results were significant at the $p < 0.05$ level, with a median of 4 for all questions, except question 2, where the general median response was 3. This indicates that participants perceived these questions as more likely than unlikely.

Table 2 shows the main statistics (n, mean, median, standard deviation, and range) for the 12 questions presented. As can be seen, the number of subjects is 35, and the range (max/min) varies between 2 and 4 points; thus, there was a lot of disparity in the responses. Both the mean and the median show values above 3, which is the midpoint on the Likert scale. Furthermore, the standard deviation varies minimally, without reaching the threshold, except in question Q10, whose value is 1.023.

Table 3 shows the value of tau_b Kendall to show the possible correlation between each pair of questions (Q1 to Q12). Significant correlations at the 0.01 level are marked with a double asterisk.

Questions	Statement
Q1	Rate the robot agent's way of speaking from 1-1 don't like it at all to 5-love it
Q2	How would you rate it from 1-1 like not at all to 5-love the main screen?
Q3	How would you rate from 1-1 like not at all to 5-love the team management screen?
Q4	How would you rate it from 1-1 like not at all to 5-love the stats screen?
Q5	How would you rate from 1-1 like not at all to 5-love the settings screen?
Q6	How would you rate from 1-1 like not at all to 5-love the create activity screen?
Q7	How would you rate from 1-1 like not at all to 5-love the activity screen?
Q8	How would you rate from 1-1 like not at all to 5-love the attend to diversity screen?
Q9	Are the screens intuitive to you (from 1-not at all to 5-very much)?
Q10	Are the screens friendly to you (from 1-not at all to 5-very much)?
Q11	Do you think your students will like the exercise with the robot agent (from 1-not at all to 5-a lot)?
Q12	Do you think your students will find the exercise with the robot agent easy (from 1-not at all to 5-very much)?

Figure 18. Likert questions in the validation questionnaire.

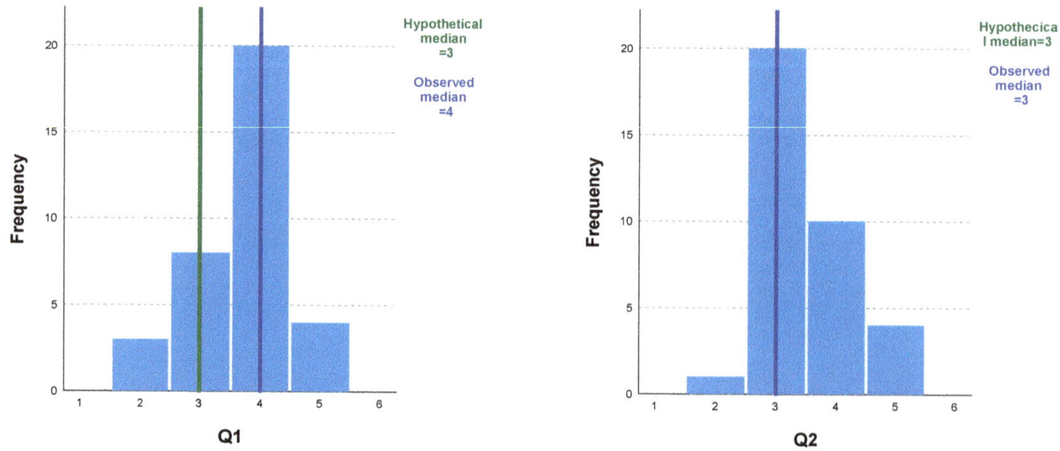

Figure 19. *Cont.*

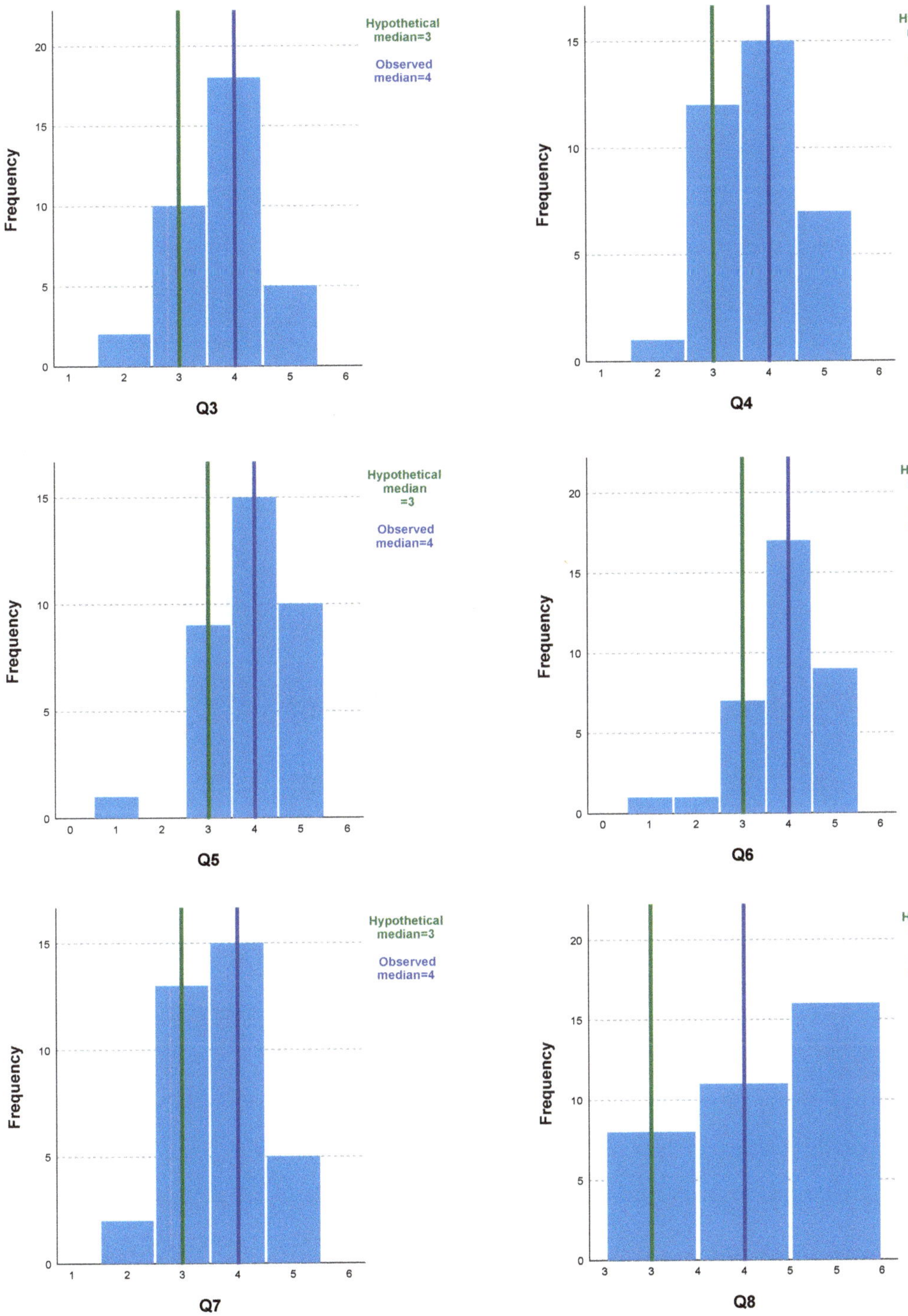

Figure 19. *Cont.*

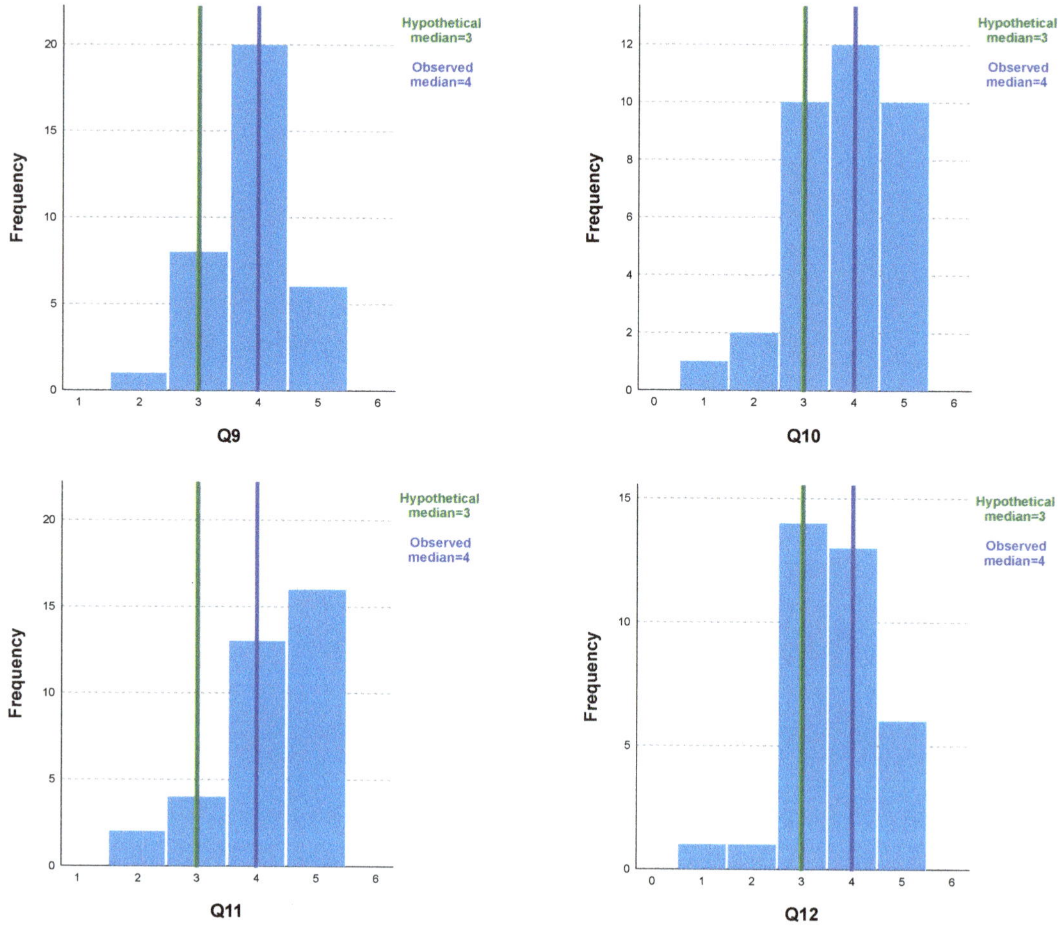

Figure 19. Bar diagrams for questions Q1 to Q12.

Table 2. Main statistics (1—mean; 2—median; 3—standard deviation; and 4—range) for the 12 questions presented.

	Q1	Q2	Q3	Q4	Q5	Q6	Q7	Q8	Q9	Q10	Q11	Q12
n	35	35	35	35	35	35	35	35	35	35	35	35
1	3.71	3.49	3.74	3.80	3.94	3.91	3.66	4.23	3.89	3.80	4.23	3.63
2	4.00	3.00	4.00	4.00	4.00	4.00	4.00	4.00	4.00	4.00	4.00	4.00
3	0.789	0.742	0.780	0.797	0.906	0.919	0.802	0.808	0.718	1.023	0.877	0.910
4	3	3	3	3	4	4	3	2	3	4	3	4

Table 3. Value of tau_b Kendall to show the possible correlation between each pair of questions (Q1 to Q12).

Q1	Q2	Q3	Q4	Q5	Q6	Q7	Q8	Q9	Q10	Q11	Q12
1.000	0.125	0.000	0.114	0.173	0.283	0.312	0.032	0.337	0.085	0.330	0.468 **
0.125	1.000	0.414 **	0.291	0.413 **	0.443 **	0.595 **	0.486 **	0.316	0.371	0.272	0.165
0.000	0.414 **	1.000	0.327	0.496 **	0.261	0.384	0.283	0.449 **	0.250	−0.052	0.078
0.114	0.291	0.327	1.000	0.458 **	0.385	0.294	0.435 **	0.298	0.226	0.179	0.243
0.173	0.413 **	0.496 **	0.458 **	1.000	0.686 **	0.501 **	0.544 **	0.400 **	0.019	0.175	0.215
0.283	0.443 **	0.261	0.385	0.686 **	1.000	0.682 **	0.506 **	0.532 **	0.021	0.316	0.394 **
0.312	0.595 **	0.384	0.294	0.501 **	0.682 **	1.000	0.474 **	0.630 **	0.189	0.278	0.308
0.032	0.486 **	0.283	0.435 **	0.544 **	0.506 **	0.474 **	1.000	0.364	0.319	0.207	0.052
0.337	0.316	0.449 **	0.298	0.400 **	0.532 **	0.630 **	0.364	1.000	0.161	0.184	0.306
0.085	0.371	0.250	0.226	0.019	0.021	0.189	0.319	0.161	1.000	0.469 **	0.097
0.330	0.272	−0.052	0.179	0.175	0.316	0.278	0.207	0.184	0.469 **	1.000	0.275
0.468 **	0.165	0.078	0.243	0.215	0.394 **	0.308	0.052	0.306	0.097	0.275	1.000

Figure 20 shows the medians of the responses to questions Q1 to Q12 separated by whether they answered "Yes" or "No" to the following question: "Do you think that the use of a robot agent like the one used could help teach programming?" From the graph, it can be seen that, in general, the subjects who answered "YES" to using the robot agent to teach programming answered all the questions with the category "more likely", with the median being 4 in all cases, except in question Q2, whose median is 3. All the responses were homogeneous. However, in the subjects who have answered that they would NOT use the robot agent, there is a lot of disparity between the answers: they vary from question Q1, whose median is 1 (dislike), with several cases of the median being 2 (Q1, Q2, and Q10), and with the rest of responses having a median of 4 and even 5.

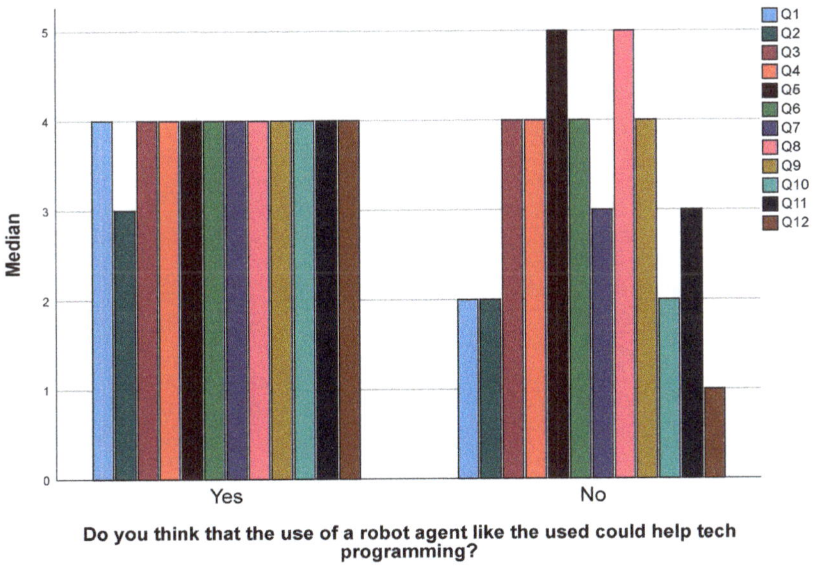

Figure 20. Relationship between Q1 through Q12 and the opinion of pre-service teachers regarding the use of a PCA to teach programming.

Finally, pre-service teachers were offered a chance of expressing any comments they would like to share freely, and they provided the following answers:

- "I think that this approach to teach programming is appropriate and can help children integrate technology in class and make them more enjoyable and didactic".
- "I think it's a great way to teach children, as it's fun and entertaining at the same time".
- "I find it very useful to make lessons more interactive and motivate children".

Figure 21 shows a tag cloud to synthesize the text of the gathered answers. As can be seen, "PCA" is one of the most used words, as well as "activity", "teach", "creating", "include", "information", "solve", and "help". Pre-service teachers, in general, considered that screens are easy to use and intuitive for children to use. They asked for difficulty levels to be considered and to allow children to have their own rhythm when interacting with the PCA. Moreover, they indicated that some teachers may be afraid of using robots for education and that they would need support from other teachers.

Figure 21. Tag cloud of the students' answer.

5. Discussion

According to the answers in the questionnaire, the answer to RQ1—"Would pre-service teachers use PCAs to teach programming in their primary education classrooms if they were involved in the creation of such technology?"—would be affirmative. In total, 97% of the survey's respondents indicated that PCAs could help children to learn programming, and 80% answered that they would like to use them in their classrooms in the future.

The answer to RQ2—"How pre-service teachers would like the PCA to teach programming in primary education?"—is that it should be intuitive, friendly, easy to use, and pay attention to diversity. Help should be provided both in the PCAs with tutorials and templates, but also with documents serving as a guide for the teachers prone to the use of PCAs. Teachers should have the possibility of creating activities for groups, managing statistics, and configuring options. Students should complete activities and fill in forms following a dialogue metaphor, in which each group is represented by an image. In general, there are some recommendations for researchers and/or teachers that would like to integrate the use of robot PCAs for teaching programming in classrooms:

1. It is necessary to provide a guide to help teachers in case they have doubts about PCAs and the activities they utilize for teaching programming.
2. The associated applications to PCAs should allow teachers to manage several teams (each team should have 2–4 students). The profile per student should at least include his/her name, age, class, and progress. Progress should register, at least, the number of activities performed correctly vs. incorrectly and the time needed to complete them.
3. When creating an activity for a PCA for teaching programming, it should include examples of possible programming activities. A template provided to the teacher should ensure that s/he knows which information should be provided, how the activity is being presented to the students, which information is provided by the student, and which information is provided by the PCA—as shown in Figures 16 and 17 of the proposed PCA.

4. When creating an activity using the PCA for teaching programming, it should include tutorials to solve doubts about how to complete all tasks. For instance, if the teacher does not understand which information should be provided, help should be provided to explain each term and what is expected in each form.
5. When creating an activity using the PCA for teaching programming, it should include a preview of how to solve the selected activity. In the case that students do not understand how to solve an activity, they could be assisted by a preview of how they are expected to complete it, so that they are prepared to tackle it later by themselves.
6. There should be a setup menu to modify the difficulty level, language, and shape of both the digital (the one in the tablet or digital whiteboard) and physical PCA (the one used by students).
7. The PCA's language should be adapted to the age of the students with short, simple, fun, nice, friendly, motivating, and respectful sentences, so that they can easily understand it and are motivated to interact with it.
8. It is also advisable to use metaphors to teach programming concepts, aimed to facilitate children's understanding.
9. If a team fails to solve a programming activity, the PCA could provide hints, suggestions, and partial solutions to help in successfully completing the activity.
10. Multimodality can help children to understand various tasks. Thus, images should always be accompanied by text to provide the same information in different channels. Audio could be helpful if children could have/use earphones to avoid disturbing the rest of the teams working in the same classroom at the same time.

These recommendations should be taken as an guide for anyone interested in using PCAs to teach programming in primary education. This study was the first approach used for finding out whether pre-service teachers would use PCAs to teach programming in their primary education classrooms if they were involved in the creation of such technology. It should be noted that more studies are needed with more pre-service and in-service teachers to keep refining the design of such PCAs. Finally, more research about exploring the use of PCAs in primary education classrooms for teaching programming [46,47] is required.

Furthermore, this research underscores the importance of user-driven designs in the development of educational technologies. Pre-service teachers felt empowered by being asked about how they would like a PCA to function. As result, teachers had a more personalized and pedagogically aligned tool, ensuring its relevance and effectiveness [46,47]. As in our case, the pre-service teachers were asked about configuring certain features of the PCAs, and they found out that, by involving future teachers in the process of decision making, educational technologists can ensure that these tools align with the needs of the teaching community, and that this could welcome and extend their use to more primary education classrooms.

However, these results are limited and preliminary as testing was carried out using a small sample of pre-service teachers with a limited set of options for configuring the used PCA. More studies are needed with a bigger sample of pre-service teachers and in-service teachers, having more possibilities for configuring the PCA being used. This is relevant research because it seems that giving teachers the freedom to choose how they would like the educational technology to function is more helpful for them that not. Moreover, with this approach, it seems that teachers adopt a better attitude towards the use of this educational technology in their classrooms.

6. Conclusions

The use of PCAs can be helpful for teaching in general; in the case of teaching programming to primary education students, the co-design with pre-service teachers seems to be the motivator for integrating such technology into their classrooms. In total, 97% of the survey's respondents indicated that PCAs could help children to learn programming, and 80% answered that they would like to use them in their classrooms in the future.

The analysis to the questions with the use of a Likert scale for finding out whether a prototype co-designed with pre-service teachers would be liked by pre-service teachers shows a significant likelihood of more than 3 points in most cases, as shown in Figure 17. Moreover, when analyzing the answers to questions Q1–Q12—which are related to the main research question of this study and regarding whether they would like to use a PCA for teaching programming—pre-service teachers who answered that they liked the screens of the prototype usually answered that they would like to use a PCA.

In conclusion, this paper contributes to the ongoing discourse on the use of conversational agents in programming education by highlighting the importance of user-driven design. Insights into the potential of conversational agents in shaping the future of programming education, particularly through the lens of pre-service teachers' perspectives, are provided. More research is needed regarding the needs of the teaching community so that primary education students can benefit from the possibilities that PCAs can bring to their classrooms. A first step in this direction could be to compare the opinions of pre-service teachers to the opinions of in-service teachers.

Author Contributions: Conceptualization, D.P.-M. and R.H.-N.; methodology, C.P.; validation, all authors; investigation, D.P.-M.; resources, R.H.-N.; data curation, C.P.; writing—original draft preparation, D.P.-M.; writing—review and editing, R.H.-N. and C.P.; funding acquisition, all authors. All authors have read and agreed to the published version of the manuscript.

Funding: This research was funded by the project with the reference number M3035 of Universidad Rey Juan Carlos and the project "Novel interactive approaches based on collaborative and visualization systems aimed at learning block-based programming" (PID2022-137849OB-I00) of the Spanish State Investigation Agency.

Data Availability Statement: The data presented in this study are available on request from the corresponding author. The data are not publicly available due to ethical restrictions.

Conflicts of Interest: The authors declare no conflicts of interest. The funders had no role in the design of this study; in the collection, analyses, or interpretation of data; in the writing of the manuscript; or in the decision to publish the results.

References

1. Johnson, W.; Rickel, J.; Lester, J. Animated Pedagogical Agents: Face-to-Face Interaction in Interactive Learning Environments. *J. Artif. Intell. Educ.* **2000**, *11*, 47–78.
2. Graesser, A.; McNamara, D. Self-regulated learning in learning environments with pedagogical agents that interact in natural language. *Educ. Psychol.* **2010**, *45*, 234–244. [CrossRef]
3. Pérez-Marín, D. A Review of the Practical Applications of Pedagogic Conversational Agents to Be Used in School and University Classrooms. *Digital* **2021**, *1*, 18–33. [CrossRef]
4. Lester, J.; Converse, S.; Kahler, S.; Barlow, S.; Stone, B.; Bhogal, R. The persona effect: Affective impact of animated pedagogical agents. In Proceedings of the Sigchi Conference on Human Factors in Computing Systems, Atlanta, GA, USA, 22–27 March 1997; ACM: New York, NY, USA, 1997.
5. Yee, N.; Bailenson, J. The Proteus effect: The effect of transformed self-representation on behavior. *Hum. Commun. Res.* **2007**, *33*, 271–290. [CrossRef]
6. Chase, C.; Chin, D.; Oppezzo, M.; Schwartz, D. Teachable agents and the Protégé effect: Increasing the effort towards learning. *J. Sci. Educ. Technol.* **2009**, *18*, 334–352. [CrossRef]
7. Sikström, P.; Valentini, C.; Kärkkäinen, T.; Sivunen, A. How pedagogical agents communicate with students: A two-phase systematic review. *Comput. Educ.* **2022**, *188*, 104564. [CrossRef]
8. Ocaña, J.M.; Morales-Urrutia, E.K.; Pérez-Marín, D.; Pizarro, C. Can a Learning Companion Be Used to Continue Teaching Programming to Children Even during the COVID-19 Pandemic? *IEEE Access* **2020**, *8*, 157840–157861. [CrossRef]
9. Wing, J.M. Computational thinking. *Commun. ACM* **2006**, *49*, 33–35. [CrossRef]
10. Pérez-Marín, D.; Hijón-Neira, R.; Bacelo, A.; Pizarro, C. Can computational thinking be improved by using a methodology based on metaphors and Scratch to teach computer programming to children? *Comput. Hum. Behav.* **2020**, *105*, 105849. [CrossRef]
11. Arfé, B.; Vardanega, T.; Ronconi, L. The effects of coding on children's planning and inhibition skills. *Comput. Educ.* **2020**, *148*, 103807. [CrossRef]
12. AlQarzaie, K.N.; AlEnezi, S.A. Using LEGO MINDSTORMS in Primary Schools: Perspective of Educational Sector. *Int. J. Online Biomed. Eng.* **2022**, *18*, 139–147. [CrossRef]

13. Bati, K. A systematic literature review regarding computational thinking and programming in early childhood education. *Educ. Inf. Technol.* **2022**, *27*, 2059–2082. [CrossRef]
14. Bucciarelli, M.; Mackiewicz, R.; Khemlani, S.S.; Johnson-Laird, P.N. The causes of difficulty in children's creation of informal programs. *Int. J. Child-Comput. Interact.* **2022**, *31*, 100443. [CrossRef]
15. Ocaña, M. MEDIE_GEDILEC: Propuesta de Metodología Para la Creación de Compañeros de Aprendizaje para la Enseñanza de la Programación en Educación Primaria. Ph.D. Thesis, Universidad Rey Juan Carlos, Móstoles, Madrid, 2021.
16. García-Peñalvo, F.J. La percepción de la Inteligencia Artificial en contextos educativos tras el lanzamiento de ChatGPT: Disrupción o pánico. *Educ. Knowl. Soc. (EKS)* **2023**, *24*, e31279. [CrossRef]
17. Cassell, J. Embodied conversational interface agents. *Commun. ACM* **2000**, *43*, 70–78. [CrossRef]
18. Kumar, R.; Rosé, C. Architecture for building conversational agents that support collaborative learning. *IEEE Trans. Learn. Technol.* **2011**, *4*, 21–34. [CrossRef]
19. Leonhardt, M.; Dutra, R.; Granville, L.; Tarouco, L. DOROTY: Una extensión en la arquitectura de un ChatterBot para la formación académica y profesional en el campo de la gestión de redes. In Proceedings of the Conferencia Mundial IFIP Sobre Computadoras en la Educación, Toulouse, France, 22–27 August 2005.
20. Graesser, A.C.; Greenberg, D.; Frijters, J.C.; Talwar, A. Using AutoTutor to track performance and engagement in a reading comprehension intervention for adult literacy students. *Rev. Signos Estud. Lingüística* **2021**, *54*, 1089–1114. [CrossRef]
21. Han, J.H.; Shubeck, K.; Shi, G.H.; Hu, X.E.; Yang, L.; Wang, L.J.; Biswas, G. Teachable Agent Improves Affect Regulation. *Educ. Technol. Soc.* **2021**, *24*, 194–209.
22. Tamayo, S.; Pérez-Marin, D. ¿Qué esperan los maestros de los Agentes Conversacionales Pedagógicos? *Educ. Knowl. Soc. (EKS)* **2017**, *18*, 59–85. [CrossRef]
23. Papert, S. *Mindstorms: Children, Computers, and Powerful Ideas*; Basic Books: New York, NY, USA, 1980.
24. Papert, S.; Harel, I. *Constructionism*; Ablex Publishing: Norwood, NJ, USA, 1991.
25. Papert, S. *Logo Philosophy and Implementation*; Logo Computer Systems: Highgate Springs, VT, USA, 1999.
26. Resnick, M.; Maloney, J.; Monroy-Hernandez, A.; Rusk, N.; Eastmond, E.; Brennan, K. Scratch: Programming for all. *Commun. ACM* **2009**, *52*, 60–67. [CrossRef]
27. Brackmann, C.; Barone, D.; Casali, A.; Boucinha, R.; Muñoz-Hernández, S. Computational thinking: Panorama of the Americas. In Proceedings of the 2016 International Symposium on Computers in Education (SIIE), Salamanca, Spain, 13–15 September 2016; pp. 1–6.
28. Papavlasopoulou, S.; Giannakos, M.N.; Jaccheri, L. Exploring children's learning experience in constructionism-based coding activities through design-based research. *Comput. Hum. Behav.* **2019**, *99*, 415–427. [CrossRef]
29. Moreno-León, J.; Robles, G. Dr. Scratch: A web tool to automatically evaluate Scratch projects. In Proceedings of the Workshop in Primary and Secondary Computing Education, London, UK, 9–11 November 2015; pp. 132–133.
30. Zygouris, N.; Striftou, A.; Dadaliaris, A.; Stamoulis, G.; Xenakis, A.; Vavougios, D. The use of LEGO Mindstorms in elementary schools. In Proceedings of the 2017 IEEE Global Engineering Education Conference (EDUCON), Athens, Greece, 25–28 April 2017; pp. 514–516. [CrossRef]
31. Morales-Urrutia, E. MEDIE_LECOE: Propuesta de Metodología para la Integración de Emociones en Compañeros de Aprendizaje Para la Enseñanza de la Programación en Educación Primaria. Ph.D. Thesis, Universidad Rey Juan Carlos, Móstoles, Madrid, 2021.
32. Pérez, J.E.; Dinawanao, D.D.; Tabanao, E.S. JEPPY: An interactive pedagogical agent to aid novice programmers in correcting syntax errors. *Int. J. Adv. Comput. Sci. Appl.* **2020**, *11*, 48–53. [CrossRef]
33. Deterding, S.; Dixon, D.; Khaled, R.; Nacke, L. From game design elements to gamefulness: Defining "gamification". In Proceedings of the Memorias del 15th International Academic MindTrek Conference: Envisioning Future Media Environments, Tampere, Finland, 28–30 September 2011; pp. 9–15.
34. Jang, S.; Chen, K. From PCK to TPACK: Developing a Transformative Model for Pre-Service Science Teachers. *J. Sci. Educ. Technol.* **2010**, *19*, 553–564. [CrossRef]
35. Roblyer, M.D. Why use technology in teaching? Making a case beyond research results. *Fla. Technol. Nology Educ. Q.* **1993**, *5*, 7–13.
36. Lim, C.; Chai, C.; Churchill, D. A framework for developing pre-service teachers' competencies in using technologies to enhance teaching and learning. *Educ. Media Int.* **2011**, *48*, 69–83. [CrossRef]
37. Stobaugh, R.; Tassell, J. Analyzing the degree of technology use occurring in pre-service teacher education. *Educ. Assess. Eval. Account.* **2011**, *23*, 143–157. [CrossRef]
38. Tondeur, J.; Braak, J.; Sang, G.; Voogt, J.; Fisser, P.; Ottenbreit-Leftwich, A. Preparing pre-service teachers to integrate technology in education: A synthesis of qualitative evidence. *Comput. Educ.* **2012**, *59*, 134–144. [CrossRef]
39. Çebi, A.; Reisoglu, I. Digital Competence: A Study from the Perspective of Pre-service Teachers in Turkey. *J. New Approaches Educ. Res.* **2020**, *9*, 294–308. [CrossRef]
40. Tárraga-Mínguez, R.; Suárez-Guerrero, C.; Sanz-Cervera, P. Digital Teaching Competence Evaluation of Pre-Service Teachers in Spain: A Review Study. *IEEE Rev. Iberoam. Tecnol. Aprendiz.* **2021**, *16*, 70–76. [CrossRef]
41. Hijón-Neira, R.; Connolly, C.; Pizarro, C.; Pérez-Marín, D. Prototype of a Recommendation Model with Artificial Intelligence for Computational Thinking Improvement of Secondary Education Students. *Computers* **2023**, *12*, 113. [CrossRef]
42. Ertmer, P. Addressing first- and second-order barriers to change: Strategies for technology integration. *Educ. Technol. Res. Dev.* **1999**, *47*, 47–61. [CrossRef]

43. Hadley, M.; Sheingold, K. Commonalties and distinctive patterns in teachers' integration of computers. *Am. J. Educ.* **1993**, *101*, 261–263. [CrossRef]
44. Hannafin, R.D.; Savenye, W.C. Technology in the classroom: The teachers new role and resistance to it. *Educ. Technol.* **1993**, *33*, 26–31.
45. Hativa, N.; Lesgold, A. Situational effects in classroom technology implementations: Unfulfilled expectations and unexpected outcomes. In *Technology and the Future of Schooling: Ninety Fifth Yearbook of the National Society for the Study of Education, Part 2*; Kerr, S.T., Ed.; University of Chicago Press: Chicago, IL, USA, 1996; pp. 131–171.
46. Ke, F.; Im, T. Adaptive Conversational Agents for Personalized Learning. *TechTrends* **2020**, *64*, 310–317.
47. Johnson, L.; Adams Becker, S.; Estrada, V.; Freeman, A. *NMC/CoSN Horizon Report: 2019 K-12 Edition*; The New Media Consortium: Austin, TX, USA, 2019.

computers

MDPI

Article

A Comparison between Online Quizzes and Serious Games: The Case of Friend Me

Lampros Karavidas, Georgina Skraparli and Thrasyvoulos Tsiatsos *

Department of Informatics, Aristotle University of Thessaloniki, GR-54124 Thessaloniki, Greece;
karavidas@csd.auth.gr (L.K.); skraparl@csd.auth.gr (G.S.)
* Correspondence: tsiatsos@csd.auth.gr; Tel.: +30 231 0998990

Abstract: The rapid changes in digital technology have had a substantial influence on education, resulting in the development of learning technologies (LTs) such as multimedia, computer-based training, intelligent tutoring systems, serious games, social media, and pedagogical agents. Serious games have demonstrated their effectiveness in several domains, while there is contradictory data on their efficiency in modifying behavior and their possible disadvantages. Serious games are games that are specifically created to fulfill a primary goal other than entertainment. The objective of our study is to evaluate the effectiveness of a serious game designed for the self-assessment of students concerning their knowledge of web technologies on students with an equivalent online quiz that uses the same collection of questions. The primary hypotheses we stated were that those utilizing the serious game would experience better results in terms of engagement, subjective experience, and learning compared to those using the online quiz. To examine these research questions, the IMI questionnaire, the total number of completed questions, and post-test grades were utilized to compare the two groups, which consisted of 34 undergraduate students. Our findings indicate that the serious game users did not have a better experience or better learning outcomes, but that they engaged more, answering significantly more questions. Future steps include finding more participants and extending the experimental period.

Keywords: serious game; online quiz; student's assessment

1. Introduction

The rapid advancements in digital technology have a profound impact on education. The introduction of the internet into our daily lives marked a transformative shift in the way individuals interact with information [1]. Furthermore, numerous studies support the fact that users have become increasingly attracted to social media platforms and online gaming [2–8]. This development has prompted inquiries into the potential role of technology in education and the possible effects of this integration.

As a result of the integration of technology into educational settings, the term learning technologies (LTs) was created. According to Jan Elen and Geraldine Clarebout [9], learning technology is defined as "a field of study and ample practices of mainly two different types: technology for learning and technology of learning. Technology for learning pertains to the use of technology during (the support of) learning processes... In line with the more general meaning of 'technology' as the application of scientific insights to solve practical problems, 'technology of learning' relates to the question on how scientific findings with respect to (supporting) learning can actually be used to support learning processes". Learning technologies comprise a combination of web tools, software applications, and mobile technologies that merge the technological and pedagogical aspects of internet advances and mobile devices [10]. Their purpose is to facilitate the entire learning process, including its design, development, delivery, and management [11]. Among the technologies explored for their integration into education are multimedia learning, computer-based training, intelligent tutoring systems, serious games, social media, and pedagogical agents [12]. In particular, Dabbagh et al. [13] identified five evolving models in the field of learning technologies (LTs): Massive Open Online Courses (MOOCs), mobile learning, social media, Augmented Reality (AR), and Game-Based Learning (GBL).

As the number of individuals with mobile phones and internet access continues to rise, technology's integration in educational settings has become more common, leading to the expansion of distance and online learning [1,13]. A notable advantage of LTs is their flexibility; that education can be delivered either synchronously or asynchronously. Additionally, LT focuses on the use of personal, portable, and handheld devices, facilitating learners' convenient access to learning resources [14].

As previously mentioned, serious games are a type of learning technology. The term "serious game" was introduced by Abt in his book "Serious Games", published in 1970, in which he characterized them as having an "explicit and carefully thought-out educational purpose and are not intended to be played primarily for amusement" [15]. While Abt originally referred to card and board games, serious games are now available in digital formats. Therefore, serious games are widely defined as games designed to serve a primary purpose beyond entertainment. The distinction between serious games and standard video games centers around their objectives. Serious games are oriented towards acquiring new knowledge, skills, or behavioral changes; while it is not mandatory for all serious games to have the feature of fun in them, it is considered essential for players to immerse themselves in the gaming experience [16]. Furthermore, there is disagreement regarding the term "game" within the context of "serious games", as it is associated with a voluntary occupation of individuals. However, in the case of serious games, individuals may be obligated to play the game, such as in a training scenario. Overall, although there is debate about the term "serious game", it has gained general acceptance [16–18].

Serious games are implemented in a wide variety of contexts and appear in fields such as business, the military, education, well-being, cultural heritage, health care, and more [17]. Extensive study has been conducted on their effectiveness, with evidence supporting their positive impact in various fields. Research demonstrates that serious games are effective in enhancing learning, promoting desirable behaviors, and offering engaging experiences, as well as providing assessment tools [19–23]. On certain occasions they are as effective as their analog counterparts, such as when assessing emotional intelligence [23]. Nevertheless, conflicting evidence exists regarding their effectiveness in generating behavioral change, and negative reactions to competitive serious games have been recorded [19,24]. Moreover, potential drawbacks such as a lack of interest, negative perceptions towards gaming, and limited computer or tablet proficiency have been identified. Thus, despite their significant promise, the creation of successful and impactful serious games remains a challenging task.

In the context of self-regulation, studies indicate that serious games could positively impact self-efficacy [25,26]. These serious games leverage effective design mechanisms, including narrative contexts, feedback, avatars, simulations, goals, a variety of difficulty levels, and social interactions [27]. It needs to be mentioned that they have shown positive results in health management, such as diabetes [28], heart failure [29], and asthma self-management [30]. Furthermore, according to Roozeboom et al. [25], serious games effectively measure generic learning features, fostering active, self-directed engagement and contributing to self-assessment and self-regulated learning.

An example of a serious game used for self-evaluation is *Serena Supergreen* [31], a point-and-click game designed for adolescents, especially girls. It aims to enhance their self-evaluation of technical competence through a problem-solving approach. Two evaluations were conducted. In the first one, 54 students from two German secondary schools, aged 13 to 15, participated by playing the game for two school hours, resulting in a positive impact on players' self-evaluations of their competence, but only when assessed through a specific perceived technical competence measure. However, there were no changes in the self-concept of their technical abilities after playing the game. The short version of the game also did not significantly impact their intrinsic motivation towards technical tasks, although it did show positive changes in task interest. In the second evaluation, 39 students (mean age 15.13) at a German secondary school played the complete version of the game (180 h). The results indicated that the game positively influenced their perceived technical competence, self-concept of their technical abilities, and intrinsic motivation towards technical tasks. In summary, the results of this game's evaluations indicate that the game increases players' perceived technical competence, self-concept of their technical ability, and intrinsic motivation with respect to technical tasks. Moreover, the feedback strategies within the game are highlighted as contributing to the positive effects on the players' self-evaluations of their competence.

In the context of software development, the use of serious games to teach software engineering has gained attention, indicating that real-world activities may include game design elements [32]. While further research is required, there is evidence to support the integration of serious games into software engineering education as a valuable adjunct to conventional teaching approaches [33]. In addition, serious games have gained specific interest in the learning of programming languages, indicating a growing trend in utilizing serious games for educational purposes [34]. Within this domain, serious games have gained attention as complementary tools to traditional teaching methods, with a focus on enhancing learning experiences and engagement [35].

The application of serious games in learning programming presents a promising approach to engaging students, incorporating motivation and enhancing the overall entertainment value of the learning process [36]. Specifically designed to facilitate a deep understanding of programming concepts and languages, these games offer an alternative and engaging way for learners to immerse themselves in simulations or experiments within the field of computer science [34]. Some examples of these serious games are *ProBot* [37] and *Py-rate Adventures* [36]. *ProBot* is a digital game designed to reinforce and improve students' abilities in terms of sequencing, defined iteration, and nesting. The game follows a problem-solving approach and implements a score-comparing mechanism to encourage students to analyze their solutions and seek better ones. The evaluation of this serious game, in which 123 engineering university students from Colombia University, aged 16-18 years old, participated as part of their core course "Programming fundamentals", demonstrated its effectiveness in enhancing the students' understanding of programming concepts. On the other hand, *Py-rate Adventures* is a 2D platform game designed to teach basic programming concepts using Python, aiming to engage and educate players with no prior programming knowledge. An evaluation, conducted with 31 graduates and postgraduate students of an Interdepartmental Programme of Postgraduate Studies in Information Systems with different bachelor degrees (economics, business administration, informatics, etc.), yielded positive results in terms of player experience and short-term learning. In summary, the increasing interest in and diverse applications of serious games in software development underscore their potential as engaging tools for teaching programming, offering a promising avenue by which to enhance learning experiences and foster student engagement.

The aim of our study is to assess the effectiveness of a serious game designed for the self-assessment of undergraduate students concerning their knowledge of web technologies, in comparison to a similar online quiz that utilizes the same set of questions. The main hypotheses we proposed were that those using the serious game would obtain greater results in terms of engagement, subjective experience, and learning, as opposed to those using the online quiz. In order to investigate these research questions, the IMI questionnaire, the overall number of answered questions, and post-test scores were employed to compare the two groups, which comprised 34 undergraduate students. Our data suggest that the users of serious games did not have an enhanced subjective experience or achieve better learning outcomes. However, they did exhibit higher levels of engagement by responding to a much larger number of questions in comparison to the users of the learning platform.

The current paper is organized in the following way: Section 2 outlines the specific Materials and Methods employed in our experiment. It discusses the presentation of the serious game "Friend Me", the similar online quiz, the research goals of the study, the tools used for measurements (questionnaires and tests), and the experimental technique that was followed. Section 3 provides an examination of the data and the outcomes of the evaluation. Section 4 comprises an in-depth discussion and the conclusions of the findings obtained in our experiment. Section 5 addresses the constraints of our investigation and outlines our forthcoming actions.

2. Research Goals, Materials, and Methods

This section presents the materials created and the procedure followed to test our hypothesis that educational games with questions tend to be more engaging and have a greater impact on academic performance than learning platform quizzes.

2.1. Research Goals

As stated before, the present study aims to compare users' subjective experience, engagement, and learning results by using either a learning platform, like Moodle, or by using a serious game like "Friend Me", to answer computer science questions.

Thus, the first research goal (RG1) of the paper is to explore the participants' subjective experience related to the main activity they performed, which involved answering multiple questions either using online quizzes or a serious game. Their experience is measured in multiple dimensions such as interest and enjoyment, perceived competence, effort and value, and usefulness, among others. The hypothesis is that serious game users will have a better experience than those using the online quiz.

The second research goal (RG2) of this article is to examine whether the participants were more engaged while using the serious game compared to using the learning platform. The hypothesis is that the serious game users will engage more compared to the online quiz users.

The third research goal (RG3) of this paper is to establish the learning impact of the serious game compared to the learning platform on participants' academic performance. The hypothesis is that the serious game users will perform better on the final test compared to the online quiz users.

2.2. Participants

To test the hypotheses of our experiment, a total of 34 undergraduate computer science students were included in the activity, all of whom were taking the same class about Virtual Learning Environments (VLEs). This common course was elective for the students. The participants' ages ranged from 21 to 41 years old, with a mean age of 21.97 years, a median age equal to 21, and a standard deviation of 3.49. Among the participants, 23.52% were female and the remaining 76.47% were male. The participants were also asked about how often they engaged in playing digital games.. The majority of them, 32.53%, play digital games at least once per week. The remaining respondents consist of 2.94% who do not engage in video gaming; 23.53% who play video games rarely, less than once a month; 20.59% who play video games on a monthly basis; and 20.59% who play video games every day.

The participants were randomly separated into two groups. The experimental group comprised 16 individuals, whereas the control group comprised 18 people. Neither group had any prior exposure to the questions utilized in the main activity.

Prior to the experiment all participants were asked to sign a consent form.

2.3. Materials

2.3.1. The "Friend Me" Serious Game

"Friend Me" [38] is a serious game designed to facilitate the learning of any programming language, either from scratch or through practice, making it particularly suitable for novice programmers. This game was evaluated by undergraduate students from the computer science department, and, after receiving their comments, a new version of the game was created, incorporating improvements based on their feedback and introducing new features [39]. As a result, the game was assessed twice [38,39] by users with the same profile as the target group of our experiment in terms of player experience, namely in the areas of Usability, Confidence, Challenge, Satisfaction, Social Interaction, Fun, Focused Attention, and Relevance, ensuring its quality and making it optimal for utilization, as it is tailored to meet the specific requirements of the course.

The research described in this paper was conducted using the improved version of the game. The current version of the game includes questions related to web development, focusing on enhancing and practicing users' Hyper Text Markup Language (HTML), Cascading Style Sheets (CSS), and PHP knowledge.

It is designed to provide teachers the ability to effortlessly update its questions regularly, and it is easy to expand. The game is accessible through a web browser or downloadable via the Google Play Store, allowing players to choose their preferred platform. However, a constant internet connection is necessary throughout gameplay.

The game employs various elements, including goal-setting, interactions, rewards, and feedback, to engage learners and motivate them to persist in their learning journey. Leveraging competition as a motivational factor, "Friend Me" encourages players to strive to pursue exceptional performance. Each player has a personal account to monitor and track their progress.

The game's scenario revolves around a character attempting to make new friends in a new school by assisting their classmates (non-players characters, NPCs), who number fifteen. These classmates assign missions to the player, which are five unique missions that are repeated. Each mission consists of a question—either theoretical or code-based—that should be answered correctly to accomplish the mission. For those learning a programming language from scratch, the game offers mini courses to cover fundamental programming concepts, which were not used in our case as the students already had some basic knowledge.

Beyond answering the questions, players must explore and interact with the game's environment, transitioning from a question-and-answer format to a more immersive gaming experience (Figure 1). The game contains three types of questions: multiple choice, putting code blocks in the right order, and writing a code's result. In each question, there is a timer at the top-left part of the screen, set to one minute, challenging players answer within the allocated time. Otherwise, their response is counted as a mistake. In addition, the game displays a title at the top of the screen to indicate the question's context.

In a multiple-choice type question (Figure 2a), users are presented with four possible answers, with only one being correct. Upon selecting their answer, players receive immediate visual and sound feedback, confirming the accuracy of their response (Figure 2b,c). If they make a mistake, the correct answer is not revealed.

In the putting-code-blocks-in-the-right-order type of question (Figure 3a), five blocks are presented on the user's screen, and only four are required, which players must arrange in the correct order. Users can adjust the order until the final block is placed, at which point the game provides visual and sound feedback, indicating correct and incorrect placements (Figure 3b). In the case of a wrong answer, the correct order is revealed (Figure 3c).

In the final question type (Figure 4a), writing the code's result, users must accurately write the output of the code as it would appear when executed. After submitting their answer by clicking the "Done" or "Unlock" button, visual and auditory feedback is provided without revealing the correct answer, in the case of users answering incorrectly (Figure 4b,c).

If players wish to answer multiple questions consecutively, they can approach the computer area. When they decide to stop answering questions, they can return to the main game by clicking the return (left arrow) button on their screens.

For users practicing their programming skills, questions are randomly selected from the database. Players can track their performance, viewing the total number of questions they have answered correctly, their rank, the top three players and their scores (scores are calculated based on the number of correct answers, with each correct answer earning

1 point), earned badges linked to learning goals, and the mood of classmates towards players, reflecting successful or unsuccessful mission outcomes.

Figure 1. "Friend Me": interactions during a mission.

(**b**) (**c**)

Figure 2. "Friend Me": multiple-choice type questions. (**a**) Demonstration of a question in the game; (**b**) visualization of a correct answer; (**c**) visualization of a wrong answer.

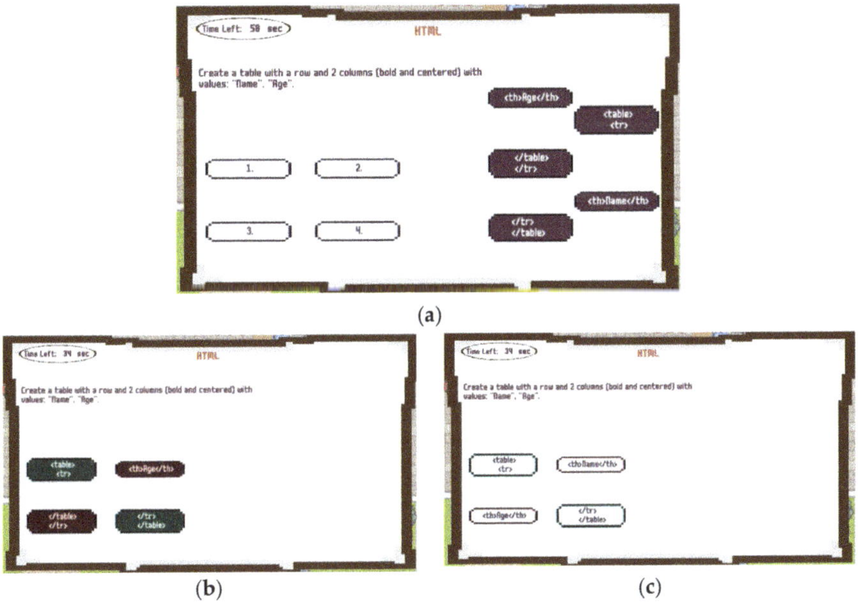

Figure 3. "Friend Me": putting-code-blocks-in-the-right-order type of question. (**a**) Demonstration of a question in the game; (**b**) visualization of correct and incorrect placements; (**c**) revelation of the correct order.

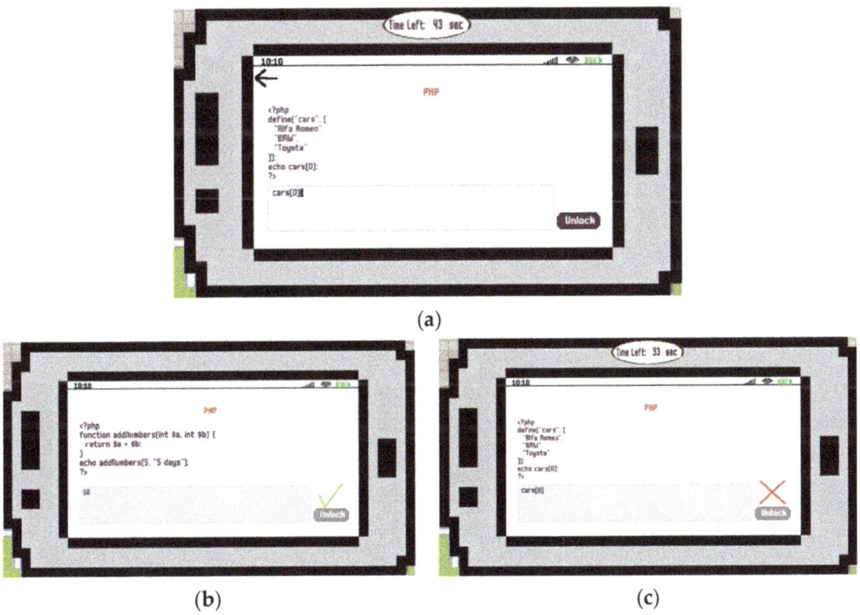

Figure 4. "Friend Me": questions that involve writing the code's result. (**a**) Demonstration of a question in the game; (**b**) visualization of correct answer; (**c**) visualization of wrong answer.

2.3.2. The Online Quiz

The online quiz was created to be similar to the serious game "Friend Me". It was created in a shared Moodle course that all the participants were registered on. On every attempt the quiz randomly showed 15 questions from the question bank created in the Moodle course. The Moodle settings that were utilized to create an interactive quiz experience like that of the game included (a) Timing, (b) Layout, (c) Question behavior, and (d) Review options.

The Timing settings were configured to enforce a time restriction of 15 min for the quiz. This was done to ensure that participants, like those who were engaged in the serious game, had an allocation of 1 min per question, given that there were 15 questions in total. In terms of the quiz's Layout options, each question was chosen to be displayed on a separate page. This was done to provide a similar experience to the serious game, where the player could only view one question at a time on their screen. In addition, concerning the Layout settings, they were adjusted to reorder the possible answers and questions in a manner comparable to the game's functionality. Moreover, instant feedback was provided to the users. Specifically, the system indicated the accuracy of a response using the textual labels "Correct", "Partially correct", or "Incorrect", as well as accompanying colored highlights that transmitted the same information.

Three sorts of questions were created, including multiple choice questions, code block ordering questions, and code result writing questions, similar to the serious game. The questions were exactly the same as those in the serious game. The questions functioned in the same manner as the questions in the serious game as well.

2.4. Instruments

The Intrinsic Motivation Inventory (IMI) questionnaire [40,41] was used to measure the subjective experience of the participants while using either the serious game or the learning platform to gain knowledge.

It consists of 45 items organized into the following seven categories: (a) Interest/Enjoyment, (b) Perceived Competence, (c) Effort/Importance, (d) Pressure/Tension, (e) Perceived Choice, (f) Value/Usefulness, and (g) Relatedness. In accordance with the construction guidelines of the questionnaire, the Relatedness category was not utilized in our study due to the absence of any interactions between participants during the experiment, meaning that the questionnaire handed to the participants consisted of 37 items. The questions were rated on a 7-point Likert scale, with the anchors being 1 for strongly disagree, 2 for disagree, 3 for slightly disagree, 4 for neither agree nor disagree, 5 for slightly agree, 6 for agree, and 7 for strongly agree.

Meanwhile, two sets of questions were prepared to serve as a pre-test and post-test questionnaire. The test was nine open-ended questions designed to assess participants' pre- and post-test knowledge of web technologies, including HTML, CSS, and the PHP programming language. All the questions assessed fundamental HTML proficiency, with six of them further evaluating CSS expertise, and the remaining three assessing participants' PHP knowledge, both in the pre-test and the post-test questionnaire.

In relation to the questions utilized in the main activity, three types of questions were created, including multiple choice questions, code block ordering questions, and code result writing questions. The generated collection of questions has a grand total of 124 questions, covering both theoretical and code-based content. The distribution of questions is as follows: there are 49 HTML questions (34 multiple choice, 12 putting code blocks in the right order, and 3 writing the code's result), 34 CSS questions (24 multiple choice and 10 putting code blocks in the right order) and 41 PHP questions (15 multiple choice, 14 putting code blocks in the right order, and 12 writing the code's result).

The course professor designed both the pre-test and post-test questionnaire, as well as the set of questions utilized in the serious game and the online quiz. The instructor of the course, who is an expert in Virtual Learning Environments (VLEs) as well as internet technologies, validated the validity of the questions.

2.5. Procedure

The research goals were achieved using a three-phase experiment, which included the Pre-test Phase, the Main Activity Phase, and the Post-test Phase. The participants were instructed to utilize different educational technology tools throughout the Main Activity Phase according to the group they were allocated to.

The participants were informed that the experiment aimed to assess the system that they utilized. They were also informed that the experiment would include some knowledge tests for statistical purposes, ensuring that they would not feel pressured to do well. Furthermore, it was explicitly stated that their participation or performance in the activity would have no impact on their overall mark in the course. The participants, after agreeing to voluntarily participate in the experiment, also possessed the right to end their involvement in the study at any given moment.

The participants were informed about each phase only after the previous one had been completed. The specifics of each phase were provided during a lecture and were also posted as announcements on the Moodle page of their shared course. The entire experiment lasted a period of three weeks.

2.5.1. The Pre-Test Phase

During the Pre-test phase, the course students that volunteered to participate in the experiment were handed a test, the pre-test questionnaire. The test aimed to assess their prior knowledge of web technologies such as HTML, PHP, and CSS, which students were expected to acquire throughout the Main Activity Phase. The test was presented in class, and it was uploaded as a Moodle quiz. It was explicitly stated that their performance would have no impact on their final mark for the course. The participants were given a two-hour timeframe to complete their test, although less time was required. Upon finishing the quiz the players did not get any feedback or a score.

While taking the test the students were randomly divided into two groups. One group served as the control group, while the other group served as the experimental group. Upon completing the test they were informed about which group they belonged to.

Afterwards, the software used in the Main Activity Phase was presented to each group. In particular, a quiz from the main activity was filled by the researchers and shown to the control group. As participants were already familiar with Moodle no further explanation was needed.

Meanwhile, the researchers in the experimental group played the serious game "Friend Me" for a period of time and demonstrated its many features. Participants were instructed to engage with the online version of the game during class. The researchers provided answers to any questions that arose. The objective of this brief session was to familiarize the participants with the game prior to its use in the main activity.

2.5.2. The Main Activity Phase

The Main Activity Phase lasted for three weeks. The participants were informed that they were able to start playing the game and start engaging with the online quiz. Each group had to fulfil a set of criteria to ensure that the participants had adequately used the software.

The individuals assigned to the control group had to answer an online quiz. The online quiz displayed a set of questions in a random sequence from the same pool of questions utilized in the serious game. The quiz had 15 questions, selected at random, and participants received immediate feedback on their responses. The participants were asked to undertake the quiz at least four times within the designated time frame. The quiz featured a strict time constraint of 15 min, allowing just one minute for each question. However, there were no restrictions on the number of attempts permitted for taking the quiz.

The experimental group was encouraged to play the game as long as they wanted to. However, in order to guarantee that they had answered a sufficient number of questions and had actively participated in the game, they were directed to refer to the Total Coverage bar, depicted in Figure 5. They were advised to aim for a score of at least twenty questions. The function of this bar is to display the player's activity by showing the number of questions they have answered correctly in relation to the total number of questions available in the database. Additionally, they were recommended to interact with a minimum of two non-player characters (NPCs). Each question had a duration of one minute.

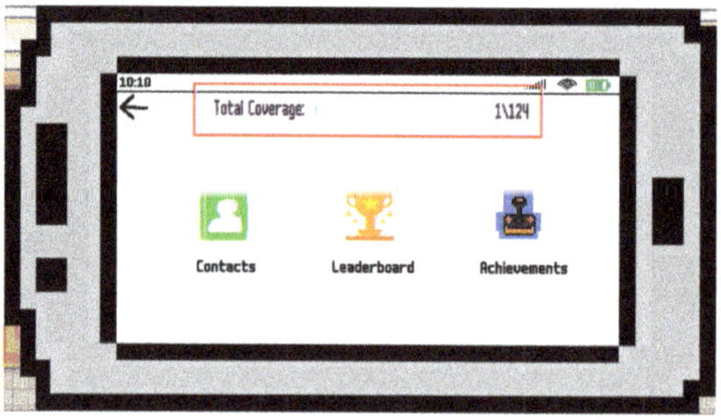

Figure 5. Total Coverage bar of the serious game "Friend Me".

For the Main Activity Phase, the participants used the software from their own personal computers whenever they wanted to and from their own space. The researchers were constantly available via email to provide any clarifications regarding the aforementioned criteria.

2.5.3. The Post-Test Phase

Following the conclusion of the three-week timeframe, the participants were given access to a final quiz. During class they were asked to complete the final assessment, known as the post-test questionnaire, which assessed their understanding of web technologies after successfully completing the main activity.

Upon the completion of the assessment by all individuals, they were subsequently given the IMI questionnaire. The survey was conducted over the internet. The participants were notified that the purpose of this questionnaire was to enhance our comprehension of their experience and gather feedback for possible improvements to the overall procedure's structure.

3. Results

3.1. Data Analysis and Results

The statistical analysis was performed using the SPSS 29 statistical package.

3.1.1. Analysis and Results of the First Research Goal (RG1)

Our main hypothesis for the first research goal was that serious game users would have a better experience than those using the online quiz. Thus, our null hypothesis was that there would be a difference in the scores of every dimension of the IMI questionnaire between the serious game and online quiz users.

Several studies have relied on the IMI questionnaire to assess the intrinsic motivation and overall experience of users when utilizing digital learning systems, including serious games [42–45] and learning management systems for e-learning [46,47]. In [48] it was used as a way to gather data regarding the intrinsic motivation of users using a course on an e-learning platform and an equivalent mobile serious game, with the objective of determining whether the serious game significantly increased users' intrinsic motivation.

Prior to any statistical analysis, a reliability test was performed for each of the seven factors of the IMI questionnaire using Cronbach's alpha measure. The Interest/Enjoyment factor score was 0.9. the Perceived Competence score was 0.87, the Effort/Importance factor score was 0.86, the Pressure/Tension score was 0.83, the Perceived Choice score was 0.85, and the Value/Usefulness score was 0.91. Therefore, every factor exhibited a level of internal consistency (measured by Cronbach's alpha) above 0.70. Ref. [49] stated that alpha coefficients of at least 0.70 are considered acceptable.

In order to investigate the first research goal (RG1), we conducted a comparison between the outcomes of the IMI questionnaire from the experimental group and the control group. The scoring instructions of the questionnaire state that some item replies should be reversed by subtracting the item response from 8 before then using the resultant number as the item score. Subsequently, a score may be computed for every factor by taking the average of all the items associated with that factor. Consequently, we obtained a score for each participant for every factor, which we utilized to compare the two groups.

Subsequently, we performed an independent samples' *t*-test comparing the two groups. The independent variable was the group variable, with a value of 0 representing the experimental group and 1 representing the control group. The dependent variables were the factor scores of each participant in the IMI questionnaire.

Given that the sample size was less than 50 ($N \leq 50$), we employed the Shapiro–Wilk test to assess whether the dependent variables of both the control and experimental groups conformed to a normal distribution. The *p*-value was more than 0.05 for the data sets for each factor in both groups, as seen in Table 1.

Table 1. Shapiro–Wilk Normality test.

Variable	Group	Sig.
Interest/Enjoyment	0	0.785
	1	0.509
Perceived Competence	0	0.769
	1	0.831
Effort/Importance	0	0.784
	1	0.964
Pressure/Tension	0	0.67
	1	0.52
Perceived Choice	0	0.964
	1	0.487
Value/Usefulness	0	0.102
	1	0.303

As a result, we could further investigate the independent samples' *t*-test. The obtained data were statistically insignificant, with a *p*-value greater than 0.05 in the 95% confidence range. The table labelled as Table 2 presents Lavene's test for the homogeneity of variance assumption, t-values, degrees of freedom, two-tailed significance *p*-values, and the effect size (Cohen's d) for each element of the IMI questionnaire in both the experimental and control group.

Table 2. Independent sample test for factors of the IMI questionnaire.

Variable	F	Sig.	t	df	Two-Sided *p*	Effect Size (Cohen's d)
Interest/Enjoyment	0.048	0.827	1.486	32	0.147	0.510
Perceived Competence	0.12	0.731	0.113	32	0.91	0.039
Effort/Importance	0.187	0.668	0.175	32	0.862	−0.06
Pressure/Tension	0.121	0.73	0.059	32	0.953	−0.02
Perceived Choice	1.627	0.211	0.359	32	0.722	0.123
Value/Usefulness	2.684	0.111	0.203	32	0.84	0.07

To conclude, an independent sample *t*-test was conducted to compare the scores in every dimension of the IMI questionnaire for serious game and online quiz users. The analysis revealed no significant difference in the scores for serious game users in the Interest/Enjoyment ($M = 5.16$, $SD = 1.05$), the Perceived Competence ($M = 4.73$, $SD = 1.06$), the Effort/Importance (M = 3.96, SD = 1.13), the Pressure/Tension (M = 2.85, SD = 1.29), the Perceived Choice (M = 5.25, SD = 0.92), and the Value/Usefulness (M = 5.43, SD = 1.27) dimensions and for online quiz users in the Interest/Enjoyment (M = 5.16, SD = 1.05), the Perceived Competence (M = 4.69, SD = 0.99), the Effort/Importance (M = 4.03, SD = 1.21), the Pressure/Tension (M = 2.88, SD = 1.35), the Perceived Choice (M = 5.11, SD = 1.30), and the Value/Usefulness (M = 5.35, SD = 0.90) dimensions.

Nevertheless, regarding the Interest/Enjoyment factor, although no significant findings were observed, the level of significance was relatively close to 0.05 ($p = 0.14$) and the effect size was equal to 0.510, which can be described as a medium effect size [50]. The descriptive statistics, alongside the medium effect size, reveal that the serious game received a higher score (Mean = 5.17, SD = 1.06) compared to the online quizzes (Mean = 4.59, SD = 1.17), even if statistical significance was not achieved. A boxplot depicting these variables is given in Figure 6.

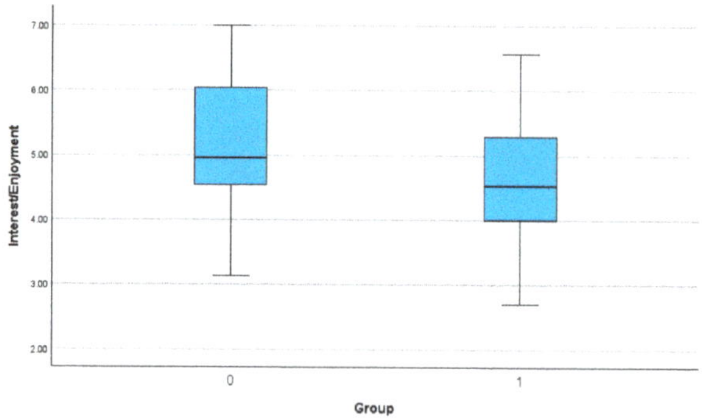

Figure 6. Boxplot of the Interest/Enjoyment variables.

Consequently, our primary hypothesis was rejected, indicating that the users of the serious game did not have a superior experience during the main activity compared to the group who used the online quiz.

3.1.2. Analysis and Results of the Second Research Goal (RG2)

The main hypothesis of our second research goal was that the users of serious games would exhibit higher levels of engagement in comparison to the users of online quizzes. Thus, our null hypothesis was that there would be a difference in the number of answered questions between the serious game and online quiz users. The number of answered questions has been utilized as a measure of engagement, serving as a shared metric for both the serious game and the online quiz. Previous studies have utilized the number of quiz attempts as an indicator of engagement with a learning module [51,52]. However, in our experiment, this measure is not applicable because the questions in the serious game were presented individually. Therefore, we have converted the quiz attempts into the number of questions answered, as the more times someone attempts a quiz more questions are answered.

The data were obtained from the log data of the serious game and the online quiz results.

A Shapiro–Wilk test indicated that both the control and experimental variables deviated from a normal distribution, as evidenced by their significances being below 0.001. Therefore, we conducted the independent samples Mann–Whitney test, which yielded a significance level of $p < 0.001$. The mean rank for the experimental group is 26, whereas the mean rank for the control group is 9.94. A boxplot of the results is depicted in Figure 7. The figure includes individuals whose values exceeded or fell below the maximum and minimum values of each boxplot, shown by asterisks. Each asterisk is accompanied with a number that serves as the ascending identifying number for each participant in the experiment.

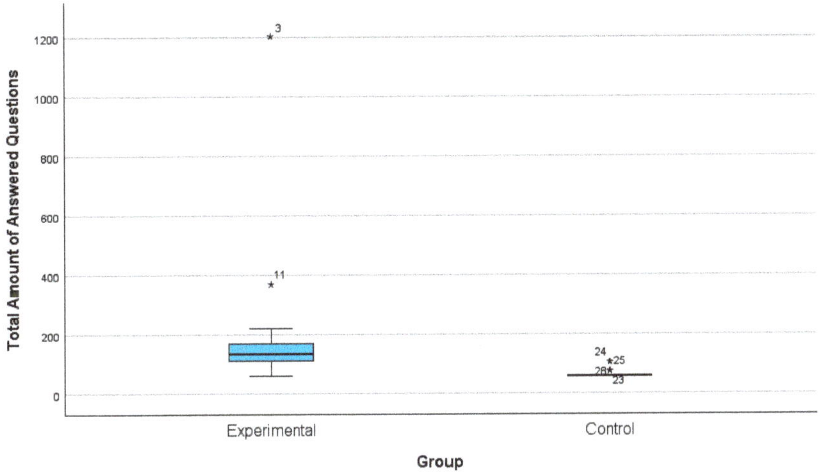

Figure 7. Boxplot of the total number of answered questions.

A Mann–Whitney U test was conducted to compare the number of questions answered by serious game and online quiz users. The analysis revealed a significant difference in the values for serious game users (Mdn = 136, IQR = 61) and online quiz users (Mdn = 60, IQR = 4): U = 8, Z = −4.865, $p < 0.001$. The results indicate that serious game users answered significantly more questions than the online quiz users.

3.1.3. Analysis and Results of The Third Research Goal (RG3)

Our third research goal had as its main hypothesis that serious game users would have a higher knowledge gain compared to online quiz users. Thus, our null hypothesis was that there would be a difference in the post-test scores between the users of serious games and online quizzes. Pre-test and post-test scores have traditionally been utilized in educational research to examine the impact of educational innovations [53]. In our study, we are using post-test scores as a measure to determine whether serious game players acquired more knowledge than online quiz users.

However, first, we should establish whether there was any significant difference in the prior knowledge of web technologies between the two groups. To do so, we conducted the independent samples Mann–Whitney U test between the two groups. The independent variable was the group variable (0 for the experimental and 1 for the control group) and the dependent variable was the score on the pre-test questionnaires.

As our sample size is smaller than 50 ($N \leq 50$), the Shapiro–Wilk test was used to examine whether the two pre-test score variables (control and experimental) did not follow a normal distribution, with significances equal to $p = 0.02 < 0.05$ and $p = 0.01 < 0.05$, respectively. Therefore, we conducted the independent samples Mann–Whitney test, which yielded a significance level of $p = 0.93 > 0.05$, which led us to retain our null hypothesis that the distribution of the pre-test scores was the same across both groups. We can see the plot of these two variables in Figure 8. This allows us to investigate further the performance of the users in the post-test questionnaire.

As the sample size is smaller than 50 ($N \leq 50$), the Shapiro–Wilk test was used to examine whether the two post-test score variables (control and experimental) did not follow a normal distribution, with significances equal to $p < 0.01 < 0.05$ and $p = 0.01 < 0.05$, respectively. Therefore, we conducted the independent samples Mann–Whitney test, which yielded a significance level of $p = 0.99 > 0.05$, which led us to retain our main hypothesis that the distribution of the post-test scores is the same across both groups. We can see the plot of these two variables in Figure 9.

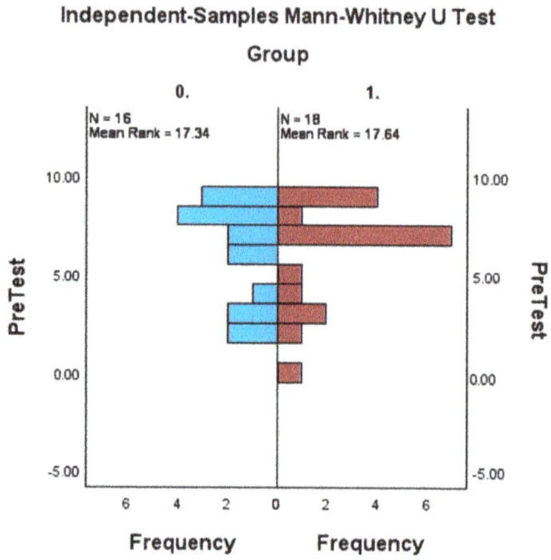

Figure 8. Independent Samples Mann–Whitney U Test of the pre-test scores.

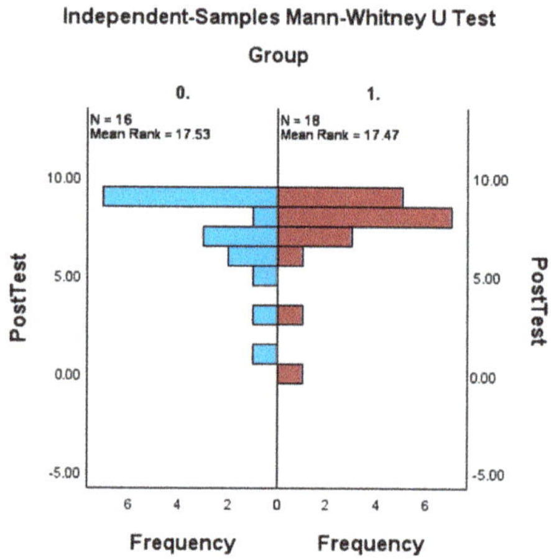

Figure 9. Independent Samples Mann–Whitney U test of the post-test scores.

An independent samples Mann–Whitney test was conducted to compare the scores on the final test between the serious game and online quiz users. Our analysis revealed no significant difference in the values for serious game users (Mdn = 7, IQR = 2.5) and online quiz users (Mdn = 7.75, IQR = 1.63): U = 143.5, Z = −0.17, p = 0.986. The results indicate that the serious game users did not perform better in their post-test questionnaire compared to the online quiz users.

4. Discussion and Conclusions

The aforementioned results are concluded and discussed in detail for each specific research goal in the following paragraphs.

4.1. First Research Goal (RG1)

Regarding the first research goal, our main hypothesis was rejected, suggesting that the participants who used the serious game did not have a superior experience in the primary activity compared to the group that utilized the online quiz. Specifically, the users of the serious game did not experience a significant increase in their sense of competence compared to the online quiz users. They reported putting in equal effort and feeling similar levels of pressure as the participants in the control group. Additionally, the perceived level of choice they had was similar to that of the online quiz users. Finally, they discovered both tools to be equally valuable.

Current research indicates that online quizzes are both motivating and able to provide a comparable experience to serious games. This aligns with the findings that Moodle, and learning platforms in general, are an effective tool for teachers to motivate students [54], particularly through the use of e-assessments [55].

Furthermore, the comparable motivation levels seen between participants taking online quizzes and those playing the serious game can be attributed to the competitive goal structure of the game, which has been found to elicit not as strong a motivation compared to games with a cooperative goal structure [56]. In our serious game, a scoreboard displaying the top three players is visible to all participants. The user's objective is to either achieve a rating that is among the top three players or to build relationships with non-player characters (NPCs) by answering questions properly. This might have resulted in the game becoming too competitive, as the player's primary objective is to answer questions properly, thus reducing its entertainment value to that of a simple online quiz.

In addition, the game inlcuded rewards such as points and badges, which usually leads to enjoyment according to [57], as was also proved in [58], but the respondents also had the choice to answer questions using a computer station in the game. By bypassing the socializing and tasks, players would be able to answer questions continually, which might have prevented them from obtaining items and exploring the game area. This may have also diminished the level of enjoyment for certain individuals.

4.2. Second Research Goal (RG2)

Regarding our second research goal (RG2), our main hypothesis was confirmed, indicating that the experimental group had a considerably greater number of answered questions compared to the control group. Consequently, the serious game effectively enhanced the participants' engagement with the activity, resulting in a significant rise in the number of questions they answered.

A recent study demonstrated that serious games have been proven to be an effective method in recent years for enhancing student engagement, among other benefits [59]. An investigation was conducted [60], utilizing serious games to improve performance during the COVID-19 period. The study found that the suggested pedagogical model received high praise from students in terms of engagement, increased motivation, and a meaningful learning experience. These findings support our own discovery that students answered a greater number of questions through the serious game compared to the online quiz during the Main Activity Phase.

The finding that the players of the serious game exhibited higher levels of engagement is substantial, as engagement in virtual learning typically leads to a pleasant learning experience and a sense of fulfilment [61]. Moreover, the findings of [62] indicate that different kinds of engagement, such as behavioral, cognitive and emotional, exhibit a substantial influence on the learning outcomes of online learning.

4.3. Third Research Goal (RG3)

Concerning our third research goal (RG3), our primary hypothesis that serious game users would perform better in the post-test questionnaire compared to the online quiz users was rejected, as the findings were not significant. This can also be easily seen through descriptive statistics, as the experimental group had a mean of 6.75 and an SD = 2.41, while the control group had a mean of 7 and an SD = 2.21.

This aligns with the findings of a conducted study [25], which utilized three empirical studies to demonstrate the efficacy of serious games compared to standard classroom instruction in terms of learning aspects and results. Although the findings indicated that the students had a higher level of competence when utilizing serious games as a tool for learning, and they reported high engagement and motivation, this improvement was not reflected in their performance on knowledge tests. The study argued that the assessment methods used on the students were not aligned with their learning experience in the serious game, which was one of the determining factors of these results.

In addition, further research [63] aimed to establish the correlation between the enjoyment of games, self-reported cognitive and motivational learning improvements, and test outcomes through an empirical investigation. The study determined that the extent to which students found studying enjoyable had a significant influence on their motivation and level of involvement, but that it did not have any noticeable impact on their measured learning outcomes.

The absence of substantial findings with regard to this research question might potentially be attributed to time constraints. The entire duration of the experiment lasted three weeks, which may have been insufficient to adequately demonstrate the potential influence of the game on academic achievement. In [64], a direct correlation between the duration of instructional minutes in an academic year and standardized test results was found at school sites. If the participants had utilized the serious game for an extended duration, it is likely that they would have exhibited improved performance, taking it as a fact that active engagement typically results in enhanced learning outcomes, as was discussed in our previous research goal.

According to the meta-analysis [65], it is difficult to verify the association between engagement and learning. Based on [66], even if the users were more engaged compared to traditional teaching, based on their feedback questionnaires, observation found no significant difference in the knowledge gains between the two groups. Although users may have been initially attracted to the idea of learning through a game and may have enjoyed it more than traditional methods, minimal knowledge gains were found due to them being distracted by the game.

4.4. Conclusions

The present study concludes that, throughout the duration of the experiment, the level of engagement exhibited by the participants utilizing the serious game was significantly higher than that of the online quiz users, as evidenced by their larger number of answered questions (RG2). This might be attributed to their heightened interest in the game, which led them to prefer continuing to play and then to respond to questions, as opposed to accessing an online quiz.

Regarding our first research goal, there were no significant findings in terms of the subjective experiences of the two groups, control and experimental. However, the fact that the Interest/Enjoyment dimension of the questionnaire had a significance level pretty close to 0.05 confirms that the game is very motivating for users and suggests that it would be advantageous to replicate the experiment with a larger sample size.

Furthermore, the absence of any noteworthy discoveries regarding the serious game in the questionnaire, even in areas where serious games are known to have an impact, may be influenced by the number of questions that participants were required to answer, as previously described. This may have significantly impacted dimensions such as the perceived pressure experienced during the utilization of the serious game in the Main Activity Phase, as well as the dimension of Perceived Choice. Although the users had the option to withdraw from the experiment without facing any consequences, individuals may have felt compelled to complete the experiment, turning it into another academic obligation.

Another element that might have affected these results was the serious game that was used. Even though the game consisted of a set of questions created by the professor of the course, who is an expert in his field, and although it had been evaluated twice regarding the players' experience, by undergraduate students and by experts, for its usability, some elements are missing that are considered to be essential to enhance multimedia learning [67]. The fact that the NPCs did not use a voice that was either human or computer-generated when the user interacted with them might have decreased the emotional engagement of the game, making it less appealing to users.

Moreover, the Pre-training principle [67] suggests that, before asking the players to answer to some questions, a brief introduction to the key concepts might be beneficial to them. As the game was tailored to the needs of the course, and it was utilized as supplementary material, similar to online quizzes with feedback, no learning was achieved through teaching, but only through self-assessing one's knowledge and through feedback, as would happen when answering online quizzes. This might have negatively affected several dimensions of the IMI questionnaire, such as the effort dimension, as both the online quiz and the serious game were equally hard for participants. However, in our case, as the serious game was customized to the course and was meant to be compared with regular quizzes on a learning platform, if the game included tips it would make it unsuitable for us to compare the two to figure out the best way to provide practice quizzes to students.

Finally, regarding the third research goal, the grades from the post-test questionnaire did not show any significant difference. The outcome may have been influenced by limitations such as the duration of the experiment and the type of post-test questions used.

5. Limitations and Future Steps

It is important to acknowledge the limitations of the current study when evaluating its results. The control and experimental groups have a limited sample size. Moreover, despite the fact that only a small sample of participants was used, no qualitative evaluation was conducted, which results in us having no comments with which to better explore the results of our research questions. Furthermore, the duration of the experiment may not have been adequate to demonstrate significant improvements in performance on the final exam and exceptional learning outcomes (RG3). The requirement for a minimal level of engagement with the materials to consider a participant as having effectively utilized them might potentially have had a negative impact on the participants' experience (RG1). Since the participants were computer science students, they could have acquired knowledge about the web technologies included in the experiment from external sources that they found on their own and might have answered relevant questions, potentially affecting the results of the post-test questionnaire (RG3). Furthermore, the study exclusively employed a serious game of a certain genre for the purpose of comparing it with online quizzes. This constraint restricts our capacity to make comprehensive generalizations regarding serious games.

Future research should include samples of participants lacking a computer science background and provide these tools, the quizzes and the serious game, alongside a set of relevant educational resources. Furthermore, we want to prolong the duration of the experimental time in which the material is applied to include an entire semester, consisting of 18 weeks. It is anticipated that the serious game players would achieve improved post-test scores due to their increased engagement, which is likely to result in enhanced learning outcomes. Ultimately, a more extensive pool of participants will be utilized, perhaps resulting in significant discoveries about the factor of Interest/Enjoyment from the IMI questionnaire.

In future work it will be essential to include a qualitative evaluation, which involves conducting interviews or focus groups, in addition to the quantitative evaluation. This would assist researchers in addressing gaps in their quantitative data findings and enhancing their comprehension of the results, if outcomes similar to those of the first and third research goals arise, without any significant findings. Utilizing a variety of serious games with distinct game mechanics, aesthetic and narrative designs, and musical scores that align with the learning objective of our present project would also be beneficial, as the results would not be affected by the particular game that was chosen by the researchers.

Author Contributions: Conceptualization, L.K. and G.S.; methodology, L.K. and G.S.; software, L.K. and G.S.; validation, L.K. and G.S.; formal analysis, L.K.; investigation, L.K.; resources, L.K. and G.S.; data curation, L.K. and G.S.; writing—original draft preparation, L.K. and G.S.; writing—review and editing, T.T.; visualization, L.K.; supervision, T.T.; project administration, T.T.; funding acquisition, T.T. All authors have read and agreed to the published version of the manuscript.

Funding: This research received no external funding.

Data Availability Statement: The data presented in this study are available upon request from the corresponding author. The data are not publicly available due to restrictions enforced by the process of the Aristotle University ethics and legislation committee.

Acknowledgments: We express our gratitude to H. Apostolidis for his invaluable assistance and to the participants in the experiment who generously dedicated their time to supporting our research efforts

Conflicts of Interest: The authors declare no conflicts of interest.

References

1. Säljö, R. Digital tools and challenges to institutional traditions of learning: Technologies, social memory and the performative nature of learning. *J. Comput. Assist. Learn.* **2010**, *26*, 53–64. [CrossRef]
2. van Rooij, A.J.; Schoenmakers, T.M.; van de Eijnden, R.J.; van de Mheen, D. Compulsive Internet Use: The Role of Online Gaming and Other Internet Applications. *J. Adolesc. Health* **2010**, *47*, 51–57. [CrossRef] [PubMed]
3. Van den Eijnden, R.; Koning, I.; Doornwaard, S.; Van Gurp, F.; Ter Bogt, T. The impact of heavy and disordered use of games and social media on adolescents' psychological, social, and school functioning. *J. Behav. Addict.* **2018**, *7*, 697–706. [CrossRef] [PubMed]
4. Dolan, R.; Conduit, J.; Frethey-Bentham, C.; Fahy, J.; Goodman, S. Social media engagement behavior: A framework for engaging customers through social media content. *Eur. J. Mark.* **2019**, *53*, 2213–2243. [CrossRef]
5. Neumann, D.; Huddleston, P.T.; Behe, B.K. Fear of Missing Out as motivation to process information: How differences in Instagram use affect attitude formation online. *New Media Soc.* **2023**, *25*, 220–242. [CrossRef]
6. Kim, K.-S.; Sin, S.-C.J.; Yoo-Lee, E.Y. Undergraduates' Use of Social Media as Information Sources. *Coll. Res. Libr.* **2014**, *75*, 442–457. [CrossRef]
7. Silaban, P.H.; Silalahi, A.D.K.; Octoyuda, E. Understanding consumers' addiction to online mobile games and in apps purchase intention: Players stickiness as the mediation. *J. Manaj. dan Pemasar. Jasa* **2021**, *14*, 165–178. [CrossRef]
8. Xu, Z.; Turel, O.; Yuan, Y. Online game addiction among adolescents: Motivation and prevention factors. *Eur. J. Inf. Syst.* **2012**, *21*, 321–340. [CrossRef]
9. Elen, J.; Clarebout, G. Learning Technology. In *Encyclopedia of the Sciences of Learning*; Seel, N.M., Ed.; Springer: New York, NY, USA, 2012; pp. 1980–1981. [CrossRef]
10. Haleem, A.; Javaid, M.; Qadri, M.A.; Suman, R. Understanding the role of digital technologies in education: A review. *Sustain. Oper. Comput.* **2022**, *3*, 275–285. [CrossRef]
11. Kitsantas, A.; Dabbagh, N. *Learning to Learn with Integrative Learning Technologies (ILT): A Practical Guide for Academic Success*; Information Age Publishing: Charlotte, NC, USA, 2010.
12. Graesser, A.C. Evolution of Advanced Learning Technologies in the 21st Century. *Theory Into Pract.* **2013**, *52* (Suppl. S1), 93–101. [CrossRef]
13. Dabbagh, N.; Benson, A.D.; Denham, A.; Joseph, R.; Al-Freih, M.; Zgheib, G.; Fake, H.; Guo, Z. Evolution of Learning Technologies: Past, Present, and Future. In *Learning Technologies and Globalization: Pedagogical Frameworks and Applications*; Dabbagh, N., Benson, A.D., Denham, A., Joseph, R., Al-Freih, M., Zgheib, G., Fake, H., Guo, Z., Eds.; Springer International Publishing: Cham, Switzerland, 2016; pp. 1–7. [CrossRef]
14. Chan, T.-W.; Roschelle, J.; Hsi, S.; Kinshuk Sharples, M.; Brown, T.; Patton, C.; Cherniavsky, J.; Pea, R.; Norris, C.; Soloway, E.; et al. One-to-one technology-enhanced learning: An opportunity for global research collaboration. *Res. Pract. Technol. Enhanc. Learn.* **2006**, *1*, 3–29. [CrossRef]
15. Abt, C.C. *Serious Games*; University Press of America: Lanham, MA, USA, 1987.
16. Marsh, T. Serious games continuum: Between games for purpose and experiential environments for purpose. *Entertain. Comput.* **2011**, *2*, 61–68. [CrossRef]
17. Laamarti, F.; Eid, M.; El Saddik, A. An Overview of Serious Games. *Int. J. Comput. Games Technol.* **2014**, *2014*, 1–15. [CrossRef]
18. Djaouti, D.; Alvarez, J.; Jessel, J.-P. *Classifying Serious Games: The G/P/S Model*; IGI Global: Hershey, PA, USA, 2011; p. 118. [CrossRef]
19. Zhonggen, Y. A Meta-Analysis of Use of Serious Games in Education over a Decade. *Int. J. Comput. Games Technol.* **2019**, *2019*, e4797032. [CrossRef]
20. Granic, I.; Lobel, A.; Engels, R.C.M.E. The benefits of playing video games. *Am. Psychol.* **2014**, *69*, 66–78. [CrossRef]
21. Giglioli, I.A.C.; Ripoll, C.d.J.; Parra, E.; Raya, M.A. EXPANSE: A novel narrative serious game for the behavioral assessment of cognitive abilities. *PLoS ONE* **2018**, *13*, e0206925. [CrossRef] [PubMed]

22. Wiemeyer, J.; Kliem, A. Serious games in prevention and rehabilitation—A new panacea for elderly people? *Eur. Rev. Aging Phys. Act.* **2011**, *9*, 41–50. [CrossRef]
23. Marengo, A.; Pagano, A.; Soomro, K.A. Serious games to assess university students' soft skills: Investigating the effectiveness of a gamified assessment prototype. *Interact. Learn. Environ.* **2024**, 1–17. [CrossRef]
24. De Troyer, O. Towards effective serious games. In Proceedings of the 2017 9th International Conference on Virtual Worlds and Games for Serious Applications (VS-Games), Athens, Greece, 6–8 September 2017; pp. 284–289. [CrossRef]
25. Bakhuys Roozeboom, M.; Visschedijk, G.; Oprins, E. The effectiveness of three serious games measuring generic learning features. *Br. J. Educ. Technol.* **2017**, *48*, 83–100. [CrossRef]
26. David, O.A.; Magurean, S.; Tomoiagă, C. Do Improvements in Therapeutic Game-Based Skills Transfer to Real Life Improvements in Children's Emotion-Regulation Abilities and Mental Health? A Pilot Study That Offers Preliminary Validity of the REThink In-game Performance Scoring. *Front. Psychiatry* **2022**, *13*, 828481. [CrossRef]
27. Nørlev, J.; Sondrup, K.; Derosche, C.; Hejlesen, O.; Hangaard, S. Game Mechanisms in Serious Games That Teach Children with Type 1 Diabetes How to Self-Manage: A Systematic Scoping Review. *J. Diabetes Sci. Technol.* **2022**, *16*, 1253–1269. [CrossRef]
28. Lieberman, D.A. Video Games for Diabetes Self-Management: Examples and Design Strategies. *J. Diabetes Sci. Technol.* **2012**, *6*, 802–806. [CrossRef]
29. Radhakrishnan, K.; Toprac, P.; O'Hair, M.; Bias, R.; Kim, M.T.; Bradley, P.; Mackert, M. Interactive Digital e-Health Game for Heart Failure Self-Management: A Feasibility Study. *Games Health J.* **2016**, *5*, 366–374. [CrossRef]
30. Sarasmita, M.A.; Larasanty, L.P.F.; Kuo, L.N.; Cheng, K.J.; Chen, H.Y. A Computer-Based Interactive Narrative and a Serious Game for Children With Asthma: Development and Content Validity Analysis. *J. Med. Internet Res.* **2021**, *23*, e28796. [CrossRef] [PubMed]
31. Kapp, F.; Spangenberger, P.; Kruse, L.; Narciss, S. Investigating changes in self-evaluation of technical competences in the serious game Serena Supergreen: Findings, challenges and lessons learned. *Metacognition Learn.* **2019**, *14*, 387–411. [CrossRef]
32. Passos, E.B.; Medeiros, D.B.; Neto, P.A.S.; Clua, E.W.G. Turning Real-World Software Development into a Game. In Proceedings of the 2011 Brazilian Symposium on Games and Digital Entertainment, Salvador, Brazil, 7–9 November 2011; pp. 260–269. [CrossRef]
33. Caulfield, C.; Xia, J.; Veal, D.; Maj, S. A Systematic Survey of Games Used for Software Engineering Education. *Mod. Appl. Sci.* **2011**, *5*, 6. [CrossRef]
34. Yassine, A.; Chenouni, D.; Berrada, M.; Tahiri, A. A Serious Game for Learning C Programming Language Concepts Using Solo Taxonomy. *Int. J. Emerg. Technol. Learn. (IJET)* **2017**, *12*, 3. [CrossRef]
35. Sideris, G.; Xinogalos, S. PY-RATE ADVENTURES: A 2D Platform Serious Game for Learning the Basic Concepts of Programming With Python. *Simul. Gaming* **2019**, *50*, 754–770. [CrossRef]
36. Xinogalos, S. Programming Serious Games as a Master Course: Feasible or Not? *Simul. Gaming* **2017**, *49*, 8–26. [CrossRef]
37. Cadavid, J. Digital Competition Game to Improve Programming Skills. *Educ. Technol. Soc.* **2012**, *15*, 288–297.
38. Skraparli, G.; Karavidas, L.; Tsiatsos, T. Dynamic Serious Game for Developing Programming Skills. In *New Realities, Mobile Systems and Applications*; Auer, M.E., Tsiatsos, T., Eds.; Springer International Publishing: Cham, Switzerland, 2022; pp. 580–592. [CrossRef]
39. Skraparli, G.; Akritidis, M.; Karavidas, L.; Tsiatsos, T. Improvement and Evaluation of Serious Game "Friend Me". In *Learning in the Age of Digital and Green Transition*; Auer, M.E., Pachatz, W., Rüütmann, T., Eds.; Springer In-ternational Publishing: Cham, Switzerland, 2023; pp. 971–981. [CrossRef]
40. Ryan, R.M.; Mims, V.; Koestner, R. Relation of reward contingency and interpersonal context to intrinsic motivation: A review and test using cognitive evaluation theory. *J. Personal. Soc. Psychol.* **1983**, *45*, 736. [CrossRef]
41. Ryan, R.M. Control and information in the intrapersonal sphere: An extension of cognitive evaluation theory. *J. Personal. Soc. Psychol.* **1982**, *43*, 450. [CrossRef]
42. Alexandrovsky, D.; Friehs, M.A.; Grittner, J.; Putze, S.; Birk, M.V.; Malaka, R.; Mandryk, R.L. Serious snacking: A survival analysis of how snacking mechanics affect attrition in a mobile serious game. In Proceedings of the 2021 CHI Conference on Human Factors in Computing Systems, Yokohama, Japan, 8–13 May 2021; pp. 1–18.
43. Bessa, D.; Rodrigues, N.F.; Oliveira, E.; Kolbenschag, J.; Prahm, C. Designing a serious game for myoelectric prosthesis control. In Proceedings of the 2020 IEEE 8th International Conference on Serious Games and Applications for Health (SeGAH), Vancouver, BC, Canada, 12–14 August 2020; pp. 1–5.
44. Guillén-Climent, S.; Garzo, A.; Muñoz-Alcaraz, M.N.; Casado-Adam, P.; Arcas-Ruiz-Ruano, J.; Mejías-Ruiz, M.; Mayordomo-Riera, F.J. A usability study in patients with stroke using MERLIN, a robotic system based on serious games for upper limb rehabilitation in the home setting. *J. Neuroeng. Rehabil.* **2021**, *18*, 41. [CrossRef] [PubMed]
45. Hashim, N.A.; Abd Razak, N.A.; Gholizadeh, H.; Abu Osman, N.A. Video game–based rehabilitation approach for individuals who have undergone upper limb amputation: Case-control study. *JMIR Serious Games* **2021**, *9*, e17017. [CrossRef] [PubMed]
46. Jurgelaitis, M.; Čeponienė, L.; Čeponis, J.; Drungilas, V. Implementing gamification in a university-level UML modeling course: A case study. *Comput. Appl. Eng. Educ.* **2019**, *27*, 332–343. [CrossRef]
47. Facey-Shaw, L.; Specht, M.; van Rosmalen, P.; Bartley-Bryan, J. Do badges affect intrinsic motivation in introductory programming students? *Simul. Gaming* **2020**, *51*, 33–54. [CrossRef]

48. Leenaraj, B.; Arayaphan, W.; Intawong, K.; Puritat, K. A gamified mobile application for first-year student orientation to promote library services. *J. Librariansh. Inf. Sci.* **2023**, *55*, 137–150. [CrossRef]
49. Nunnally, J.C. *Psychometric Theory*, 2nd ed.; McGraw-Hill: New York, NY, USA, 1978.
50. Cohen, J. *Statistical Power Analysis for the Behavioral Sciences*; Academic Press: Cambridge, MA, USA, 2013.
51. Doherty, C. An investigation into the relationship between multimedia lecture design and learners' engagement behaviours using web log analysis. *PLoS ONE* **2022**, *17*, e0273007. [CrossRef]
52. O'Dowd, I. Using learning analytics to improve online formative quiz engagement. *Ir. J. Technol. Enhanc. Learn.* **2018**, *3*, 30–43. [CrossRef]
53. Dugard, P.; Todman, J. Analysis of pre-test-post-test control group designs in educational research. *Educ. Psychol.* **1995**, *15*, 181–198. [CrossRef]
54. Aikina, T.; Bolsunovskaya, L. Moodle-based learning: Motivating and demotivating factors. *Int. J. Emerg. Technol. Learn. (IJET)* **2020**, *15*, 239–248. [CrossRef]
55. Elshareif, E.; Mohamed, E.A. The Effects of E-Learning on Students' Motivation to Learn in Higher Education. *Online Learn.* **2021**, *25*, 128–143. [CrossRef]
56. Peng, W.; Hsieh, G. The influence of competition, cooperation, and player relationship in a motor performance centered computer game. *Comput. Hum. Behav.* **2012**, *28*, 2100–2106. [CrossRef]
57. Plass, J.L.; Homer, B.D.; Kinzer, C.K. Foundations of game-based learning. *Educ. Psychol.* **2015**, *50*, 258–283. [CrossRef]
58. King, D.L.; Delfabbro, P.H.; Griffiths, M.D. The role of structural characteristics in problematic video game play: An empirical study. *Int. J. Ment. Health Addict.* **2011**, *9*, 320–333. [CrossRef]
59. Yu, Z.; Sukjairungwattana, P.; Xu, W. Effects of Serious Games on Student Engagement, Motivation, Learning Strategies, Cognition, and Enjoyment. *Int. J. Adult Educ. Technol. (IJAET)* **2022**, *13*, 1–15. [CrossRef]
60. Arias-Calderón, M.; Castro, J.; Gayol, S. Serious games as a method for enhancing learning engagement: Student perception on online higher education during COVID-19. *Front. Psychol.* **2022**, *13*, 889975. [CrossRef] [PubMed]
61. Farrell, O.; Brunton, J. A balancing act: A window into online student engagement experiences. *Int. J. Educ. Technol. High. Educ.* **2020**, *17*, 25. [CrossRef]
62. Wang, C.; Mirzaei, T.; Xu, T.; Lin, H. How learner engagement impacts non-formal online learning outcomes through value co-creation: An empirical analysis. *Int. J. Educ. Technol. High. Educ.* **2022**, *19*, 1–26. [CrossRef]
63. Iten, N.; Petko, D. Learning with serious games: Is fun playing the game a predictor of learning success? *Br. J. Educ. Technol.* **2016**, *47*, 151–163. [CrossRef]
64. Jez, S.J.; Wassmer, R.W. The impact of learning time on academic achievement. *Educ. Urban Soc.* **2015**, *47*, 284–306. [CrossRef]
65. Girard, C.; Ecalle, J.; Magnan, A. Serious games as new educational tools: How effective are they? A meta-analysis of recent studies. *J. Comput. Assist. Learn.* **2013**, *29*, 207–219. [CrossRef]
66. Wrzesien, M.; Raya, M.A. Learning in serious virtual worlds: Evaluation of learning effectiveness and appeal to students in the E-Junior project. *Comput. Educ.* **2010**, *55*, 178–187. [CrossRef]
67. Mayer, R.E. Multimedia learning. In *Psychology of Learning and Motivation*; Academic Press: Cambridge, MA, USA, 2002; Volume 41, pp. 85–139.

computers

MDPI

Article

Enhancing Collaborative Learning and E-Mentoring in a Smart Education System in Higher Education

Loan Nguyen [1], Sarath Tomy [2] and Eric Pardede [3,*]

[1] Faculty of Informatics and Foreign Languages, The Army Academy, Da Lat, Lam Dong 66000, Vietnam; loan.nguyenthithanh.aa@gmail.com
[2] Department of Computer Science and Information Technology, School of Computing, Engineering and Mathematical Sciences, Bendigo Campus, La Trobe University, Bendigo, VIC 3552, Australia; s.tomy@latrobe.edu.au
[3] Department of Computer Science and Information Technology, School of Computing, Engineering and Mathematical Sciences, Melbourne Campus, La Trobe University, Melbourne, VIC 3086, Australia
* Correspondence: e.pardede@latrobe.edu.au

Abstract: The requirement to develop a smart education system is critical in the era of ubiquitous technology. In the smart education environment, intelligent pedagogies are constructed to take advantage of technological devices and foster learners' competencies which undoubtedly assist learners in dealing with knowledge and handling issues in a dynamic society more effectively and productively. This research suggests two effective learning strategies: (1) collaborative learning, which helps learners improve their knowledge and skills by exchanging resources and experiences, and (2) e-mentoring, which connects learners to a wide range of professional communities. This research first proposes a model to show how these two learning methods help learners achieve their goals, along with a set of hypotheses that are explained in detail. Then, a smart education system is proposed which comprises the two learning strategies with the necessary features. Lastly, two questionnaires, one for facilitators and the other for learners, are used to evaluate the usefulness and the feasibility of the proposed model in a real-world educational environment. The great majority of respondents agreed with all the statements, demonstrating the efficiency of the research for educators and learners.

Keywords: collaborative learning; e-mentoring; smart education; smart learning environment; smart learners; smart pedagogies

1. Introduction

Technology has had a positive impact on most aspects of society, including education and learning [1,2]. The technological transformation of education has not only had an impact on learning materials and classroom boundaries, but it also offers learners various opportunities to acquire a range of skills and knowledge by connecting to a wide professional learning network [2,3]. Educators and learners are no longer limited by learning borders due to advances in technology, which has made online learning and hybrid learning possible, giving learners greater flexibility, a wide selection of courses, accessibility, and cost-effective options [4]. Online and hybrid learning also open the door to learning communities around the world, where learners can build a network and develop an international mindset [4].

In particular, in the era of the fourth industrial revolution, known as Industry 4.0, the development of digitalisation and the increasingly convergent boundaries between humans and machines are expected to produce a qualified and highly educated workforce [5,6]. Learners are required to acquire holistic competencies, including technical and non-technical skills that cannot be attained by learning from books and lectures alone [5]. Hence, designing a smart education system is of critical importance to offer learners the opportunity to choose the learning pathway that is the most effective for them.

The smart education paradigm is one of the most effective and promising directions for educational development. The purpose of smart education is to cultivate a smart learner generation by immersing learners in intelligent pedagogies facilitated by smart environments with the support of technological advances [7]. There are three key factors contributing to a complete smart education system: smart learners, smart pedagogies, and smart environments. Smart learners not only possess sustainable hard skills, but also need to achieve the necessary soft skills, both in terms of personal skills (complex problem-solving, critical thinking, creativity, out-of-the-box thinking, emotional intelligence, and cognitive flexibility), and social skills (communication, teamwork, negotiation, and leadership skills) [8]. A smart environment and smart pedagogy support smart learners on their learning pathways. A smart environment is shaped by both software and hardware technological support, digital resources, and the contribution of smart pedagogies that are designed based on a learner-centric paradigm to shape learners who have different backgrounds, levels, and interests to enhance their necessary knowledge skills [7]. Consequently, two major pedagogical strategies, collaborative learning and e-mentoring, are designed to improve learners' knowledge, experience, and skills by not only encouraging them to actively communicate and exchange valuable learning resources but also helping them connect with professional communities.

Collaborative learning encourages learners to develop their capabilities by exchanging knowledge and experience with peers [9]. The paradigm provides learners with the opportunity to build a group themselves with common goals or to search for an existing group which has the same goals as the learner [10]. They engage in the learning process using a joint workspace where they can share resources, learn new concepts, and discuss and deal with uncertain theories and construct ideas together, especially in the case of learners in disparate locations [9]. Moreover, collaborative learning applications enable them to learn in both synchronous and asynchronous ways using a range of multimedia and devices [11]. Since collaboration takes place between learners with different backgrounds and characteristics and diverse fields of specialisation, learners can acquire new knowledge and cultivate advanced skills, such as intensive judgment and negotiation skills, wise emotional intelligence, and effective communication skills, contributing to building a stronger learning community [7].

Another effective learning strategy is to study with mentors who are experts in their field, with unique experiences and skills. E-mentoring takes place between mentors and mentees who desire to achieve mutual growth [12]. This approach consists of a matching mentor–mentee stage and learning process with flexible curriculums. By connecting with professional communities, learners are able to search for suitable mentors who can guide them, develop ideas, build knowledge, and encourage and assist them in their learning development [13]. Mentors with valuable experience, knowledge and skills can develop suitable programs and activities that can be flexibly adjusted as the learners progress. Hence, learners gradually acquire competencies to deal with complex problem-solving and decision-making.

In a smart education environment, both collaborative learning and e-mentoring are supported by technological advances that are breaking the barriers of learning space and time. A more immersive environment has been created with various dynamic media: virtual classrooms, a huge number of digital resources, and flexible tools and systems have been employed to improve collaboration. Subsequently, this paper focuses on "How effective is an integrated model that combines collaborative learning and e-mentoring in engaging learners with diverse backgrounds, characteristics, and interests?" and "How can technological advances be harnessed to enhance collaborative learning and e-mentoring strategies within a smart education context?".

This paper first discusses the importance of implementing two effective learning strategies, collaborative learning and e-mentoring, in the smart education environment.

Furthermore, it proposes a research model with a set of hypotheses to explain how these two learning modes engage learners so that they can achieve their goals effectively. Then, the implementation part presents a smart education system visually, focusing on collaborative learning and e-mentoring deployed in a higher education learning environment. This section proposes models with should-have features to provide a thorough understanding of how the system supports participants in teaching and learning, the way users interact with the system, and perform learning processes. Finally, this research illustrates the usefulness and feasibility of the framework in a real educational environment by evaluating the effectiveness of the functionalities from the perspective of the participants who are learning and teaching in a higher education environment.

2. Literature Review

To adapt to the changes and the requirements of the workforce in a digital and intelligent society, the key factors in the success of the new learner generation are classified into two categories: hard skills (analytical skills and research skills) and soft skills (critical thinking, problem-solving, decision-making, creativity, emotional intelligence, communication skills, teamwork skills, negotiation skills, ability to transfer knowledge, and leadership skills) [8]. Progressively, smart educational systems need to focus on creative, innovative, and communicative activities rather than routine activities with monitoring duties, which evolve and consider many promising trends, including opportunities to learn at diverse times and places, personalised learning based on students' capabilities, the use of technological advances and resources, the use of experiential and collaborative learning, student involvement in curriculum design, and increased mentoring approaches [14]. Zhu and He [7] proposed a research model in smart education with three essential elements: (1) smart learners; (2) smart environments; and (3) smart pedagogies (Figure 1), in which smart environments play a vital role in influencing smart pedagogies, and smart pedagogies are one of the key factors contributing to smart environments. The skills and knowledge enhancement of smart learners are supported by smart pedagogies and smart environments.

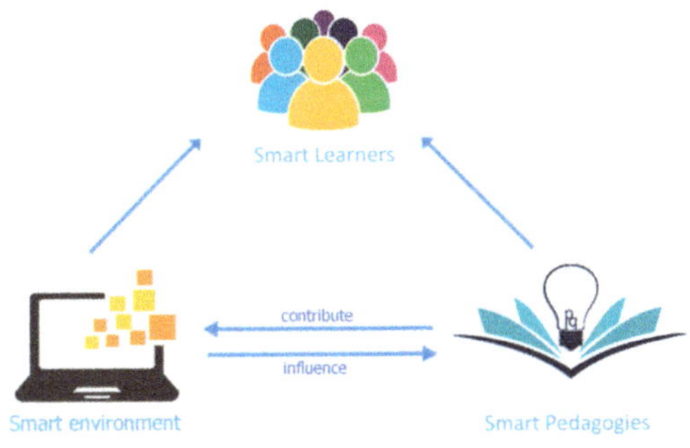

Figure 1. Smart education.

2.1. Smart Learners

Learners in a smart learning environment are demanded to learn smarter to acquire competencies to adapt to a modern and dynamic society. They are required to actively look for the knowledge and learning approaches that are appropriate for them [15] and build their own knowledge and skills by interacting with their peers, instructors, technological advancements, and learning resources [16]. Achieving success in a smart learning environment is difficult and depends heavily on learners' academic characteristics, such as collaboration, self-motivation, persistency, curiosity, and risk-taking, as well as the skills of time management, effective reading, creativity and innovation, and learning through co-operation [17]. Hence, to meet the needs of the smart education system, learners must master the following four skills [7]:

(1) Basic knowledge and core skills, which provide a foundation for skill development and setting future goals, and this is instrumental in the process of understanding concepts [18].
(2) Comprehension such as critical thinking and problem solving.
(3) Personalised expertise which challenges learners to think and suggest new ideas in studying and working to contribute to innovation.
(4) Collective intelligence refers to the abilities of a group of individuals to share and gather their knowledge and skills to perform tasks or deal with problems. This collective intelligence can be constructed by accumulating, arranging, and refining individual learning content followed by communication and collaboration between the learners [19].

2.2. Smart Pedagogies

Pedagogy is defined as a science that is constantly evolving and looking for a better way to teach and engage learners in the process of knowledge building. SMART stands for Self-Monitoring Analysis and Reporting Technology. In the contemporary society, wherein technology is integrated into education, smart refers to smart devices [20]. Zhu et al. [7] argue that, if the goal of the educational process is learners, then, for smart pedagogies, which focus on smart learners, technology is a supporting factor influencing the learning environment. A dynamic and intelligent society requires the future workforce to possess holistic competencies, such as strong logical thinking and decision-making, judgment and negotiation skills, organisational leadership and management qualities, and interpersonal and high-level communication skills, which are fostered by practice and problem-based learning approaches. Learners should be experienced in applying effective learning strategies, namely, having the ability to actively use theoretical knowledge in practice, engage in open discussion, understand problems from different perspectives, and learn from more experienced people; moreover, within interdisciplinary groups, with teamwork and practice, develop the soft skills needed for cooperation and communication in solving common tasks. Furthermore, each individual learner with a different background, education level, and interest deserves suitable and flexible curriculums which ignite their passion and promote their understanding [21]. Hence, learning collaboratively and mentoring are the two most important learning strategies that provide opportunities for learners to broaden their views and gain comprehensive knowledge.

2.2.1. Collaborative Learning

In a smart learning environment, facilitators are required to design their teaching strategies flexibly, enhance the quality of the teaching content, and evaluate the impact of the learning process on students' outcomes [22] to motivate learners to study actively. Therefore, collaborative learning has become one of the most effective pedagogical approaches in the design of a smart learning environment. Knowledge acquired from lectures is a key fundamental of core knowledge and the basic skills required for learners in their learning pathway. However, in higher education, to develop core knowledge, enhance advanced comprehension abilities, and, especially, engage in flexible problem-solving, learners need to step out of their comfort zones by actively exchanging knowledge and skills and studying with their peers.

As shown in Figure 2, collaborative learning is an educational strategy where learners are encouraged to study and work in a group to perform tasks together and achieve common goals. Karin et al. [9] stated that this kind of study provides an opportunity for learners to develop both cognitive skills, such as analytical skills, research skills, critical thinking, problem-solving, and decision-making, and pro-social behaviour, like understanding, communicating, negotiating, helping, sharing, and cooperating. Moreover, learners who study in a group achieve a significantly better understanding in comparison with those who study individually. In the group learning context, learners engage in high-quality social interaction, such as discussing contradictory information, explaining and questioning one another critically, recognizing misconceptions, and strengthening the connections between new information and previously learned knowledge. Additionally, it is an advisable strategy that helps facilitators recognize a poor-performing student and help them find a solution to improve their learning performance and engagement.

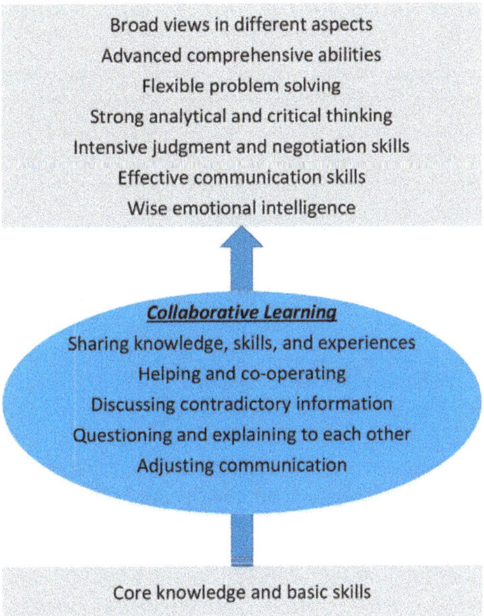

Figure 2. Collaborative learning enhances knowledge and skills.

2.2.2. E-Mentoring

Mentoring is mostly conceptualised as a learning process where the experienced mentor provides guidance, instruction, encouragement, role modelling, and emotional support to a younger person [23]. Mentoring is also defined as a collaborative learning and mutually beneficial relationship where both mentors and mentees foster their personal and professional development by engaging in professional activities [12]. In higher education, the role of mentors is critical because they direct mentees on the path to success, enhance their academic achievements, reduce their stress, and inspire them to engage in a cycle of learning [3]. There are many types of mentoring relationships, such as traditional mentoring, peer mentoring, group mentoring, reserve mentoring, and situation mentoring, which depend on many factors, such as the purpose and goal of learning, the organisation's circumstances, willingness, availability, and appropriateness according to the individual's situations, as well as the length of the learning time [24]. The key factor to success in an e-mentoring program is the establishment of a strong personal relationship based on trust, self-motivation, flexibility, communication skills, and technological skills. Two important elements need to be considered: (1) matching appropriate mentors and mentees [25] and (2) building a strong relationship between mentors and mentees [26].

E-mentoring is a process where a virtual platform is used to facilitate mentoring relationships. Participants not only engage in synchronous and asynchronous online dialogue through various aspects of the course but can also be introduced to social and professional networks, providing a valuable opportunity to connect to a pool of mentors and mentees [26]. However, Colky and Young [27] suggested that understanding the mentoring process established in a traditional learning environment is necessary for effective mentoring in a virtual environment. There are four phases to a mentoring relationship: (1) initiation, which involves identifying and matching mentors-mentees; (2) training, where the success of a mentoring program is dependent on the training given to both the mentors and mentees and aims to familiarise all the partners with the techniques and the overall goals of the mentoring program; (3) monitoring, to assess if the mentoring process is working well or if there is a need for retraining; (4) evaluation, which involves evaluating the mentoring results and obtaining recommendations to improve the first three steps [28].

2.3. Smart Learning Environment

Huang et al. [29] pointed out that the objective of a smart learning environment is to promote easy learning, engaged learning, and effective learning. Consequently, it is necessary to design a smart learning environment technically and pedagogically. It should be expanded in space, time, technology, interaction, and control [8] to facilitate and engage learners to experience a seamless learning process and perform tasks in an easy and natural way. Technology covers both hardware and software. Hardware includes tangible technological devices such as IQ boards, projection screens, interactive LCD/LED touchscreens using cloud computing, ubiquitous computing, IoT technology, and smart audio–visual systems. Software includes learning tools, online resources, new supporting applications using virtual reality technology, and learning analytics. From a pedagogical perspective, a learning environment is implemented to assist facilitators in designing and conducting lessons and learning activities effectively and supports learners to enhance their knowledge and skills with the additional flexibility and diversity of the learning practice [6].

Many researchers have found that a smart learning environment has considerably changed the way learners and facilitators interact with each other, enabling collaboration in a flexible environment [10,30–32]. Learning processes are maintained from building groups to monitoring students' progress and adjusting curriculums accordingly to suit the student's needs. A smart learning environment supports learners to form the right group by finding suitable partners in a wide range of learning communities. Learners receive opportunities to experience virtual learning environments where they can study both asynchronously and synchronously, have access to shared repositories with diverse valuable resources, and join in common learning workspaces. The learning progress is monitored and evaluated to identify the strengths and weaknesses of the learners and the curriculum for improvement (as shown in Figure 3).

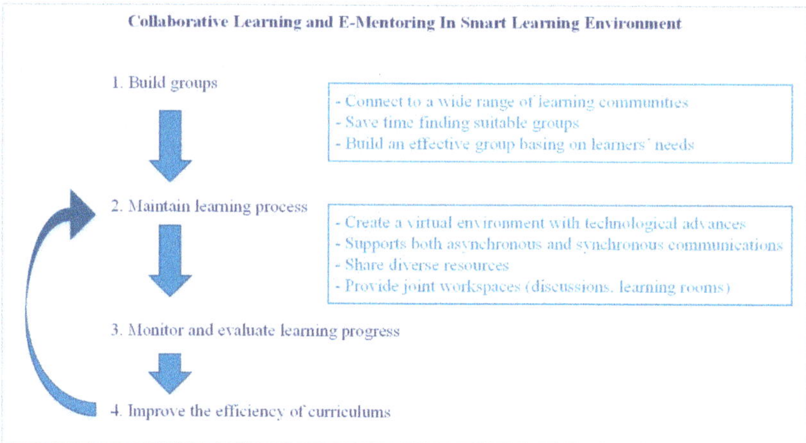

Figure 3. Collaborative learning and e-mentoring in a smart learning environment.

Smart education is becoming a promising trend to ensure the development of a new generation of the smart workforce who need to be equipped with valuable competencies, involving sustainable knowledge and flexible skills. Smart pedagogies are designed to focus more on learners, influencing a learning environment that is supported by technology and intelligent devices to be flexible, diverse, and smart [7]. As a result, two learning approaches, collaborative learning and e-mentoring, are considered as effective learning strategies for learners to adapt to future requirements. To further explain the theory, the next section proposed a model to show how collaborative learning and e-mentoring help learners reach their goals effectively in a smart education environment.

3. Research Model

Learners are expected to study within a collaborative environment, sharing their knowledge and skills to enhance their performance in critical thinking and improve their problem-solving skills [7]. The knowledge imparted and the lessons delivered by experts and experienced facilitators are necessary for learners to gradually advance their careers [29]. It is clear that collaborative learning and e-mentoring are the two most efficient approaches to smart pedagogies, in which learners and facilitators exchange knowledge productively to achieve their ongoing learning goals. The exchange of knowledge is a dynamic and social process that incorporates various forms of knowledge from multiple sources [33]. The process is achieved through peer interaction and diverse resource sharing. Additionally, in e-mentoring, learners have opportunities to interact with professional communities, wherein they can find not only facilitators, instructors, and professors in their institutions but also experts in the specific fields that they require. Learners are also engaged in flexible curriculums, which are adjusted to suitably enhance their improvements. Mentors share wisdom, experience, deep knowledge, and also their successes and failures [23] to help mentees achieve their goals and objectives [34], connect knowledge to handle situations logically, and build new knowledge with the aim of succeeding in their learning pathway [35] (as shown in Figure 4).

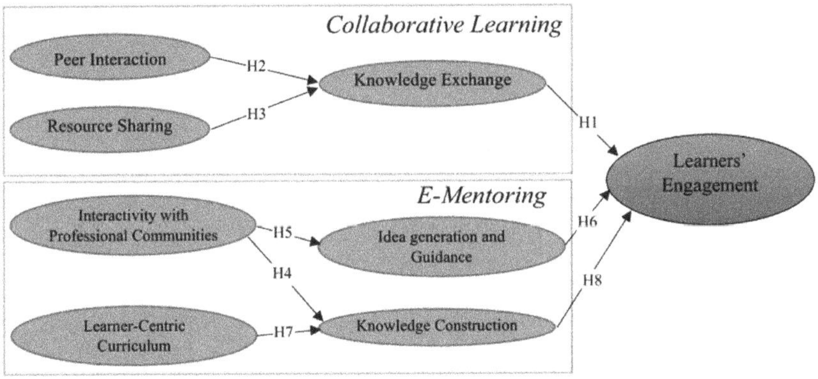

Figure 4. Proposed research model.

Core knowledge and basic skills from books and lessons are key fundamentals that help learners develop other advanced skills. However, cognitive skills, such as analytical skills, research skills, critical thinking, problem-solving, and decision-making, as well as pro-social behaviour, like understanding, communicating, negotiating, helping, sharing, and co-operating, cannot be attained by self-learning but by engaging in high-quality social interaction, in which knowledge is exchanged actively, contradictory information is discussed and explained critically, and misconceptions are identified and handled effectively, so that new information and previously learned knowledge will be connected strongly [9]. Chi et al. [11] stated that actively engaging in an exchange with peers, such as watching a tutorial video or solving a problem together using each other's knowledge and experience, helps learners construct an in-depth understanding and enhance their knowledge in a way that is similar to directly receiving the guidance from a highly experienced instructor. In addition, Pangil [36] pointed out that knowledge grows when it is shared and used but depreciates in value when being kept to oneself. Sharing knowledge can stimulate learners' creativity by generating new knowledge. Consequently, learners have a greater opportunity to acquire the necessary skills and achieve their goals when learning collaboratively.

Therefore, we hypothesise:

H1: *Active knowledge sharing in collaborative learning effectively improves learners' engagement.*

Individuals often possess distinctive experience and expertise that should be combined, especially, to complete tasks that require the combination of different knowledge bases [10]. A smart education environment that incorporates technological advances assists learners at right the first stage, which is to form a suitable group. By using the intelligent features of a learning system, learners input their requirements as they want to find the best match partners or facilitators; then, the system should sort out collaborators with appropriate criteria based on their expertise and background [10]. This stage is the key factor in all collaborations because partners who are appropriately matched not only exchange their new knowledge and perspectives but also provide constructive feedback and motivational encouragement to each other [22], especially in relation to peer-reviewed works.

Additionally, along with learning processes, learning applications with ubiquitous mediums support participants in experiencing new ways of learning, which facilitates their constant interactions, regardless of the distance. Since then, learners have more opportunities to understand each other and deal with tasks effectively. Learners need a space in which they are assisted to continually discuss, refer to others' ideas, develop solutions together, keep track of prior discussions, and create a synergy of individual contributions [37]. Hence, the following hypothesis is proposed:

H2: *A learning environment that facilitates peer interaction will positively affect knowledge sharing.*

Collaboration refers to a situation where participants share their resources, knowledge, and experience with others. This exchange process can be performed directly or indirectly via a knowledge repository, where members provide and access each other's knowledge resources such as data, information, and knowledge [38]. In shared repositories, partners can easily exchange and organize diverse resources regardless of their location [10]. Furthermore, learners would like to study in a dynamic learning environment with the support of technological advances to assist them in both synchronous and asynchronous communications, in which they are given opportunities to understand new concepts or phenomena more visually, which can foster their in-depth knowledge to engage in real-world problem-solving [31]. Knowledge resource sharing saves time and energy for all partners and helps them explore problems and solutions more deeply through shared ideas from others. Hence, we propose the following hypothesis:

H3: *A learning environment that facilitates resource sharing will positively affect knowledge sharing.*

Knowledge is not static, it exists and is codified through collaborative processes [39]. According to Kaplan [40], nearly 70% of the knowledge that an employee needs to be successful is cultivated outside of formal training. Forming a community connection is one way to create and structure opportunities where learners interact, capture, formalize, and disseminate implicit knowledge. Additionally, knowledge productivity appears not to be an inborn capability, but, rather, is accumulated by professional knowledge building [41] that produces a deeper understanding in more complicated domains than knowledge exchange [42]. Being a professional involves producing solutions for actions and building knowledge progressively using a knowledge base; however, knowledge and action seem to be distinct or disconnected. Communication with professionals who grasp the nature of knowledge and who have a view on how it will be acquired and organized in the mentoring process is the way to unfold knowledge and collaboratively build knowledgeable action in practice situations [41]. Consequently, the following hypothesis is proposed:

H4: *A learning environment that facilitates sufficient interactivity with professional communities positively affects knowledge construction.*

In a broad professional community, knowledge, experience, and wisdom from older and more experienced professionals are valuable sources of learning that cannot be ignored. Mentoring is an efficient learning strategy used in higher education environments to enable learners to connect to a pool of intellectual knowledge and to take advantage of these valuable resources [3]. Mentors have more experience and should guide the mentee with patience, positivity, and openness to provide help, instruction, encouragement, role modelling, and emotional support [23].

Depending on many criteria, such as the learning goals, the organisational factors (culture, structure, strategies, or policies), or individual situations, mentoring occurs in different forms of learning, namely, traditional mentoring, peer mentoring, group mentoring, reverse mentoring, or situation mentoring [24]. Regardless of any type of learning, the success of a mentoring process is measured based on the satisfaction of both partners and their achievements. These outcomes depend on the establishment of a solid relationship between mentors and mentees, which is built by matching the right mentor with the right mentee, and needs to be maintained along the learning pathway [26]. It is not intended that a mentor provides solutions to various problems, but that they actively listen to ascertain the learners' interests and needs, determine the goals together, and build trust. After this, the mentor assists the learners in finding resources, imparting knowledge, explaining, discussing, and developing ideas, sharing experiences and mistakes, observing learning processes, providing constructive feedback, and also encouraging and inspiring learners to reach their goals [43]. Hence, the following hypothesis is proposed:

H5: *A learning environment that facilitates sufficient interactivity with professional communities positively affects idea generation and guidance.*

For a successful mentoring process, establishing the goals to pursue may be especially important and should be a collaborative progress. Depending on the learners' knowledge base, experience, and improvement throughout the mentoring relationship, partners need to keep the learning progress on track, as well as clarify and constantly reconsider the learning goals to achieve a satisfactory outcome [34]. The consentaneous target results in a higher quality mentor–mentee relationship and a greater sense of attainment [44]. By receiving support and guidance from facilitators, learners can be oriented to smarter goals, be inspired in the cycle of learning, and be guided to stay on the right track to success. Moreover, they not only receive valuable knowledge and experience, but they also acquire skills, gain mastery, and develop maturity [24].

Thus, this paper proposes the following hypothesis:

H6: *Idea generation and guidance in e-mentoring effectively improve learners' engagement.*

A learner-centric approach, which is referred to as the outcome-based approach or what the learner is expected to achieve at the end of the learning period, has become an international trend in education [45]. Moreover, "smart" in a smart learning environment refers to the flexibility and adaptability framing the learners' targets [7]. This means pedagogies can be adjusted suitably depending on the learners' progress, which needs to be monitored and evaluated regularly. These processes are complex, difficult to perform, and take much time and effort. However, partners who immerse themselves in a smart learning environment should be assisted in monitoring their learning progress, such as recognizing how much work the learners have done or knowing about peers' contributions, which can prompt learners to adjust their behaviours or give ideas to mentors in relation to modifying the curriculum [46]. In doing so, the mentor will understand a learner's perceived capacity and how they interpret knowledge; hence, the learner will be guided to correct any misconceptions and will accumulate knowledge and experience for new understandings and interpretations [47]. Thus, this paper proposes the following hypothesis:

H7: *A learning environment that facilitates a learner-centric curriculum improves knowledge construction.*

Knowledge construction in higher education is important because it ensures that students are experiencing meaningful learning [48]. People may often understand and interpret the same things in different ways [49,50]. The ability to exchange information, develop arguments and justifications, and make decisions are attributes that help learners become critical thinkers with the ability to construct knowledge at high levels [48]. In the mentoring process, a facilitator's role, wisdom, experience, and ability help to link knowledge into a structure to guide, support, and direct students as they advance their understanding of learning. Thereby, the location of the knowledge base is shifted from the "outsider", or expert perspectives, to "insider" perspectives [51]. In this way, learners achieve rich and coherent knowledge structures, which appear as a deeper understanding of a field and an easier activation of new knowledge [35]. Hence, the following hypothesis is proposed:

H8: *Knowledge construction in e-mentoring effectively improves learners' engagement.*

The research model focuses on the principal ideas of collaborative learning and e-mentoring, which provide learners with various opportunities to immerse themselves in a broad professional learning environment. Knowledge, experience, and skills are accumulated naturally via active and flexible pedagogies. Along with research theory, this paper also concentrates on developing these efficient pedagogies in a smart education environment, supported by advanced technologies in which learning activities are logically organized to engage learners in an efficient learning pathway. As a proof of concept, the model is implemented as a web application to provide a clear and practical method that allows a multifaced concept to be explained visually and easily.

4. Implementation

In this section, the model is visualized as a web application to demonstrate the effectiveness and flexibility of two smart pedagogies, collaborative learning and e-mentoring. The application is built using the PHP programming language with the My SQL database for reliability and flexibility. The user interfaces are designed using a front-end framework, Bootstrap, to create a dynamic, consistent, and responsive web application. The application dashboards are classified into two sessions based on the two types of users involved in the learning process, namely, learners and teachers. This framework is designed to be governed by the admin, who assigns appropriate rights to certain users. All the users have the same rights to access collaborative learning functions, just different ones between team leaders and members. However, mentors and mentees are responsible for specific tasks, as mentors manage all learning activities and mentees have permission to conduct activities that mentors assign to them.

As shown in Figure 4, the different components contributing to collaborative learning and e-mentoring help learners succeed in their learning pathways. However, collaborative learning and e-mentoring take place in separate processes. The following sections explain each component that is integrated into the learning process in more detail to raise awareness of the way to conduct learning activities effectively and provide an in-depth understanding of the proposed model in this research.

4.1. Collaborative Learning

Collaborative learning occurs when a group of students or a group of teachers are guided by a facilitator to solve a problem, carry out a task, or learn a new concept. Goal achievement is driven by exchanging knowledge and experience (as addressed in H1), in which peer interaction and resource-sharing activities are key aspects supporting learners in the learning process (H2 and H3). As stated in H2 and H3, the implementation should involve the design of a learning environment that assists learners to work in a productive group wherein they maintain positive communication and share resources effectively.

However, not all groups foster effective collaboration because of the differing cognitive, social, emotional, and academic status of the participants [22], resulting in a lack of collaborative skills, free-riding behaviour, or unequal participation [19]. Therefore, it is important to build the right group at the beginning of the process because an effective group strengthens collaboration and avoids internal competition. As shown in Figure 5, the application offers users two flexible choices to join the most suitable group, namely, (1) sending a request to an existing group and becoming a member after the request is accepted or (2) being added to a new group. Collaboration activities occur after the group has been formed successfully and are completed when the common goal has been achieved.

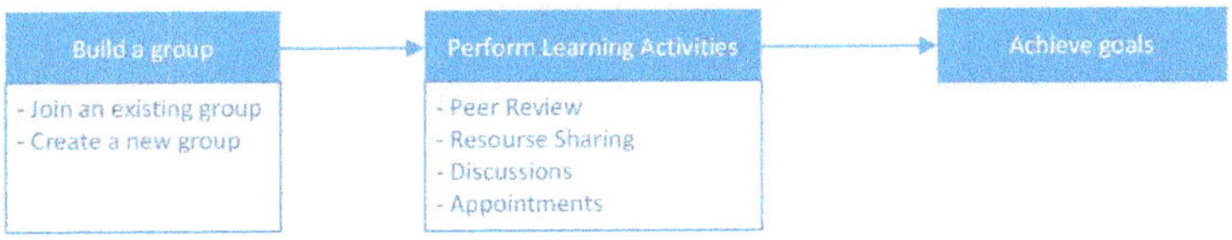

Figure 5. Collaborative learning process.

The application is designed to help members engage in the learning process with multiple detailed activities. Firstly, they can engage in peer interactions (addressed in H2) in a joint workspace asynchronously with discussion boards to handle issues and keep track of each other's contributions to achieve a common goal or synchronously with video conferences and appointments. Moreover, they can easily share diverse resources and access those of others using a shared repository (H3). Peer review is a specific collaboration activity where users assist peers to improve the overall quality of their academic work. Figure 5 illustrates the collaborative learning process.

As shown in Figure 6 above, a user can successfully perform collaborative learning processes from building a group to completing their group's activities. A user can join an existing group by selecting "Search Groups" and sending requests that are managed in "Manage Group Requests". Moreover, a user can create a new group and send requests to other users asking if they want to participate. The "Manage My Requests" function manages all the requests sent directly to the user, which the user can choose to join the group or decline. A member of a group has permission to conduct all learning activities via "Manage Group detail", "Peer Reviews", and learning synchronously with appointments. To clarify H1, H2, and H3, this section visualizes several specific processes using user interfaces, in particular, (1) joining an existing group by making a request, (2) creating a new group, and (3) peer reviewing.

Figure 6. Functional organization of collaborative learning.

4.1.1. Join an Existing Group by Making a Request

In cases where a user wants to participate in an existing group, the application should support the user easily using the following steps: (1) searching groups with several criteria, as shown in Figure 7, (2) sending a request directly to a group or viewing the detail of a group and then sending a request, and (3) waiting for the approval, as it can be accepted or declined.

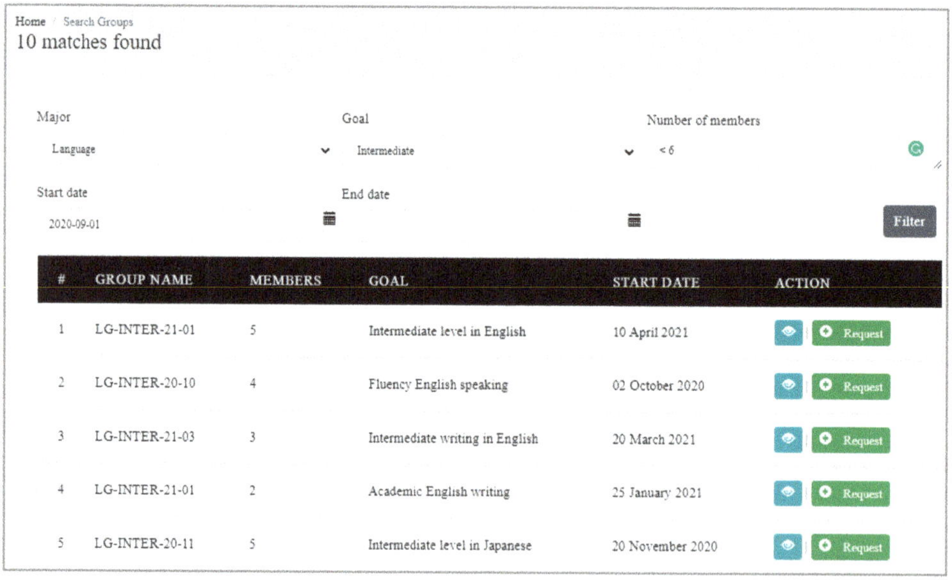

Figure 7. Search groups.

Requests to join a group are displayed when members open the group's details (Figure 8). Members can view the details of the request (Figure 9); however, only the team leader has the right to accept or decline requests. After being accepted, the user becomes a member of the group. Otherwise, the declined requests are sent back to the user with suitable reasons.

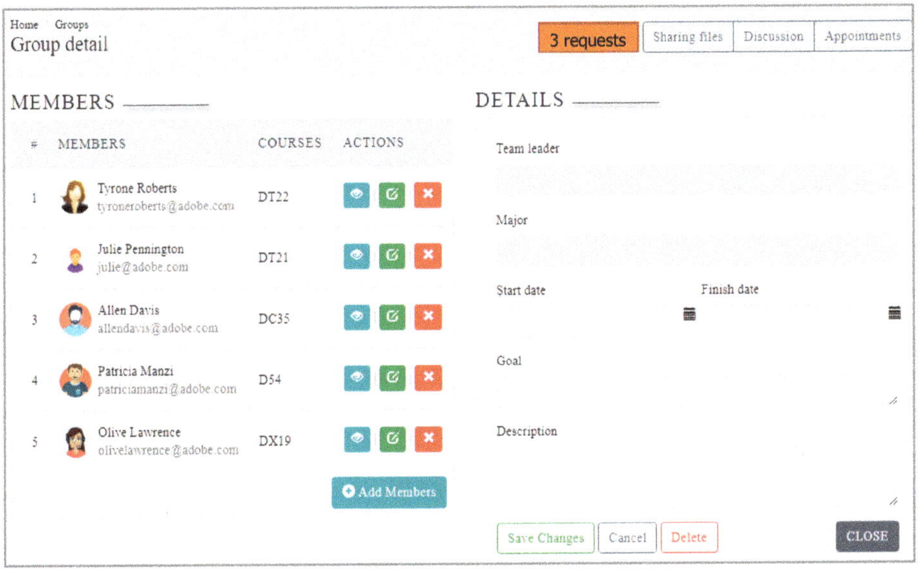

Figure 8. Details of the group.

Figure 9. Details of the requests.

4.1.2. Create a New Group

At the beginning of a learning process, a new group is usually created with detailed information (major, learning's goal, start day of learning, description). The creator of the group will add new members by searching for peers and sending requests to ask members to join the group. As shown in Figure 10, a new group is built using the following steps: (1) inputting and saving the details of the group, (2) searching for peers using specific criteria, and (3) sending requests to learners asking them to join the group.

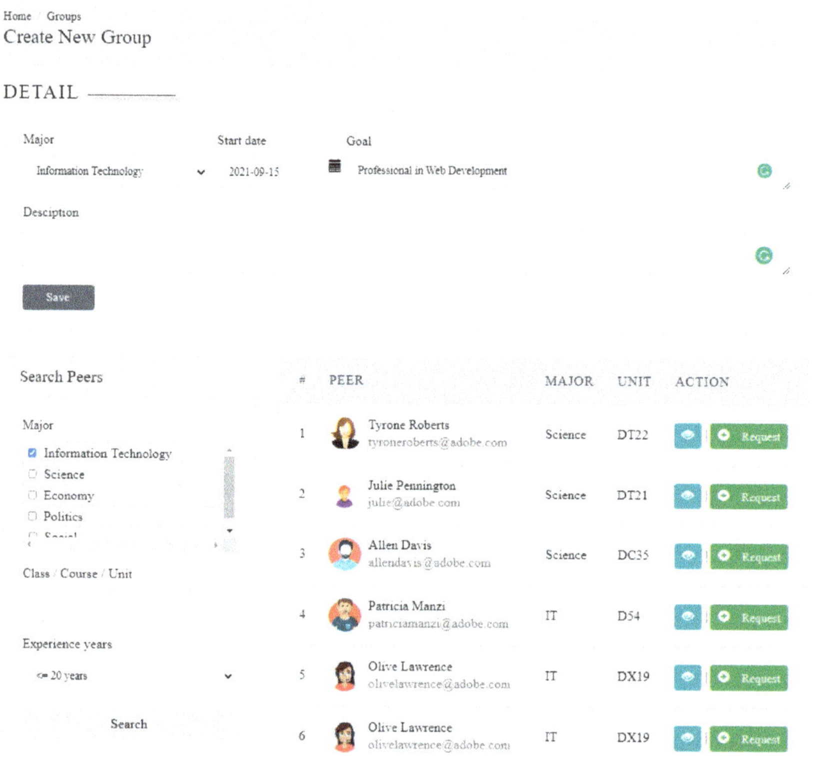

Figure 10. Create a new group.

All the requests to join a group are sent directly to the user with the group list (Figures 11 and 12). The user views the detailed information and chooses to join the group or decline with their reasons.

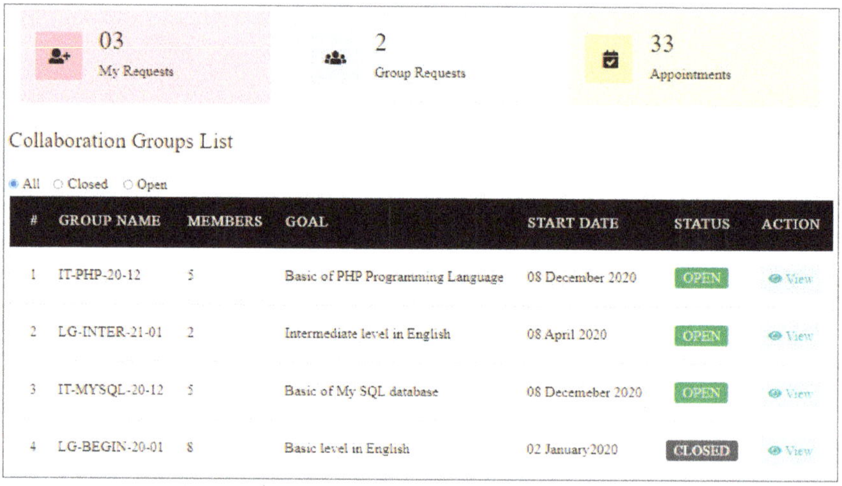

Figure 11. Group list.

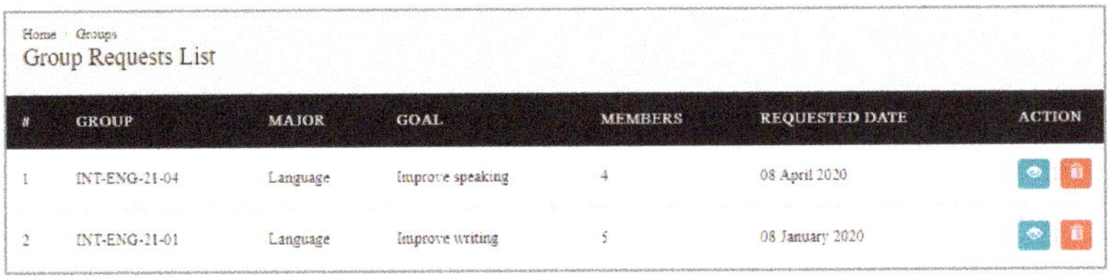

Figure 12. Group requests.

After becoming a member of a group, users engage in learning activities directly using the group's detail interface (see Figure 8). Learners have the opportunity to share resources with each other and participate in interactions by joining discussions and meetings.

4.1.3. Peer Review

Peer review is a specific kind of collaboration, with the objective of improving the overall quality of an academic task. Figure 13 shows the details of a review work. After receiving and accepting a request to be a reviewer, the user undertakes the process by viewing the details of a peer's work, downloading the paper, and leaving comments or uploading the reviewed file.

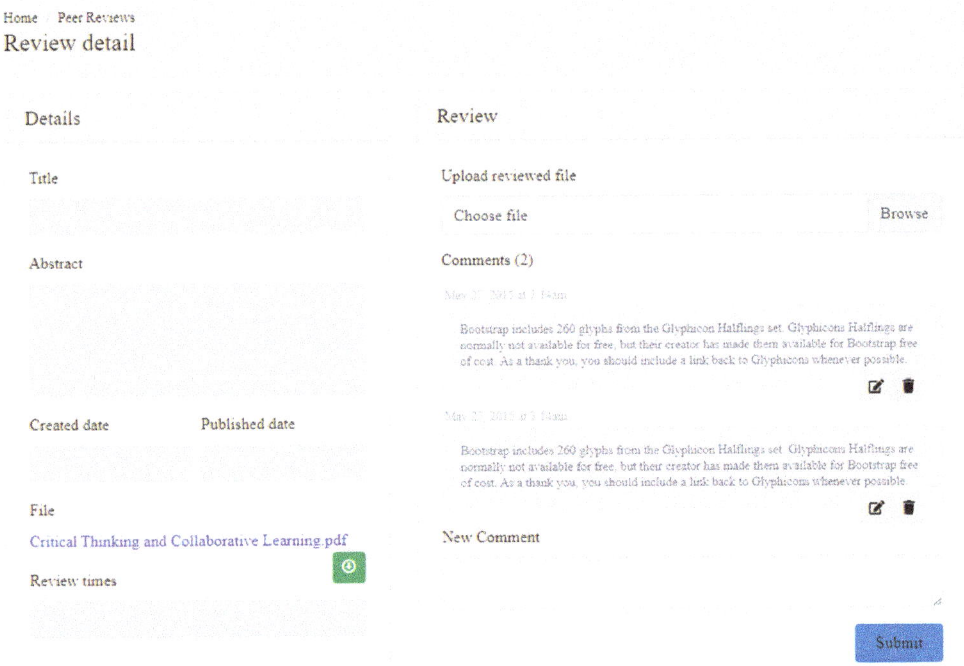

Figure 13. Reviewed peer paper.

The authors are able to easily follow all the reviews by viewing the details (Figure 14). After each review, the author can upload the most recent file and send another review request. This process is conducted iteratively until all the work has been accepted and the paper is published.

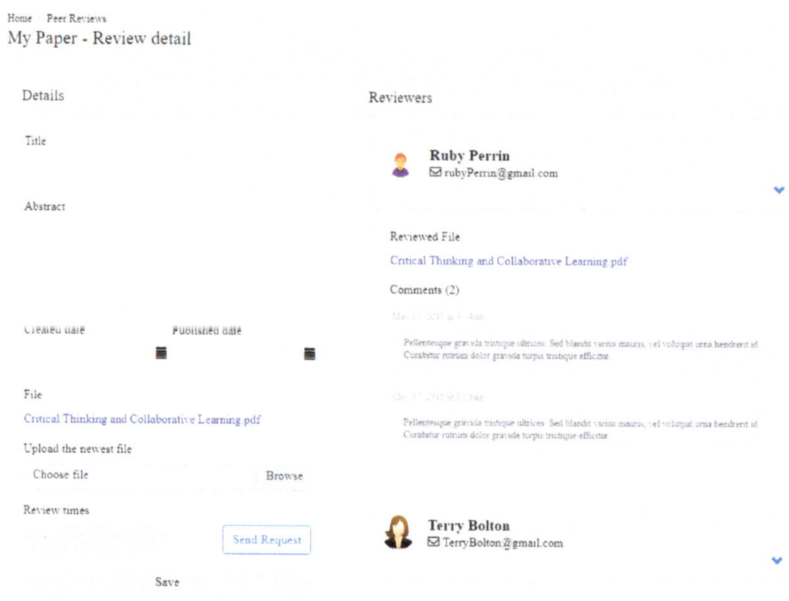

Figure 14. View review detail.

4.2. E-Mentoring

As shown in Figure 4, interactivity with professional communities (addressed in H4 and H5) and learner-centric curriculums (H7) are two core features contributing to the success of the mentoring process. Therefore, by being immersed in e-mentoring, learners should be supported to engage in a learning environment that facilitates a broad connection with professional communities and flexible learner-centric curriculums.

A mentoring and learning process begins after mentors and mentees have been matched successfully. Mentees engage in learning activities, such as conducting lessons and assessments and joining in online classes and discussions. During a learning process, mentors monitor the improvement of mentees and then adjust curriculums to be more effective for learners, focusing on the learners' goals. By that, the implementation logicizes mentoring processes as the model below (Figure 15)

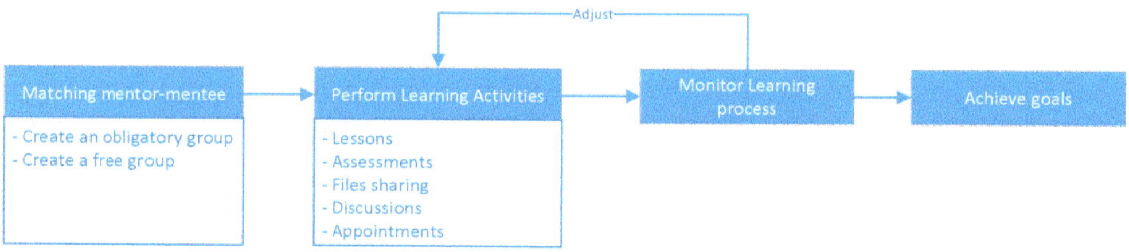

Figure 15. E-mentoring process.

When engaging in the e-mentoring process, although mentors and mentees carry out some tasks similarly in comparison with collaborative learning, the responsibilities of mentors and mentees are disparate. As shown in Figure 16, a mentor who can be a facilitator, an instructor, or a supervisor has a right to create a group of mentees by performing the "Match Mentoring Group" function. The mentor organizes learning activities by managing mentoring details, setting up appointments, and adjusting lessons and assignments according to learners' progress. Another way for a mentee to participate in a mentoring process is to search for a mentor who is suitable for the mentee's requirements and send requests, which are managed in "Manage My Requests" (as shown in Figure 17). These requests can be accepted or declined by the mentor using the "Manage Mentoring Requests" function (Figure 16). The mentee completes learning activities in "View Mentoring detail" and tracks the results of completed lessons and assignments in "View Learning progress" (Figure 17).

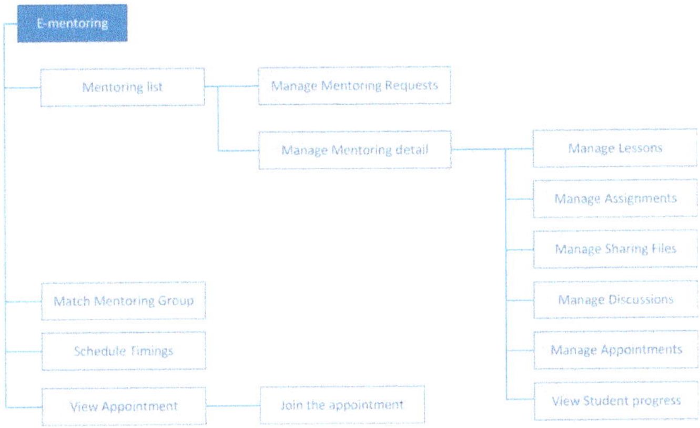

Figure 16. Functional organization of e-mentoring for mentors.

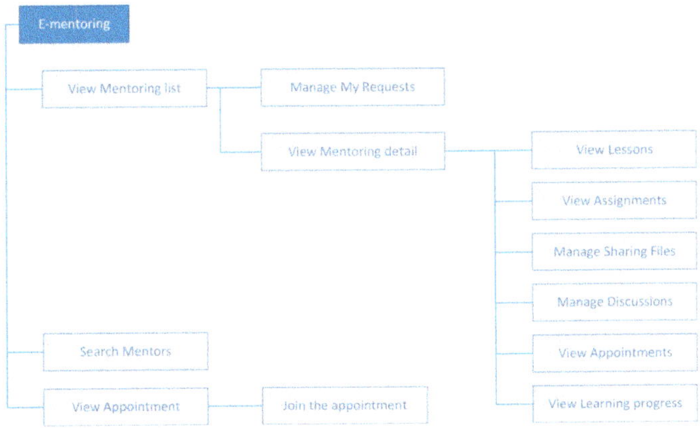

Figure 17. Functional organization of e-mentoring for mentees.

This section explains the process of matching a mentor with a mentee, which is the first and most important process in ensuring the effectiveness of the interactions between the mentor and the mentee (H4 and H5). Moreover, this section clarifies the adjustment of learner-centric curriculums in H7 using the monitor-learning process interface.

4.2.1. Matching Mentor–Mentee

Ragins and Kram [13] proposed that an initial match has a significant effect on the relationship between mentors and mentees and the e-mentoring process. Approximately 95% of participating mentors and mentees are satisfied with mentoring processes if they are able to search for the most suitable matches. Hence, to help learners interact effectively with a wide range of professional communities, the application should offer users the chance to look closely at the online matching system, in which both mentors and mentees complete their profiles with their interests and preferences. Suggestions based on common preferences, such as majors, interests, and research fields are given. Then, using a sophisticated computer algorithm, the system presents some potential matches and gives the mentee the opportunity to select the most suitable one.

The tasks of matching appropriate mentors and mentees should be based on trust and flexibility. Based on the different types of mentoring, such as traditional mentoring, peer mentoring, group mentoring, or situation mentoring, the application supports the matching process in two ways, namely, (1) creating an obligatory mentoring group and (2) creating a free mentoring group.

4.2.2. Creating an Obligatory Mentoring Group

An obligatory mentoring group is a group that requires participants to join the mentoring process. Only mentors have permission to create a matching, as illustrated in Figure 18. Mentors and mentees are added to the mentoring group by being searched according to the criteria or directly by name. With the input information, the group is created, and the mentoring process has begun.

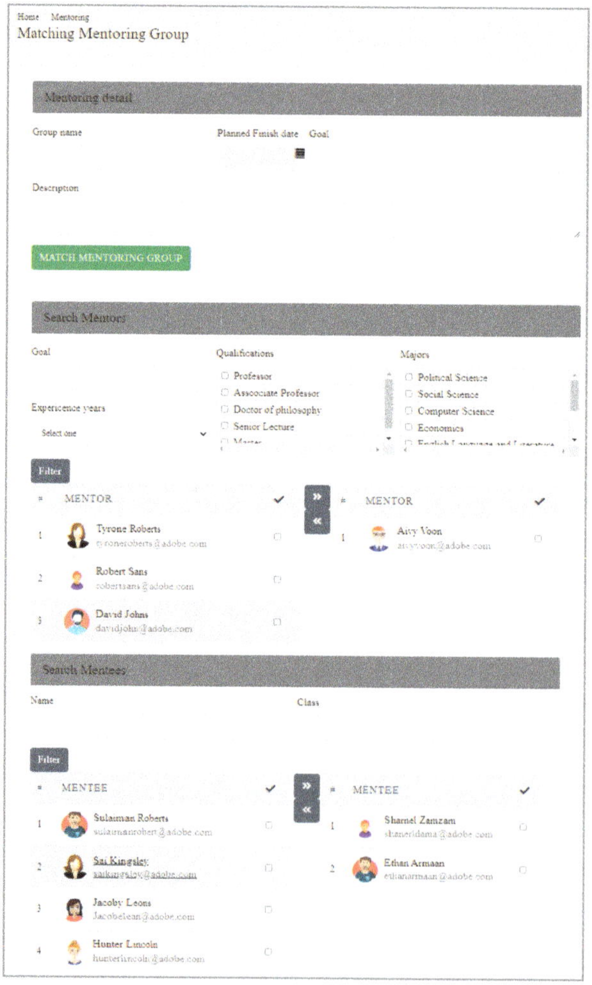

Figure 18. The process of matching mentors and mentees.

4.2.3. Creating a Free Mentoring Group

The matching process in a free mentoring group is performed by the learners. If learners want to be mentored in relation to a particular skill or if they want to learn a new concept, they can easily search for mentors by inputting specific criteria, such as the skills the learners want to improve and the requirements the mentors must possess. Then, the learners choose an appropriate mentor and send a request (Figure 19). However, the mentoring process starts when the mentor accepts the request. Otherwise, the learners continue with the matching process to find a suitable mentor.

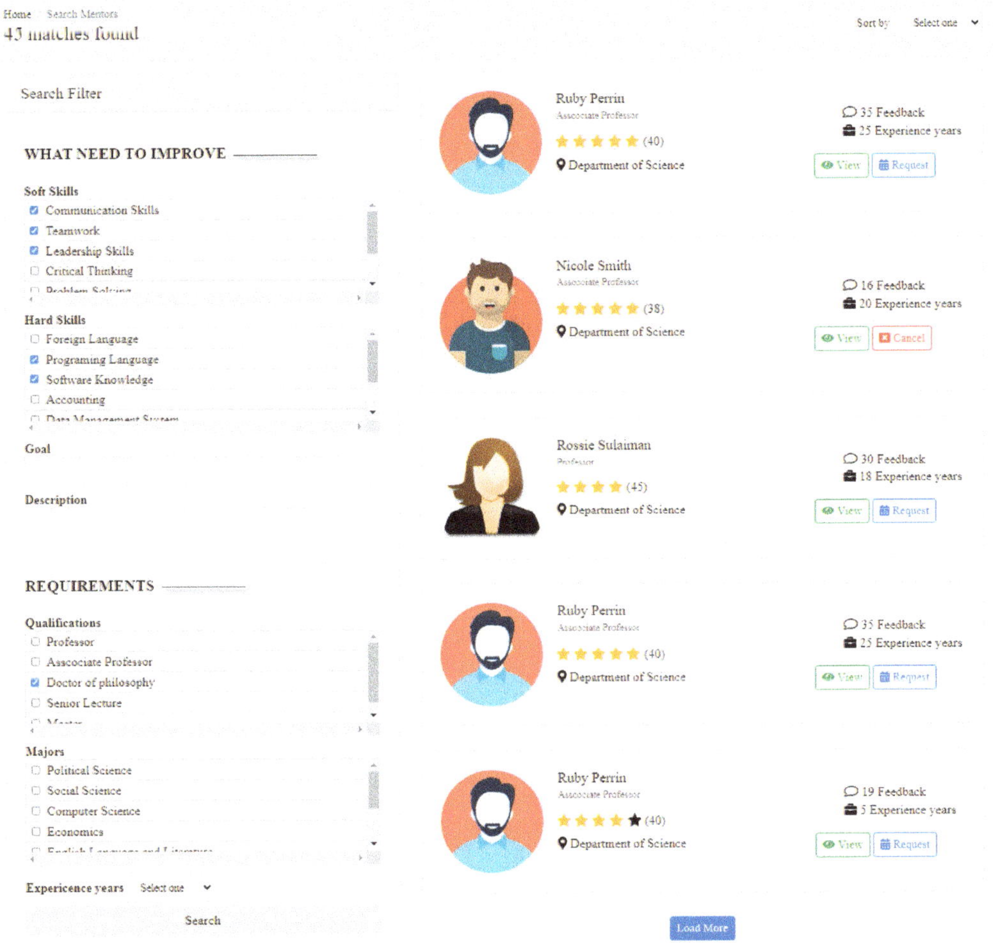

Figure 19. Search mentors.

Similar to collaborative learning, mentees engage in learning activities that are designed and adjusted by mentors to support learners in reaching their goals more effectively. After this, the mentees have the responsibility to carry out all the tasks, including participating in lessons and completing assignments, which will be used to evaluate their learning process. Moreover, they can share their own resources and manage their discussions (shown in Figure 20).

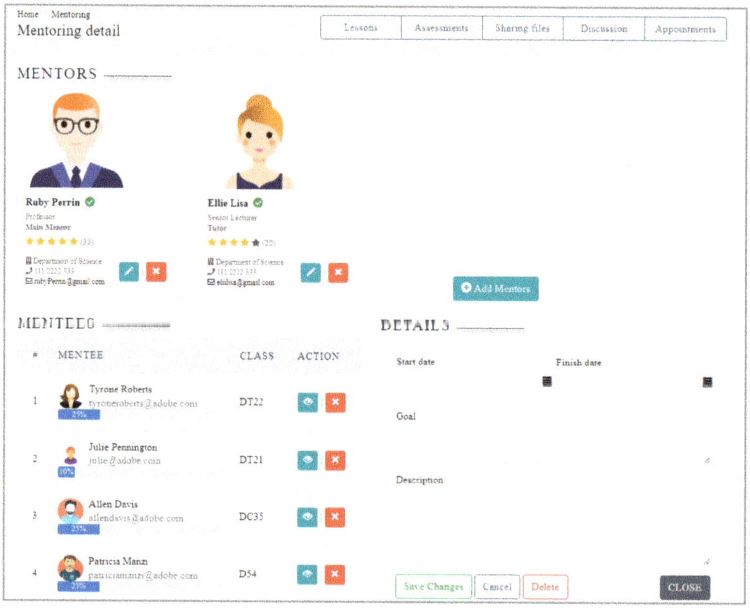

Figure 20. Mentoring detail.

4.2.4. Monitor the Learning Process

At the beginning of the mentoring process, a mentor decides what pedagogies are suitable to help the mentees achieve their goals. Throughout the learning process, the mentor monitors the mentees' progress (shown in Figure 20) and adjusts the objectives of the lessons and activities to suit the learners' goals. The evaluation is based on how well the learners complete the tasks based on the due date and the level they achieve for each activity (Figures 20 and 21).

Figure 21. Learning progress.

This implementation section shows how collaborative learning helps learners acquire knowledge from their interactions with peers and resource sharing. Moreover, learners are able to achieve their goals more easily and effectively through their connection with a wide professional community and suitable curriculum adjustments in the e-mentoring process. However, to demonstrate the usefulness of the proposed model and the feasibility of its implementation, evaluation is necessary. The evaluation stage is detailed in the next section.

5. Evaluation

This research centres on enhancing collaborative learning and e-mentoring in a smart education system in the higher education sector to foster the learners' skills. The evaluation stage plays an important role in demonstrating the feasibility and efficiency of the proposed model. Hence, we conducted surveys with the facilitators and learners who are currently working or pursuing a postgraduate qualification in eleven universities and academies in the Vietnamese military. The reason for conducting the surveys in these institutions is due to their plans to develop a smart education environment and the need to connect learning communities in specific fields. It was anticipated that the questionnaires would uncover useful ideas and varying opinions from the participants on their experience of moving from a traditional learning method to a smart learning approach. The questionnaires were designed using the Google Form application because they are easily created and shared online; moreover, participants can use any mobile device, tablet, or computer to respond, and the results can be analysed in real time.

Two surveys were used for the evaluation, one for facilitators and the other for learners; this is because the success of applying a new learning strategy is evaluated based on the satisfaction and effective collaboration between learners and facilitators. Data analysis was performed using SPSS, and the statements and descriptive statistics are shown in Tables 1–3. The two questionnaires had the same structure, but the questions varied. All the questions were translated into Vietnamese to ensure the ideas were transparent and to avoid misunderstanding. The questionnaires comprised two sections with optional textboxes for the participants to comment on how the two learning strategies could be improved. The first section focuses on initial ideas about how the system is mainly developed and how the framework supports their learning. The second section provides an opportunity for the learners to indicate their level of satisfaction with all the main functionalities that the tool supports, which are (1) collaborative learning: search groups and join an existing group, create new group, collaborative learning activities, and peer reviews, and (2) e-mentoring: create an obligatory mentoring group, create a free mentoring group, manage and conduct mentoring activities, and monitor the learning process. We provided step-by-step instructions with screenshots of the main interfaces of the experiment tool before they attempted the survey questions and were given the URL of the platform to participants. Therefore, participants had a clear view of how to conduct collaborative learning and e-mentoring tasks before experiencing the main features through the tool. The participants were required to express their level of agreement or disagreement using a 5-point Likert scale from 1–5 to indicate their response as either strongly disagree, disagree, neutral, agree, or strongly agree, respectively.

Table 1. Descriptive statistics of the facilitators' agreement with each statement of the survey.

#	Question	#	Question
Section 1			
1. Learners should actively discuss and maintain interactions to acquire in-depth knowledge and accumulate soft skills for their future work.		2. Maintaining interactions with each other will help learners exchange knowledge and experience.	

Table 1. *Cont.*

# Question	# Question
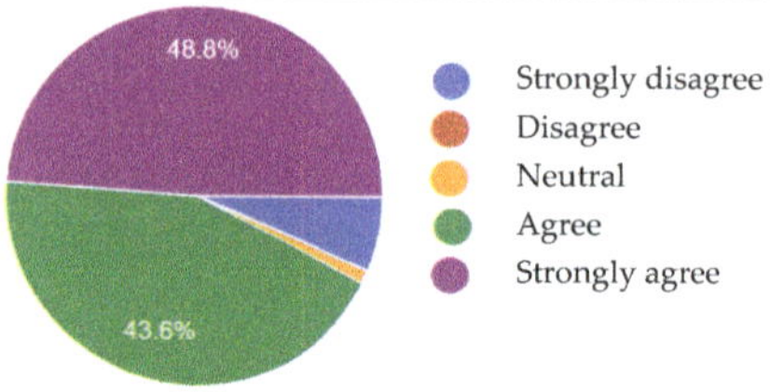	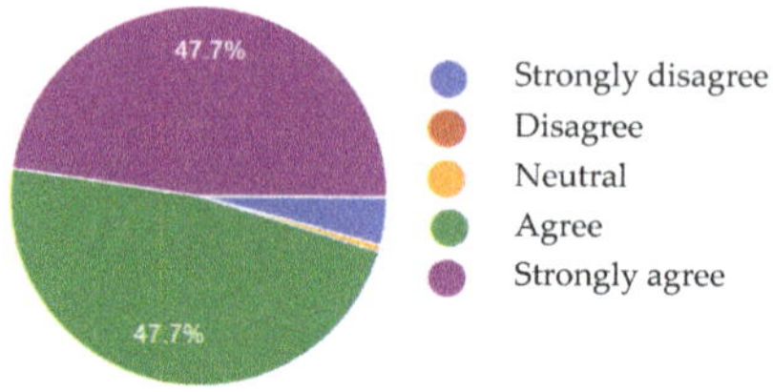
3. Resource-sharing repositories help learners exchange knowledge and experience.	4. The support of mentors to construct knowledge is vitally important for learners to achieve their goals.
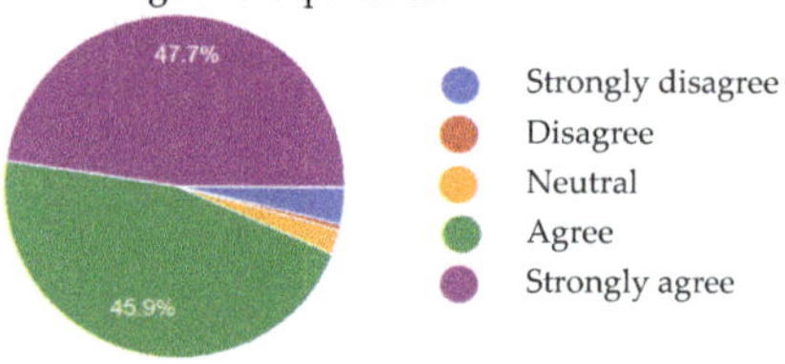	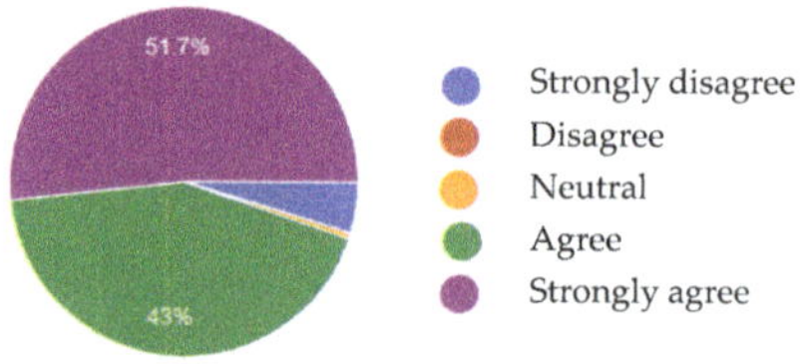
5. Connecting to a wide range of professional communities gives learners the opportunity to receive effective guidance.	6. Connecting to a wide range of professional communities enables learners to construct knowledge.
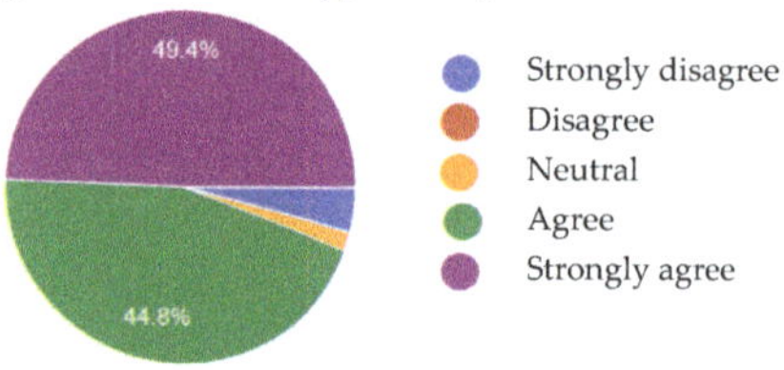	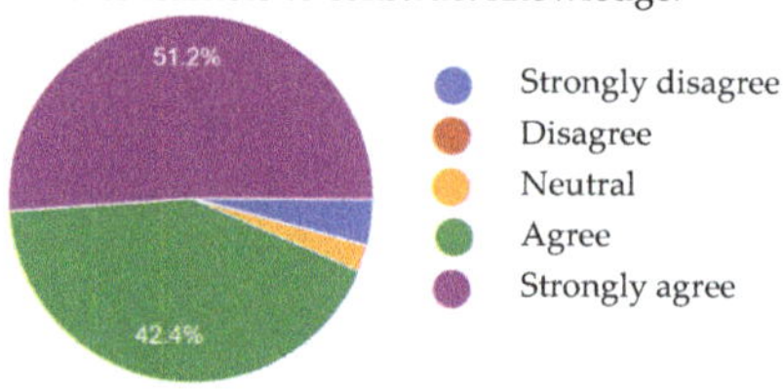
7. An effective method to help learners acquire valuable knowledge and skills is to provide feedback and guide them to generate ideas rather than to simply give them the solutions.	8. An effective method to assist learners in achieving their goals is to design a specific curriculum based on their levels and improvements.
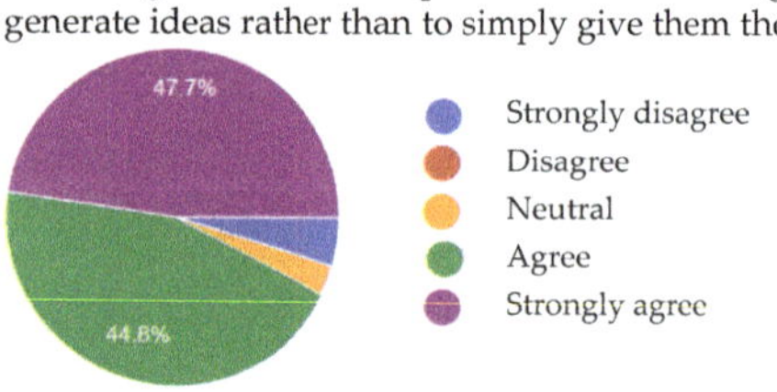	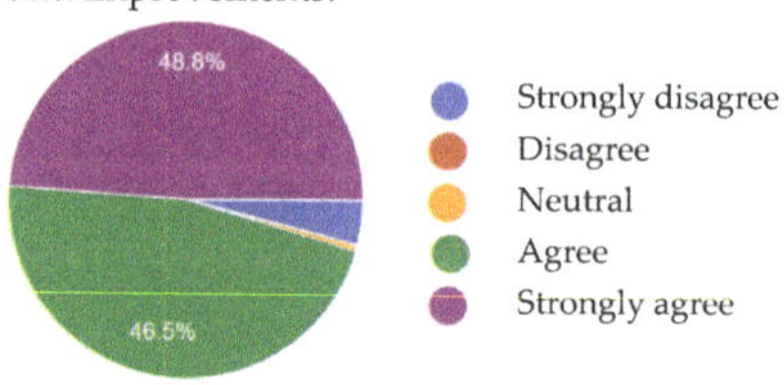

Table 2. Histogram showing the results of the facilitators' survey when using the tool.

# Question	# Question
Section 2 1. The tool would help me find an existing group.	2. The tool would help me build an effective learning group.
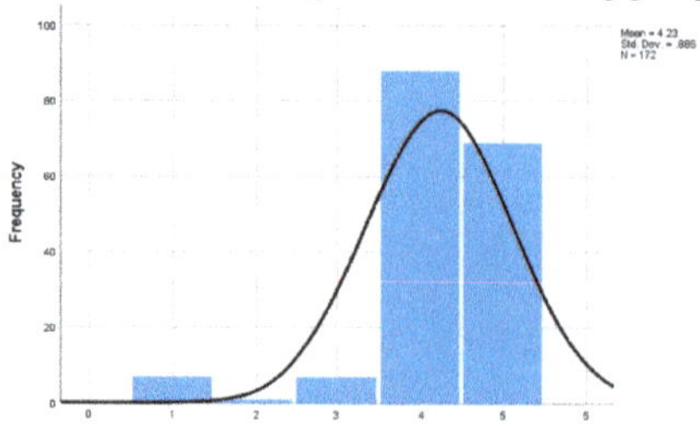	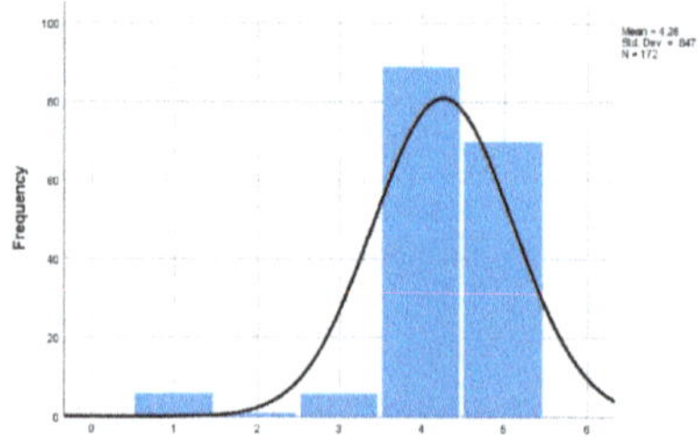

Table 2. *Cont.*

#	Question	#	Question
3. The tool would help me manage the peer review easily and effectively. 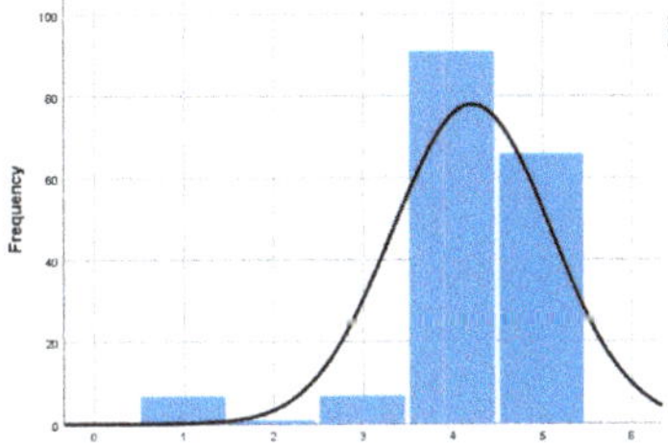		4. The tool would provide a clear view of the learners' background and their goals. 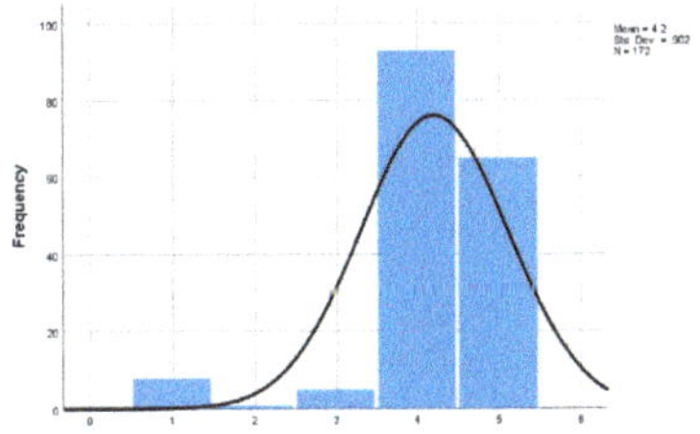	
5. The tool would help me organize lessons and resources more effectively. 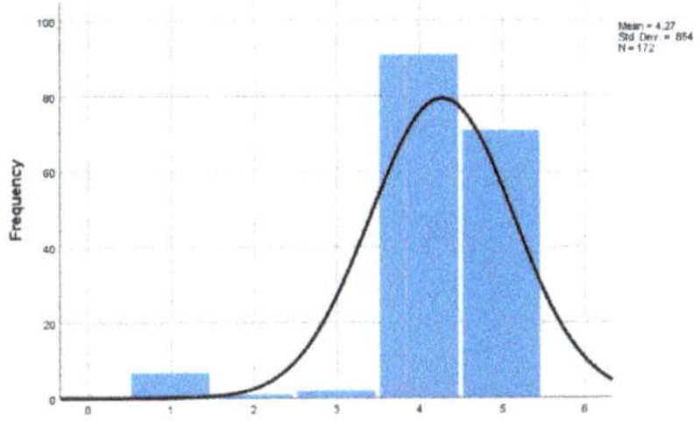		6. The tool would help me to monitor each learner's improvement process. 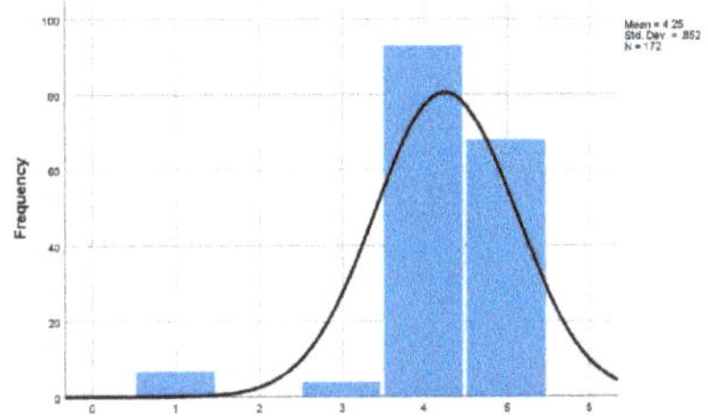	

Table 3. Descriptive statistics of the learners' agreement with each statement of the survey.

#	Question	N	Min	Max	Mean	Std. Dev.
Section 1						
1	Exchanging knowledge and experience would foster my in-depth understanding and necessary skills.	388	1	5	4.29	1.165
2	Interactions amongst peers would effectively help me exchange knowledge and experience.	388	1	5	4.26	1.082
3	Resource-sharing repositories would effectively help me exchange knowledge and experience.	388	1	5	4.18	1.147
4	The guidance and support of mentors in generating ideas are vitally important for me to stay on the right path to success.	388	1	5	4.30	1.085
5	The support of mentors in constructing knowledge is vitally important for me to achieve my goals.	388	1	5	4.29	1.049
6	Connecting to a wide range of professional communities would provide me with the opportunity to receive effective guidance.	388	1	5	4.25	1.062
7	Connecting to a wide range of professional communities would provide me with the opportunity to construct knowledge effectively.	388	1	5	4.24	1.070
8	A flexible curriculum which is adjustable based on my level and improvement would help me enhance my knowledge.	388	1	5	4.30	1.078
Section 2						
9	The tool would help me find an existing group easily.	388	1	5	4.12	1.037
10	The tool would help me build an effective group of learning.	388	1	5	4.08	1.013
11	The tool would help me maintain interactions constantly and conveniently.	388	1	5	4.13	1.010
12	The tool would help me share and access resource repositories easily.	388	1	5	4.16	0.972
13	The tool would help me to perform a peer review easily and effectively.	388	1	5	4.13	0.998
14	The tool would provide me with the opportunity to connect to a wide range of professional communities.	388	1	5	4.12	1.010
15	The tool would help me to choose mentors who are well-matched with my requirements.	388	1	5	4.18	0.957

A total of 172 completed questionnaires were received from the facilitators. Interestingly, the participants expressed diverse views in their responses to the questionnaire, but the majority of respondents agreed with most of the questions in the questionnaire. The first three questions evaluated to what extent they agreed with the idea that collaborative learning helps learners achieve their goals (addressed in H1, H2, and H3). The first question evaluated whether learners should discuss and actively maintain interactions with facilitators to acquire in-depth knowledge and soft skills to benefit them in their future careers. The second question evaluated the idea that the interactions would help learners exchange knowledge and experience. The third question evaluated whether resource-sharing repositories would help learners exchange knowledge and experience. About 92% to 95% of the participants agreed and strongly agreed with the ideas presented in questions 1–3, while less than 6.4% disagreed.

The next five questions evaluated the respondents' level of agreement that e-mentoring assists learners in succeeding in their learning pathways. To evaluate H8, the fourth question asked the respondents to rate their level of agreement on the importance of the mentors' support in constructing knowledge in relation to the learners' success. Nearly 95% of the participants answered that this support is extremely important for learners. The fifth and sixth questions evaluated the respondents' level of agreement with the notion that connecting to the wider professional community provides learners with more opportunities to receive guidance and to be assisted in constructing knowledge (addressed in H5 and H4). The majority of respondents (94.2% and 93.6%) agreed with questions 5 and 6, respectively. The seventh question evaluated whether an effective method to help learners acquire valuable knowledge and skills is to provide feedback and to guide them to generate ideas rather than to give them the solutions (H6), receiving a 92.5% positive response. The eighth question evaluated to what degree the respondents agreed that an effective method to assist learners in achieving their goals is to design a specific curriculum based on their levels and improvements (H7), receiving a 95.3% positive response.

In the second section, after performing a set of tasks and experiencing the features of the tool while following the given instructions, the participants were asked to rate the statements on a five-point Likert scale. As shown in Table 2, there are six statements in the second section, three addressing the effectiveness of the application in supporting learners in a collaborative learning setting and the other three addressing the effectiveness of the tool in assisting learners in e-mentoring. Statement 1 and statement 2 address the first stage in collaborative learning, where learners want to participate in a suitable group by finding and asking to join an existing group or build a new group. Most participants indicated that they thought the tool supported learners easily, with 91.3% finding an existing group, and 92.4% forming a new efficient group. Moreover, 91.3% of the participants strongly agreed and agreed with the effectiveness of managing the peer-review works, which is addressed in statement 3.

The last three statements required the participants to evaluate the effectiveness of several specific features of e-mentoring. The majority of participants agreed with the statements. In response to statement 4, 91.9% of participants agreed that the tool provided a clear view of the learners' backgrounds and goals. Because organizing lessons and learning resources are similar in collaborative learning and e-mentoring, statement 5 asked the participants to indicate what they thought of this feature in the tool. Only 4.7% of participants stated that the tool did not assist them in managing lessons and resources effectively, whereas 94.2% provided contrary responses. For the last statement, 93.6% of participants indicated that they felt the tool helped them to monitor each learner's improvement effectively.

As for the learners' survey, in total, 388 completed responses were received. The content of the first section of eight questions for the learners was the same as the first section for the facilitators; however, it focused on the learners' perspective. The results shown in Table 3 with mean values greater than 4.20 indicate a high level of agreement for all the questions. Moreover, the next seven statements in the second section evaluated the satisfaction of learners in experiencing collaborative learning and e-mentoring. Learners were provided with detailed instructions on how to find an existing group or create a new group with common goals, as well as the ways they maintain interactions, share resources, perform peer-review works, connect to a wide range of professional communities, and choose mentors who are well-matched to their requirements. Considering the mean and standard deviation scores for each statement, most items have a mean value of between 4.08 and 4.18 and a standard deviation of around 1, which indicates that the participants agreed with all the statements and formed similar opinions, while the minority rated the application as not really effective in terms of supporting their learning.

Two open-ended questions invited participants to write comments about the tool. Of the 172 surveys completed by the facilitators, a total number of 97 responses were received for collaborative learning, and 92 responses were received for e-mentoring. The results show that almost all facilitators were interested in the way the application supported them in exchanging and learning with their colleagues and more experienced professors and guiding their learners. Some of their positive feedback statements are "It is great that we have been given various opportunities to connect to experts in different fields", "Reviewing academic work is much quicker and more effective as authors and reviewers can do the work directly with the tool", "The tool helps us to monitor and evaluate the learning processes visually; also, discussion boxes encourage learners to share their thoughts naturally which enhances our professional ethics and pedagogical skills". We also received some useful comments to improve the application, for example: "The team leader should understand the strengths and the weaknesses of each member to assign suitable tasks"; "Each member in a group should take a specific responsibility which would be checked regularly to ensure the efficiency of the group"; "If a mentor declines a learner's request, the tool should suggest other mentors who are suitable in relation to the learner's criteria".

Of the 388 responses from the learners, 177 responses were received for collaborative learning, and 174 responses were received for e-mentoring. Similar to the facilitators' surveys, most of the learners expected to experience new learning approaches that would help them reach their goals by flexibly connecting them with a wide range of professional communities and providing various opportunities to communicate and exchange knowledge. Many of the learners' comments express their positive experience with the tool: "The tool helps us to not only be receivers of knowledge but also sharers which ignites our passion and helps us to assert ourselves"; "The tool provides us with a comfortable learning environment as facilitators or mentors accompany us through the learning process"; "We were really impressed with the e-mentoring strategy which suggests suitable mentors based on our requirements with useful information, so we could make an effective choice". Moreover, several comments aiming to improve the tool are "The team leader should take the responsibility to monitor, give instructions, and manage the group's activities to ensure the effectiveness of the group", "Resource sharing should be reviewed and approved before updating to the common repository to ensure the scientific quality of resources", "For each group, the number of members should be limited to make effective use of each member's responsibility", "To perform the two learning strategies effectively, besides the flexibility, the learning program should be varied with diverse activities to engage learners, or combine different learning strategies flexibly".

The large number of positive results and feedback indicates the feasibility and effectiveness of the research. Both learners and facilitators are expecting an educational transformation to more modern and flexible learning approaches, as collaborative learning and e-mentoring become two learning strategies that effectively assist them in succeeding in their learning pathways. Moreover, the designed functions ensure that the learning processes are smoother and more effective, and participants strongly believe that the proposed framework will meet their expectations. However, the learners' suggestions indicate that the framework should be improved to assist facilitators and learners more efficiently and more rigorously in assigning members' roles, limiting group numbers, and improving the quality of the resources in shared workplaces, where the integration of supporting tools can be considered if deemed necessary.

6. Conclusions

Implementing a smart education system is important in today's era of digital transformation. A smart learning system comprises intelligent pedagogies in a sophisticated learning environment supported by technological advances to foster a competent workforce. In addition to mastering foundation knowledge and skills, learners are required to acquire certain competencies to successfully perform all the tasks associated with the changes in today's highly technological society. Learners are no longer studying alone, or within the boundaries of their training institutions, but are exposed to valuable opportunities to learn from colleagues or strengthen their knowledge and skills by connecting to a wide body of professional communities. The purpose of this research is to propose a smart learning system that enhances collaborative learning and e-mentoring in higher education. The framework comprises two effective learning strategies, namely, collaborative learning and e-mentoring.

To address the theory effectively, we proposed a model with a set of hypotheses. We argued that a learner's achievement and motivation can be enhanced by collaborative learning and e-mentoring. Furthermore, when engaging in high-quality social interaction and resource sharing, learners are exposed to valuable opportunities to exchange knowledge and experience. E-mentoring assists learners in overcoming difficulties in gaining mastery of new skills and knowledge by providing a learning environment where they can connect to professional communities and experience flexible curriculums that are adjusted to be more suitable for learners' improvement. Through e-mentoring, learners receive personalised guidance in generating ideas and constructing knowledge to improve their skills and develop self-confidence [29].

The paradigm has been implemented as a web application to demonstrate the effectiveness of the proposed model in a smart education environment. The collaborative learning framework enables users to build a group with common goals or to search for a group that has the same goals as they do. They engage in learning using a joint workspace where they can share resources, learn new concepts, discuss and deal with uncertain theories, and construct ideas together. Moreover, the application enables them to learn both synchronously and asynchronously using a range of multimedia and devices.

Similarly, in this framework, e-mentoring assists learners from the matching stage onward to maintain mentor–mentee relationships and evaluate the results. Mentees can be required to participate in the mentoring process, or they can proactively search for mentors who meet their requirements. Learners engage in the learning process by following curriculums designed by mentors, including lectures and activities. The progress of learners is monitored and evaluated based on their achievements and improvement, which provides helpful evidence that can be used by mentors to access and improve their learning programs.

To demonstrate the usefulness and feasibility of the proposed model, two surveys with similar structures were conducted to evaluate the proposed framework and its functionality from the perspective of facilitators and learners. The questionnaires were divided into two parts, one focusing on the theory, which relates to the hypotheses about participants, and the other, focusing on the implementation part. The questionnaires were designed in the Google Form application in the Vietnamese language because all participants are working and pursuing postgraduate programs in Vietnamese military academies. Our purpose was to collect feedback on whether facilitators and learners agreed with the statements describing how collaborative learning and e-mentoring assist learners to be successful. The great majority of respondents agreed with all the statements with constructive comments. Thus, the research model is effective in addressing the requirement of developing a smart education environment for a future high-quality workforce.

This study analyses how collaborative learning and e-mentoring support learners in higher education. The evaluation was conducted in a specific learning environment, namely, Vietnamese military institutions, because this organization is pushing for the implementation of a smart education platform and the requirements of working cooperatively and connecting across the organization. To broaden the intelligent features of these two learning approaches so they are applicable to different learning environments, future research will examine whether they support learners in other learning environments, such as vocational education or secondary education, and more responses from various types of learners will be collected.

The framework also helps learners complete learning activities, as they can study synchronously or asynchronously, and question, refer, and respond to one another's ideas via discussion boxes. However, participants require diverse activities to motivate and engage them in the learning process. Learners with different levels of knowledge and experience may expect specific activities that not only build teamwork skills but also immerse learners in interactive problem-solving scenarios. One of the growing trends of education that needs to be considered as a learning activity in future research is the gamification of virtual reality, especially in the case of training practice skills for specialists using modern digital solutions, such as in the mining [52] and medical fields. A successful course includes a vibrant mix of activities, which requires future work to identify which will be the most suitable for learners and integrate supporting components to the tool as necessary.

Additionally, the framework helps learners by suggesting groups or mentors that are a suitable match based on specific criteria, such as their goals, required qualifications, majors, and years of experience. Without assistance from the framework, learners may experience difficulties searching for an appropriate mentor or group from a large professional community. Throughout the learning process, the facilitators monitor the ways learners complete assigned tasks and evaluate and adjust the curriculum to better suit the learners' goals. For this reason, to provide learners with a more sophisticated learning environment, future work will integrate AI and machine learning algorithms to undertake an advanced analysis on the platform to recommend a better matching process and suggest the most suitable learning curriculums for individuals based on their requirements, personality traits, and learning habits.

In this research, the main focus was on two learning approaches, collaborative learning and e-mentoring, both of which help learners achieve their academic goals by connecting them to a wide range of professional communities. However, there are countless pedagogies that can engage learners and help them develop higher-order thinking skills and understand how to relate their learning to the world around them. Flexibly implementing different pedagogical techniques in a smart educational environment is of vital importance to ensure that learners can tackle learning in a way that best meets their needs. Future work will investigate other learning strategies to gain a deeper grasp of which pedagogy best suits learners in specific circumstances. Pedagogical approaches for higher education that can be considered are constructivist learning, inquiry-based learning, integrative learning, and the reflective approach.

Author Contributions: Conceptualization, L.N., S.T. and E.P.; methodology, L.N.; software, L.N.; validation, L.N., S.T. and E.P.; formal analysis, L.N.; investigation, L.N.; resources, L.N.; data curation, L.N.; writing—original draft preparation, L.N.; writing—review and editing, S.T. and E.P.; visualization, L.N.; supervision, S.T. and E.P.; project administration, L.N. All authors have read and agreed to the published version of the manuscript.

Funding: This research received no external funding.

Institutional Review Board Statement: All subjects gave their informed consent for inclusion before they participated in the study. Please note that the survey was conducted in Vietnamese institution and no Ethics Committee approval is required.

Data Availability Statement: The data presented in this study are available on request from the corresponding author.

Conflicts of Interest: The authors declare no conflict of interest.

References

1. Azam, M.; Nouman, M.; Gill, A.R. Impacts of information technology on society in the new century. *Preprints. Org.* **2022**, *2022*, 2022070283.
2. Haleem, A.; Javaid, M.; Qadri, M.A.; Suman, R. Understanding the role of digital technologies in education: A review. *Sustain. Oper. Comput.* **2022**, *3*, 275–285. [CrossRef]
3. Laverick, D.M. *Mentoring Processes in Higher Education*; Springer: Berlin/Heidelberg, Germany, 2016.
4. Parchure, A.; Gosavi, S. Learning strategies: Impact of emerging hybrid model of learning. *TMV's Knowl. Resour. Cent. Digit. Repos.* **2022**, *24*, 41–46.
5. Azmi, A.N.; Kamin, Y.; Noordin, M.K.; Nasir, A.N.M. Towards industrial revolution 4.0: Employers' expectations on fresh engineering graduates. *Int. J. Eng. Technol.* **2018**, *7*, 267–272.
6. Lase, D. Education and industrial revolution 4.0. *J. Handayani Pgsd Fip. Unimed.* **2019**, *10*, 48–62. [CrossRef]
7. Zhu, Z.-T.; Yu, M.-H.; Riezebos, P. A research framework of smart education. *Smart Learn. Environ.* **2016**, *3*, 1–17. [CrossRef]
8. Nafea, R.M.F.D.; Toplu, F.K. Future of Education in Industry 4.0: Educational Digitization. A Canadian Case Study. In *Research Anthology on Digital Transformation, Organizational Change, and the Impact of Remote Work*; IGI Global: Hershey, PA, USA, 2021; pp. 1977–1997.
9. Scager, K.; Boonstra, J.; Peeters, T.; Vulperhorst, J.; Wiegant, F. Collaborative learning in higher education: Evoking positive interdependence. *CBE—Life Sci. Educ.* **2016**, *15*, ar69. [CrossRef] [PubMed]
10. Jeong, H.; Hmelo-Silver, C.E. Seven affordances of computer-supported collaborative learning: How to support collaborative learning? How can technologies help? *Educ. Psychol.* **2016**, *51*, 247–265. [CrossRef]
11. Chi, M.T.; Roy, M.; Hausmann, R.G. Observing tutorial dialogues collaboratively: Insights about human tutoring effectiveness from vicarious learning. *Cogn. Sci.* **2008**, *32*, 301–341. [CrossRef]
12. Aderibigbe, S.A.; Colucci-Gray, L.; Gray, D. Mentoring as a collaborative learning journey for teachers and student teachers: A critical constructivist perspective. *Teach. Educ. Adv. Netw. J.* **2014**, *6*, 17–27.
13. Ragins, B.R.; Kram, K.E. *The Handbook of Mentoring at Work: Theory, Research, and Practice*; Sage Publications: New York, NY, USA, 2007.
14. Elbestawi, M.; Centea, D.; Singh, I.; Wanyama, T. SEPT learning factory for industry 4.0 education and applied research. *Procedia Manuf.* **2018**, *23*, 249–254. [CrossRef]
15. Ibrahim, N.; Al Ani, I.I. Smart Learner-Centric Learning Systems. In Proceedings of the Information Science and Applications 2017, Macau, China, 20–23 March 2017; pp. 577–584.
16. Asoodar, M.; Vaezi, S.; Izanloo, B. Framework to improve e-learner satisfaction and further strengthen e-learning implementation. *Comput. Hum. Behav.* **2016**, *63*, 704–716. [CrossRef]
17. MirsaeedGhazi, T.; Kharrat, M.; Kardan, A.; Eghbali, N. A framework for learner preparation and support in academic e-learning environment. *Int. J. Inf. Commun. Technol.* **2011**, *3*, 33–41.
18. Madhusudhana, K. Learner Cognitive Behavior and Influencing Factors in Web-based Learning Environment. *Int. J. Adv. Comput. Sci. Appl.* **2018**, *9*, 542–546. [CrossRef]
19. Le, H.; Janssen, J.; Wubbels, T. Collaborative learning practices: Teacher and student perceived obstacles to effective student collaboration. *Camb. J. Educ.* **2018**, *48*, 103–122. [CrossRef]
20. Zhang, Q.; Long, L. Didactics of smart pedagogy: Smart pedagogy for technology enhanced learning. In *Innovations in Education and Teaching International*; Daniela, L., Ed.; Springer: Cham, Switzerland, 2021.
21. Tomlinson, C.A.; McTighe, J. *Integrating Differentiated Instruction & Understanding by Design: Connecting Content and Kids*; ASCD: Alexandria, VA, USA, 2006.
22. Kallel, I.; Chniter, M. Building Collaborative e-Learning Teams in a Smart Education Environment. In Proceedings of the 2019 IEEE International Smart Cities Conference (ISC2), Casablanca, Morocco, 14–17 October 2019; pp. 324–329.
23. Quinnell, K. Mentoring organically. In *Beyond Mentoring*; Elsevier: Amsterdam, The Netherlands, 2017; pp. 5–18.
24. Mullen, C.A. Alternative mentoring types. *Kappa Delta Pi Rec.* **2016**, *52*, 132–136. [CrossRef]
25. Sohn, M.; Kwon, Y.M.; Lee, H.J. Context-based hybrid semantic matching framework for e-mentoring system. In Proceedings of the 2012 15th International Conference on Network-Based Information Systems, Melbourne, Australia, 26–28 September 2012; pp. 691–696.
26. Neely, A.R.; Cotton, J.; Neely, A.D. E-mentoring: A model and review of the literature. *AIS Trans. Hum. Comput. Interact.* **2017**, *9*, 220–242.
27. Lavin Colky, D.; Young, W.H. Mentoring in the virtual organization: Keys to building successful schools and businesses. *Mentor. Tutoring* **2006**, *14*, 433–447. [CrossRef]
28. Gay, B. What is mentoring? *Educ. Train.* **1994**, *36*, 4–7. [CrossRef]
29. Tinoco-Giraldo, H.; Torrecilla Sanchez, E.M.; García-Peñalvo, F.J. E-mentoring in higher education: A structured literature review and implications for future research. *Sustainability* **2020**, *12*, 4344. [CrossRef]
30. Cho, Y.H.; Lim, K.Y. Effectiveness of collaborative learning with 3 D virtual worlds. *Br. J. Educ. Technol.* **2017**, *48*, 202–211. [CrossRef]
31. Moskaliuk, J.; Bertram, J.; Cress, U. Training in virtual environments: Putting theory into practice. *Ergonomics* **2013**, *56*, 195–204. [CrossRef]

32. Miller, M.; Hadwin, A. Scripting and awareness tools for regulating collaborative learning: Changing the landscape of support in CSCL. *Comput. Hum. Behav.* **2015**, *52*, 573–588. [CrossRef]
33. Ward, V.; Smith, S.; House, A.; Hamer, S. Exploring knowledge exchange: A useful framework for practice and policy. *Soc. Sci. Med.* **2012**, *74*, 297–304. [CrossRef] [PubMed]
34. Zachary, L.J.; Fischler, L.A. *The Mentee's Guide: Making Mentoring Work for You*; John Wiley & Sons: Hoboken, NJ, USA, 2009.
35. Aarnio, M. Collaborative Knowledge Construction in the Context of Problem-Based Learning: Exploring Learning from Conflicting Ideas and Knowledge. Ph.D. Thesis, University of Helsinki, Helsinki, Finland, 2015.
36. Pangil, F.; Mohd Nasurddin, A. Knowledge and the importance of knowledge sharing in organizations. In Proceedings of the Conference on Business Management Research, Malaysia, Sintok, 11 December 2013.
37. Bartholomé, T.; Stahl, E.; Pieschl, S.; Bromme, R. What matters in help-seeking? A study of help effectiveness and learner-related factors. *Comput. Hum. Behav.* **2006**, *22*, 113–129. [CrossRef]
38. Fulk, J.; Monge, P.; Hollingshead, A.B. Knowledge resource sharing in dispersed multinational teams: Three theoretical lenses. In *Managing Multinational Teams: Global Perspectives*; Emerald Group Publishing Limited: Bingley, UK, 2005.
39. Learning, C. Foundations for a CSCL Community. In Proceedings of the CSCL, Boulder, CO, USA, 7–11 January 2002; pp. 7–11.
40. Kaplan, S. *Strategies for Collaborative Learning: Building eLearning and Blended Learning Communities*; iCohere, Inc.: Walnut Creek, CA, USA, 2002.
41. Tillema, H.; van der Westhuizen, G.J.; Smith, K. *Mentoring for Learning: Climbing the Mountain*; Springer: Berlin/Heidelberg, Germany, 2015.
42. Van Aalst, J. Distinguishing knowledge-sharing, knowledge-construction, and knowledge-creation discourses. *Int. J. Comput. Support. Collab. Learn.* **2009**, *4*, 259–287. [CrossRef] [PubMed]
43. Center for Health Leadership & Practice. "Guía de Mentoría: Guía para Mentores" (2003). Ethics in Science and Engineering National Clearinghouse. 305. Available online: https://scholarworks.umass.edu/esence/305 (accessed on 28 December 2023).
44. DuBois, D.L.; Karcher, M.J. *Handbook of Youth Mentoring*; Sage Publications: Thousand Oaks, CA, USA, 2013.
45. Scheurs, J.; Dumbraveanu, R. A shift from teacher centered to learner centered approach. *Learning* **2014**, *1*, 31–37.
46. Janssen, J.; Erkens, G.; Kanselaar, G. Visualization of agreement and discussion processes during computer-supported collaborative learning. *Comput. Hum. Behav.* **2007**, *23*, 1105–1125. [CrossRef]
47. Bada, S.O.; Olusegun, S. Constructivism learning theory: A paradigm for teaching and learning. *J. Res. Method Educ.* **2015**, *5*, 66–70.
48. Shukor, N.; Tasir, Z.; van der Meijden, H.; Harun, J. Exploring students' knowledge construction strategies in computer-supported collaborative learning discussions using sequential analysis. *J. Educ. Technol. Soc.* **2014**, *17*, 216–228.
49. Bernáld, H.; Cajander, Å.; Daniels, M.; Laxer, C.; Bernáld, H.; Cajander, Å.; Daniels, M.; Laxer, C. Reasoning about the value of cultural awareness in international collaboration. *J. Appl. Comput. Inf. Technol.* **2011**, *15*, I2.
50. Parker-Katz, M.; Bay, M. Conceptualizing mentor knowledge: Learning from the insiders. *Teach. Teach. Educ.* **2008**, *24*, 1259–1269. [CrossRef]
51. Abu-Abed, F.; Zhironkin, S. New Game Artificial Intelligence Tools for Virtual Mine on Unreal Engine. *Appl. Sci.* **2023**, *13*, 6339. [CrossRef]
52. Kumar, A.; Saudagar, A.K.J.; Alkhathami, M.; Alsamani, B.; Khan, M.B.; Hasanat, M.H.A.; Ahmed, Z.H.; Kumar, A.; Srinivasan, B. Gamified Learning and Assessment Using ARCS with Next-Generation AIoMT Integrated 3D Animation and Virtual Reality Simulation. *Electronics* **2023**, *12*, 835. [CrossRef]

computers

MDPI

Article

Optimization and Scalability of Educational Platforms: Integration of Artificial Intelligence and Cloud Computing

Jaime Govea [1], Ernesto Ocampo Edye [2], Solange Revelo-Tapia [3] and William Villegas-Ch [1,*]

1 Escuela de Ingeniería en Ciberseguridad, Facultad de Ingenierías Ciencias Aplicadas, Universidad de Las Américas, Quito 170125, Ecuador; jaimealejandro.govea@udla.edu.ec
2 Departamento de Informática, Universidad Católica del Uruguay, Montevideo 11600, Uruguay; eocampo@ucu.edu.uy
3 Departamento de Educación Básica, Colegio San Gabriel, Quito 170521, Ecuador; solange.revelo@csgabriel.edu.ec
* Correspondence: william.villegas@udla.edu.ec; Tel.: +593-098-136-4068

Abstract: The intersection between technology and education has taken on unprecedented relevance, driven by the promise of transforming teaching and learning through advanced digital tools. This study proposes a comprehensive exploration of how cloud computing and artificial intelligence converge to impact education, focusing on accessibility, efficiency, and quality of learning. A mixed-research design identified a 25% improvement in the personalization of educational content thanks to AI and a 60% increase in simultaneous user capacity through cloud computing. Additionally, a significant reduction in administrative errors and improvements in scalability were observed without sacrificing quality. The results demonstrate that these technologies not only improve efficiency and accessibility in education but also enrich the learning experience. By comparing these findings with previous research, this study highlights the synergistic value of these technologies and positions itself as a critical resource to guide future developments and improvements in the education sector in a digitally advanced world.

Keywords: artificial intelligence in education; cloud computing and scalability; optimization of educational platforms

1. Introduction

In today's digital age, technology has permeated every corner of our lives, reshaped entire sectors, and redefined how we interact with the world and each other. One of the domains that has undergone monumental changes thanks to technological advances is education. Traditionally seen as face-to-face interaction in classrooms, education has transformed, incorporating digital tools that promise to improve both the delivery of content and the student learning experience [1]. To fully understand the impact of these tools, it is essential to ask ourselves how and to what extent the integration of advanced technologies, such as artificial intelligence (AI) and cloud computing, is really affecting the educational process [2].

From the introduction of the first computer in a classroom to modern online learning platforms, technology has promised to revolutionize education. However, it is crucial to distinguish between simply adding technology to the educational process and using it to transform education [3]. The former can be a simple additive, while the latter can completely redefine how educational content is delivered and consumed. Historically, technological advances have been viewed with optimism, from using radio and television in education to adopting personal computers. Each innovation brought with it the promise of revolutionizing learning. However, as [4,5] have pointed out, the true power of technology lies in its ability to complement and enrich existing pedagogical methodologies rather than simply replacing them. Along these lines, adopting cloud computing and AI is not merely a fad; it is founded on a tradition of continuous improvement in education delivery, as previous studies have highlighted [6,7]. However, despite the rich history of educational technologies, the confluence of cloud computing and AI presents largely uncharted territory. While previous works, such as [8,9], have examined these technologies in isolation, the intersection of the two promises to unlock synergies that could exceed the sum of their parts. This research is situated at this intersection, seeking to decipher the collective potential of these technologies in educational transformation.

In this sense, cloud computing and AI are two of the most promising technologies for this transformation. The cloud offers scalability and accessibility, eliminating physical and geographic barriers. At the same time, AI promises personalization and efficiency, adapting content to each student's individual needs and offering educators valuable insights. While many studies have focused on exploring the effectiveness of personal digital tools or investigating the potential of specific online platforms, there is a gap in the literature regarding how the combination of cloud computing and AI can be leveraged to maximize educational benefits [10]. Furthermore, many of these studies have observed these impacts from a purely quantitative perspective, leaving aside qualitative analyses that could offer a deeper understanding of the student experience.

In this study, we look at technology integration, questioning whether these tools are making a difference and how and why. Specifically, we seek to understand how cloud computing and AI, together, can improve the accessibility, efficiency, and quality of learning. However, despite technological optimism, it is imperative to examine how these technologies translate into tangible educational impacts closely [11]. This study, therefore, explores and quantifies such results.

The results obtained are enlightening, where it is discovered that cloud computing has played an instrumental role in ensuring that educational platforms can serve a massive number of users without compromising the quality of service [12]. On the other hand, AI has proven to be a powerful tool, particularly in areas such as predictive analysis, evaluation, and administrative support, with significant reductions in errors and palpable improvements in content personalization [13].

The novelty of this study lies in its holistic approach. While others have focused on individual pieces in the educational field, in this work, we try to obtain a complete picture, integrating multiple variables and considering both quantitative and qualitative data. This approach allows us to identify the tangible benefits of these technologies and understand the underlying reasons behind these benefits, offering valuable insights for educators, developers, and other stakeholders in the educational domain.

This article is organized as follows: Section 1 presents the Introduction, Section 2 delves into the "Materials and Methods", describing our methodology and approach. The primary findings emerge in Section 3, "Results", where the collected data are presented. In Section 4, "Discussion", we interpret and confront our findings with previous research. Finally, in Section 5, "Conclusions", we summarize our study's key insights and contributions to the field.

2. Materials and Methods

The methodology adopted in this research is based on a mixed approach, combining quantitative and qualitative techniques to provide a holistic and multifaceted analysis of the study problem. This combination allows you to capitalize on the objectivity and precision of quantitative methods while incorporating the depth and contextual richness of qualitative approaches [14]. In terms of scope, the study was designed with an exploratory and descriptive nature [15]. While the experimental dimension seeks to identify and understand new areas, trends, or patterns in computer-assisted learning, the descriptive component focuses on detailing and characterizing current practices and tools, thus establishing a complete overview of the current situation.

2.1. Description of the Problem

Cloud computing has emerged as a promising tool in the educational sphere. It offers outstanding potentialities, such as accessibility from anywhere in the world, the ability to store large volumes of data and resources, and a platform for real-time collaboration. However, although its application has extended the geographical boundaries of learning, it has also revealed scalability problems [16]. As educational institutions seek to reach larger audiences, they face the challenge of ensuring that the quality of education is not diluted and that each student receives a personalized and enriching learning experience.

On the other hand, AI has proven to be a revolutionary tool in many sectors, including education. The promise of AI lies in its ability to adapt and personalize educational content based on students' individual needs [17]. However, its application in distance education is still in its early stages, and there are many unresolved issues about implementing it in a practical, ethical, and accessible way.

The problem manifests itself at the intersection of these two technologies. How can we effectively merge the scalability of cloud computing with the personalization of AI to create a robust, student-centered distance education system? While each technology alone has the potential to address specific aspects of the problem, their combination is the key to resolving the inherent limitations of each. Furthermore, the rapid transition to online learning modalities, accelerated by global events such as the COVID-19 pandemic, has exacerbated these concerns [18]. Educators and administrators found themselves navigating uncharted waters, searching for tools and platforms that can serve a growing number of online learners without compromising quality. The demand for immediate solutions led to a hasty adoption of technologies, some of which were not fully prepared to meet distance education's complex and multifaceted needs [19].

At the core of this work lies the aspiration to imagine the interactions and possibilities at the confluence of cloud computing and AI within education. The exploration seeks to discern how these emerging technologies can enhance distance education, offering scalable and personalized solutions that respond to the growing demands of contemporary society. Therefore, the methodological choice reflects this intention, oriented towards discovering deep and applicable insights in online educational contexts.

2.2. Review of Similar Works

Computer-assisted learning has undergone rapid evolution with the emergence of new technologies and teaching methods, which promise to transform education at unprecedented levels. The convergence of cloud computing and artificial intelligence has been one of the most prominent trends in this change.

The study in ref. [10] illustrates how cloud computing has enabled unprecedented democratization in access to educational resources. Institutions, particularly in developing countries, have been able to transcend geographic and infrastructure limitations. However, this work also emphasizes a critical observation: although scalability is a clear advantage of cloud computing, customization and adaptability remain challenges.

On the other hand, ref. [11] highlighted the benefits of cloud-powered virtual classrooms, highlighting the ability of these platforms to adapt to changing scenarios, such as the hasty transition to distance education during the recent pandemic [9]. However, despite its flexibility and scalability, the study also pointed out a lack of personalization of learning.

Entering the domain of AI [13] demonstrated how artificial intelligence can infuse a level of personalization into the educational process that was previously unattainable. They observed that systems that adapt content based on student behavior and responses improve academic performance and student satisfaction. This sentiment was reiterated by Zou and Chen, who described automatic adaptability systems, proposing a more individual-centered education [14]. However, an evident gap in the existing literature is the exploration of the confluence between cloud computing and AI in education. While ref. [15] addresses learning analytics using advanced AI techniques and highlights the value of interventions based on real-time data, it falls short by not fully integrating the benefits of cloud computing.

Other works, such as [20], examined how AI can improve the management and administration of virtual classrooms. Their study found that AI-based systems can automatically optimize administrative tasks, freeing up valuable time for educators. Still, the lack of a robust cloud-based infrastructure limited the large-scale implementation of their proposed solutions. Furthermore, ref. [21] investigated the application of deep learning algorithms in analyzing student behavior in virtual learning environments. They found that AI has significant potential to predict student performance and provide early interventions. However, their study also emphasized the need for more robust computing infrastructures, such as those that cloud computing can provide, to process and analyze large datasets in real-time.

It is essential to mention the work of ref. [22], which focused on developing MOOCs using AI and cloud computing. His study provided a preliminary insight into how integrating these two technologies could create more effective and personalized virtual learning environments. Given this review, it is evident that while there is extensive research in individual areas of cloud computing and AI, there is a lack of studies that fully integrate the two to transform computer-assisted learning. Our research seeks to fill this gap, providing a holistic view of how these technologies can redefine the educational process.

2.3. Previous Concepts

To fully understand the scope and nature of the intersection between cloud computing and AI in the context of distance education, it is essential to become familiar with some key concepts [23]. These terms and definitions provide the theoretical and practical basis for our study and have a solid background in the scientific literature.

- Cloud computing refers to providing computing services, including storage, processing, and intelligence, over the Internet. Resources are rented as needed and accessed over the web, allowing flexibility, scalability, and access from anywhere. This flexibility is crucial to ensuring that AI-based applications perform optimally, accessing resources as needed, and is supported by research such as [24,25].
- Machine learning, a subfield of AI, refers to the study of algorithms and statistical models that machines use to improve their performance on a specific task. These algorithms and models, such as neural networks, identify patterns and make decisions without being specifically programmed to do so, allowing personalized adaptations in real time [26].
- Distance education is a teaching method in which teachers and students are not physically present in a traditional classroom. Instead, they use technology to facilitate interaction and access to course content, allowing learning without geographical restrictions. Works such as [9] have shown how the cloud has enhanced the adaptability of distance education.
- Educational analytics involves collecting, analyzing, and presenting data related to learning and teaching. It often relies on Big Data and AI tools, as seen in studies such as [15], to provide valuable insights and further personalize the learning experience.
- Scalability refers to the ability of a system to handle an increase in workload or demand. This is especially relevant in educational contexts where there may be peak demand, and a system that can adapt quickly without losing quality of service is needed [27].

These concepts represent the basis of this exploration at the intersection of cloud computing and artificial intelligence in education [28]. Each of them contributes to the development of the method, helping to contextualize and focus this study on areas with the most significant potential to drive innovation and positive change.

2.4. Method Design

In the methodological design of this research, a quantitative approach is adopted, using numerical data to analyze and model the interactions between cloud computing and artificial intelligence in educational contexts. These tools allow impacts and trends to be measured and quantified accurately. Regarding the scope, the investigation is oriented in an exploratory and descriptive manner [29]. This means that while identifying and describing emerging characteristics and patterns, we also seek to understand the implications and possible applications of the findings in technology-enhanced distance education.

Figure 1 presents the critical phases of the research sequentially, from the selection of participants to the recognition of limitations. Its structure highlights rigor in the data collection and analysis, underlines the centrality of ethical considerations, and anticipates a self-critical perspective by identifying study restrictions.

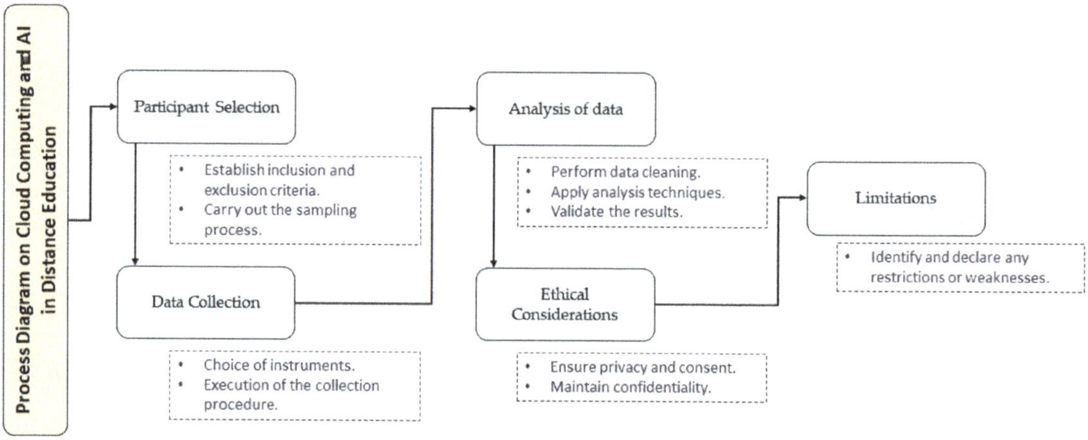

Figure 1. Methodological process for cloud computing and artificial intelligence in distance education.

The design of the method seeks to understand the confluence and synergy between cloud computing and artificial intelligence in an educational environment. The use of the cloud in the educational sector has democratized access to learning resources, allowing students and teachers to access them anytime, anywhere [30]. This flexibility and scalability are especially critical for educational institutions. However, beyond simple content delivery, AI integration allows for an in-depth, real-time analysis of user interaction patterns with these resources.

For example, with AI models, it is possible to identify how students approach content, identify problem areas or topics that present more incredible difficulty, and provide, in almost real time, personalized feedback or recommendations to improve the learning experience. At the institutional level, AI can also forecast trends, such as the risk of student attrition or emerging areas of interest, based on data collected in the cloud.

The proposed method is aimed at evaluating the cloud infrastructure. To achieve this, it is necessary to understand the architecture, capacity, performance, and security of the cloud environment of the educational institute. With the integration of AI, it is possible to investigate how and to what extent AI is incorporated in this cloud environment and what specific tools are being used, for example, recommendation systems, predictive analysis, and automatic problem detection. For the evaluation, the collection and analysis of data is essential; this considers the use of surveys, interviews, and platform records, as well as the identification of concrete evidence of the impact of this integration on the educational experience.

Figure 2 presents sequentially the flow of operations that integrates cloud computing capabilities with artificial intelligence in an academic environment. This begins with data collection in the cloud, which captures the essence of user access and interaction with educational resources hosted in a virtual environment. AI integration then addresses the processing and analysis of this data to extract behavioral patterns and areas of interest or difficulty [27]. These insights generate personalized feedback and recommendations, providing students with an adapted and optimized learning experience. In the predictive analysis phase, future trends are projected as possible academic challenges or emerging topics. Finally, updating resources in the cloud reflects a cycle of continuous improvement, where educational resources adapt and evolve based on the feedback and analysis carried out.

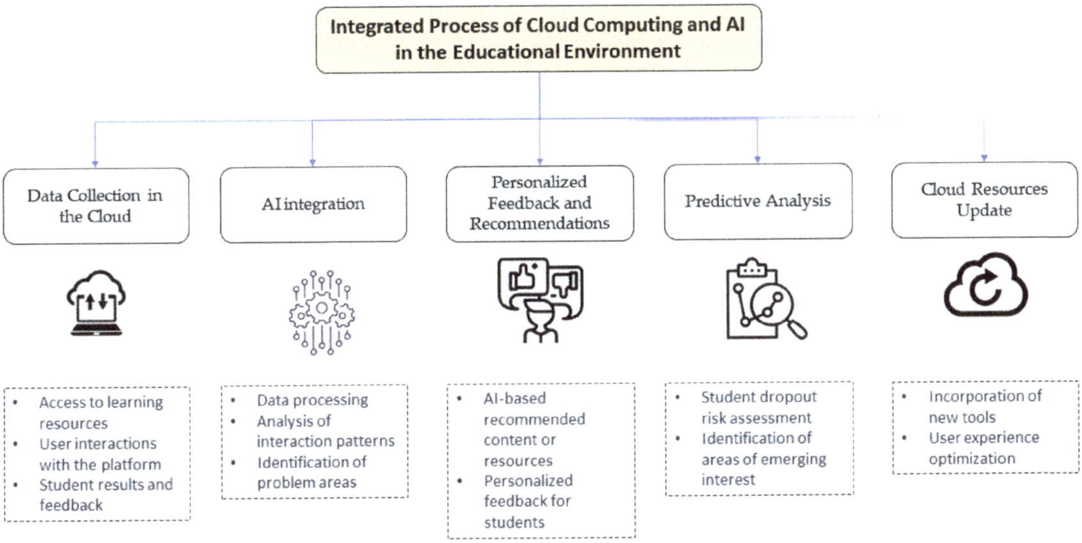

Figure 2. How the integration of cloud computing and AI works in an educational environment.

2.5. Participant Selection

For selecting participants, it is necessary to establish the environment in which this work is carried out, in which a technological institute of higher education participates with a student population of approximately 3000 students and a teaching staff of 50 professors. The institution emphasizes the importance of integrating cutting-edge technologies into its programs [24]. It has modern infrastructure, digital classrooms, and an online learning platform that continues to grow and adapt to the demands of the current educational environment.

Inclusion criteria:

- Students enrolled in training programs during the current semester.
- Teachers teaching at least one subject in online or blended mode.
- Active users of the online learning platform during the semester under study.

Exclusion criteria:

- Students who have not accessed the online platform in the last three months.
- Teachers who exclusively teach subjects in person and do not use digital resources.
- Administrative and technical support staff of the institute.

To ensure an equitable representation of students and teachers, stratified sampling was chosen. Of the student population, 10% were randomly selected, resulting in 300 students. A sample of 20% of the teaching staff was taken, that is, ten teachers. This sample size was considered adequate to represent the diversity of the academic community and the variety in the use of technological tools at the institute [25]. With these selection criteria and methodology, it is intended that the study participants reflect the reality of the institute that participates in the study, thus providing a robust basis to develop and evaluate the proposed method.

2.6. Data Collection

The data collection process is carried out in a digitalized environment, facilitated by the institution's cloud-based LMS. The academic semester is expected to accumulate approximately five terabytes of data derived from student activities. The platform's interaction logs have been considered among the primary data sources [31]. These files record each student's interactions, including access time, duration of sessions, and actions performed. The accumulated data volume is around two terabytes from these logs.

Each student can take up to 20 evaluations during the semester. With 3000 students, it is expected that 60,000 test results will be collected. This would represent around 500 gigabytes of data. Regarding surveys, these are textual and quantitative responses from students. With a monthly frequency and a participation rate of 80%, approximately 24,000 reactions are accumulated, equivalent to 1.5 terabytes of data. These data include test results, access times, and other data with a defined structure, representing about 60% of the total data volume. Unstructured data encompass open-ended survey responses and comments; they constitute approximately 40% of the entire data volume.

Several critical parameters and metrics will be adopted to evaluate the effectiveness of the integration between the cloud platform and AI tools. These parameters include the accuracy of AI predictions, error rate, and response time [32]. Specific hyperparameters for the AI model will be tuned using a combination of grid search and Bayesian optimization. For example, hyperparameters in a neural network model include the learning rate, the number of hidden layers, and the number of neurons per layer.

2.7. Analysis of Data

The data analysis is essential to extracting meaningful insights from the large amount of information collected. Given the complex nature of data and the integration of cloud and AI, it is vital to ensure a rigorous and systematic analysis. The cleaning procedure begins with identifying missing data, for which automated algorithms identify records with missing or incomplete fields [33]. An imputation approach using the mean or median is adopted for quantitative data, such as test scores. Qualitative data, such as comments or survey responses, will be flagged for manual review.

Outlier elimination is carried out using outlier detection techniques, such as the IQR or Z-score method, for which data that deviate significantly from the general behavior are identified, eliminated, or corrected. Normalization and standardization, depending on the analysis techniques to be applied, are carried out by adjusting the data between 0 and 1 or standardization (adjusting the mean to 0 and the standard deviation to 1) to guarantee consistency and improve the effectiveness of the data—AI models.

As an analysis technique, a fundamental statistical analysis is used to identify the data's distribution, central tendency, and dispersion. Supervised algorithms, such as logistic regression and neural networks, are also used to predict behaviors or ratings based on past patterns [34]. For open-survey responses, an AI-based sentiment analysis is used to gain insights into student perception and experience.

Cross-validation techniques are employed to ensure that AI models are robust and generalizable, splitting the data into training and test sets multiple times. Another tool is the confusion matrix; this will allow us to visualize the model's performance, identifying true positives, true negatives, false positives, and false negatives [35]. As performance metrics, we will evaluate precision, sensitivity, specificity, and F1-score to obtain a complete view of how the model performs in different aspects. Integrating these methods and techniques ensures comprehensive and reliable data analyses, providing robust and reliable results that can guide future pedagogical and technological decisions.

Mathematical equations representative of some key procedures employed in our research are presented below to clarify the analysis methods. These equations form the backbone of our analytical process.

Imputation using the mean:

Where $\mathcal{X}_{missing}$ is the imputed value for missing data and $\mathcal{X}_i$ are the observed values of the dataset.

$$\mathcal{X}_{missing} = \frac{1}{N}\sum_{i=1}^{n} \mathcal{X}_i \quad (1)$$

Z-score for outlier detection:

$$Z = \frac{x - x_{min}}{x_{max} - x_{min}} \quad (2)$$

where:

- x is the value of the observation;
- μ is the mean of the population or sample;
- σ is the standard deviation of the population or sample.

Standardization

$$x' = \frac{x - x_{min}}{x_{max} - x_{min}}, \quad (3)$$

where:

- x' is the normalized value;
- x is the original value;
- x_{max} and x_{min} are the minimum and maximum values of the dataset, respectively.

Logistic regression equation (a simple model mentioned):

$$P(Y = 1) = \frac{1}{1 + e^{(\beta_0 + \beta_1 x)}}, \quad (4)$$

where:

- $P(Y = 1)$ is the probability of the dependent variable;
- β_0 is the intercept;
- β_1 is the slope of the relationship;
- x is the independent variable.

*F*1-score:

$$F1 = 2 \times \frac{precision \times recall}{precision + recall}, \quad (5)$$

where:

- *Precision* is the precision of the model;
- Sensitivity (or *recall*) is the sensitivity of the model.

2.8. Ethical Considerations and Limitations of the Study

Before data collection, it is necessary to ask participants to provide informed consent. It was guaranteed that their participation would be voluntary and that they could withdraw at any time without repercussions; for this, all data collected must be anonymized to ensure no individual can be identified. The databases used for the analyses have been encrypted, and security measures have been implemented to prevent unauthorized access. Additionally, the data collected should only be used for the specific purposes of the study. They should not be shared for any other purpose without the explicit consent of the participants.

3. Results

Within the presentation of the results, it is essential to highlight that significant patterns were identified in the scalability of digital educational systems after applying advanced cloud analysis techniques powered by AI. These findings, intrinsically linked to the primary objectives of our study, provide valuable insights into how cloud computing can positively transform the educational experience.

3.1. Simulation Environment and Methods

The simulations were carried out on high-performance machines with the following specifications: 3.6 GHz Intel i9 processors, 64 GB RAM, and NVIDIA RTX 3090 graphics cards with 24 GB GDDR6X. These features enable handling large volumes of data and efficiently performing complex operations. From a software perspective, it was operated on systems with Ubuntu 20.04 LTS, optimized for artificial intelligence and cloud computing operations. The AI frameworks used were TensorFlow 2.4 and PyTorch 1.7, known for their robustness and versatility in deep learning tasks. The datasets used included "Dataset EduTech A" with 500,000 records and "Dataset B Learning Cloud" with 300,000 records.

The initial preparation of the simulation required meticulous setup. Initial parameters, such as cloud configuration and AI variables, were set based on previous studies and recommendations from experts in the field. The choice of these initial parameters was crucial to ensuring that the simulations were representative and relevant. The simulation was initially tuned with precise parameters. The cloud configuration was set with a limit of 10 TB of storage and 20 vCPUs. AI variables such as learning rate were set to 0.001 and batch size to 64, based on optimal results from previous research.

Simulation procedure: Once the configuration was established, the simulations were executed. Each simulation was developed following a clearly defined sequence of events, ensuring the process's coherence and replicability. Throughout the simulations, decisions were made based on the data dynamics and intermediate results, following previously established protocols. The execution involved a total of 50,000 iterations for each simulation. Each iteration had an average response time of 200 ms, ensuring smooth interaction with the system and consistent data collection.

Evaluation criteria: To evaluate the results, specific metrics were defined. These metrics, selected for their relevance and usefulness in the study context, offered an objective evaluation of the simulation results. Each metric provided valuable information about different aspects of the process and its impacts. The metrics used to evaluate the results included precision, reaching at least 95%, and loss, with a reduction goal below 0.05. These metrics were essential to understanding the effectiveness of the methods used.

Results validation: The results obtained from the simulations were subjected to a rigorous validation process. To do this, they were compared with findings from previous simulations, and cross-validation techniques were used. This step ensured that the results were not just the product of anomalies or random variations but reflected genuine patterns and trends. In addition to cross-validation, which used a separate dataset of 20% of the total, the k-fold method with $k = 10$ was implemented to ensure the results' robustness.

3.2. General Results

In the analysis, a significant sample of data was studied, covering the interactions, usability, and effectiveness of the cloud platform regarding assisted learning methods. Among the data, I identified the average accessibility as being 89%. This suggests that most students and teachers accessed and used the cloud platform with ease. The accessibility standard deviation of 7% is relatively low and indicates that accessibility was consistently high across users, with few outliers. Furthermore, the system showed optimal performance for 95% of simultaneous users, indicating robust traffic management capabilities.

The standard deviation of scalability is 5%; this figure highlights that the system mostly operated to its average performance without large spikes in overload or downtime. The range of AI use is between 70 and 100%; these values represent the minimum and maximum percentage of students and teachers who benefited from the functions enhanced by artificial intelligence on the platform. Figure 3 shows a bar chart comparing accessibility and scalability at different points in the study, allowing for a clear visualization of how the cloud platform performed over time.

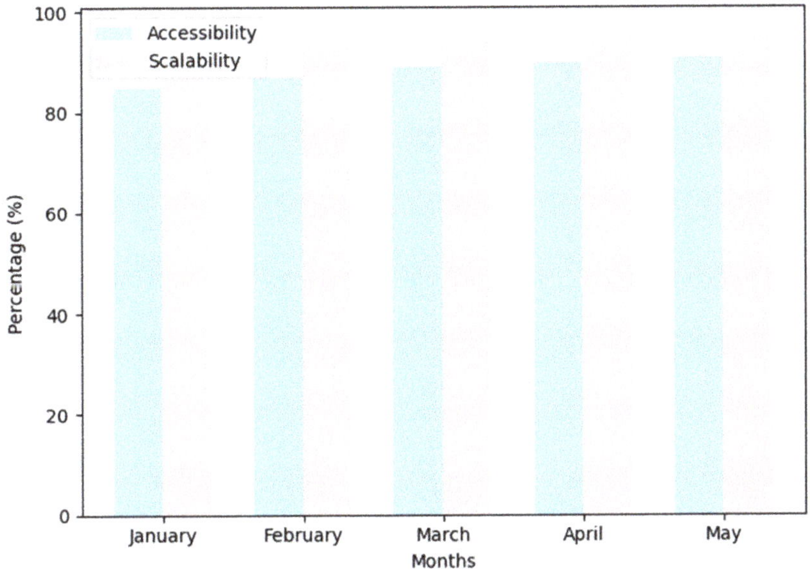

Figure 3. Comparison of accessibility and scalability by month.

Table 1 presents a detailed view of the tangible impact of implementing artificial intelligence in different areas of a cloud-based educational platform. Notably, all areas benefited in some way from the integration of AI, although to different magnitudes. For example, the "Predictive Analytics" area shows an impressive 30% improvement in efficiency, suggesting that AI's ability to analyze and predict trends in student behaviors and needs has dramatically enhanced the adaptability and reactivity of the platform. In addition, it is relevant to highlight the "Reduction of errors" in the "Evaluations" segment, where a 30% decrease was experienced. This could be attributed to AI's ability to evaluate more accurately and consistently than traditional methods. However, there are areas such as "Administrative Support" where the benefits, although present, are more modest, which could indicate that there are still opportunities for improvement in these segments. Overall, these data support the premise that when properly applied, artificial intelligence can lead to significant advances in the efficiency and accuracy of online educational platforms.

Table 1. Summary of artificial intelligence usage metrics in impact areas.

Impact Areas	Affected Users (n)	Efficiency Improvement (%)	Error Reduction (%)
Access to resources	2500	15	25
Collaboration	2100	20	18
Evaluations	2800	12	30
Real-time assistance	2300	22	20
Predictive analysis	1700	30	10
Content adaptation	2200	25	28
Interface customization	1900	20	15
Progress tracking	2600	18	22
Administrative support	1500	10	12
Resource optimization	2400	28	25

The metrics presented in Table 1 were obtained through a rigorous evaluation and analysis. The "Affected Users (n)" column represents the number of users who directly interacted with the AI features within each impact area, and these data were collected directly from the platform's interaction logs. "Efficiency Improvement (%)" was calculated by comparing the speed and performance of tasks before and after implementing AI-based functions. To ensure accuracy, these measurements were carried out using in-platform monitoring tools and an A/B analysis. The "Error Reduction (%)" column was derived from user feedback reports and platform error logs, comparing error frequency before and after AI integration. It is essential to mention that all metrics underwent an internal validation process and were adjusted considering user variability and the context of use.

3.3. Detailed Results

The data are presented as detailed results that show the platform's ability to handle a greater number of concurrent users without degrading performance.

3.3.1. Impact of Cloud Computing on the Accessibility and Scalability of the Educational Platform

With the growing demand for distance education and the need for a robust platform to manage the increase in user traffic, an imperative requirement was observed to guarantee accessibility and scalability. By migrating the educational forum to a cloud-based solution, we seek to precisely address these challenges.

The data collected post-migration highlight the significantly improved ability of the platform to handle increased numbers of concurrent users. Before deployment, notable performance degradations were observed when more than 1500 users accessed the platform simultaneously. Following the transition, the forum has been shown to support up to 3000 concurrent users with no evidence of degradation in user experience. A summary of the results is presented in Table 2.

Table 2. Comparison of performance pre-migration and post-migration to the cloud.

Metrics	Pre-Migration	Post-Migration
Maximum concurrent users	1500	3000
Response time (seconds)	4–5	1–2
CPU usage (%)	80–90	50–60
Memory Usage (%)	85–95	55–65
Downtime (hours per month)	10	2
Operation cost (USD/month)	USD 1200	USD 900

The metrics presented in the Table 2 emerged from extensive system monitoring before and after migration to the cloud. The "Maximum Concurrent Users" metric indicates the maximum number of users the system could support simultaneously without degrading the user experience. "Response time" reflects the time the system takes to respond to a user request, which is a critical indicator of a system's efficiency. The "CPU Usage" and "Memory Usage" percentages show the number of resources consumed by the system in its operations, with lower percentages indicating more efficient resource management after migration. "Downtime" means the total monthly hours that the system was unavailable to users due to technical issues or maintenance. Finally, "Operation cost" compares the monthly costs before and after the migration, indicating the profitability of the transition to the cloud solution. These metrics were meticulously recorded and validated through system monitoring tools and user feedback, ensuring their accuracy and relevance to this study.

Figure 4 presents a clear comparison between the performance metrics before and after migrating the educational platform to the cloud. A notable improvement is observed in the post-migration response time, with an approximate reduction of 66%, going from an average of 4.5 s to 1.5 s. This improvement indicates a smoother and more efficient experience for users. Regarding resource use, both the CPU and memory experience a significant decrease in consumption after the migration. The CPU usage decreases from 85% to 55%, suggesting that the cloud platform manages computational resources more efficiently. Likewise, the memory usage is reduced from 90% to 60%, which implies that more resources are available for future scalability. These results evidence the tangible benefits of adopting cloud solutions, highlighting improvements in efficiency and performance and the platform's ability to accommodate more users effectively without compromising the quality of service.

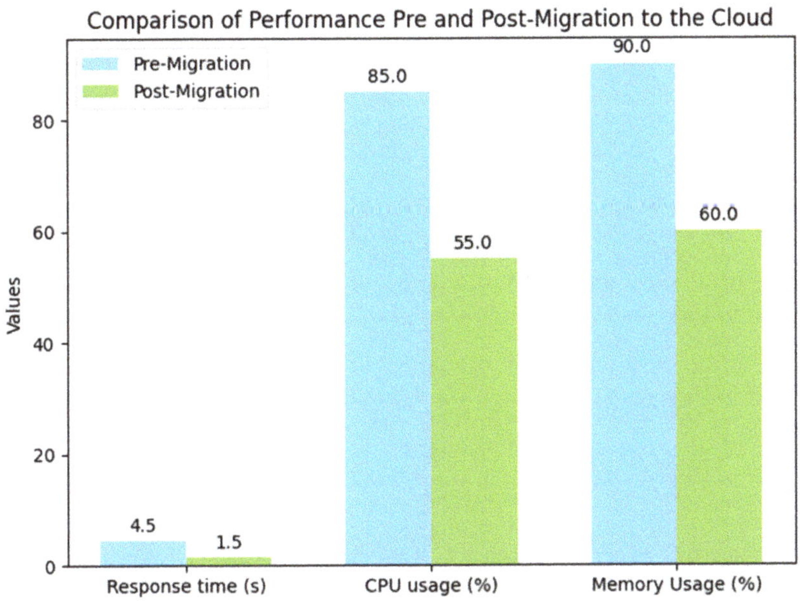

Figure 4. Response time and resource usage (CPU and Memory) before and after migration to the cloud.

These findings underscore the importance and effectiveness of adopting cloud-based solutions for online educational environments. Not only do they ensure that a greater number of users can access the platform simultaneously, but they also ensure a smooth and uninterrupted experience. Migration to the cloud has allowed the educational platform to accommodate more users and improved overall efficiency, guaranteeing accessibility, especially during times of high demand, such as registration, exams, or assignment delivery.

3.3.2. Efficiency of the Integration of Artificial Intelligence in Specific Functions

With the integration of AI into the educational platform, there have been significant changes in the efficiency and accuracy of certain vital functions. These advances have been particularly notable in predictive analytics, assessments, and administrative support.

Table 3 shows the significant advantages of integrating AI into the educational platform. For example, in predictive analyses, a drastic reduction in errors has been observed, going from 18% to 5%. Additionally, this feature now operates with increased efficiency, saving an average of 10 min per task. A similar pattern is seen in automated assessments and administrative support. Additionally, virtual student assistance, a crucial component in improving the user experience, has reduced errors from 15% to 4%, and content management has improved substantially. These results highlight the potential and effectiveness of AI in enhancing and optimizing operations in digital educational environments. Even with these advances, areas of opportunity for future improvements are recognized, including the adaptability of AI to changing user needs and the integration of deep learning to personalize the educational experience further.

Table 3. Specific Feature Improvements with AI Integration.

Function	Errors before AI (%)	Errors after AI (%)	Time Saved (Minutes per Task)
Predictive Analysis	18	5	10
Automated Assessments	25	7	15
Automatic Administrative Support	20	6	12
Virtual Student Assistance	15	4	8
Content Management	10	3	5

The table details the improvements achieved in various functions after implementing artificial intelligence. For each feature listed, a breakdown of errors pre- and post-AI integration is presented, as is the time saved per task due to this addition. The "Errors before AI" and "Errors after AI" metrics provide a clear view of artificial intelligence's impact on reducing inaccuracies in different areas. These metrics were obtained through the systematic review and comparison of records and system logs before and after the incorporation of AI. On the other hand, "Time saved per task" indicates the efficiency gained when performing specific processes and was determined by monitoring the execution time of tasks before and after the integration. It is notable, for example, how implementing AI in predictive analytics significantly reduced errors and enabled considerable time savings per task. Each metric and value in the table was derived from empirical testing and statistical analyses, ensuring its accuracy and reliability in the study context.

3.3.3. Evaluation of the Quality of Learning through the Use of AI

In education, the desired result is not simply operational efficiency or the ability to scale; ultimately, we seek to improve student learning quality. Therefore, the evaluation of the impact is carried out through different indicators.

Student engagement data: Since implementing AI-based tools, active student engagement has shown an upward trend. Feedback about the platform indicates an appreciation for personalized features and recommendations based on individual learning patterns. In Table 4, it is evident the positive impact that the implementation of AI-based tools has had on student participation. The participation rate in courses such as Mathematics has increased considerably, going from 75% to 92%. Programming, an essential discipline in today's technological era, also showed a notable increase in participation, from 68% to 90%. Artificial intelligence course, being inherently technical and advanced, has seen a rise from 82% to 95%, which indicates that AI features not only engage students but also facilitate their engagement with inherently complex materials. These increases suggest that the personalization and adaptability provided by AI may significantly contribute to greater student engagement in the learning process.

Table 4. Student participation rate in courses with and without AI features.

Module	Participation without AI (%)	Engagement with AI (%)
Math	75	92
Programming	68	90
Artificial intelligence	82	95

The table reflects the change in student participation rates in different courses after implementing AI-based features. The metrics presented as "Engagement without AI" and "Engagement with AI" were obtained by recording and analyzing the number of students actively engaged in course activities compared to the total enrolled before and after integrating AI tools. The figures indicated in the "Participation without AI" column represent student engagement based on traditional teaching systems. In contrast, the figures in "Participation with AI" reflect the increase in participation once the AI characteristics were integrated. It is important to note that these percentages were derived through a constant platform analysis, considering frequent access to course materials, interactions in discussion forums, and submission of assignments and exams. These metrics highlight the potential of AI to improve the educational experience, evidencing increased student motivation and engagement with content. These figures' level of detail and precision is based on empirical data collected over time and carefully analyzed to ensure their validity.

Table 5 identifies a positive trend in student grades after incorporating AI functions into the educational process. Specifically, in algebra course, the average rates experienced an increase from 78 to 87, which implies a substantial improvement in the student's understanding and mastery of the content. For databases, a subject that requires analytical and practical skills, the jump from 80 to 92 shows how the adaptability and personalization enabled by AI can positively influence the student's ability to absorb and apply complex concepts. In the case of robotics, an intricate discipline, the increase in scores from 75 to 89 suggests that AI is not only effective in improving academic performance but can also be instrumental in helping students overcome challenges in areas of technique. These results indicate that integrating AI-based tools can significantly benefit education, optimizing learning and facilitating academic success.

Table 5. Average student grades in courses with and without AI features.

Course	Rating without AI	AI Grading
Algebra	78	87
Databases	80	92
Robotics	75	89

The table clearly illustrates how the incorporation of artificial intelligence tools has directly impacted student learning quality. It is essential to understand that behind these numbers are educational methodologies that, enhanced by artificial intelligence, have adapted better to each student's pace and learning style. In the case of algebra course, the improvement in grades reflects a greater understanding and retention of essential mathematical concepts. In the case of databases, the increased performance suggests that students have integrated analytical thinking more effectively with the practical skills required. For robotics, the notable increase highlights how AI-based tools can simplify complex and technical concepts, making learning more accessible. These figures demonstrate "that the tool, in combination with an appropriate pedagogical approach, has been decisive in strengthening the educational process."

The evidence suggests that the integration of AI-based tools has positively influenced the quality of learning. Not only has there been an increase in student engagement, but there has also been a palpable improvement in academic performance. While AI has been a valuable tool, combining these technologies with effective pedagogical strategies has led to these encouraging results. Therefore, investment in AI has operational benefits and, when appropriately implemented, improves the quality of education.

3.4. Comparisons and Contrasts

To evaluate the effectiveness of implementing AI and cloud computing in the educational platform, it was considered essential to systematically compare groups that use these technologies and those that do not. These comparisons provide a clearer view of the differences and similarities in academic performance, user experience, and platform efficiency. Table 6 illustrates a marked difference in academic performance between the two groups. Students who used the platform with AI and cloud functions had, on average, almost 10 points higher grades and a 9% higher passing rate than those who used the traditional version.

Table 6. Comparison of academic performance.

Group	Average Mark	Pass Rate
With AI and Cloud	89.2	94%
Without AI and Cloud	79.5	85%

Regarding statistical tests, a *t*-test was performed to determine if the differences observed in the average scores between the two groups were significant. The results indicated that $p < 0.05$ confirmed a statistically significant difference in academic performance between students who use the platform with emerging technologies and those who do not.

3.5. Additional Analysis Results

In addition to the results found, several additional analyses were carried out to explore secondary and specific aspects of the impact of AI and cloud computing in the educational environment. These analyses provided valuable insights, offering more a profound insight into trends and patterns that were not previously considered. For example, a post hoc analysis was conducted on active platform participation to determine if there were notable differences in students' active involvement depending on the time of day. These findings help optimize platform upgrades and maintenance times.

Figure 5 illustrates student activity on the platform throughout different times of the day, both before and after implementing AI-based tools. It is observed that, after the integration of AI, there is a notable increase in student activity at practically all hours of the day. The post-AI activity significantly exceeds the pre-AI activity during morning and afternoon peak hours, suggesting that AI has improved platform efficiency and incentivized greater student interaction. It is also notable that evening activity, although lower than the rest of the day, shows a slight increase with AI, which could indicate improved platform adaptability for evening students or those in different time zones. Taken together, the figure identifies the positive impact that the integration of AI has had on the active participation of students on the educational platform.

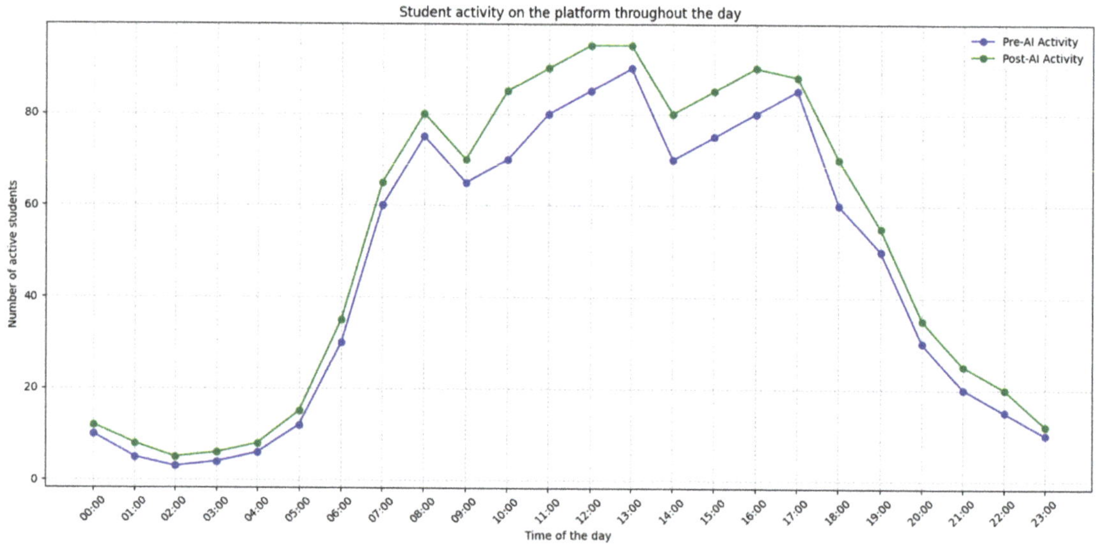

Figure 5. Student activity on the platform throughout different times of the day.

Furthermore, it was decided to explore whether the age of the students had any impact on their adaptability and efficiency when using AI-based tools. Table 7 indicates that younger students appear to adapt more quickly to new AI-powered tools, although the differences are not huge. However, all age groups showed relatively quick adaptation, suggesting that the tools are intuitive and user-friendly.

Table 7. T Adaptability of students according to age.

Age Range	Average Adaptation Time (Days)
18–24	5.2
25–34	6.1
35–44	7.3

3.6. *Validation Results*

The validation of the results, AI techniques, and machine learning models implemented on the platform through specific tests and metrics: To evaluate the effectiveness of our models, we used an independent validation dataset not used during the model training or optimization phases. This division guarantees that the results reflect the model's performance in unseen scenarios.

Metrics used to validate model's performance:

- Precision: This indicates the proportion of correct identifications. Within the framework of our platform, it reflected the model's ability to provide relevant recommendations and analyses to users.
- Recall: This indicates the proportion of actual positives that were correctly identified. It is essential to capturing the most opportunities or areas for improvement.
- F1-score: This provides a balance between precision and recall, offering a composite metric that considers both dimensions. It is beneficial when classes are unbalanced.
- AUC (area under the ROC curve): this metric evaluates the ability of the model to discriminate between positive and negative classes, being especially relevant when working with probabilities.

The values presented in Table 8 show the model's high performance, with an accuracy of 92% and an AUC of 0.95, indicating excellent discriminative capacity. These results validate the effectiveness of AI integration into the platform and the reliability of the recommendations and analyses provided to users.

Table 8. Validation metrics.

Metrics	Value
Precision	0.92
Accuracy	0.89
F1-score	0.90
AUC	0.95

4. Discussion

Integrating advanced techniques such as AI and cloud computing in education has been a recurring theme in recent years. Previous studies have explored the potential and challenges associated with these technologies. Still, few have managed to carry out a profound and contextualized analysis in a specific environment, such as a higher education institute. Our work was inspired by the growing need to adapt educational institutions to technological and sociocultural changes [2,36]. Previous studies have pointed out how AI can transform education by personalizing learning, providing instant feedback, and improving administrative efficiency. Simultaneously, cloud computing has been recognized for making educational systems more accessible and scalable.

Aligning this work with these perspectives, the research was approached by analyzing how integrating these technologies could benefit a specific educational institute. With the migration to the cloud, the educational platform demonstrated remarkable resilience and flexibility, especially during periods of high demand [37]. These findings corroborate previous work that has indicated that cloud computing can improve IT infrastructure in educational institutions, allowing for faster adaptation to changing needs.

Predictive analyses, evaluations, and administrative support showed a considerable error reduction and increased post-AI integration efficiency. These findings align with previous research that has proposed that AI can be a valuable tool in the educational field, mainly when applied for a specific purpose [38]. The positive impact of AI on student performance and experience is perhaps one of the most encouraging results [4]. Although several studies have suggested that AI has the potential to improve personalized education, our work provides empirical evidence in a real-world context, linking AI integration with tangible improvements in learning.

Beyond these findings, our study has made a substantial contribution to the methodology. By combining quantitative and qualitative data collection and analysis techniques, we have provided a holistic approach to evaluating technology integration in educational institutions. However, like any study, this work is not without limitations. Although we have obtained significant results in our specific context, generalization to other educational settings may require adaptations [39]. Furthermore, the accelerated pace of technological development means that solutions and techniques implemented today could soon be surpassed.

It is evident that while specific findings align with the existing literature, others present novelties. For example, the increase in the efficiency and capacity of educational platforms goes beyond simple geographic accessibility. Furthermore, the depth of personalization provided by the AI tools in our study appears to be more advanced and predictive than previous implementations cited in [7,8]. One possible reason for these differences may be these technologies' constant and rapid evolution, allowing for more efficient and adaptive integration. It is crucial, therefore, to consider the temporality and technological context in which these studies are carried out.

By analyzing the results obtained in this work, the idea is reinforced that integrating advanced technologies such as AI and cloud computing in the educational field is not just a passing trend but a necessary evolution [10,30]. Through detailed and contextualized research, we have demonstrated how these technologies can be used to improve both educational administration and the student learning experience. With this, we hope our study serves as a reference point and guide for future research and implementation in the exciting intersection between technology and education.

5. Conclusions

This study has highlighted the transformative capacity of technology, particularly AI and cloud computing, in the educational field. These technologies not only allow for greater accessibility to and scalability of educational platforms but also enhance the quality and efficiency of the teaching and learning process. We saw a significant impact on student performance after implementing AI-based features. This validates the theoretical statements about the potential of AI in education and highlights the importance of its correct implementation to maximize its benefits.

As the world becomes increasingly digital, integrating advanced technologies in the educational field is consolidated not as an option but as a necessity. Institutions that adapt and adopt these tools will be better equipped to meet future challenges and provide quality education.

Building on the previous literature and work discussed, this study expands and refines our understanding of how cloud computing and AI can work together to revolutionize distance learning. While other studies have outlined the possibilities and benefits of these technologies separately, this work has integrated both to discover their synergistic potential. The novelty of our research lies in this integration, exploring how combining the scalability and accessibility of the cloud with the adaptability and personalization of AI can offer an unprecedented educational experience. This contribution is crucial for computer-assisted learning and sets a new standard for future research in the field.

Integrating cloud computing and artificial intelligence in education has proven to be more than just a technological addition; it has the potential to transform distance education radically. Our simulation results provide concrete evidence of this potential. We see tangible improvements in content customization, administrative efficiency, and system scalability. AI proved to be fundamental in adapting educational content to the needs of students, reflecting a 25% improvement in personalization and adaptability. Content management and administrative tasks also benefited, with a 40% reduction in errors, indicating a smoother and more efficient user experience. On the other hand, cloud computing has proven its value by providing scalability. The system could serve 60% more simultaneous users during testing without compromising service quality. This level of scalability ensures that educational institutions can accommodate a growing number of students, which is especially relevant in the current global landscape of distance education growth.

With the rapid evolution of technology, it is crucial to keep an eye on new emerging tools and techniques. Future studies could explore the integration of emerging technologies, such as virtual or augmented reality, in the educational field and its possible impact on learning. While we have scratched the surface of what AI can do regarding personalization, there is so much more to explore. A promising area of research would be the creation of AI systems that can adapt to the individual needs of each student, offering a fully personalized learning path.

While our results are promising, it is essential to conduct longitudinal studies to understand the long-term impact of these technologies on student performance and well-being. Furthermore, it would be beneficial to replicate this study in different educational contexts, from primary schools to vocational training, to understand how the particularities of each environment can influence the effectiveness of these technologies.

Author Contributions: Conceptualization, W.V.-C.; methodology, J.G.; software, J.G.; validation, S.R.-T. and E.O.E.; formal analysis, W.V.-C.; investigation, S.R.-T. and E.O.E.; data curation, W.V.-C. and J.G.; writing—original draft preparation, S.R.-T.; writing—review and editing, W.V.-C. and E.O.E.; visualization, S.R.-T.; supervision, W.V.-C. and E.O.E.; All authors have read and agreed to the published version of the manuscript.

Funding: This research received no external funding.

Data Availability Statement: Not applicable.

Conflicts of Interest: The authors declare no conflict of interest.

References

1. Li, Q.; Cui, D.; Fu, Q.; He, J. Application of Parallel Computing Thought in Training Model for Computer Talents. In Proceedings of the 2021 2nd International Conference on Information Science and Education, ICISE-IE 2021, Chongqing, China, 26–28 November 2021.
2. Liu, B. The Integration and Innovation of Modern Information Technology with Landscape Architecture Teaching under the Emerging Engineering. In Proceedings of the 2021 2nd International Conference on Education, Knowledge and Information Management, ICEKIM 2021, Xiamen, China, 29–31 January 2021.
3. Wang, N. Exploration of College English Blended Learning Model under the Background of Educational Information. In Proceedings of the 2021 2nd International Conference on Big Data and Informatization Education, ICBDIE 2021, Hangzhou, China, 2–4 April 2021.
4. Chard, R.; Chard, K.; Wolski, R.; Madduri, R.; Ng, B.; Bubendorfer, K.; Foster, I. Cost-Aware Cloud Profiling, Prediction, and Provisioning as a Service. *IEEE Cloud Comput.* **2017**, *4*, 48–59. [CrossRef]
5. Hammad, S. Determining the Factors That Affect the Use of Virtual Classrooms: A Modification of the UTAUT Model. *J. Inf. Technol. Educ. Res.* **2021**, *20*, 117.
6. Sithipolvanichgul, J.; Chen, C.; Land, J.; Ractham, P. Factors Affecting Cloud Computing Adoption and Continuance Intention of Students in Thailand. *Int. J. Innov. Technol. Manag.* **2021**, *18*, 2150037. [CrossRef]
7. Pesek, I.; Nosovic, N.; Krasna, M. The Role of AI in the Education and for the Education. In Proceedings of the 2022 11th Mediterranean Conference on Embedded Computing, MECO 2022, Hotel Budva, Montenegro, 7–11 June 2022.

8. Haleem, A.; Javaid, M.; Asim Qadri, M.; Pratap Singh, R.; Suman, R. Artificial Intelligence (AI) Applications for Marketing: A Literature-Based Study. *Int. J. Intell. Netw.* **2022**, *3*, 119–132. [CrossRef]
9. Garg, S.; Bag, T.; Mitschele-Thiel, A. Decentralized Machine Learning Based Network Data Analytics for Cognitive Management of Mobile Communication Networks. In Proceedings of the IEEE/IFIP Network Operations and Management Symposium 2022: Network and Service Management in the Era of Cloudification, Softwarization and Artificial Intelligence, NOMS 2022, Budapest, Hungary, 25–29 April 2022.
10. Lee, B.-H.; Park, S.-H. A Study on the NCS Based Curriculum for Educating Technical Director for VFX Industry with Artificial Intelligence. *Cartoon. Animat. Stud.* **2021**, *63*, 417–450. [CrossRef]
11. Yang, Y.; Yu, D. Research and Exploration on the Training of New Engineering Personnel from the Perspective of Artificial Intelligence. In Proceedings of the 2022 2nd Asia Conference on Information Engineering, ACIE 2022, Haikou, China, 15–17 January 2022.
12. Rani, S.; Bhambri, P.; Kataria, A. Integration of IoT, Big Data, and Cloud Computing Technologies: Trend of the Era. In *Big Data, Cloud Computing and IoT: Tools and Applications*; Taylor & Francis: Abingdon, UK, 2023.
13. Liu, H.; Tai, Y.; Lin, H.; Du, X. Analysis of Technology Hotspots in Artificial Intelligence Field Based on Patent Map. In Proceedings of the 2022 International Seminar on Computer Science and Engineering Technology, SCSET 2022, Indianapolis, IN, USA, 8–9 January 2022.
14. Zou, J.; Chen, Y. Online Aesthetic Education Information Teaching System Based On Big Data Cloud Platform. In Proceedings of the IEEE International Conference on Knowledge Engineering and Communication Systems, ICKES 2022, Chikkaballapur, India, 29–31 December 2022.
15. Doughan, Z.; Al Mubasher, H.; El Bizri, M.; Haidar, A. The metaverse: A virtual world in the palm of your hand. *BAU J. Sci. Technol.* **2022**, *4*, 10. [CrossRef]
16. Luo, X.; Xie, L. Research on Artificial Intelligence-Based Sharing Education in the Era of Internet. In Proceedings of the 3rd International Conference on Intelligent Transportation, Big Data and Smart City, ICITBS 2018, Xiamen, China, 25–26 January 2018; Volume 2018.
17. Azzolini, D.; Marzadro, S.; Rettore, E.; Engelhardt, K.; Hertz, B.; Wastiau, P. Raising Teacher Retention in Online Courses through Personalized Support. Evidence from a Cross-National Randomized Controlled Trial. *J. Res. Educ. Eff.* **2023**, *16*, 300–325. [CrossRef]
18. Appolloni, A.; Colasanti, N.; Fantauzzi, C.; Fiorani, G.; Frondizi, R. Distance Learning as a Resilience Strategy during COVID-19: An Analysis of the Italian Context. *Sustainability* **2021**, *13*, 1388. [CrossRef]
19. Li, Y.; Wu, F. Design and Application Research of Embedded Voice Teaching System Based on Cloud Computing. *Wirel. Commun. Mob. Comput.* **2023**, *2023*, 7873715. [CrossRef]
20. Soodtoetong, N.; Rattanasiriwongwut, M. Educational Transformation with Virtual Classroom: Integrated between TTF and Social Motivation. *TEM J.* **2022**, *11*, 439–445. [CrossRef]
21. Chen, H.C.; Prasetyo, E.; Tseng, S.S.; Putra, K.T.; Prayitno; Kusumawardani, S.S.; Weng, C.E. Week-Wise Student Performance Early Prediction in Virtual Learning Environment Using a Deep Explainable Artificial Intelligence. *Appl. Sci.* **2022**, *12*, 1885. [CrossRef]
22. Tzeng, J.W.; Lee, C.A.; Huang, N.F.; Huang, H.H.; Lai, C.F. MOOC Evaluation System Based on Deep Learning. *Int. Rev. Res. Open Distance Learn.* **2022**, *23*, 21–40. [CrossRef]
23. Kamruzzaman, M.M.; Alruwaili, O. AI-Based Computer Vision Using Deep Learning in 6G Wireless Networks. *Comput. Electr. Eng.* **2022**, *102*, 108233. [CrossRef]
24. Hou, Y. Foreign Language Education in the Era of Artificial Intelligence. In *Big Data Analytics for Cyber-Physical System in Smart City, Proceedings of the BDCPS 2019, Shenyang, China, 28–29 December 2019*; Springer: Singapore, 2020; Volume 1117.
25. Ge, Z.; Hu, Y. Construction of Smart Service Platform in the Perspective of Smart City Development. In *2020 International Conference on Applications and Techniques in Cyber Intelligence: Applications and Techniques in Cyber Intelligence (ATCI 2020)*; Springer International Publishing: Berlin/Heidelberg, Germany, 2021; Volume 1244.
26. Tzevelekakis, K.; Stefanidi, Z.; Margetis, G. Real-Time Stress Level Feedback from Raw Ecg Signals for Personalised, Context-Aware Applications Using Lightweight Convolutional Neural Network Architectures. *Sensors* **2021**, *21*, 7802. [CrossRef] [PubMed]
27. Mustapha, R. The Impact of Industrial Revolution 4.0 on Educational Technology, Digital Innovation and Future Learning. In Proceedings of the International Conference on Learning Innovation in Science and Technology, Barcelona, Spain, 7–9 December 2018.
28. Xu, J. An Accurate Management Method of Public Services Based on Big Data and Cloud Computing. *J. Cloud Comput.* **2023**, *12*, 80. [CrossRef]
29. Rico-Bautista, D.; Maestre-Gongora, G.; Guerrero, C.D. Smart University: IoT Adoption Model. In Proceedings of the World Conference on Smart Trends in Systems, Security and Sustainability, WS4 2020, London, UK, 27–28 July 2020.
30. Xia, P. Design of Personalized Intelligent Learning Assistant System Under Artificial Intelligence Background. In Proceedings of the Advances in Intelligent Systems and Computing, Azores, Portugal, 30 March–2 April 2021; Volume 1282.
31. Villegas-Ch, W.; Luján-Mora, S. Analysis of Data Mining Techniques Applied to LMS for Personalized Education. In Proceedings of the IEEE World Engineering Education Conference (EDUNINE), Santos, Brazil, 19–22 March 2017; pp. 85–89.

32. Yanhua, Z. The Application of Artificial Intelligence in Foreign Language Teaching. In Proceedings of the 2020 International Conference on Artificial Intelligence and Education, ICAIE 2020, Ifrane, Morocco, 6–10 July 2020.
33. Meng, H. Research on Innovation and Practice of University-Industry Cooperation under AI Environment. In Proceedings of the E3S Web of Conferences, Strasbourg, France, 5–7 May 2021; Volume 251.
34. Gong, Y.; He, Y.; Xie, D.; Chen, J. Research on Path Selection of Digital Governance of Online Education. *Mod. Econ.* **2021**, *12*, 123024. [CrossRef]
35. Yu, S. A Research on University Students' Behavioral Intention to Use New-Generation Information Technology in Intelligent Foreign Language Learning. In *ACM Transactions on Asian and Low-Resource Language Information Processing*; Association for Computing Machinery: New York, NY, USA, 2022. [CrossRef]
36. Bongomin, O.; Gilibrays Ocen, G.; Oyondi Nganyi, E.; Musinguzi, A.; Omara, T. Exponential Disruptive Technologies and the Required Skills of Industry 4.0. *J. Eng.* **2020**, *2020*, 4280156. [CrossRef]
37. Jingyi, Q.; Hua, L.; Xiu, C.; Wen, F. Explore and Practice of China's Intelligent "New Engineering"—Based on the Grounded Theory. *Int. J. Inf. Educ. Technol.* **2020**, *10*, 632–640. [CrossRef]
38. Yankson, E. The ILA Study Group on the Role of Cities in International Law City Report: Arusha. *Int. Law Assoc.* **2021**, *14*, 14–18.
39. Rani, S.; Mishra, R.K.; Usman, M.; Kataria, A.; Kumar, P.; Bhambri, P.; Mishra, A.K. Amalgamation of Advanced Technologies for Sustainable Development of Smart City Environment: A Review. *IEEE Access* **2021**, *9*, 150060–150087. [CrossRef]

computers

MDPI

Article

Enhancing Automated Scoring of Math Self-Explanation Quality Using LLM-Generated Datasets: A Semi-Supervised Approach

Ryosuke Nakamoto [1,*], Brendan Flanagan [2,*], Taisei Yamauchi [1], Yiling Dai [3], Kyosuke Takami [3,4] and Hiroaki Ogata [3]

1 Graduate School of Informatics, Kyoto University, Kyoto 606-8501, Japan
2 Center for Innovative Research and Education in Data Science, Institute for Liberal Arts and Sciences, Kyoto University, Kyoto 606-8501, Japan
3 Academic Center for Computing and Media Studies, Kyoto University, Kyoto 606-8501, Japan
4 Education Data Science Center, National Institute for Educational Policy Research, Tokyo 100-8951, Japan
* Correspondence: s0527225@gmail.com (R.N.); flanagan.brendanjohn.4n@kyoto-u.ac.jp (B.F.)

Abstract: In the realm of mathematics education, self-explanation stands as a crucial learning mechanism, allowing learners to articulate their comprehension of intricate mathematical concepts and strategies. As digital learning platforms grow in prominence, there are mounting opportunities to collect and utilize mathematical self-explanations. However, these opportunities are met with challenges in automated evaluation. Automatic scoring of mathematical self-explanations is crucial for preprocessing tasks, including the categorization of learner responses, identification of common misconceptions, and the creation of tailored feedback and model solutions. Nevertheless, this task is hindered by the dearth of ample sample sets. Our research introduces a semi-supervised technique using the large language model (LLM), specifically its Japanese variant, to enrich datasets for the automated scoring of mathematical self-explanations. We rigorously evaluated the quality of self-explanations across five datasets, ranging from human-evaluated originals to ones devoid of original content. Our results show that combining LLM-based explanations with mathematical material significantly improves the model's accuracy. Interestingly, there is an optimal limit to how many synthetic self-explanation data can benefit the system. Exceeding this limit does not further improve outcomes. This study thus highlights the need for careful consideration when integrating synthetic data into solutions, especially within the mathematics discipline.

Keywords: self-explanation; automated scoring; semi-supervised learning; language learning model (LLM); data augmentation

1. Introduction

The emergence of digital learning platforms has opened a plethora of opportunities for researchers to investigate and comprehend learning behaviors through abundant system interaction data [1]. A notable area of interest among various learning facets is self-explanation, identified as a robust active learning technique. This strategy has been particularly effective in bolstering comprehension in subjects like mathematics [1–3]. Self-explanation can be described as a mechanism where learners articulate explanations, elucidate concepts, expand on methods, and immerse in problem-solving to enhance their grasp and absorb fresh insights [4,5].

With the proliferation of computer-driven learning platforms, self-explanation has gained renewed attention and application. Contemporary learning innovations place a premium on self-explanation by crafting intuitive interfaces, creating assessment models rooted in self-explanation behaviors, and formulating tactics to extract profound self-explanations [6,7]. Tools like the one formulated by Crippen and Earl [8] highlight the centrality of self-explanation in methodical problem-solving. Ongoing studies persistently explore the versatile applications of self-explanation in education [9,10], like the adoption of template-driven self-explanations. Such templates equip learners with pre-set frameworks, serving as built-in guides to bolster their explanation processes [1,11,12].

Furthermore, the domain of self-explanation practices reaches beyond traditional boundaries. These methods involve understanding a concept and facilitating multiple educational tools such as feedback systems, crafting practice quiz responses, and generating valuable datasets for automated evaluations [10]. Within this framework, automated assessments play a pivotal role. By analyzing and interpreting self-explanations, both educators and automated systems can delve deeper into the intricacies of a learner's thought patterns. This knowledge equips them with the capability to tailor educational strategies to better cater to individual needs. Such insights are crucial for tasks like classifying learner responses, which provide a clear view of their comprehension levels. Additionally, they allow for the easy detection of recurring mistakes or topics that consistently stump students [9,10].

However, devising a system capable of automatically grading diverse styles of self-explanation is challenging. A major concern is that self-explanation, due to its time-intensive nature [13], poses a feasibility issue for mass data collection. Additionally, crafting a quality self-explanation requires proficiency in both the specific subject matter and general writing [14,15]. Given these challenges, amassing a vast and diverse collection of self-explanation samples is demanding. This predicament further complicates the development of systems designed to aid learning through extensive sets of self-explanation examples.

To address these challenges and enhance automated scoring of self-explanations, we propose a semi-supervised approach that leverages the LLM. While popular LLMs such as OpenAI's GPT-3 [16] are commonly employed in English language settings, due to the nature of the target problem we specifically focus on the Japanese variant of the model developed by CyberAgent [17], based on GPT-NeoX [18]. This approach aims to explore the model's potential for generating self-explanation sentences, which will serve as the foundation for our regression models designed to predict self-explanation scores. By incorporating the semi-supervised methodology and leveraging advanced language models, we aim to improve the accuracy and effectiveness of auto-scoring in the self-explanation learning domain. Our research is anchored by two pivotal questions:

RQ1: To what extent can the integration of self-explanations generated by the LLM Japanese model and mathematical material be used to enhance the accuracy of the predictive regression model for self-explanation scores?

RQ2: What is the optimal quantity of artificially generated pseudo-self-explanation data required to effectively improve the predictive performance of the model?

These research questions provide insights into maximizing the utility of the LLM Japanese model and refining data augmentation techniques. The core findings from our research are twofold. First, we propose a strategy for advancing automated scoring in math education by synergizing LLM-generated content and mathematical material. Second, we highlight the ideal quantity of artificial self-explanation data for peak predictive accuracy.

2. Related Work

2.1. Automated Scoring of Self-Explanations: The Imperative for Rich Data

Self-explanation, widely recognized for amplifying learning outcomes in various fields, notably mathematics, has found its stride in the digital learning environment [1,4,5]. Emblematic tools like the iSTART tutoring system have been devised to foster and elevate learners' grasp and performance [19]. Such platforms urge students to think critically, mirroring the analytical strategies of experts. Notably, the iSTART system utilizes natural language processing (NLP) in its pioneering approach to gauge and rate self-explanations, bolstering understanding across a gamut of texts.

The endeavor to automate the scoring of self-explanation quality has seen the integration of NLP tools and cutting-edge neural network architectures [20]. Techniques like latent semantic analysis (LSA) and recurrent neural network (RNN) interfaced with machine learning underscore the capabilities of automated systems, often outshining traditional manual evaluation in both effectiveness and efficiency [14,20–24]. Furthermore, semi-supervised learning techniques, which capitalize on abundant unlabeled data, have exhibited the potential to refine scoring accuracy [25]. Yet, the quest for more representative samples of self-explanations, especially in languages other than English, remains a prevailing challenge.

2.2. Augmenting Mathematical Self-Explanations Using Large Language Models

Consistent data shortages and imbalances have long impeded automated classification. Techniques like the synthetic minority oversampling technique (SMOTE), adaptive synthetic (ADASYN), and its derivatives aim to counteract these with synthetic data generation [26–29], but their effectiveness wanes for scant datasets. Although a variety of synthetic data tools and research exist [30–35], their applicability is often curtailed when facing complex domain-specific data, particularly in predicting student outcomes [35–37]. Navigating this landscape, large language models (LLMs) have made a compelling case as tools for text data augmentation. For instance, Dai et al.'s AugLLM [38] capitalizes on ChatLLM [16] to generate supplemental text, emphasizing the rising importance of LLMs in the realm of mathematical content [39].

However, in the context of mathematical education, the accurate auto-scoring of self-explanations presents stark challenges. Crafting these self-explanations is not just labor-intensive but demands expertise in both the subject and linguistic expression. Coupled with the lack of diverse and representative self-explanation samples, particularly in languages other than English, the task becomes even more daunting.

This paper aims to navigate these challenges by adopting a semi-supervised learning technique anchored by the Japanese variant of LLM. Our objective is twofold: to generate enriched self-explanation content and to amplify the accuracy of automated grading tailored for Japanese mathematical education. The emphasis here is a meticulous alignment with the intricacies of the Japanese language, paired with the nuances of mathematical challenges. In essence, our work hopes to bridge the existing data gap, presenting a more robust and linguistically attuned auto-scoring system.

3. Problem Setting: The Learning Task

In this chapter, we primarily introduce the original human-labeled data, which serves as a foundation for the subsequent pseudo-labeling of the unlabeled samples, thereby bolstering the training process. Prior to delving into methodological details, it is pivotal to define the distinct learning task under examination, which underpins our methodological foundation.

3.1. Collecting Self-Explanations

Self-explanations from learners are gathered via online platforms, as represented in Figure 1. The scope of this approach includes diverse mathematical challenges or quizzes that require written elaboration. We utilized the LEAF platform [40], composed of BookRoll (a digital reading application), and LAViEW (a tool for learning analytics), enabling students and teachers to monitor and reflect on their educational progress. This platform, having been successfully implemented in a Japanese secondary school for several years, captures handwritten responses in vector form, portraying the precise coordinates and velocity of each pen stroke.

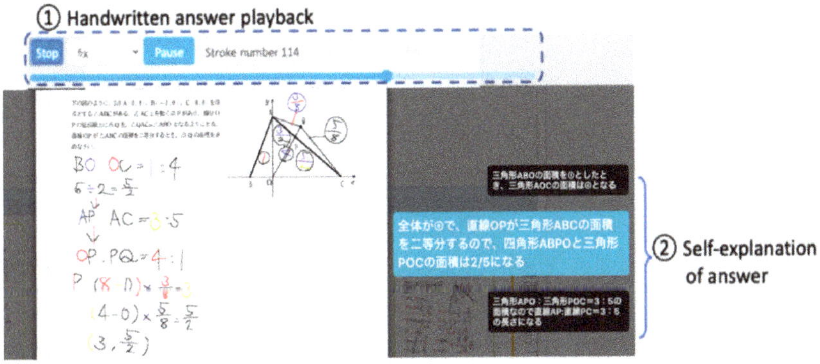

Figure 1. Handwritten answer review playback and self-explanation input user interface. The self-explanation of the answer section includes the following: If triangle ABO's area is 1, then triangle AOC's area is 4. Given that the total area is five and straight-line OP bisects the area of triangle ABC, the joint area of quadrilateral ABPO and triangle POC is 2/5. Hence, the area ratio of triangle APO to triangle POC is 3:5, leading to a length ratio of straight-line AP to straight-line PC of 3:5.

The learners interacted with the quiz and recorded their answers using a tablet computer, employing a stylus for handwriting. As shown in Figure 1, the handwritten answer playback and self-explanation input process require students to input an explanation sentence after completing a step of their answer during playback.

3.2. Assessment of Self-Explanation Quality

Self-explanations in our study were assessed based on three main criteria: coherence, clarity, and relevance. Specifically, 'coherence' gauges the logical flow of the explanation, 'clarity' measures its understandability, and 'relevance' ensures the inclusion of all pertinent knowledge concepts and procedural elements. For consistent evaluation, we adapted the rubric and scoring definitions from Nakamoto et al. [10], as depicted in Tables 1 and 2, which are well-suited for tasks with varied solutions or strategies [41]. Instead of a detailed sentence-by-sentence breakdown, our approach evaluates explanations on a holistic, quiz-by-quiz basis, offering a comprehensive insight into the learner's understanding of the topic.

Table 1. Rubrics and a sample answer of self-explanation in a quiz.

Numbers	Rubric	Sample Answer of Self-Explanations
Step 1	Be able to find the equation of a linear function from two points.	Substituting the y-coordinate of p into the equation of the line AC.
Step 2	Be able to find the equation of the line that bisects the area of a triangle.	Find the area of triangle ABC, then find the area of triangle OPC.
Step 3	Be able to represent a point on a straight-line using letters (P-coordinates).	With the line OC as the base, find the y-coordinate of p, which is the height. P's coordinate is (t, −1/2t + 4).
Step 4	Be able to represent a point on a straight-line using letters (Q-coordinate).	Since the coordinates of P are (3,5/2), the line OP is $y = \frac{5}{6}x$, and the coordinates of Q are (t,5/6).

Table 2. Score grading definitions.

Graded Score	Description
1 (Unacceptable)	The number of steps for which self-explanation is filled in for the steps required for the solution is minimal, and there were problematic expressions in the students' self-explanation (e.g., mistaken patterns, boredom).
2 (Poor)	Self-explanation is mainly provided for the steps required for the solution. Still, they are more like bullet points than explanations.
3 (Fair)	Self-explanation is mainly provided for the steps required for the answer—the average self-explanation level among all respondents.
4 (Very Good)	Self-explanation is provided for most of the steps required for the answer, but there is room for improvement as an explanation (logic, expressions).
5 (Excellent)	Self-explanation is mainly provided for the steps required for the answer, and the explanation is logical and well-written.

For the evaluation process, two independent evaluators employed these rubrics to rate the collected 2205 self-explanations, scoring them on a scale ranging from 1 to 5. A quadratic weighted Cohen's kappa coefficient [42] of 0.749 between the evaluators indicated a significant level of agreement. The subsequent analysis used the mean score derived from both evaluators, which categorized the self-explanation scores for a roughly uniform distribution. Descriptive statistics of the collected self-explanations are presented in Table 3.

Table 3. Descriptive statistics of graded self-explanations.

Data Type	Num of Quiz	Variations in Math Units	Total Answers	Sentence Length (Character Count)		Quality Score	
				Mean	SD	Mean	SD
Train	40	8	1420	67.8	56.8	2.94	1.34
Valid	37	8	355	67.3	59.3	2.92	1.31
Test	8	3	431	63.7	53.2	2.81	1.25

In anticipation of the machine learning methodologies outlined in the subsequent chapters, our dataset was segmented into three distinct categories. The train dataset, which incorporates 1420 self-explanations, forms the fundamental basis for both training our models and for LLM data augmentation. Meanwhile, the valid dataset, comprising 355 self-explanations, is earmarked for the crucial tasks of fine-tuning our models' parameters. It also plays a significant role in the evaluation of model accuracy and in ensuring model robustness. Lastly, the test dataset, which consists of 431 self-explanations, is designated to provide a measure of the performance of our finalized models.

3.3. The Text Regression Model Description

Inspired by the work of Wang et al. [43], we employ BERT [44] and a pre-trained BERT Japanese model [45] as the backbone for our regression models, which are intended to predict the quality scores of self-explanations. Wang et al.'s methodology of injecting rubrics into the system influenced the architecture of our model, making it specifically attuned to the grading of short responses. BERT's deep learning model, grounded on a transformer architecture, has been recognized for surpassing most preceding models in diverse natural language processing tasks [46]. Given its robust performance and compatibility with the Japanese language, BERT is an ideal choice for our study. Our model takes as the input the preprocessed self-explanation text and the corresponding quiz title (Figure 2) and yields as the output the predicted quality score for each self-explanation.

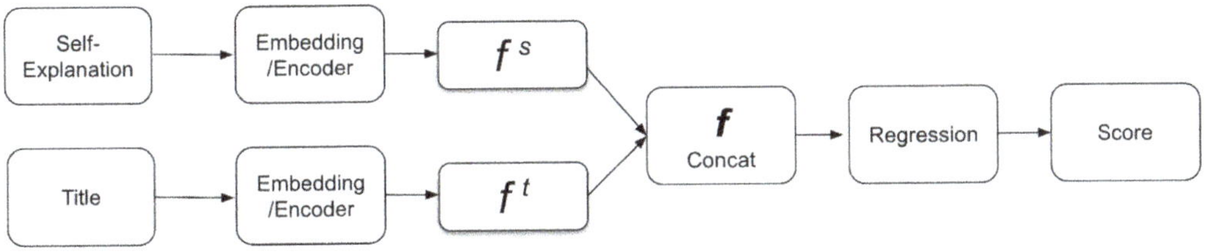

Figure 2. Workflow for the BERT regression models.

4. The Proposed Method

4.1. Overview or Pseudo-Labeling

In this section, we delve into our proposed method, building on the foundation laid out in Section 3. Our approach, illustrated in Figure 3, seamlessly blends human-labeled mathematical text data described in Section 3 and LLM-generated data to enhance our machine-learning model. Drawing from Cascante–Bonilla's semi-supervised framework [25], we utilize pseudo-labeling as our primary technique. For human-labeled data, we lean on mathematical self-explanations, while the LLM and mathematical content texts help in producing pseudo-labeled samples to complement them. We gathered over 1420 self-explanation samples for the training model from undergraduate math students, which were further utilized in the Japanese LLM (Step 1). Figure 3 provides a comprehensive visual overview of this pseudo-training mechanism and its integrated phases.

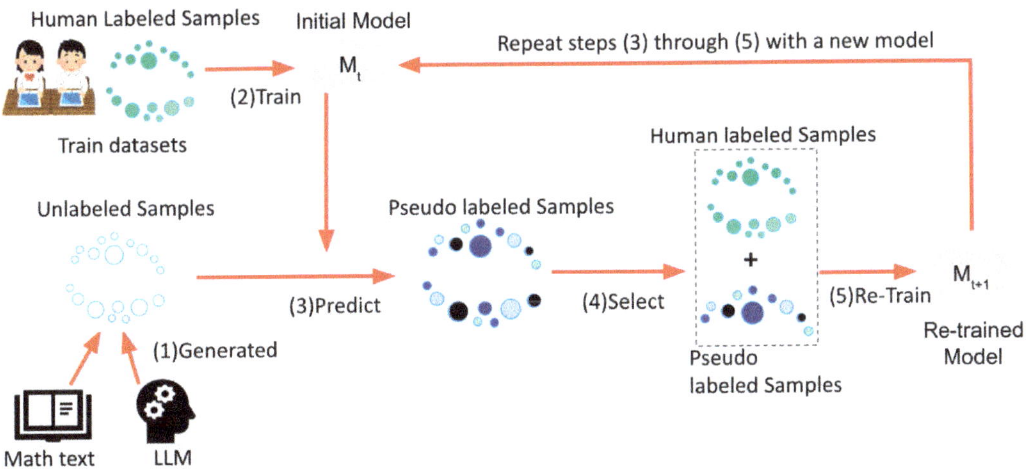

Figure 3. The overview of pseudo-training process.

The pseudo-labeling technique commences with the training of an initial model using the labeled dataset (Step 2). This model then assigns labels to the unlabeled data, producing what we term 'pseudo' labels (Step 3). These newly formed pseudo-labels are then amalgamated with the original labeled dataset, initiating a cycle of continuous model enhancement (Steps 4–5). As the model's predictive prowess escalates, the caliber of the pseudo-labels also elevates.

4.2. Pseudo-Labeling Training Algorithm: Dataset Categorization, Function Definitions, and Model Learning

In Figure 3, we present our methodology which combines both human and pseudo-labeled samples to form a mathematically relevant dataset. Using the pseudo-labeling training algorithm (Algorithm 1), we integrate human-labeled datasets, LLM, and math texts and functions.

The human-labeled datasets act as the primary foundation for our machine learning training, and the pseudo-labeled datasets further refine and expand it. A comprehensive breakdown and flow are described in detail in the following sections as definitions and pseudo-code. Figure 4 offers an illustrative representation of the training process, harmonizing with the methodology laid out in Figure 3.

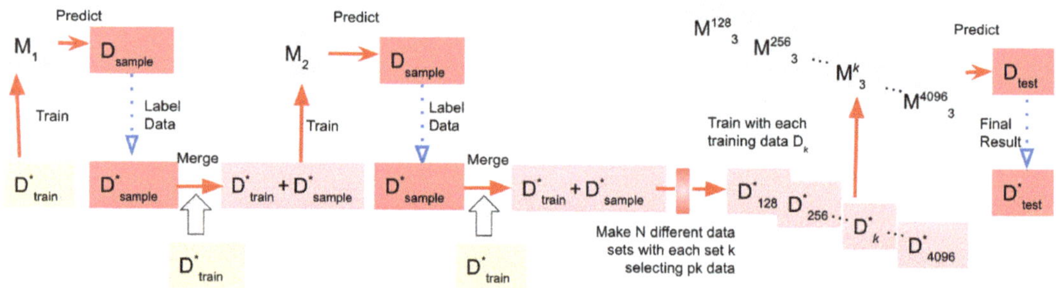

Figure 4. The detail of pseudo-training process.

(1) Dataset categorization:

Hereafter $\mathbb{D}_{type}$ represents an unlabeled dataset pertaining to a particular *type*, and $\mathbb{D}^*_{type}$ does a labeled dataset of the same category as $\mathbb{D}_{type}$. $\mathbb{D}_{\text{provided}}$ is the composite dataset given to the model for training and evaluation, which includes the labeled training set $\mathbb{D}^*_{\text{train}}$, test dataset $\mathbb{D}_{\text{test}}$, and the generated unlabeled sample dataset $\mathbb{D}_{\text{sample}}$.

$$\mathbb{D}_{\text{provided}} = \mathbb{D}^*_{\text{train}} + \mathbb{D}_{\text{test}} + \mathbb{D}_{\text{sample}} \tag{1}$$

(2) Function definitions:

$$\mathscr{Model}(\theta,\ \mathbb{D}^*) = M \tag{2a}$$

$$\mathscr{Test}(M,\ \mathbb{D}_{\text{test}}) = \mathbb{D}^*_{\text{test}} \tag{2b}$$

$$\mathscr{Select}(\mathbb{D}, k) = \mathbb{D}_k \text{ (where } \mathscr{Select}(\mathbb{D}, n(\mathbb{D})) = \mathbb{D}) \tag{2c}$$

- $\mathscr{Model}(\theta,\ \mathbb{D}^*)$: A function that takes a set of parameters, denoted by θ, and a labeled dataset $\mathbb{D}^*$ to yield a learned model M.
- $\mathscr{Test}(M,\ \mathbb{D}_{\text{test}})$: A function that accepts a model M and a non-labeled test dataset $\mathbb{D}_{\text{test}}$, subsequently outputting a labeled test dataset $\mathbb{D}^*_{\text{test}}$.
- $\mathscr{Select}(\mathbb{D}, k)$: A function that takes in a dataset $\mathbb{D}$ and a numerical value k where $0 \leq k \leq n(\mathbb{D})$ ($n(\mathbb{D})$ refers to the total number of data points in dataset $\mathbb{D}$), outputting a selected subset $\mathbb{D}_k \subseteq \mathbb{D}$.

(3) Model learning and final test:

$$M_1 = \mathscr{Model}(\theta, \mathbb{D}^*_{\text{train}}) \tag{3a}$$

$$M_{t+1} = \mathscr{Model}\left(\theta, \mathbb{D}^*_{\text{train}} + \mathscr{Select}\left(\mathscr{Test}\left(M_t, \mathbb{D}_{\text{sample}}\right), k_t\right)\right) \tag{3b}$$

$$\mathbb{D}^*_{\text{test}} = \mathscr{Test}(M_T, \mathbb{D}_{\text{test}}) \text{ (where } T \text{ is sufficient number of } t\text{)} \tag{3c}$$

The model learning procedure follows an iterative process. Initially, the model M_1 is trained using θ and the labeled training dataset $\mathbb{D}^*_{\text{train}}$. In each subsequent timestep, a new model M_{t+1} is developed with an updated training set, comprising the original labeled dataset $\mathbb{D}^*_{\text{train}}$ and a selected subset of the pseudo-labeled $\mathbb{D}_{\text{sample}}$. After the model learning process has been iterated T times, the final model M_T is evaluated on the original test dataset $\mathbb{D}_{\text{test}}$ to output the pseudo-labeled test dataset $\mathbb{D}^*_{\text{test}}$. This dataset, enriched with pseudo-labels, serves as a vital resource for subsequent analyses and performance evaluations.

(4) Parameter setting in our study:

Figure 4 provides a comprehensive outline of our experimental approach. Our dataset consists of both human-annotated and unlabeled samples. For the training process, we amassed 2205 self-explanation samples from student contributors. In our setting, θ stands for a model built using logistic regression with text representation acquired from BERT, a state-of-the-art transformer-based model renowned for its superior performance on numerous NLP tasks. The iterative process continues for 3 timesteps; in other words, T is set to 3. The selection size at each timestep t, denoted by k_t, varies as follows: k_1 is equal to the total number of data points in $\mathbb{D}_{\text{sample}}$, such as $n\left(\mathbb{D}_{\text{sample}}\right)$, whereas for the second time step, k_2 could be any one of the following: 128, 256, 512, 1024, 2048, or 4096. To distinguish them, we defined the $(t+1)$th model, which is the same as M_{t+1} in Formula (3b), which was learned with selected k_t training data as $M_t^{k_t}$. The following formula represents the concrete model learning method in the study:

$$M_1 = \mathscr{Model}(\theta, \mathbb{D}^*_{\text{train}}) \tag{4a}$$

$$M_2 = \mathscr{Model}\left(\theta, \mathbb{D}^*_{\text{train}} + \mathscr{Select}\left(\mathscr{Test}\left(M_1, \mathbb{D}_{\text{sample}}\right), n\left(\mathbb{D}_{\text{sample}}\right)\right)\right) \tag{4b}$$

$$M_3^{2^{i+7}} = \mathscr{Model}\left(\theta, \mathbb{D}^*_{\text{train}} + \mathscr{Select}\left(\mathscr{Test}\left(M_2, \mathbb{D}_{\text{sample}}\right), 2^{i+7}\right)\right) \text{(where } 0 \le i \le 5\text{)} \tag{4c}$$

$$\mathbb{D}^*_{\text{test}} = \mathscr{Test}\left(M_3^{2^{i+7}}, \mathbb{D}_{\text{test}}\right) \text{(where } 0 \le i \le 5\text{)} \tag{4d}$$

Algorithm 1: Semi-supervised learning with pseudo-labeling

Input:

- *Labeled dataset:* $\mathbb{D}^*_{\text{train}}$
- *Unlabeled dataset:* $\mathbb{D}_{\text{sample}}$
- *Test dataset:* $\mathbb{D}_{\text{test}}$
- *Maximum number of iterations:* T
- *Confidence threshold for pseudo-labeling:* $confidence$
- *Convergence threshold for change in consecutive scores:* ε

Output:

- *Trained model:* $NLP\ model$
- *Final score of the model on* $\mathbb{D}_{\text{test}}$: s

Procedure:
Initialize model:
$NLP\ model \leftarrow trained\ NLP\ model\ with\ \mathbb{D}^*_{\text{train}}$

Initialize values:
$previous\ score \leftarrow 0$
$iteration \leftarrow 0$
$convergence\ achieved \leftarrow$ False

While $iteration < T$ **and not** $convergence\ achieved$ **do**
a. **Predict pseudo-labels:**
$predictions \leftarrow$ predicted labels of $\mathbb{D}_{\text{sample}}$ using $NLP\ model$
$confidence \leftarrow$ threshold when labeling of $\mathbb{D}_{\text{sample}}$ using $NLP\ model$
b. **Filter high confidence predictions:**
$\mathbb{D}^*_{\text{sample}} \leftarrow \{sample \mid sample$ in $\mathbb{D}_{\text{sample}}$ and $confidence\ of\ the\ sample > confidence\}$
c. **Merge labeled and pseudo-labeled data:**
$\mathbb{D}^*_{\text{train}} \leftarrow \mathbb{D}^*_{\text{train}} + \mathbb{D}^*_{\text{sample}}$
d. **Retrain the model:**
$NLP\ model \leftarrow$ trained $NLP\ model$ with $\mathbb{D}^*_{\text{train}}$
e. **Evaluate current model performance:**
$current\ score \leftarrow$ Evaluation metrics when labeling $\mathbb{D}_{\text{test}}$ using $NLP\ model$
f. **Check for convergence:**
If $|current\ score - previous\ score| < \varepsilon$:
$convergence\ achieved \leftarrow$ True
$previous\ score \leftarrow current\ score$
g. **Update iteration count:**
$iteration \leftarrow iteration + 1$
End Procedure

4.3. Pseudo-Data Preparation: LLM Usage and Mathematical Material

We employed a pseudo-labeling technique to enrich our dataset, sourcing additional self-explanation data via the Japanese LLM and mathematical material.

Given alternatives such as OpenAI's GPT-3 [16], our preference leaned towards Cyberagent's LLM [17] due to its open-source availability and its adeptness in the Japanese language, perfectly complementing our dataset. To gather data, the LLM tackled mathematical contexts and formulated pertinent explanations. Our methodology was as follows:

- Random data selection: We began our process by randomly selecting 30% from our human-labeled training dataset to capitalize on the rich diversity of student-generated self-explanations.
- Keyword extraction: Ten keywords were extracted from each self-explanation, encapsulating its essence, guiding LLM to produce contextually relevant data.
- LLM generation: Armed with the extracted keywords, we then proceeded to prompt the LLM [47]. Specifically, each set of 10 keywords was used as seed input, directing

the LLM to generate contextually coherent pseudo-self-explanation data. The model was given a directive to 'elaborate based on the provided keywords', ensuring the generated content-maintained relevance to the original self-explanation context.

Approximately 19,000 entries were generated, with a random subset of 4096 used for experiments. This combination of pseudo- and human-labeled data broadened our training set, enhancing the automated scoring system's performance without compromising quality.

We also leveraged the math quiz texts dataset, populated with standard mathematical solutions. Its rich mathematical material and contextual problem-solving methods made it invaluable for generating mathematical self-explanations.

4.4. Comparative Analysis of Original and LLM-Generated Dataset

In Table 4 and Figure 5, a detailed comparative analysis between the original and the synthetically generated datasets is elucidated. Upon examination, it becomes evident that the augmented datasets exhibit a modest augmentation in their average quality metrics relative to the foundational dataset.

Table 4. Comparative metrics for original and generated datasets.

Data Type	Counts	Mean Score	Std
Original	2205	2.91	1.33
LLM	4096	3.39	1.44
Math	4096	3.87	1.77

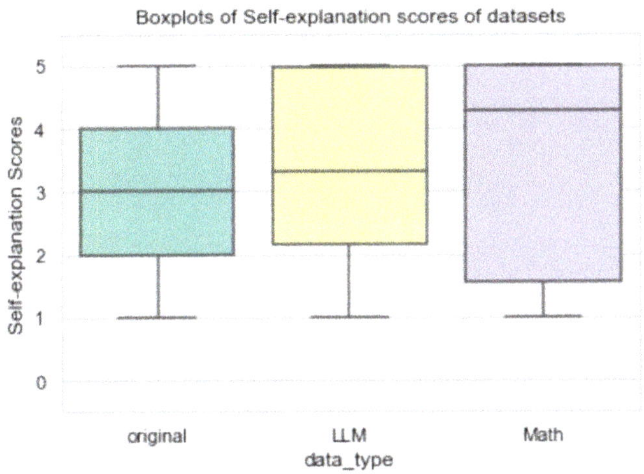

Figure 5. Boxplots of self-explanation scores.

Table 5 showcases a range of these samples with their respective translations in English, alongside the scores predicted by our automated system. It is evident from the samples that as the complexity of the self-explanation increases, so does the predicted score. For instance, the first sample, which delves into the relationship between solutions and coefficients, is accorded a high score of 5.00 due to its comprehensive self-explanation. Conversely, the final example, which is a brief reflection on an error and an attempt to rectify it, receives a lower score of 1.23, reflecting its succinct nature. Table 6 offers various math texts that were considered during our study. These texts, extracted from educational resources, shed light on various mathematical principles and theorems. The predicted self-explanation score gives an indication of the depth and comprehensiveness of the self-explanation provided in each math text. For instance, the math text delving into the 'angle bisector and ratio, using Ceva's theorem' provides a nuanced exploration of the topic, earning it a top score of 5.00. In contrast, the examination of the sizes of the three angles of a triangle is more straightforward, reflected in its score of 2.66. The varied scores underline the diverse complexity levels present in math texts.

Table 5. LLM-generated samples.

LLM-Generated Samples (Original)	LLM-Generated Samples (English Translation)	Predicted Self-Explanation Score
その後、$\alpha + \beta = -a-2$と$\alpha\beta = 2a$の関係から解と係数の関係が分かる。次に、問題で言及されたαとβを用いて式を展開し整理し、右辺を0にする。さらに式を工夫して代入が可能な形にする。そして、関係式$\alpha + \beta = -a-2$と $\alpha\beta = 2a$を式に代入して簡略化し、a^2 + a−6 = 0となる。これを因数分解してaの解を求めると、a = −3と a = 2が得られる。その後、a = 2を代入すると解が重解になり、解が一つしかなくなるため問題に合わない。したがって、正しい答えはa = −3である。その後、重積算や累乗などいろいろな計算が解に出てきて混乱するだろうから丁寧に説明していく。	After that, $\alpha + \beta = -a-2$ and $\alpha\beta = 2a$ can be understood from the relationship between the solutions and coefficients. Next, expand and organize the expressions using the α and β mentioned in the problem, and set the right side to 0. Further manipulate the equation to transform it into a form that allows for substitution. Then, substitute the relationship $\alpha + \beta = -a-2$ and $\alpha\beta = 2a$ into the equation and simplify it, resulting in a2 + a−6 = 0. Factorize this to find the solutions for a, which are a = −3 and a = 2. Afterward, when a = 2 is substituted, the answer becomes a repeated root, which means there is only one solution, making it inconsistent with the problem. Therefore, the correct answer is a = −3. Afterward, various calculations such as product of roots and exponentiation may appear in the solution, and it may be confusing, so I will explain it carefully.	5.00
代入してみたら、平方根の中が計算できた。αとβを求めた。αに−2を代入した。解を吟味して、答えは−3だった。その後、a = −4.7x^5 + 7として計算したが誤差があった。そこで右側の5を左側の4に変形すると正しい値が求められた（ただし小数点以下を切り捨て）。この問題は高校数学の範囲外であるが、中学　高校で習った知識で解くことができたので紹介したい。	Substituted it into the formula for solutions. Calculated the value inside the square root. Found α and β. Substituted $\alpha = -2$. Examined the solution, and the answer was −3. Afterward, calculated it as a = −4.7x^5 + 7, but there was an error. So I rearranged the 5 on the right side to 4, and the correct value was obtained (with the decimal part truncated). This problem is beyond the scope of high school mathematics, but it could be solved using knowledge learned in middle and high school, so I want to introduce it.	4.08
グラフを書いた傾きが−4のy = x^2の接線を求めた。その後、接点を原点とし両辺に点a,bを代入すると「sin-cos」と出たので、「COS(1)」で求めた。これで式の意味が分かったと思う。−5は角度が変化しないからゼロでないといけないのだ！	Used the slope obtained from graphing to find the tangent of y = x^2 with slope −4. Took the point of tangency as the origin and substituted points a and b on both sides. 'Sin-cos' was obtained, so I calculated it using 'COS(1)'. I think I understood the meaning of the equation now. −5 does not change the angle, so it must be nonzero!	3.02
x = 3 を代入する。方程式を解き進める。解の吟味を書く。間違いに気づき、修正する。最終的な答えを書く。その後、再帰的に解く。	Substituted x = 3. Proceeded to solve the equation. Wrote the examination of the solutions. Noticed the mistake and corrected it. Wrote the final answer. Afterward, solve it recursively.	2.18
前のは間違えたため、全部消した。その後、通分してみた。	Since the previous one was incorrect, I deleted everything and then performed the common denominator. Afterwards, something like this.	1.23

Table 6. Math texts samples.

Math Texts Samples	Predicted Self-Explanation Score
Angle bisector and ratio, using Ceva's theorem: Revised version succeed math A problem 349 Δ (Triangle), let Δ have the angle bisector of ∠ and the point where it intersects the side, and the point that divides the side in the ratio. When the line intersects at point, find the length of the side.	5.00
Using Menelaus's theorem: Segment ratio and area ratio, revised version succeed math A problem 350 Δ, let be the point where it divides the side in the ratio, and the point where the segment is divided in the ratio, and the point where the extension of the segment intersects the side. Find the following segment ratios and area ratios Δ:Δ	4.93
Using the relationship between sides and angles: Range of values for side length in a triangle, revised version succeed math A problem 355, determine the range of values for so that a triangle with the following side lengths exists.	3.84
Using the relationship between the sizes of three sides: Proving inequalities related to segment lengths, revised version succeed math A important example 66, take point inside Δ, and join and prove that . Abbreviated.	3.13
Examining the sizes of the three angles of a triangle, revised version succeed math A important example 64, examine the sizes of the three interior angles of Δ.	2.66

The inherent variability in the complexity of mathematical texts and self-explanations, as illustrated by Tables 5 and 6, underscores the importance of our automated scoring system. It demonstrates the system's capability to adaptively discern and quantify the nuances in self-explanation quality.

5. Experiments and Evaluations

5.1. Exploring the Influence of Self-Explanation Augmentation on Model Efficiency

We embarked on an exploration to discern the influence of self-explanation augmentation on the efficiency of an automated self-explanation scoring model across diverse datasets. We used mean absolute error (MAE) metrics [48,49] to evaluate model performance, giving insights into the extent of error deviation and the efficacy for individual items. Tables 7 and 8 lay out the results of our experiments, contrasting performances across different dataset permutations. When we introduced augmented datasets into the mix, distinct variations in performance emerged.

Table 7. Datasets overview.

Dataset	Base_Line	LLM	Math	Mixed	Only_LLM_Math
Original (N = 1420)	•	•	•	•	
LLM-generated (N = 4096)		•		•	•
Math texts (N = 4096)			•	•	•
Total Number of Data	1420	5516	5516	9612	8192

Table 8. Model performance for various datasets (MAE).

Data Type	Base_Line	LLM	Math	Mixed	Only_LLM_Math
Test	0.749	0.699	**0.646**	0.692	1.135
Val	0.602	0.341	0.358	**0.336**	1.033

Remarkably, our model, when nurtured with a blend of the 'math' and 'original dataset', consistently delivered the most desirable MAE results. This underlines its superior predictive precision in assessing self-explanation quality. Such results lend credence to the efficacy of the model when trained with this specific data amalgamation. On another note, the 'mixed' model—which weaves together human-graded samples, LLM-crafted pseudo-sentences, and mathematical content—also demonstrated notable improvements. This outcome underscores the model's robustness and flexibility when fed with diverse data sources. Yet, the model named 'only_LLM_math', which exclusively depended on LLM-created sentences, trailed behind the foundational model in terms of performance. This observation underscores the criticality of harmonizing human-judged and machine-produced data to achieve optimal results.

5.2. Evaluating Optimal Quantity of Pseudo-Self-Explanation Data

The data from Tables 9 and 10, as well as the visual cues from Figures 6 and 7, underline the importance of calibrating the amount of added pseudo-self-explanation data. While adding more datasets often improves performance, there is a saturation point beyond which the returns diminish. This trend underscores the need for a balanced approach, optimizing the amount of data incorporated to ensure robust and generalizable results. It also emphasizes the intricate interplay between different datasets, with 'LLM' and 'mixed' data offering particularly promising outcomes.

Table 9. Test MAE with varying amounts of added pseudo-self-explanation sata.

Dataset	Number of Datasets Added					
	128	256	512	1024	2048	4096
base_line	0.75					
LLM	0.67	**0.63**	0.72	0.72	0.71	0.7
math	**0.64**	0.66	0.67	**0.64**	0.65	0.65
mixed	0.68	**0.66**	0.71	0.68	0.73	0.69
only_LLM_math	1.19	0.96	1.02	0.89	1.15	1.14

Table 10. Validation MAE with varying amounts of added pseudo-self-explanatory data.

Dataset	Number of Datasets Added					
	128	256	512	1024	2048	4096
base_line	0.60					
LLM	0.57	**0.35**	0.51	0.49	0.40	0.34
math	0.40	0.50	0.43	**0.35**	0.40	0.36
mixed	0.59	**0.32**	0.52	0.44	0.40	0.34
only_LLM_math	1.19	0.90	0.96	**0.81**	1.02	1.03

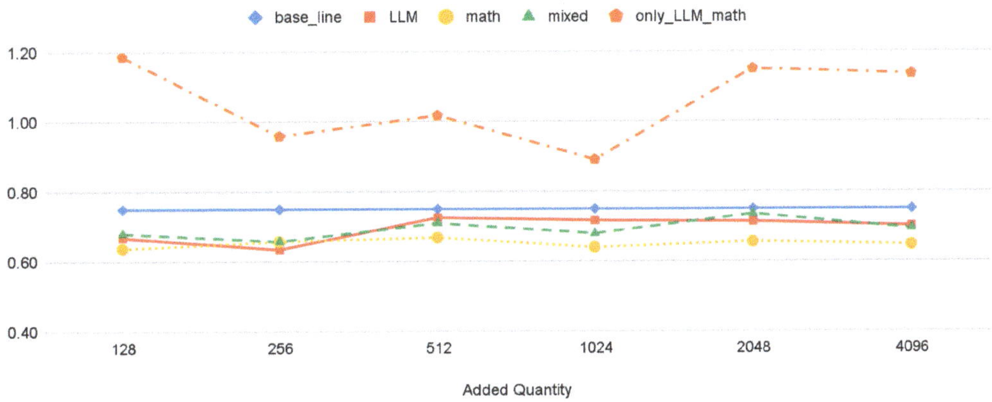

Figure 6. Test MAE plot.

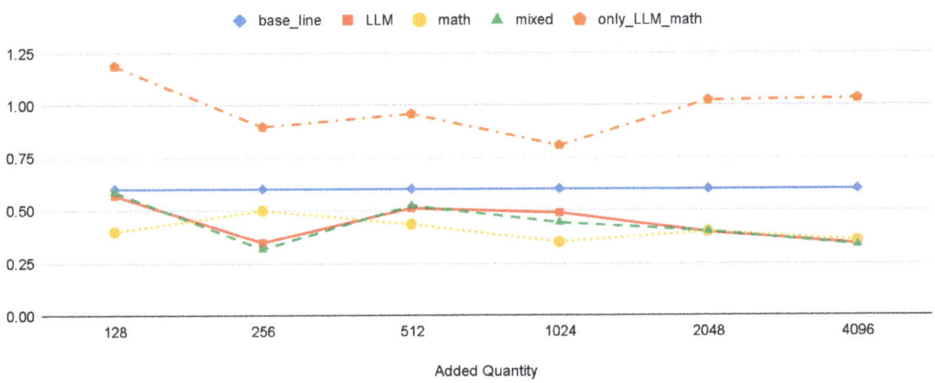

Figure 7. Validation MAE plot.

The 'baseline' row signifies the MAE when the model is trained only on the original dataset, devoid of any pseudo-self-explanation data. Each subsequent row shows the MAE when the model is trained with an increasing volume of pseudo-self-explanation data, ranging from 128 to 4096 datasets.

Upon examining the 'LLM' model, we note an enhancement in performance when the added datasets increase from 128 to 256. Beyond this, the further addition of generated data does not significantly reduce the MAE, suggesting an optimal balance between data augmentation and model efficacy with an addition of 256 datasets. The 'math' model displays a similar trend, with the lowest MAE achieved when 1024 datasets are added. Beyond this point, no substantial performance enhancement is observed with extra data.

For the 'mixed' model, we see a consistent improvement in performance with increased data, but this plateaus beyond 2048 datasets, where the MAE slightly increases. Conversely, the 'only_LLM_math' model shows erratic trends. Its performance varies noticeably with the quantity of added data and consistently exceeds the baseline model's MAE, regardless of the added data volume. This reveals potential difficulties when exclusively relying on generated pseudo-self-explanation data.

6. Discussion

6.1. Detailed Analysis of Results (RQ1)

Regarding Research Question 1, an in-depth analysis of the results displayed in Table 8 reveals several noteworthy observations regarding the influence of self-explanation augmentation on the model's performance. In the test category, we observe an improvement in the model's performance when transitioning from the baseline to the LLM and math models. Notably, the math model achieves the lowest MAE at 0.646, which aligns with Dai et al.'s [36] proposition that data augmentation at the semantic level improves robustness and consistency. However, the performance slightly deteriorates in the mixed model and substantially plummets in the 'only_LLM_math' model. This suggests that an excessive concentration of LLM-generated self-explanations could impair the model's predictive proficiency.

A similar pattern emerges when examining individual topics within the 'test' category. For instance, the model delivers optimal performance for 'quadratic equations' with the LLM-generated model, but the performance markedly deteriorates when solely relying on LLM-generated self-explanations. The validation category follows a similar trajectory, with the LLM, math, and mixed models outshining the baseline model. Once again, the mixed model achieves the smallest error. However, the 'only_LLM_math' model experiences a decline in performance, further highlighting the advantages of using a diverse dataset that encompasses both human-evaluated and machine-generated explanations.

6.2. Findings and Observations (RQ2)

Regarding Research Question 2, the results presented in Tables 9 and 10 provide valuable insights into determining the optimal quantity of generated pseudo-self-explanation data that can enhance the model's performance. For the 'LLM' model, an initial improvement in model performance is observed as the number of added datasets increases from 128 to 256. Beyond this point, further augmentation of the generated data does not lead to a significant reduction in MAE, suggesting that adding 256 datasets strikes an optimal balance between data augmentation and model performance. The 'math' model exhibits a similar pattern, with the lowest MAE observed when 1024 datasets are added, and no significant performance improvements resulting from further data augmentation. The 'mixed' model, on the other hand, shows a general trend of performance enhancement with increased data augmentation, up to a threshold of 2048 datasets, beyond which the MAE slightly increases. In contrast, the 'only_LLM_math' model does not present a consistent trend. Its performance fluctuates significantly as the volume of added data increases, and its MAE consistently surpasses that of the baseline model, regardless of the amount of added data. This underscores the challenges of solely leveraging generated pseudo-self-explanation data for augmentation, particularly when the model might lack domain-specific expertise, echoing concerns raised by Dai et al. [36].

Our study underscores that while weaving in generated pseudo-self-explanation data offers potential advantages, there is a point of diminishing returns. Beyond a certain threshold, piling on more data does not invariably translate to superior outcomes. This stunted impact might have its roots in the constraints imposed by our evaluation dataset's size and imbalance. The compact nature of our training and test datasets might curtail the model's expansive learning capabilities. Intriguingly, despite the mathematical underpinnings in the LLM and math texts, the 'only_LLM_math' model does not match up to either the baseline or its proposed counterparts. The divergences might be attributable to the caliber of the generated self-explanations coupled with the characteristics of the datasets utilized in the training and testing phases.

In conclusion, while integrating generated pseudo-self-explanation data shows potential in enhancing model performance, our results suggest there is a limit. Oversampling methods, such as SMOTE and ADASYN, can expand small datasets and provide a broader learning spectrum for models [29]. Although our focus has been on LLM pseudo-labeling, merging this with oversampling could be a promising direction for future research, aiming to further refine our models. Our study underscores the importance of careful and context-aware adjustments when adopting data augmentation strategies in developing self-explanation auto-scoring models.

6.3. Limitations and Future Research

In our research, several limitations of our study should be highlighted.

- Subject scope: Our dataset is restricted to mathematics, potentially constraining the generalizability of our findings to other subjects.
- Dependency on LLM: Our methodology hinges on the LLM's ability to generate pseudo-self-explanation data. This dependence may introduce noise and errors into our system.
- Data quality and representativeness: The performance of our approach is contingent on the quality and representativeness of labeled data. Poor or biased data could compromise model efficacy.
- Model performance variability: We identified noticeable disparities in our model's performance across various mathematical categories. For instance, it predicted the 'property of a circle' (0.242) more accurately than 'quadratic functions' (0.419) within the validation datasets. These results indicate that self-explanation augmentation's effectiveness may be influenced by the inherent complexity of a topic and the linguistic nuances present within the self-explanations.
- Evaluation dataset categories and size: The evaluation dataset for some categories is comparatively small, which poses challenges in drawing definitive conclusions. It is essential to consider the ease of inference as it pertains to various mathematical concepts, including linear functions, shapes, equations, and square roots. Certain subjects may be inherently more challenging for machine training due to their linguistic or conceptual intricacies.

Author Contributions: R.N., B.F., T.Y., Y.D., K.T. and H.O. contributed to the research conceptualization and methodology. Data collection was performed by R.N. R.N. analyzed the data and wrote the manuscript. B.F., Y.D. and H.O. provided comments to improve the manuscript. All authors have read and agreed to the published version of the manuscript.

Funding: This research was partly funded by the JSPS Grant-in-Aid for Scientific Research (B) JP20H01722 and JP23H01001, (Exploratory) JP21K19824, (Early Career) JP23K17012, (A) JP23H00505, and NEDO JPNP20006.

Data Availability Statement: The data of this study are not open to the public due to participant privacy.

Acknowledgments: We used LLM for the English proofreading of this paper and this fact has been explicitly mentioned for transparency. As this study involves the use of student data, we acknowledge the importance of obtaining approval from the Institutional Review Board (IRB). We have taken the necessary steps to ensure compliance with ethical guidelines, and the study has been submitted to and approved by the IRB. Consent for using the students' data in our research is obtained from their guardians at the beginning of each academic year. We provide detailed information about the purpose of data collection, how it will be used, and the measures taken to ensure confidentiality and privacy. The guardians have the right to decline consent or withdraw their consent at any time without any negative consequences for the students.

Conflicts of Interest: The authors declare no conflict of interest. The funders had no role in the design of the study, in the collection, analyses.

References

1. Rittle-Johnson, B.; Loehr, A.M.; Durkin, K. Promoting self-explanation to improve mathematics learning: A meta-analysis and instructional design principles. *ZDM* **2017**, *49*, 599–611. [CrossRef]
2. Rittle-Johnson, B. Developing Mathematics Knowledge. *Child Dev. Perspect.* **2017**, *11*, 184–190. [CrossRef]
3. Renkl, A. Learning from worked-examples in mathematics: Students relate procedures to principles. *ZDM* **2017**, *49*, 571–584. [CrossRef]

4. Chi, M.T.; Leeuw, N.D.; Chiu, M.; LaVancher, C. Eliciting Self-Explanations Improves Understanding. *Cogn. Sci.* **1994**, *18*, 439–477.
5. Rittle-Johnson, B. Promoting transfer: Effects of self-explanation and direct instruction. *Child Dev.* **2006**, *77*, 1–15. [CrossRef] [PubMed]
6. Conati, C.; VanLehn, K. Toward Computer-Based Support of Meta-Cognitive Skills: A Computational Framework to Coach Self-Explanation. *Int. J. Artif. Intell. Educ.* **2000**, *11*, 389–415.
7. Bisra, K.; Liu, Q.; Nesbit, J.C.; Salimi, F.; Winne, P.H. Inducing Self-Explanation: A Meta-Analysis. *Educ. Psychol. Rev.* **2018**, *30*, 703–725. [CrossRef]
8. Crippen, K.J.; Earl, B.L. The impact of web-based worked examples and self-explanation on performance, problem solving, and self-efficacy. *Comput. Educ.* **2007**, *49*, 809–821. [CrossRef]
9. Nakamoto, R.; Flanagan, B.; Takami, K.; Dai, Y.; Ogata, H. Identifying Students' Stuck Points Using Self-Explanations and Pen Stroke Data in a Mathematics Quiz. In Proceedings of the 29th International Conference on Computers in Education, Online, 22–26 November 2021; Volume 2021, pp. 22–26.
10. Nakamoto, R.; Flanagan, B.; Dai, Y.; Takami, K.; Ogata, H. Unsupervised techniques for generating a standard sample self-explanation answer with knowledge components in a math quiz. *Res. Pract. Technol. Enhanc. Learn.* **2024**, *19*, 016. [CrossRef]
11. Berthold, K.; Eysink, T.H.; Renkl, A. Assisting self-explanation prompts are more effective than open prompts when learning with multiple representations. *Instr. Sci.* **2009**, *37*, 345–363. [CrossRef]
12. Berthold, K.; Renkl, A. Instructional Aids to Support a Conceptual Understanding of Multiple Representations. *J. Educ. Psychol.* **2009**, *101*, 70–87. [CrossRef]
13. McEldoon, K.L.; Durkin, K.L.; Rittle-Johnson, B. Is self-explanation worth the time? A comparison to additional practice. *Br. J. Educ. Psychol.* **2013**, *83*, 615–632. [CrossRef] [PubMed]
14. Panaite, M.; Dascalu, M.; Johnson, A.M.; Balyan, R.; Dai, J.; McNamara, D.S.; Trausan-Matu, S. Bring It on! Challenges Encountered While Building a Comprehensive Tutoring System Using ReaderBench. In Proceedings of the International Conference on Artificial Intelligence in Education, London, UK, 27–30 June 2018.
15. Hodds, M.; Alcock, L.; Inglis, M. Self-explanation training improves proof comprehension. *J. Res. Math. Educ.* **2014**, *45*, 62–101. [CrossRef]
16. CyberAgent. Open-Calm-7B [Software]. Hugging Face. 2023. Available online: https://huggingface.co/cyberagent/open-calm-7b (accessed on 1 June 2023).
17. Andonian, A.; Anthony, Q.; Biderman, S.; Black, S.; Gali, P.; Gao, L.; Hallahan, E.; Levy-Kramer, J.; Leahy, C.; Nestler, L.; et al. GPT-NeoX: Large Scale Autoregressive Language Modeling in PyTorch (Version 0.0.1) [Computer Software]. 2021. Available online: https://zenodo.org/record/7714278 (accessed on 1 June 2023).
18. Brown, T.B.; Mann, B.; Ryder, N.; Subbiah, M.; Kaplan, J.; Dhariwal, P.; Neelakantan, A.; Shyam, P.; Sastry, G.; Askell, A.; et al. Language Models are Few-Shot Learners. *arXiv* **2020**, arXiv:2005.14165.
19. McNamara, D.S.; Levinstein, I.B.; Boonthum, C. iSTART: Interactive strategy training for active reading and thinking. Behavior Research Methods. *Instrum. Comput.* **2004**, *36*, 222–233. [CrossRef]
20. Funayama, H.; Asazuma, Y.; Matsubayashi, Y.; Mizumoto, T.; Inui, K. Reducing the Cost: Cross-Prompt Pre-finetuning for Short Answer Scoring. In Proceedings of the International Conference on Artificial Intelligence in Education, Tokyo, Japan, 3–7 July 2023.
21. Crossley, S.A.; Kim, M.; Allen, L.K.; McNamara, D.S. Automated Summarization Evaluation (ASE) Using Natural Language Processing Tools. In Proceedings of the International Conference on Artificial Intelligence in Education, Chicago, IL, USA, 25–29 June 2019.
22. Özsoy, M.G.; Alpaslan, F.N.; Çiçekli, I. Text summarization using Latent Semantic Analysis. *J. Inf. Sci.* **2011**, *37*, 405–417. [CrossRef]
23. León, J.A.; Olmos, R.; Escudero, I.; Cañas, J.J.; Salmerón, L. Assessing short summaries with human judgments procedure and latent semantic analysis in narrative and expository texts. *Behav. Res. Methods* **2006**, *38*, 616–627. [CrossRef]
24. Panaite, M.; Ruseti, S.; Dascalu, M.; Balyan, R.; McNamara, D.S.; Trausan-Matu, S. Automated Scoring of Self-explanations Using Recurrent Neural Networks. In Proceedings of the European Conference on Technology Enhanced Learning, Delft, The Netherlands, 16–19 September 2019.
25. Cascante-Bonilla, P.; Tan, F.; Qi, Y.; Ordonez, V. Curriculum Labeling: Revisiting Pseudo-Labeling for Semi-Supervised Learning. In Proceedings of the AAAI Conference on Artificial Intelligence, New York, NY, USA, 7–12 February 2020.
26. Chawla, N.; Bowyer, K.; Hall, L.O.; Kegelmeyer, W.P. SMOTE: Synthetic Minority Over-sampling Technique. *arXiv* **2002**, arXiv:1106.1813. [CrossRef]
27. Han, H.; Wang, W.; Mao, B. Borderline-SMOTE: A New Over-Sampling Method in Imbalanced Data Sets Learning. In Proceedings of the International Conference on Intelligent Computing, Hefei, China, 23–26 August 2005.
28. He, H.; Bai, Y.; Garcia, E.A.; Li, S. ADASYN: Adaptive synthetic sampling approach for imbalanced learning. In Proceedings of the 2008 IEEE International Joint Conference on Neural Networks (IEEE World Congress on Computational Intelligence), Hong Kong, China, 1–8 June 2008; pp. 1322–1328.
29. Salazar, A.; Vergara, L.; Safont, G. Generative Adversarial Networks and Markov Random Fields for oversampling very small training sets. *Expert Syst. Appl.* **2021**, *163*, 113819. [CrossRef]

30. Rubin, D.B. Statistical disclosure limitation. *J. Off. Stat.* **1993**, *9*, 461–468.
31. Antulov-Fantulin, N.; Bošnjak, M.; Zlatić, V.; Grčar, M.; Šmuc, T. Synthetic Sequence Generator for Recommender Systems–Memory Biased Random Walk on a Sequence Multilayer Network. In *Discovery Science. DS 2014. Lecture Notes in Computer Science*; Džeroski, S., Panov, P., Kocev, D., Todorovski, L., Eds.; Springer: Cham, Switerland, 2014; Volume 8777. [CrossRef]
32. El Emam, K. Seven Ways to Evaluate the Utility of Synthetic Data. *IEEE Secur. Priv.* **2020**, *18*, 56–59. [CrossRef]
33. Ping, H.; Stoyanovich, J.; Howe, B. DataSynthesizer: Privacy-Preserving Synthetic Datasets. In Proceedings of the 29th International Conference on Scientific and Statistical Database Management, Chicago, IL, USA, 27–29 June 2017.
34. Dahmen, J.; Cook, D.J. SynSys: A Synthetic Data Generation System for Healthcare Applcations. *Sensors* **2019**, *19*, 1181. [CrossRef] [PubMed]
35. Berg, A.; Mol, S.T.; Kismihók, G.; Sclater, N. The Role of a Reference Synthetic Data Generator within the Field of Learning Analytics. *J. Learn. Anal.* **2016**, *3*, 107–128. [CrossRef]
36. Peña-Ayala, A. Learning analytics: A glance of evolution, status, and trends according to a proposed taxonomy. *Wiley Interdiscip. Rev. Data Min. Knowl. Discov.* **2018**, *8*, e1243. [CrossRef]
37. Flanagan, B.; Majumdar, R.; Ogata, H. Fine Grain Synthetic Educational Data: Challenges and Limitations of Collaborative Learning Analytics. *IEEE Access* **2022**, *10*, 26230–26241. [CrossRef]
38. Dai, H.; Liu, Z.; Liao, W.; Huang, X.; Cao, Y.; Wu, Z.; Zhao, L.; Xu, S.; Liu, W.; Liu, N.; et al. AugGPT: Leveraging ChatGPT for Text Data Augmentation. *arXiv* **2023**, arXiv:2302.13007.
39. Lightman, H.; Kosaraju, V.; Burda, Y.; Edwards, H.; Baker, B.; Lee, T.; Leike, J.; Schulman, J.; Sutskever, I.; Cobbe, K. Let's Verify Step by Step. *arXiv* **2023**, arXiv:2305.20050.
40. Flanagan, B.; Ogata, H. Learning analytics platform in higher education in Japan. *Knowl. Manag. E-Learn. Int. J.* **2018**, *10*, 469–484.
41. Thompson, D.R.; Senk, S.L. Using rubrics in high school mathematics courses. *Math. Teach. Learn. Teach. PK–12* **1998**, *91*, 786–793. [CrossRef]
42. Cohen, J. A Coefficient of Agreement for Nominal Scales. *Educ. Psychol. Meas.* **1960**, *20*, 37–46. [CrossRef]
43. Wang, T.; Inoue, N.; Ouchi, H.; Mizumoto, T.; Inui, K. Inject Rubrics into Short Answer Grading System. In Proceedings of the Conference on Empirical Methods in Natural Language Processing, Hong Kong, China, 3–7 November 2019.
44. Vaswani, A.; Shazeer, N.M.; Parmar, N.; Uszkoreit, J.; Jones, L.; Gomez, A.N.; Kaiser, L.; Polosukhin, I. Attention is All you Need. In Proceedings of the 31st International Conference on Neural Information Processing Systems, Long Beach, CA, USA, 4–9 December 2017; NIPS'17, 6000-6010. Curran Associates Inc.: Red Hook, NY, USA, 2017. ISBN 9781510860964.
45. Suzuki, M. Pretrained Japanese BERT Models, GitHub Repository. 2019. Available online: https://github.com/cl-tohoku/bert-japanese (accessed on 1 April 2021).
46. Devlin, J.; Chang, M.W.; Lee, K.; Toutanova, K. BERT: Pre-training of Deep Bidirectional Transformers for Language Understanding. In Proceedings of the 2019 Conference of the North American Chapter of the Association for Computational Linguistics: Human Language Technologies, Minneapolis, MN, USA, 2–7 June 2019; Association for Computational Linguistics: Minneapolis, MN, USA, 2019; Volume 1, pp. 4171–4186.
47. Liu, P.; Yuan, W.; Fu, J.; Jiang, Z.; Hayashi, H.; Neubig, G. Pre-train, Prompt, and Predict: A Systematic Survey of Prompting Methods in Natural Language Processing. *ACM Comput. Surv.* **2021**, *55*, 1–35. [CrossRef]
48. Chai, T.; Draxler, R.R. Root mean square error (RMSE) or mean absolute error (MAE)?–Arguments against avoiding RMSE in the literature. *Geosci. Model Dev.* **2014**, *7*, 1247–1250. [CrossRef]
49. Hodson, T.O. Root-mean-square error (RMSE) or mean absolute error (MAE): When to use them or not. Geoscientific Model Development. *Geosci. Model Dev.* **2022**, *15*, 5481–5487. [CrossRef]

computers

MDPI

Article

Predictive Modeling of Student Dropout in MOOCs and Self-Regulated Learning

Georgios Psathas [1,*], Theano K. Chatzidaki [2] and Stavros N. Demetriadis [1,*]

[1] School of Informatics, Aristotle University of Thessaloniki, 541 24 Thessaloniki, Greece
[2] Department of Economics, University of Macedonia, 156 Egnatia Street, 546 36 Thessaloniki, Greece; theano@uom.edu.gr
* Correspondence: gpsathas@csd.auth.gr (G.P.); sdemetri@csd.auth.gr (S.N.D.)

Abstract: The primary objective of this study is to examine the factors that contribute to the early prediction of Massive Open Online Courses (MOOCs) dropouts in order to identify and support at-risk students. We utilize MOOC data of specific duration, with a guided study pace. The dataset exhibits class imbalance, and we apply oversampling techniques to ensure data balancing and unbiased prediction. We examine the predictive performance of five classic classification machine learning (ML) algorithms under four different oversampling techniques and various evaluation metrics. Additionally, we explore the influence of self-reported self-regulated learning (SRL) data provided by students and various other prominent features of MOOCs as potential indicators of early stage dropout prediction. The research questions focus on (1) the performance of the classic classification ML models using various evaluation metrics before and after different methods of oversampling, (2) which self-reported data may constitute crucial predictors for dropout propensity, and (3) the effect of the SRL factor on the dropout prediction performance. The main conclusions are: (1) prominent predictors, including employment status, frequency of chat tool usage, prior subject-related experiences, gender, education, and willingness to participate, exhibit remarkable efficacy in achieving high to excellent recall performance, particularly when specific combinations of algorithms and oversampling methods are applied, (2) self-reported SRL factor, combined with easily provided/self-reported features, performed well as a predictor in terms of recall when LR and SVM algorithms were employed, (3) it is crucial to test diverse machine learning algorithms and oversampling methods in predictive modeling.

Keywords: Massive Open Online Courses (MOOCs); self-regulated learning (SRL); prediction; self-reported data; oversampling

1. Introduction

This study aims to examine the factors that contribute to the early prediction of MOOC dropout to identify at-risk students and facilitate their successful completion through supportive interventions. Emphasis is placed on the SRL factor, which is often overlooked in MOOC dropout prediction studies. The motivation for this research lies in the persistent issue of high dropout rates in MOOCs and the investigation of the SRL factor in addressing this problem, given that students with higher SRL indices have been shown to achieve better learning outcomes. Additionally, the study explores the impact on the prediction performance of the employment of different oversampling techniques to address the class imbalance problem. Therefore, a variety of oversampling techniques and algorithms to compare prediction performance and identify the best combinations for the specific dataset were used.

1.1. Massive Open Online Courses (MOOCs)

MOOCs are a new distance education model established in 2008 by George Siemens. Many MOOC platforms offer educational design with video lectures, announcements, forums, and assessments (quizzes, assignments, etc.) [1,2]. Some MOOCs allow students to progress at their own pace, while others follow a predetermined schedule [3]. The acquisition of completion certificates serves as a motivation for many students [4]. Most students fail to complete MOOCs successfully, even if they intend to do so [5]. The challenges of MOOCs include the absence of a supporting and guiding instructor [6], limited social interaction between teachers and students [7], and the most critical challenge lies in the high dropout rates observed within the MOOC environment [3]. In the literature, dropout rate percentages are cited as 93.5% [8] or 91–93% [9].

Many studies have extensively explored the phenomenon of dropout rates in MOOC courses. Several researchers have indicated significantly low percentages in completion rates, falling below 10% and even as low as 5% [3,10–12]. Although these figures may appear alarming, such an assessment is based on the assumption that enrollment in a MOOC is comparable to enrolling in a traditional course, which is not always the case, as the intentions of individuals enrolling in a MOOC differ—some seek professional development. In contrast, others pursue simple information or entertainment [11]. However, it is essential to acknowledge some positive exceptions to the high dropout rates. For instance, programming MOOCs demonstrated retention rates above 60% [3,13].

Identifying and exploring factors directly influencing the attrition of students from MOOCs will enable researchers and educators to examine novel strategies and techniques to enhance students' persistence and successful course completion. Dalipi et al. [14] have categorized these factors contributing to high dropout rates into those associated with students (such as lack of motivation, poor time management, inadequate background knowledge, and skills) and those related to MOOCs (course design, lack of interactions, hidden costs).

Ihantola et al. [3] conducted a study to investigate the attrition rates of students in MOOCs with flexible versus strict scheduling. The findings revealed that students enrolled in MOOCs with flexible scheduling were more likely to drop out early compared to those in MOOCs with rigid schedules. In their study, approximately 17% of students abandoned the course within the first week, while the corresponding rate for the flexible MOOC was 50%. However, after the initial week, the dropout behavior between the two versions of MOOCs became nearly similar.

Furthermore, the researchers observed that both versions of MOOCs had students who completed all computer programming assignments within a week but did not continue further, possibly due to perceiving a heavy workload. Therefore, the authors suggest that identifying the profiles of students who benefit from each type of MOOC could lead to novel, more effective methods of organizing and grading courses. Previous studies have also identified that the lack of a sense of community and ineffective social interactions and collaborations contribute to the high attrition rates in MOOCs [7,14,15].

Hone and El Said [16] also investigated factors influencing retention in MOOCs and found that 32.2% of students successfully completed their preferred courses, a rate surpassing the average completion rate. The main driver for their completion was the satisfaction derived from the course content, which was perceived as unique and not readily available elsewhere. However, non-completers identified several reasons for their discontinuation, including feelings of isolation due to inadequate communication channels, perceived complexity and technical difficulties of the courses, and a lack of engagement. A related study by Zhang [17] explored how to enhance MOOC attractiveness by aligning courses with students' regulatory foci. The observations made in this study indicate that students with promotion-focused mindsets were more influenced by advocates emphasizing gains and positive outcomes, while prevention-focused students responded better to advocates stressing the avoidance of losses.

1.2. Prediction of Dropout and the SRL Factor

According to Gardner and Brooks (2018) [2], regarding the statistical models used to map features to predictions, supervised learning techniques are extensively used in predictive student modeling in MOOCs, compared to unsupervised approaches, as student dropout/stopout is easily observable. In supervised learning, machines are trained using well "labelled" training data, and on the basis of that data, machines predict the output. Authors chose to present indicatively popular techniques for MOOC learner modeling, with very good empirical performance in large-scale MOOC modeling studies, (e.g., Dass et al., 2021 [18]). LR and SVM are among the most used, while NB, kNN, and DT are less frequently used in surveys ([2]). There is no pattern found for an algorithm to be distinguished compared to others. According to Herrmannova et al., 2015 [19], each model captures different properties of input data and the results are complementary.

Self-regulated learning (SRL) is a complex multidimensional phenomenon often described by a set of individual cognitive, social, metacognitive, and behavioral processes embedded in a cyclical model. Students with limited application of SRL strategies do not perform well [1,20–22]. Zimmerman [23] proposed a cyclical model consisting of three interrelated phases of the learning process. In the forethought phase, self-regulated learners set learning goals and design the strategy for their learning. This is followed by the performance and control phase, during which self-regulated learners employ strategies to process the learning material. They seek help when needed, manage their time, structure their environment, and monitor their learning processes. In the third phase of self-reflection, self-regulated learners evaluate their performance and adjust their strategies to achieve their learning goals [1,18,22,24,25].

Research using questionnaires has shown positive correlations between the mentioned SRL activity and the completion of MOOCs [24]. Despite the limitations of self-reported data [26], the large sample size enhances their usefulness. On the other hand, the use of trace data in measuring SRL has increased, but their interpretation remains challenging [26]. Jansen et al. [24] propose the combined use of SRL data from traces and questionnaires. Timely SRL support interventions in MOOCs should be considered significant pedagogical tools that contribute to achieving positive outcomes for students [20,21].

The features of MOOCs, such as internet-based massiveness, openness, and flexible learning, create a unique blend of a large number of learners, making the prediction of learner success (as well as providing support based on these predictions) particularly challenging. Several researchers have developed prediction models by employing machine learning (ML) algorithms [27] and adopting supervised, unsupervised, and semi-supervised architectures [28]. Deep learning methods are also utilized for predicting dropout. For instance, Moreno-Marcos et al. [29] applied a combination of random forest (RF), generalized linear model (GLM), support vector machines (SVM), and decision trees (DT). Feng et al. [10] utilized logistic regression (LR), support vector machine with a linear kernel (SVM), random forest (RF), gradient boosting decision tree (GBDT), and a three-layer deep neural network (DNN) for their analysis.

Diverse features, even in limited quantities, provide a more comprehensive, multidimensional view of learners and can improve the quality of predictive models. Collecting additional data, especially during the initial weeks of a course, enhances prediction performance [2,28]. For successful timely interventions, predictive models need to be transferable, meaning they perform well on new course iterations by utilizing historical data [30–32]. Some researchers have examined specific aspects of SRL and observed its impact on predicting success, including goal setting and strategic planning [6], student-programmed plans [33], the combination of self-reported SRL strategies and patterns of interaction sequences, demographic features, and intentions [34]. For example, Kizilcec et al. (2017) [6] investigated which specific SRL strategies predict the attainment of personal course goals and how they are mapped in specific interactions with MOOCs' online content. Yielding to form a longitudinal account of SRL, authors combined learners' self-reported SRL strategies and characteristics, achievement data, and records of individual's engagement with the course's content. Using multiple linear and logistic regression modeling, Maldonado-Mahauad et al. (2018) [34] concluded that specific self-reported SRL strategies ("goal setting", "strategic planning", "elaboration" and "help seeking"), complex behavioral data on MOOC's platform like meaningful online activity sequence patterns, self-reported prior experience and level of interest in MOOC's assessments as well as total time spent online belong to factors that contribute to the prediction of MOOC learners' success.

1.3. Handling Imbalanced Classes in Dropout Prediction

Due to the very high rates of student dropout, imbalance in the classes is a common phenomenon in MOOCs and can result in a bias toward the majority class [35], while the class of interest typically has fewer samples [36]. Although it is strongly recommended to pay attention to this issue when training an ML model for dropout prediction [37,38], according to Nagrecha et al., 2017 [35], very few studies in the MOOCs domain refer the consideration of the imbalanced problem (e.g., [39]). Barandela et al. (2004) [40] suggest oversampling the minority class when the imbalance is severe and undersampling the majority class in the opposite case. Most of the MOOC domain studies refer to the employment of oversampling SMOTE techniques to overcome imbalance (e.g., [18,41]).

Effective techniques to improve the performance of classifiers in the presence of a class imbalance in training data [42] include data-level approaches such as undersampling, oversampling, and their combinations [43,44]. In the context of this study, the majority class consists of successful students, and this asymmetry can lead a classifier to primarily predict that students do not drop out of the MOOC, which is an undesirable situation as students at risk are incorrectly identified as non-dropouts, resulting in them not receiving the necessary support intervention. Therefore, oversampling is preferred in this study to avoid neglecting important samples from the majority class [44,45]. To address the problem of overfitting in random oversampling, where minority class samples are repeated to increase their size [46], Chawla et al. [47] proposed the synthetic minority over-sampling technique (SMOTE). SMOTE generates synthetic samples along the line segments between minority class instances and a specified number, k (typically k = 5), of their nearest neighbors, thereby expanding the decision region [44]. This technique has found widespread use [36]. The newly generated synthetic samples contribute essential information to the minority class, mitigating misclassification issues of these samples [46].

Efforts to improve SMOTE include Borderline-SMOTE and ADASYN techniques. Han et al. [44] proposed the Borderline-SMOTE technique, which performs oversampling only on instances near the decision boundary between the two classes, as they are more likely to be misclassified, aiming to create a clearer decision boundary [36]. The technique has two variations: Borderline-SMOTE1, which only uses minority class samples as neighbors, and Borderline-SMOTE2, which additionally uses samples from the majority class to generate synthetic data [36]. As a variation of the SMOTE technique, He et al. [48] proposed ADASYN (adaptive synthetic sampling method), which generates more synthetic data for the instances that are more difficult to learn [49]. Improved predictive performance of classification models through the combined use of PCA and resampling techniques has been reported (e.g., [42]).

Brandt and Lanzén (2021) [49] examined the performance of SMOTE and ADASYN using different classification models and evaluation metrics and found that both techniques improved the performance in most cases. Authors conclude that none of the pre-processing methods they examined consistently outperformed the other, confirming the literature of imbalanced techniques comparison and the existence of a variety of results, where such pre-processing techniques may even decrease the performance. Therefore, in our study, we examine different oversampling methods, in addition to commonly used SMOTE in the MOOCs domain.

1.4. Rationale and Research Questions

Based on the above theoretical background, this study supports the idea that it is interesting to investigate the early prediction of dropout in the MOOC "Programming in Python for Non-Programmers", taking into consideration primarily the SRL (self-regulated learning) factor, after using various oversampling techniques. For this purpose, we employ five classic educational models [50] commonly used in the literature for comparing oversampling techniques when dealing with class imbalance [36,37,42,46] predictive models (NB, LR, SVM, DT, kNN), and we consider data from student questionnaires regarding their SRL, as well as other typical data, easily provided for this purpose, aiming to identify at-risk students as early as possible and support them with appropriate interventions to complete the course.

The research questions addressed in this study are as follows:

1. What is the performance of the five classic models (NB, LR, SVM, DT, kNN) in predicting dropout before and after oversampling for various oversampling methods?
2. What appear to be the important predictors for students' MOOC dropout and why?
3. What is the impact of the SRL factor, as determined by self-reported student data, on the performance of dropout prediction?

2. Materials and Methods

2.1. Context

We deployed the xMOOC "Programming in Python for Non-Programmers" that was offered in the Greek language during two time periods: 16 November 2020, to 20 December 2020 (referred to as MOOC1), and 22 February 2021, to 28 March 2021 (referred to as MOOC2). This initiative was a collaboration between the Department of Informatics at AUTH, EKETA, and GUnet, as part of the European-funded project "colMOOC: Integration of Dialogic Agents and Learning Analytics in MOOCs" (https://colmooc.eu/). It had a duration of 5 weeks, specific start and end dates, and included an equal number of 5 thematic modules, organized in each of the weeks. The course curriculum comprised various components aimed at augmenting the learning experience, encompassing video lectures, mini-quizzes, weekly quizzes, weekly assignments, and chat activities. We integrated chat-based collaborative activities with the support of a conversational agent [51], aiming to facilitate productive peer dialogue [52]. These chat activities involved students engaging in dyadic collaboration to collectively respond to open-ended questions with a shared goal, and they were encouraged to interact with a preconfigured conversational agent during their discussions. To foster individual accountability, support on students' SRL, and awareness of peers' progress, a learning analytics module was provided, enabling students to reflect on their own and their partner's performance and compare metrics with other students who completed the same activity, thereby allowing for potential adjustments in learning strategies to enhance their performance and SRL skills. During the second week, an email was disseminated to notify students about the existence of the learning analytics module.

Participants had the flexibility to study the educational material and complete assessments and activities at their own pace within the duration of the MOOC. A certificate of completion was granted to participants with a minimum score of 60%, based on weekly quizzes, assignments, collaborative activities, and a final quiz. After enrollment, students were required to complete a questionnaire, which was essential for receiving the certificate (provided they met the grading criteria). This questionnaire, available only during the first week, collected demographic data, participation intention (degree of engagement with the educational material), programming and Python experience, prior MOOC experience, and their self-regulated learning (SRL) profile).

2.2. Description of the Data Set

The initial dataset comprises 1543 rows and 232 columns, consisting of data from students in MOOC1 (1324 rows) and MOOC2 (219 rows). Our focus was on actively engaged students, defined as those who registered and remained active until the conclusion of the first week, completed the introductory questionnaire, and submitted the first week's programming assignment. This subset consisted of 935 students for MOOC1 and 134 students for MOOC2 (Table 1).

Table 1. Dataset.

	MOOC1	MOOC2
Enrolled	1.324	219
Started	935	134
%	0.70	0.61

According to a study by Stein and Allione [53], completing an assessment within the first week is a significant predictor of retention in the MOOC. The success completion rates for these specific subsets of students in the two MOOCs were 88.40% and 87.30%, respectively. It is important to note that there exists an imbalance in the distribution of classes among students who submitted and completed the MOOC and those who did not.

2.3. Procedure

Using the Python/sci-kit ecosystem, we fitted a predictive model on the data from MOOC1 by applying the NB, LR, SVM, DT, and kNN algorithms. We evaluate the performance of these models in predicting dropout in the MOOC2 dataset. Default settings were used for all algorithms. In a case study by Gardner and Brooks [2], parameter tuning showed minimal impact compared to the results obtained from different features or algorithms. The dependent variable DROPOUT categorizes students into the categories 1 (dropout) and 0 (non-dropout) as follows: those who participated in less than 10% of the activities are considered dropouts. The approach followed in this study to investigate the research questions involves the following steps:

1. Retrieval of data.
2. Preprocessing and cleaning of the data.
3. Selection of significant features.
4. Normalization, dimensionality reduction using PCA, and oversampling.
5. Training and testing the models using stratified 10-kfold cross-validation.
6. Comparative evaluation of the models for different oversampling techniques.

2.3.1. Data Retrieval

The student data from the 2 MOOCs, the potential independent variables (Table 2), and the dependent variable were retrieved.

Table 2. The variables used in the predictive models.

Features (Corresponding Question in the Questionnaire)	Type	Values
Performance_A1 (Grade in programming assignment at the end of the first module)	Continuous that was discretized	1–10
Gender	Categorical	1. Male 2. Female
Age	Categorical	1. <17 2. 18–25 3. 26–35 4. 36–45 5. 46–55 6. 56+

Table 2. *Cont.*

Features (Corresponding Question in the Questionnaire)	Type	Values
Employment (Are you employed?)	Categorical	1. Yes 2. No
Studies	Categorical	1. Doctorate 2. Master's degree 3. Higher Educational Institution/Higher Technological Educational Institution/Technological Educational Institution 4. Vocational Training Institution 5. High School (upper secondary education) Diploma 6. Gymnasium (lower secondary education) Diploma 7. Primary School Diploma 8. None of the above
MOOC Experience (What is your prior experience in MOOCs?)	Categorical	1. It is my first time attending a MOOC 2. I have attended 1–3 MOOCs in the past 3. I have attended more than 3 MOOCs in the past
Programming Experience (Previous experience in any programming language)	Categorical	1. None, complete beginner 2. Basic programming knowledge 3. Moderate programming knowledge 4. Advanced programming knowledge
Python Experience (Previous experience in Python)	Categorical	1. None, complete beginner 2. Basic programming knowledge 3. Moderate programming knowledge 4. Advanced programming knowledge
UseOfChatTools (Frequency of use of chat tools like Skype, Messenger, or Google Hangouts)	Categorical	1. I do not use such tools 2. Occasionally (e.g., once a week) 3. Moderately (e.g., 2–3 times a week 4. Frequently (e.g., more than 3 times a week 5. Daily
Intention_to_Participate Which of the following best matches your intended way of participating in the course?	Categorical	1. I intend to attend the entire course, complete assignments/tasks, and obtain the certificate of successful completion 2. I intend to attend the entire course, and complete assignments/tasks, but I am not interested in obtaining the certificate of successful completion at the moment 3. I intend to attend the course and complete assignments/tasks to the extent that I can, without being particularly interested in its completion 4. I plan to review the course material at the beginning and decide later on whether and how much I will attend 5. I intend to watch only the educational videos of the course and I am not interested in the assignments/tasks 6. I registered out of curiosity to obtain access to the material. I am currently unsure whether and how much I will attend 7. None of the above
SRL START num (SRL profile in the intro questionnaire)	Continuous	1–7

2.3.2. Preprocessing and Data Cleaning

The dataset consists of students who completed the intro questionnaire, submitted the first week's programming assignment, and received the general intervention (control group). Missing values were handled by deleting the corresponding students from the dataset.

2.3.3. Feature Selection

Different features are likely to incorporate different aspects of the same information. On the other hand, there may be interdependence among features and their coexistence in predictive modeling should be avoided. In this study, the user selects as candidate predictors the feature or combination of features that are desired, in order to arrive at subsets of significant features that contribute to the predictive performance. The results of filtering techniques that evaluate and rank candidate features are taken into account. It is common for variables to be ranked differently by heterogeneous filters, but ultimately, a stronger subset of features is identified [54]. Various statistical tests can be used to determine the features with the strongest relationship with the output variable. We apply the SelectKBest filter type method from the sci-kit-learn library, using chi-square for feature ranking (Figure 1a). Additionally, we can assess the importance of each feature using tree-based classifiers (Figure 1b). We utilize the sklearn built-in extra tree classifier. The higher the score of a feature, the more significant or relevant it is to the output variable [55].

	Specs	Score
3	Performance_A1	4.568921
9	Intention	2.070005
6	MOOC_exp	1.772722
8	Python_exp	1.436890
1	Age	1.264993
2	Employment	1.015339
4	Education	0.525901
10	SRL START num	0.468577
5	UseOfChatTools	0.159368
0	Gender	0.080138
7	Program_exp	0.005047

(**a**)

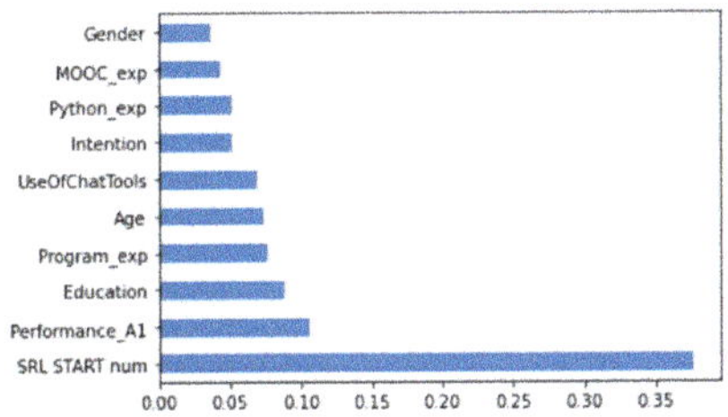

(**b**)

Figure 1. Ranking of features (**a**) using chi-square test; (**b**) using decision tree.

2.3.4. Normalization, Dimension Reduction with PCA and Oversampling

The principal component analysis (PCA) technique in feature extraction aims to reduce the dimensionality of the dataset by identifying and selecting features with higher variance, which carry significant information, especially when dealing with noisy data that can adversely affect model accuracy [36]. Holland [56] suggests determining the number of principal components to retain based on their collective ability to explain a predetermined percentage of the total variance, typically set at 90% in this context. A crucial prerequisite before employing PCA is data normalization, as emphasized by Mourdi et al. [26]. In our study, we ensured data remained on the same scale through scaling, adjusting only the value range. Our analytical pipeline involved the sequential application of normalization, PCA for dimensionality reduction, and oversampling, a commonly employed practice in the literature (e.g., [57]), to overcome imbalance and avoid neglecting important samples from the majority class.

2.3.5. Training and Testing

Data splitting into training and testing sets mimics the application of the model to new data and evaluates its performance [27]. We train the models using the MOOC1 dataset and apply the stratified 10-kfold cross-validation technique, which is suitable for classification problems with class imbalance (e.g., [36]).

2.3.6. Prediction Performance Evaluation of Models

Model evaluation is a crucial component of predictive modeling research in the context of learning analytics. Suitable performance metrics for the field (e.g., [58,59]) include accuracy, precision, recall, F1 score, as well as the confusion matrix (e.g., [44]). Due to the high number of dropouts in MOOCs, minimizing the number of false negatives (FN) [27] and focusing on the recall metric, which summarizes how well students at risk (i.e., the positive class) are predicted, is critical to ensure that they are not missed. This metric indicates missed positive predictions.

3. Results

Results for recall values ≥0.8 on the validation data of MOOC2 before and after oversampling are presented in Tables 3 and 4, respectively. Except for recall, various popular evaluation metrics are also presented. Comparing Tables 3 and 4, we observe that oversampling significantly improves the performance of the models in terms of recall. The kNN algorithm achieves the highest recall performance when data are imbalanced. All algorithms used appear in Table 4 but kNN appears more frequently. Programming assignment performance at the end of the first module of the MOOC seems a significant predictor for MOOC completers rather than dropouts as it performs high in terms of precision rather than recall. In the context of imbalanced data, it is essential to recognize that high accuracy values do not necessarily translate to superior predictive performance of a model. Through the process of oversampling, we identified Employment and UseOfChatTools as the most significant predictors associated with the risk of DROPOUT, as evidenced by their respective recall values. Specifically, both aforementioned features demonstrate a minor adverse correlation with the occurrence of DROPOUT (Spearman's correlation coefficient = −0.09, p = 0.007, and −0.03, p = 0.341, respectively).

Table 3. MOOC2 (test) data, imbalanced.

Features	Alg.	Roc_auc	Acc.	Prec.	Rec.	f1
SRL START num	LR	0.50	0.87	0.00	0.00	0.00
	DT	0.50	0.79	0.13	0.11	0.13
SRL START num, Employment	LR	0.50	0.87	0.00	0.00	0.00
	DT	0.55	0.78	0.20	0.24	0.22
Intention_to_Participate	kNN	0.56	0.72	0.18	0.35	0.24
SRL START num, Intention_to_Participate	LR	0.50	0.87	0.00	0.00	0.00
UseOfChatTools	kNN	0.59	0.69	0.07	0.35	0.12
Intention_to_Participate, SRL START num, Employment, Age	DT	0.54	0.77	0.18	0.24	0.20
	kNN	0.63	0.89	0.56	0.29	0.39
Performance_A1	NB	0.50	0.87	0.00	0.00	0.00
	LR	0.50	0.87	0.00	0.00	0.00
	SVM	0.50	0.87	0.00	0.00	0.00
	DT	0.50	0.87	0.00	0.00	0.00
	kNN	0.56	0.88	0.67	0.12	0.20
SRL START num, Performance_A1	LR	0.50	0.87	0.00	0.00	0.00
Intention_to_Participate, Performance_A1, SRL START num	LR	0.49	0.89	0.00	0.00	0.00
	SVM	0.50	0.87	0.00	0.00	0.00
	DT	0.52	0.77	0.16	0.18	0.17

Table 3. *Cont.*

Features	Alg.	Roc_auc	Acc.	Prec.	Rec.	f1
Intention_to_Participate, Performance_A1, SRL START num, Age	kNN	0.58	0.88	0.60	0.17	0.27
Intention_to_Participate, Performance_A1, SRL START num, Employment	NB	0.46	0.80	0.00	0.00	0.00
	LR	0.50	0.87	0.00	0.00	0.00
	SVM	0.50	0.87	0.00	0.00	0.00
	DT	0.44	0.72	0.04	0.06	0.05
	kNN	0.51	0.85	0.20	0.06	0.09
Intention_to_Participate, Performance_A1, Programming Experience	kNN	0.59	0.80	0.26	0.29	0.28
Intention_to_Participate, Performance_A1, SRL START num, Programming Experience	DT	0.59	0.80	0.26	0.29	0.28

With gray shading we distinguish the 2 highest values of the recall and roc_aucmetrics and the corresponding application algorithm.

Table 4. MOOC2 (test) data, balanced. Contains recall values >0.8.

Features	Alg.	Oversampling Method, k = 5	Roc_auc	Acc.	Prec.	Rec.	f1
Employment	kNN	ADASYN, SMOTE, Borderline-SMOTE1, Borderline-SMOTE2	0.50	0.13	0.13	1.00	0.23
UseOfChatTools	NB	Borderline-SMOTE2	0.59	0.28	0.15	1.00	0.26
UseOfChatTools	NB, LR	ADASYN	0.50	0.13	0.13	1.00	0.23
Programming experience, Gender	kNN	SMOTE	0.54	0.25	0.14	0.94	0.24
Intention, Education	LR	ADASYN	0.59	0.37	0.16	0.89	0.26
Python experience, MOOC experience	kNN	Borderline-SMOTE2	0.56	0.32	0.14	0.89	0.25
Python experience, MOOC experience	kNN	ADASYN	0.53	0.27	0.14	0.88	0.23
Python experience, MOOC experience	kNN	SMOTE	0.56	0.32	0.14	0.88	0.25
Python experience, MOOC experience	kNN	Borderline-SMOTE1	0.55	0.29	0.14	0.88	0.24
Education	SVM	SMOTE, Borderline-SMOTE1	0.57	0.38	0.15	0.82	0.25
Python experience, Gender	NB	Borderline-SMOTE1	0.57	0.38	0.15	0.82	0.25
Python experience, Gender	LR	Borderline-SMOTE1	0.57	0.37	0.15	0.82	0.25
Python experience, Gender	SVM	Borderline-SMOTE2	0.57	0.37	0.15	0.82	0.25
Python experience, Gender	SVM	SMOTE	0.56	0.37	0.15	0.82	0.25
Python experience, Gender	DT	SMOTE	0.58	0.40	0.15	0.82	0.26
Python experience, Gender	DT, kNN	Borderline-SMOTE2	0.58	0.40	0.15	0.82	0.26

Table 4. *Cont.*

Features	Alg.	Oversampling Method, k = 5	Roc_auc	Acc.	Prec.	Rec.	f1
Programming experience, Gender	NB, SVM, DT	Borderline-SMOTE1	0.51	0.27	0.13	0.82	0.22
Python experience, Gender, Intention	NB	SMOTE	0.64	0.51	0.18	0.82	0.30
Python experience, Gender, Intention	LR	Borderline-SMOTE1	0.57	0.37	0.15	0.82	0.25
MOOC experience, Gender	kNN	Borderline-SMOTE1	0.62	0.46	0.17	0.82	0.28
MOOC experience, Gender	LR	Borderline-SMOTE2	0.61	0.46	0.17	0.82	0.28

However, it is noteworthy that not all oversampling techniques employed yielded high recall values for the same algorithm and feature set, underscoring the importance of exploring alternative oversampling approaches. For example, when the UseOfChat feature and SMOTE or Borderline-SMOTE1 were used, the recall value on MOOC4 validation data is 0,11 when NB or LR are employed, while the use of ADASYN or Borderline-SMOTE2 yields to corresponding recall value 1.0. When Intention to Participate and Education features combined with Borderline-SMOTE2 were used, the recall value on MOOC4 validation data is 0,47 when LR is employed while the use of ADASYN yields to corresponding recall value 1.0. Similarly, this observation extends to the choice of algorithms, necessitating the exploration and incorporation of diverse algorithms to achieve improved model performance.

Table 5 also presents validation data of MOOC2 but focuses specifically on the prediction performance of the SRL factor in terms of recall. We observe in Table 5 that the SRL factor, combined with other self-reported features, seems a good predictor in terms of recall when LR and SVM algorithms are used.

Table 5. SRL factor performance on MOOC2 (test) data, balanced.

Features	Alg.	Oversampling Method, k = 5	Roc_auc	Acc.	Prec.	Rec.	f1
SRL, MOOC experience, UseOfChat	LR	ADASYN	0.61	0.50	0.17	0.77	0.28
SRL, MOOC experience	LR	ADASYN, Borderline-SMOTE1	0.64	0.59	0.19	0.71	0.30
SRL, MOOC experience	LR	SMOTE	0.63	0.57	0.19	0.71	0.29
SRL, Education	SVM	ADASYN	0.61	0.54	0.17	0.71	0.28
SRL, Programming experience	DT	SMOTE	0.66	0.66	0.22	0.65	0.33
SRL, Programming experience	NB	Borderline-SMOTE2	0.65	0.65	0.21	0.65	0.32
SRL, Intention	LR	Borderline-SMOTE2	0.62	0.60	0.19	0.65	0.29
SRL	kNN	SMOTE	0.61	0.62	0.19	0.59	0.28
SRL	LR	ADASYN, SMOTE	0.57	0.55	0.16	0.59	0.25
SRL	LR	Borderline-SMOTE1	0.57	0.56	0.16	0.59	0.25

4. Discussion

We utilize MOOC data to examine the dropout predictive performance of five classic classification ML algorithms under different oversampling techniques (e.g., ADASYN, SMOTE, Borderline-SMOTE1, and Borderline-SMOTE2, for k = 5 neighbors) and evaluation metrics. We also investigate the impact on the performance of self-reported SRL data by students and other popular MOOC features. Using the Python/sci-kit version 0.24.1 ecosystem, we perform predictive modeling on the data from MOOC1 by applying the NB, LR, SVM, DT, and kNN algorithms. We evaluate the performance of these models in predicting dropout in another similar (MOOC2) dataset.

Oversampling may significantly improve the performance of the models in terms of recall. kNN on the Employment feature and NB, LR on UseOfChatTools achieve excellent recall performance, the latter under particular oversampling techniques. Therefore, employing different oversampling methods and classic ML algorithms is useful to compare performance and identify the best combinations for the specific dataset. Intention to Participate, Education, and Experience features (MOOC, Python, Programming) contribute to predictive performance. SRL's contribution to MOOC dropout prediction performance emerges with LR and SVM algorithms in terms of recall (maximum value according to Table 5: 0.77). SRL factor as a sole feature yielded moderate recall values (0.59), but, combined with other, easily provided data, performs better.

Research Question 1: The datasets of the two Massive Open Online Courses (MOOCs) exhibited significant class imbalances, necessitating the utilization of oversampling techniques to enhance the predictive capabilities of the algorithms. Notably, the employment of a combination of principal component analysis (PCA) and an oversampling method emerged as the most influential factor contributing to the overall performance of all algorithms when employing readily available features such as employment status, frequency of chat tool usage, gender, education level, prior experiences, and intentions. An intriguing observation from our findings is that no discernible pattern emerged favoring one oversampling method over others, confirming the literature of imbalanced techniques comparison. This suggests that the choice of the appropriate oversampling technique may depend on the specific characteristics of the dataset under investigation. Consequently, we advocate for the adoption of diverse oversampling methods and algorithms to better accommodate the heterogeneity inherent in different datasets.

Our investigation further revealed that all algorithms demonstrated commendable performance in terms of recall values. Particularly, the k-nearest neighbors algorithm exhibited exceptional recall for employment-related features, while Naive Bayes and logistic regression excelled in capturing the frequency of chat tool usage. These outcomes indicate the efficacy of the selected algorithms in identifying potential dropout cases, especially concerning specific predictive aspects.

In conclusion, our study contributes valuable insights into the performance of classic predictive models in the context of dropout prediction, shedding light on the interplay between oversampling techniques and algorithm selection. Our findings are consistent with the literature on imbalance methods comparison and the existence of a variety of results in the prediction performance, indicating the need to examine different imbalance techniques (e.g., [49]). By embracing a diverse range of oversampling methods and algorithms, researchers can capitalize on the strengths of different approaches and improve the accuracy and robustness of their predictive models for dropout identification in MOOCs.

Research Question 2: The discussion of the second research question, which aims to identify the important predictors for students' MOOC dropout, yielded significant findings through the incorporation of readily available student features. Notably, variables such as self-reported employment status emerged as crucial indicators in predicting dropout rates, with the utilization of kNN (k-nearest neighbors) and variables such as UseOfChat with the utilization of LR (logistic regression), and NB (Naive Bayes) algorithms resulting in highly prediction performance, particularly in terms of recall. On the other hand, the NB algorithm exhibited enhanced performance when specific oversampling methods were applied, indicating its sensitivity to the data distribution and the potential to be more effective under certain conditions.

Moreover, the utilization of easily accessible student profile attributes, including experiences, gender, education level, and intention to participate, also proved to be valuable in predicting MOOC dropout rates. These attributes contributed to commendable recall rates when employing various traditional machine learning classification algorithms in conjunction with appropriate oversampling methodologies.

The significance of these findings lies in their practical implications for MOOC platform providers and educators. By identifying the key predictors of dropout, interventions can be designed and implemented to mitigate attrition rates effectively. For instance, targeted support and tailored interventions can be offered to students with specific employment statuses or chat tool usage patterns, thereby fostering a supportive learning environment and increasing the likelihood of course completion.

Research Question 3: The present study aimed to investigate the impact of the self-regulated learning (SRL) factor, as determined through self-reported student data, on the performance of dropout prediction. Our investigation focused on addressing the third research question, which sought to explore the potential contribution of the SRL factor to the predictive accuracy of dropout prediction models.

The discussion of our research findings indicates that the self-reported student self-regulated learning (SRL) factor, when combined with other widely recognized self-reported features, has demonstrated considerable predictive power in terms of recall when utilized with the LR and SVM algorithms. The inclusion of the SRL factor as a predictor offers valuable insights into the dynamics of dropout prediction.

5. Conclusions

This study addresses the challenging problem of early MOOC dropout prediction, which has implications for student retention and success, considering the significant issue of mitigating the imbalanced problem when training an ML model for dropout prediction. We explored a variety of oversampling techniques and classic supervised ML algorithms to compare performance using various evaluation metrics and identify the best combinations for the specific dataset. We also examined the factors that contribute to the early prediction of MOOC dropout in order to identify and support at-risk students. We investigated the self-reported SRL factor as well as various other prominent features of MOOCs as potential indicators of early stage dropout prediction.

The main conclusions are: (1) prominent predictors, including employment status, frequency of chat tool usage, prior subject-related experiences, gender, education, and willingness to participate, exhibit remarkable efficacy in achieving high to excellent recall performance, particularly when specific combinations of algorithms and oversampling methods are applied, (2) self-reported SRL factor, combined with easily provided/self-reported features, performed well as a predictor in terms of recall when LR and SVM algorithms were employed, (3) it is crucial to test diverse classification machine learning algorithms and oversampling methods in predictive modeling.

Researchers in the MOOC domain are suggested to consider thoughtfully the imbalance issue at the pre-processing stage and employ different imbalance mitigation techniques to overcome it, even of the same general category (in our study, oversampling) as we confirmed the literature of imbalanced techniques comparison about the existence of a variety of results in the context of MOOC dropout prediction performance.

Our results also suggest that the self-reported SRL factor contributes significantly to the accuracy of dropout prediction models. However, there is room for further enhancement and refinement of predictive capabilities by delving deeper into the identification of the SRL factor. For instance, complementing self-reported data with trace data could yield more precise and comprehensive insights into students' self-regulated learning behaviors.

6. Limitations and Future Research

The present study acknowledges certain limitations that warrant consideration. Firstly, the algorithms' hyperparameters were employed with default settings, and we did not explore their optimization for the specific dataset. Consequently, there exists potential for further investigation into fine-tuning the algorithms' performance to enhance predictive accuracy and robustness.

It is crucial to recognize that this research constitutes a case study centered on a specific Massive Open Online Course (MOOC) offering. The investigation focused on the subject of "Python for non-programmers" and was conducted in a particular language. As a result, generalizability beyond this specific context should be approached with caution, and caution must be exercised when extending the findings to other MOOCs or diverse academic domains.

Another important consideration is that the data obtained from questionnaires primarily provide insights into students' perceptions regarding their utilization of self-regulated learning (SRL) strategies. While valuable for understanding student perspectives, such self-reported data may not fully capture the actual SRL behaviors demonstrated by the students. Particularly noteworthy is the fact that the introductory questionnaire was administered early in the MOOC, potentially rendering the responses more reflective of behavioral intentions rather than realized SRL practices.

While the current findings contribute valuable insights into the predictive potential of the self-reported SRL factor, this research could be extended in several ways. To overcome this limitation and gain a more accurate understanding of the SRL factor, future research may consider employing a combination of trace data and self-referential information. The use of a shorter questionnaire, possibly targeting specific, effective strategies (dimensions) of SRL in the MOOC context, could be investigated and contribute to adaptive scaffolding research. This comprehensive approach could provide a more nuanced and reliable assessment of students' self-regulatory practices throughout the duration of the course. Future studies might explore the integration of additional factors, such as socio-economic background and prior academic performance, to further enhance the accuracy and robustness of dropout prediction models. Additionally, employing more advanced machine learning techniques (e.g., deep learning), employing a variety of imbalance mitigation techniques as well as exploring the use of longitudinal data could lead to more sophisticated and precise predictions.

Notwithstanding these limitations, the present study offers valuable insights into the role of the self-reported SRL factor within the specific context of the investigated MOOC. It provides a foundation for further explorations in the realm of dropout prediction and the design of tailored interventions to support student success in online learning environments. As the field of educational data mining and learning analytics progresses, more advanced techniques and larger datasets can be leveraged to refine and expand upon these findings, thus fostering advancements in the understanding and application of SRL strategies for enhanced educational outcomes.

Author Contributions: Methodology, T.K.C.; Writing—original draft, G.P. and T.K.C.; Writing—review & editing, G.P., T.K.C. and S.N.D.; Supervision, G.P. and S.N.D. All authors have read and agreed to the published version of the manuscript.

Funding: This research received no external funding.

Data Availability Statement: The data presented in this study are available on request from the corresponding author. The data are not publicly available due to privacy restrictions.

Conflicts of Interest: The authors declare no conflict of interest.

References

1. Hsu, S.Y. An Experimental Study of Self-Regulated Learning Strategies Application in MOOCs. Ph.D. Thesis, Teachers College, Columbia University, New York, NY, USA, 2021.
2. Gardner, J.; Brooks, C. Student success prediction in MOOCs. *User Model. User-Adapt. Interact.* **2018**, *28*, 127–203.
3. Ihantola, P.; Fronza, I.; Mikkonen, T.; Noponen, M.; Hellas, A. Deadlines and MOOCs: How Do Students Behave in MOOCs with and without Deadlines. In Proceedings of the 2020 IEEE Frontiers in Education Conference (FIE), Uppsala, Sweden, 21–24 October 2020; IEEE: Piscateville, NJ, USA, 2020; pp. 1–9.
4. Chuang, I.; Ho, A. HarvardX and MITx: Four years of open online courses-fall 2012-summer 2016. 2016. Available online: https://papers.ssrn.com/sol3/papers.cfm?abstract_id=2889436 (accessed on 1 June 2023).
5. Kizilcec, R.F.; Schneider, E. Motivation as a lens to understand online learners: Toward data-driven design with the OLEI scale. *ACM Trans. Comput.-Hum. Interact. (TOCHI)* **2015**, *22*, 1–24.
6. Kizilcec, R.F.; Pérez-Sanagustín, M.; Maldonado, J.J. Self-regulated learning strategies predict learner behavior and goal attainment in Massive Open Online Courses. *Comput. Educ.* **2017**, *104*, 18–33.
7. Zheng, S.; Rosson, M.B.; Shih, P.C.; Carroll, J.M. Designing MOOCs as interactive places for collaborative learning. In Proceedings of the Second (2015) ACM Conference on Learning@ Scale, Vancouver, BC, Canada, 14–18 March 2015; pp. 343–346.
8. Jordan, K. Initial trends in enrolment and completion of massive open online courses. *Int. Rev. Res. Open Distrib. Learn.* **2014**, *15*, 133–160. [CrossRef]
9. Peng, D.; Aggarwal, G. Modeling mooc dropouts. *Entropy* **2015**, *10*, 1–5.
10. Feng, W.; Tang, J.; Liu, T.X. Understanding dropouts in MOOCs. *Proc. AAAI Conf. Artif. Intell.* **2019**, *33*, 517–524.
11. Eriksson, T.; Adawi, T.; Stöhr, C. "Time is the bottleneck": A qualitative study exploring why learners drop out of MOOCs. *J. Comput. High. Educ.* **2017**, *29*, 133–146. [CrossRef]
12. Reich, J. MOOC completion and retention in the context of student intent. *EDUCAUSE Rev. Online* 2014.
13. Lepp, M.; Luik, P.; Palts, T.; Papli, K.; Suviste, R.; Säde, M.; Tõnisson, E. MOOC in programming: A success story. In Proceedings of the International Conference on e-Learning, Belgrade, Serbia, 28–29 September 2017; pp. 138–147.
14. Dalipi, F.; Imran, A.S.; Kastrati, Z. MOOC dropout prediction using machine learning techniques: Review and research challenges. In Proceedings of the 2018 IEEE Global Engineering Education Conference (EDUCON), Santa Cruz de Tenerife, Spain, 17–20 April 2018; IEEE: Piscateville, NJ, USA, 2018; pp. 1007–1014.
15. Zheng, S.; Rosson, M.B.; Shih, P.C.; Carroll, J.M. Understanding student motivation, behaviors and perceptions in MOOCs. In Proceedings of the 18th ACM Conference on Computer Supported Cooperative Work and Social Computing, Vancouver, BC, Canada, 13–18 March 2015; pp. 1882–1895.
16. Hone, K.S.; El Said, G.R. Exploring the factors affecting MOOC retention: A survey study. *Comput. Educ.* **2016**, *98*, 157–168.
17. Zhang, J. Can MOOCs be interesting to students? An experimental investigation from regulatory focus perspective. *Comput. Educ.* **2016**, *95*, 340–351.
18. Dass, S.; Gary, K.; Cunningham, J. Predicting student dropout in self-paced MOOC course using random forest model. *Information* **2021**, *12*, 476. [CrossRef]
19. Herrmannova, D.; Hlosta, M.; Kuzilek, J.; Zdrahal, Z. Evaluating weekly predictions of at-risk students at the open university: Results and issues. In Proceedings of the EDEN 2015 Annual Conference Expanding Learning Scenarios: Opening out the Educational Landscape, Barcelona, Spain, 9–12 June 2015.
20. Callan, G.L.; Longhurst, D.; Ariotti, A.; Bundock, K. Settings, exchanges, and events: The SEE framework of self-regulated learning supportive practices. *Psychol. Sch.* **2021**, *58*, 773–788. [CrossRef]
21. Sebesta, A.J.; Bray Speth, E. How should I study for the exam? Self-regulated learning strategies and achievement in introductory biology. *CBE—Life Sci. Educ.* **2017**, *16*, ar30. [CrossRef] [PubMed]
22. Zimmerman, B.J. Self-efficacy: An essential motive to learn. *Contemp. Educ. Psychol.* **2000**, *25*, 82–91. [CrossRef] [PubMed]
23. Zimmerman, B.J. Investigating self-regulation and motivation: Historical background, methodological developments, and future prospects. *Am. Educ. Res. J.* **2008**, *45*, 166–183. [CrossRef]
24. Jansen, R.S.; van Leeuwen, A.; Janssen, J.; Conijn, R.; Kester, L. Supporting learners' self-regulated learning in Massive Open Online Courses. *Comput. Educ.* **2020**, *146*, 103771. [CrossRef]
25. Zimmerman, B. Becoming learner: Self-regulated overview. *Theory Into Pract.* **2002**, *41*, 64–70. [CrossRef]
26. Winne, P.H. Learning analytics for self-regulated learning. In *Handbook of Learning Analytics*; SOLAR, Society for Learning Analytics and Research: New York, NY, USA, 2017; pp. 241–249.
27. Cunningham, J.A. Predicting Student Success in a Self-Paced Mathematics MOOC. Ph.D. Thesis, Arizona State University, Tempe, AZ, USA, 2017.
28. Mourdi, Y.; Sadgal, M.; El Kabtane, H.; Fathi, W.B. A machine learning-based methodology to predict learners' dropout, success or failure in MOOCs. *Int. J. Web Inf. Syst.* **2019**, *15*, 489–509. [CrossRef]
29. Moreno-Marcos, P.M.; Munoz-Merino, P.J.; Maldonado-Mahauad, J.; Perez-Sanagustin, M.; Alario-Hoyos, C.; Kloos, C.D. Temporal analysis for dropout prediction using self-regulated learning strategies in self-paced MOOCs. *Comput. Educ.* **2020**, *145*, 103728. [CrossRef]
30. Kuzilek, J.; Zdrahal, Z.; Fuglik, V. Student success prediction using student exam behaviour. *Future Gener. Comput. Syst.* **2021**, *125*, 661–671. [CrossRef]

31. Wan, H.; Liu, K.; Yu, Q.; Gao, X. Pedagogical intervention practices: Improving learning engagement based on early prediction. *IEEE Trans. Learn. Technol.* **2019**, *12*, 278–289. [CrossRef]
32. Kuzilek, J.; Hlosta, M.; Herrmannova, D.; Zdrahal, Z.; Vaclavek, J.; Wolff, A. OU Analyse: Analysing at-risk students at The Open University. *Learn. Anal. Rev.* **2015**, *LAK15-1*, 1–16.
33. Yeomans, M.; Reich, J. Planning prompts increase and forecast course completion in massive open online courses. In Proceedings of the Seventh International Learning Analytics and Knowledge Conference, Vancouver, BC, Canada, 13–17 March 2017; pp. 464–473.
34. Maldonado-Mahauad, J.; Pérez-Sanagustín, M.; Kizilcec, R.F.; Morales, N.; Munoz-Gama, J. Mining theory-based patterns from Big Data: Identifying self-regulated learning strategies in Massive Open Online Courses. *Comput. Hum. Behav.* **2018**, *80*, 179–196. [CrossRef]
35. Nagrecha, S.; Dillon, J.Z.; Chawla, N.V. MOOC dropout prediction: Lessons learned from making pipelines interpretable. In Proceedings of the 26th International Conference on World Wide Web Companion, Perth, Australia, 3–7 April 2017; pp. 351–359.
36. Bajer, D.; Zonć, B.; Dudjak, M.; Martinović, G. Performance analysis of SMOTE-based oversampling techniques when dealing with data imbalance. In Proceedings of the 2019 International Conference on Systems, Signals and Image Processing (IWSSIP), Osijek, Croatia, 5–7 June 2019; IEEE: Piscateville, NJ, USA, 2019; pp. 265–271.
37. Buraimoh, E.; Ajoodha, R.; Padayachee, K. Importance of Data Re-Sampling and Dimensionality Reduction in Predicting Students' Success. In Proceedings of the 2021 International Conference on Electrical, Communication, and Computer Engineering (ICECCE), Kuala Lumpur, Malaysia, 12–13 June 2021; IEEE: Piscateville, NJ, USA, 2021; pp. 1–6.
38. Fei, M.; Yeung, D.Y. Temporal models for predicting student dropout in massive open online courses. In Proceedings of the 2015 IEEE International Conference on Data Mining Workshop (ICDMW), Atlantic City, NJ, USA, 14–17 November 2015; IEEE: Piscateville, NJ, USA, 2015; pp. 256–263.
39. Al-Shabandar, R.; Hussain, A.; Laws, A.; Keight, R.; Lunn, J.; Radi, N. Machine learning approaches to predict learning outcomes in Massive open online courses. In Proceedings of the 2017 International Joint Conference on Neural Networks (IJCNN), Anchorage, AK, USA, 14–19 May 2017; IEEE: Piscateville, NJ, USA, 2017; pp. 713–720.
40. Barandela, R.; Valdovinos, R.M.; Sánchez, J.S.; Ferri, F.J. The imbalanced training sample problem: Under or over sampling? In Proceedings of the Structural, Syntactic, and Statistical Pattern Recognition: Joint IAPR International Workshops, SSPR 2004 and SPR 2004, Lisbon, Portugal, 18–20 August 2004; Springer: Berlin/Heidelberg, Germany, 2004; pp. 806–814.
41. Mulyani, E.; Hidayah, I.; Fauziati, S. Dropout prediction optimization through smote and ensemble learning. In Proceedings of the 2019 International Seminar on Research of Information Technology and Intelligent Systems (ISRITI), Yogyakarta, Indonesia, 5–6 December 2019; IEEE: Piscateville, NJ, USA, 2019; pp. 516–521.
42. Revathy, M.; Kamalakkannan, S.; Kavitha, P. Machine Learning based Prediction of Dropout Students from the Education University using SMOTE. In Proceedings of the 2022 4th International Conference on Smart Systems and Inventive Technology (ICSSIT), Tirunelveli, India, 20–22 January 2022; IEEE: Piscateville, NJ, USA, 2022; pp. 1750–1758.
43. Mduma, N.; Kalegele, K.; Machuve, D. Machine learning approach for reducing students dropout rates. International Journal of Advanced Computer Research. 9. 10.19101/IJACR.2018.839045. 2019. Available online: https://www.researchgate.net/publication/333016151_Machine_Learning_Approach_for_Reducing_Students_Dropout_Rates (accessed on 1 June 2023).
44. Han, H.; Wang, W.Y.; Mao, B.H. Borderline-SMOTE: A new over-sampling method in imbalanced data sets learning. In *International Conference on Intelligent Computing*; Springer: Berlin/Heidelberg, Germany, 2005; pp. 878–887.
45. Rahman, M.M.; Davis, D.N. Addressing the class imbalance problem in medical datasets. *Int. J. Mach. Learn. Comput.* **2013**, *3*, 224. [CrossRef]
46. Shelke, M.S.; Deshmukh, P.R.; Shandilya, V.K. A review on imbalanced data handling using undersampling and oversampling technique. *Int. J. Recent Trends Eng. Res* **2017**, *3*, 444–449.
47. Chawla, N.V.; Bowyer, K.W.; Hall, L.O.; Kegelmeyer, W.P. Smote: Synthetic minority over-sampling technique. *J. Artif. Intell. Res.* **2002**, *16*, 321–357. [CrossRef]
48. He, H.; Bai, Y.; Garcia, E.A.; Li, S. ADASYN: Adaptive synthetic sampling approach for imbalanced learning. In Proceedings of the 2008 IEEE International Joint Conference on Neural Networks (IEEE World Congress on Computational Intelligence), Hong Kong, China, 1–8 June 2008; IEEE: Piscateville, NJ, USA, 2008; pp. 1322–1328.
49. Brandt, J.; Lanzén, E. A comparative review of SMOTE and ADASYN in imbalanced data classification. (Dissertation). 2021. Available online: https://urn.kb.se/resolve?urn=urn:nbn:se:uu:diva-432162. (accessed on 1 June 2023).
50. Brooks, C.; Thompson, C. Predictive modelling in teaching and learning. In *Handbook of Learning Analytics*; SOLAR, Society for Learning Analytics and Research: New York, NY, USA, 2017; pp. 61–68.
51. Demetriadis, S.; Tegos, S.; Psathas, G.; Tsiatsos, T.; Weinberger, A.; Caballé, S.; Dimitriadis, Y.; Sánchez, G.E.; Papadopoulos, M.; Karakostas, A. Conversational agents as group-teacher interaction mediators in MOOCs. In Proceedings of the 2018 Learning With MOOCS (LWMOOCS), Madrid, Spain, 26–28 September 2018; pp. 43–46.
52. Tegos, S.; Demetriadis, S.; Papadopoulos, P.M.; Weinberger, A. Conversational agents for academically productive talk: A comparison of directed and undirected agent interventions. *Int. J. Comput.-Support. Collab. Learn.* **2016**, *11*, 417–440. [CrossRef]
53. Stein, R.M.; Allione, G. *Mass attrition: An analysis of drop out from a Principles of Microeconomics MOOC*; PIER Working Paper Archive 14-031; Penn Institute for Economic Research, Department of Economics, University of Pennsylvania: Philadelphia, PA, USA, 2014.

54. Haq, A.U.; Zhang, D.; Peng, H.; Rahman, S.U. Combining multiple feature-ranking techniques and clustering of variables for feature selection. *IEEE Access* **2019**, *7*, 151482–151492. [CrossRef]
55. Shohag, S.I.; Bakaul, M. A Machine Learning Approach to Detect Student Dropout at University. *Int. J. Adv. Trends Comput. Sci. Eng.* **2021**, *10*.
56. Holland, S.M. *Principal Components Analysis (PCA)*; Department of Geology, University of Georgia: Athens, GA, USA, 2008; pp. 30602–32501.
57. Mulla, G.A.; Demir, Y.; Hassan, M. Combination of PCA with SMOTE Oversampling for Classification of High-Dimensional Imbalanced Data. *Bitlis Eren Üniversitesi Fen Bilim. Derg.* **2021**, *10*, 858–869. [CrossRef]
58. Umer, R.; Susnjak, T.; Mathrani, A.; Suriadi, S. Prediction of students' dropout in MOOC environment. *Int. J. Knowl. Eng.* **2017**, *3*, 43–47. [CrossRef]
59. Pelánek, R. Metrics for Evaluation of Student Models. *J. Educ. Data Min.* **2015**, *7*, 1–19.

computers

MDPI

Article

Effect of Digital Game-Based Learning on Student Engagement and Motivation

Muhammad Nadeem *, Melinda Oroszlanyova and Wael Farag

College of Engineering and Technology, American University of the Middle East, Egaila 54200, Kuwait; melinda.oroszlanyova@aum.edu.kw (M.O.); wael.farag@aum.edu.kw (W.F.)
* Correspondence: muhammad.nadeem@aum.edu.kw

Abstract: Currently, academia is grappling with a significant problem—a lack of engagement. Humankind has gone too far into exploring entertainment options, while the education system has not really kept up. Millennials love playing games, and this addiction can be used to engage and motivate them in the learning process. This study examines the effect of digital game-based learning on student engagement and motivation levels and the gender differences in online learning settings. This study was conducted in two distinct phases. A game-based and traditional online quizzing tools were used to compare levels of engagement and motivation, as well as to assess the additional parameter of gender difference. During the first phase of the study, 276 male and female undergraduate students were recruited from Sophomore Seminar classes, and 101 participated in the survey, of which 83 were male and 18 were female. In the second phase, 126 participants were recruited, of which 107 (63 females and 44 males) participated in the anonymous feedback surveys. The results revealed that digital game-based learning has a more positive impact on student engagement and motivation compared to traditional online activities. The incorporation of a leaderboard as a gaming element in the study was found to positively impact the academic performance of certain students, but it could also demotivate some students. Furthermore, female students generally showed a slightly higher level of enjoyment toward the games compared to male students, but they did not prefer a comparison with other students as much as male students did. The favorable response from students toward digital game-based activities indicates that enhancing instruction with such activities will not only make learning an enjoyable experience for learners but also enhance their engagement.

Keywords: gamification; digital game-based learning; engagement; pedagogy design; motivation; leaderboard; emerging technologies

1. Introduction

The world of academia is currently facing a serious crisis—a crisis of engagement [1–4]. Humankind has gone too far into exploring entertainment options, while the education system has not really kept up and has barely progressed beyond 1900. The traditional methods used for engagement no longer hold our attention the way they once did because we have become used to so much engagement per second. This situation is exacerbated when teaching online or in large classes at universities, where there is little or no interaction between students and teachers. COVID-19 compelled the academic sector to embrace online learning as a means of survival [4]. This abrupt shift left instructors stranded on how to engage students in this mode of setting and facilitate learning. Many instructors faced difficulty in engaging students in a meaningful way during the online delivery [5]. This might be due to distractions, lack of supervision, and nonacademic use of digital devices mainly for interacting with social media and playing games. Furthermore, the lack of learning of interaction with the teacher and in-person loss of learning is sometimes critical for a student in need of assistance. Strategies such as scaffolding the learning material, synchronous class meetings, use of breakout rooms, use of quizzing programs, and polling helped overcome the pyramid of challenges posed by remote teaching [6]. The implementation of these strategies necessitates the employment of technology; fortunately, numerous applications are at our disposal. The integration of online activities has been highly effective in fostering student engagement during in-person teaching, as this approach was previously uncommon for students and succeeded in capturing their attention [3,7,8]. Initially, online activities were instrumental in engaging students during the COVID-19 pandemic owing to their innovative nature. However, their appeal gradually diminished as these methods became routine, resulting in a decline in motivation and making it challenging for students to concentrate on course content, whether in online or in-person classes. Therefore, it is crucial to explore alternative digital technologies, such as AI-generated applications [9], chatbots [10], podcasting [11], interactive whiteboards, augmented reality [12,13], and gamification [14]. Many of these technologies have been explored extensively, while others are emerging and not quite mature yet. AR and gamification are two relatively new technologies that have the potential to attract and engage students, thereby promoting active learning. The deployment of AI-generated applications has many ethical issues that need to be solved before they can be used freely in class. The value of interpersonal communication and human engagement in the classroom might be diminished by the usage of chatbots. Podcasting is not an active method, and interactive whiteboards are not only expensive, but also fragile, and their use is problematic in large classrooms, especially for backbenchers. AR is a relatively new technology, but it has its own issues which make it hard to implement in the classroom. It requires a device with higher computation power, a high-speed internet connection, long battery life, and greater data storage capacity. Furthermore, there is a lack of tools or apps that can quickly be adopted for instruction design. On the other hand, with the increasing popularity of video games across all age groups, digital game-based learning can prove to be a valuable tool in energizing students and encouraging active learning in the classroom. Game-based or gamified activities have been utilized for a considerable period to create courses that not only make learning enjoyable but also engage and motivate students in both traditional and online learning environments [15]. Furthermore, playing games also improves decision-making, and those who play action-based video games make judgments 25% faster than the average person while maintaining the same level of accuracy. The gamers make decisions and take actions up to six times per second, which is four times quicker than the average person [16]. In the future, the immersive and interactive elements of gamification may be improved with the help of AR and VR technologies, which also opens up new opportunities and problems. We believe that augmented reality game-based learning (ARGBL) will become increasingly relevant in technology-enhanced learning as the above-mentioned issues are resolved.

Digital game-based learning involves linking subject content to gameplay, enabling students to apply their knowledge in real-world scenarios, thereby making learning more engaging and enjoyable. Through game-based activities, students are presented with challenges and obstacles that motivate them to work harder, increasing their sense of accomplishment and self-esteem upon overcoming these obstacles. Additionally, games involve social interactions with other players, allowing students to establish relationships and a sense of community, which can be crucial in online learning environments where students may feel isolated [17]. Most importantly, games are entertaining, and, when students enjoy themselves, they are more likely to be motivated to continue learning. Overall, game-based activities can be a highly effective way to engage and motivate students, enabling them to invest more in their learning and achieve better outcomes.

The incorporation of game-like characteristics into a non-game environment is referred to as gamification. The most commonly used gamification elements are points, badges, and leaderboards. Leaderboards are a vital component of game design and a powerful tool for motivating users through competition [18]. However, certain studies suggest that the use of leaderboards can demotivate students [19,20].

Game-based learning often requires specialized hardware or software, which can be expensive and time-consuming to set up and maintain. Technical issues such as glitches or system crashes can also interfere with learning and frustrate students [21]. If it is too tedious or expensive, then the instructor might not be motivated to implement them in the class. Therefore, instructors have to analyze factors such as cost, developing tasks, and availability of digital resources before using games in the classroom. In addition, games should be compatible with the course curriculum and learning goals. The games that educators choose to use must be pertinent and successful in reaching learning objectives [22]. Considering these arguments, we enhanced the online teaching instruction with simple game-based activities implementing sorting games such as Vortex for exploring student engagement and motivation. Furthermore, gender is one of the many factors that can influence an individual's perception of game-based learning, but it is not the only factor. Research has shown that both males and females can have positive perceptions of game-based learning, but the specific games and learning outcomes that appeal to each gender may vary. Therefore, it is important to explore the differences in gender perception toward Vortex-based quizzes.

To sum up, research has shown that, when students have ownership of an educational tool, it can enhance their attitude, motivation, interest, and learning outcomes [23]. Many online activities and games provide opportunities for students to take control, which is why they often return to these games to practice. Additionally, these activities require minimal teacher intervention, as the game itself usually provides answers or results. This promotes students' self-reliance when using digital resources and minimizes disruptions to their work.

1.1. Research Question

The goal of this study is to ascertain how using Vortex as a game in a non-game learning setting has an effect from the viewpoints of university undergrads. Specifically, it examines student motivation and engagement levels, as well as gender differences, when using a digital game-based quiz tool and a conventional tool. The study was conducted in two phases, where two different digital platforms were used in the first phase to compare engagement and motivation as well as the impact of the leaderboard. We used a game-based platform only during the second phase to examine gender differences. Inspired by Keller's motivational design process, the lecture component of an online course was redesigned to include game-based learning activities. Students can complete these activities in class using personal devices. The students were provided time to complete the activity at the beginning, middle, and end of the lecture. This study answers the following research questions:

- RQ 1: How are students' engagement and motivation affected by the usage of game-based activities?
- RQ 2: What is the impact of the leaderboard on student motivation and behavior?
- RQ 3: Do males or females have the same perception toward game-based activities?

1.2. Literature Review

More than 2.6 billion people enjoy video or computer games worldwide, and the number is growing daily. For instance, according to the NPD Group (NPD, 2019), the number of individuals playing computer games increased by 6% between 2018 and 2019. Every other person aged 6 to 64 who lived in the five main European nations of France, Italy, Germany, Spain, and the UK played video games, according to statistics gathered by the Interactive Software Federation of Europe [24]. The information showed that players of all ages enjoyed playing games on the computer, these are especially popular among young people. Among young poll participants, the percentage of players reached 70% (15–25 years old). The typical player's weekly gaming time was estimated to be 9.5 h, and 47% of all players who took part in the survey identified as female. The Statistical Office of the European Union [25] carried out a larger poll in 2019 that covered the majority of

European nations. According to this survey's data, which was gathered in 2018, 33% of all individuals between the ages of 16 and 74 had played video games.

Several educational and psychological theories support the use of game-based learning. Constructivism theory suggests that students learn the best when they actively construct their knowledge through experiences and interactions [26]. Games provide an opportunity for students to explore, experiment, and make decisions that impact the outcomes of the game. This also helps them to construct their knowledge in a meaningful way. The experiential learning theory [27] emphasizes the importance of direct experience and reflection in the learning process. Games provide an opportunity for students to experience different scenarios and to reflect on their decisions, leading to a deeper understanding of the contents being learned. The flow theory [28] describes a state of deep engagement and enjoyment that can be achieved when a person is completely immersed in an activity. It suggests creating a balance between skill level and challenge to avoid anxiety and continue the flow of the game.

Many pieces of research have shown that most people enjoy playing games, and this enjoyment can lead to an increase in engagement and motivation during educational activities [29]. The concept of gamification has gained extensive attention in recent years as a possible way to make learning more enjoyable and engaging. Gamification involves incorporating game-like structures, such as points, badges, and leaderboards, into educational activities to increase motivation and engagement. Several studies in the academic literature have emphasized the advantages of incorporating gamification into the educational process, such as an enhancement of students' capacity to acquire new competencies, attendance, motivation, and participation in undergraduate course activities by using points, leaderboards, levels, and badges [30–33]. Although various gamification methods have been applied and implemented in educational contexts during the last decade to achieve certain goals, their effect on student performance and motivation is still questionable [18,19,34–36].

Many of the existing student response systems (SRSs) have incorporated game features to boost student engagement such as Space Race games in Socrative [37]. Kahoot! was the first to offer a gaming experience using game design concepts from the theory of intrinsic motivation [38] and game flow [39]. It has been used in a variety of ways to enhance teaching/learning in a fun and interactive way for engaging students and make learning more enjoyable and memorable [40–47]. Although these SRSs can be a useful tool for promoting engagement and assessing knowledge in the classroom, they cannot be used outside the classroom due to their synchronous nature as they always require a facilitator. In addition, they are time-consuming and have a limit on participants. Using such tools is fun but hampers the learning process. Therefore, they are suitable for occasional use but not as permanent instruction methods. The Vortex sorting game, on the other hand, is simple and has been used for improving vocabulary which is crucial for learning new topics [48].

A strong conclusion that arises from literature is the importance of the context. A contextualization strategy is generally thought to result in improved comprehension. Learners respond differently to the same gamification setup; effectiveness in one context may not be the same in another context. This vagueness about the use of gaming elements in educational settings makes it important to stress context-specific studies for a better understanding of its impact on student performance and motivation [35,49–52].

Leaderboards are the most commonly used method for course gamification [18]. Usefulness and relative easiness of setup are some of the apparent reasons for their frequent use. Leaderboards provide comparative feedback to the students of a gamified course about their performance against other students using points and ranks. Many studies have reported that leaderboards can positively impact the achievements of learners [18,53,54], engagement [30], and the amount of completed work [21,36,55], while maintaining performance [56] and course attendance [57]. While gamifying a course with leaderboards, the aforementioned favorable verdicts come with some concerns that need to be handled. These concerns can lead to affecting student participation, possibly even resulting in high drop-out rates if the course leaderboards can only sustain engagement for a short time period [18,58]. If students focus on achieving the extrinsic goals offered by a leaderboard instead of the assigned tasks, this could distract the student learning and result in low-quality work [21,56,59].

The competitive nature of a leaderboard may attract higher-performing competitive students but can backfire with low-performing students [18,32,33,53,60]. Short-term performance gains from an extrinsically rewarding leaderboard may come at the cost of students' intrinsic motivation [19,56,58,60]. The authors in [19,56] reported a significant improvement in the learning performance of students in the gamified condition in programming and language courses. The latter also discovered that the students' focus on the extrinsic rewards used by the leaderboard uplifted their performance until the point they achieved the threshold and diminished consequently. They also pointed out that the use of points, rank, and forced social comparison to control behavior resulted in a shift from intrinsic to extrinsic motivation. However, the authors of [61] suggested otherwise, stating that incorporating competitive gaming elements, such as badges and leaderboards, may hurt low-performance students.

Students' personalities [62] and genders [22] affect their perception of game elements in an educational context, and gender disparities can impact students' academic performance. For instance, the authors of [63] discovered that female students excelled more than male students in a particular learning task. Likewise, the authors of [17] found that female students had higher academic achievements compared to male students. Despite both genders having comparable levels of intellectual capacity, this outcome was attributed to variations in their personality traits. It was shown by the authors of [64] that feedback might be more helpful to females than males, while less extroverted students may find progress bars more useful than those who are more extroverted and see the value in badges in gamified courses than their counterparts.

1.3. Vortex Sorting Game

Schwabe and Goth defined the criteria for creating gamifying instruction material to engage them in a meaningful way [65]. They underlined six structural elements that should characterize the game to achieve the goals in a fun way: rules, objectives and goals, outcome and feedback, competition and challenges, interaction, and story. We adhered to these criteria when selecting the game, called Vortex, for integration with teaching activities.

Vortex is the most recent game template released by ClassTools for designing online games, in which participants must classify words or phrases into up to four categories. When students play a Vortex game, they must sort terms that appear on the screen as quickly as possible. This game has very simple rules which make it very easy for students to follow without any cognitive overloading. The objective is to familiarize the students with the vocabulary of technical terms, definitions, and key points of the topic as soon as a topic is covered. The goal is to engage the students with the course material, and this retrieval-based learning strategy helps students learn faster. It can also work as a multiple-choice question or true–false quiz, forcing the student to choose the right option only. This also provides immediate feedback to students on their learning, as wrong answers are not accepted by the game, and the music generated indicates that the student's response is wrong. This type of confirmatory feedback reduces ambiguity about the concepts learned and helps in the attainment of goals. The scores are based on how quickly and accurately the terms are sorted. This also provides feedback on their retention of knowledge as a low score indicates that the student did not make many mistakes, indicating that the student has a good grasp of the topic. The student is not only competing against their previous efforts but also their fellow students as the scores are displayed on the leaderboard. This not only poses a challenge but also creates a competitive environment. This creates an opportunity to interact and opens a channel of communication with fellow students—another important element of course design.

Students can play Vortex game-based quiz activities (GBQAs) asynchronously during lectures, at the end of the day, near assessment times, and during their free time reviewing the material. Moreover, Vortex is simple to use, develops activities easily and quickly, is free for instructors and students, is compatible with a wide range of devices, and is suitable for a variety of teaching and learning styles. Therefore, Vortex seems to offer great potential for involving and evaluating students while remaining simple to use, inexpensive, and adaptable. Digital devices such as smartphones, tablets, and laptops support Vortex-based formative assessment activities. These activities do not need the installation of any application and only require access to the Internet. A screenshot of the activity related to the topic of ethics is shown in Figure 1.

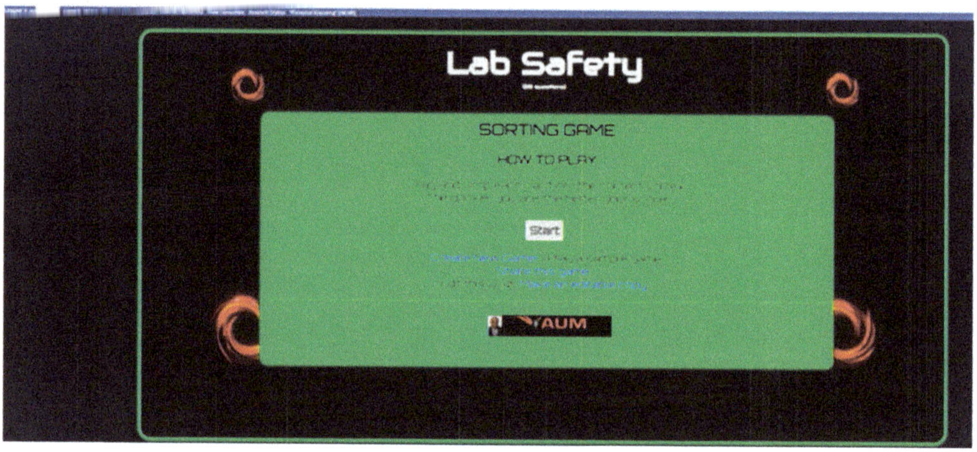

Figure 1. Screenshot of Vortex-based activity.

2. Materials and Methods

2.1. Research Subject

This study was conducted in two phases to achieve the objectives listed in the previous section. During the first phase, the research subject comprised over 276 students (aged 19–22 years) enrolled in five parallel classes of an undergraduate engineering seminar course taught by different instructors. This course was offered online during the spring semester of 2022 by the Department of Electrical Engineering, of which only 101 students participated in the survey, including both males (82.0%) and females (18.0%), and the majority of them belonged to the sophomore year. Similarly, more than 120 students registered for this course offered during the summer of 2022, and two parallel classes taught by the same teacher took part in the activities, of which 107 participated in the study, including both males (42.1%) and females (58.9%). It can be noted that a significantly higher number of students participated in the survey during the summer of 2022 because students take fewer courses during the relatively short summer semester and devote their time and effort to this course. In addition, this course does not have a final exam, meaning that students have more free time in the end and can afford to spend some time completing the survey. Furthermore, the instructor allocated time to complete the survey at the start and end of the lecture. The participants were under no obligation to participate in the research as part of their coursework, and it was completely voluntary. The objective was to explore the effect of game-based and gamified quizzes on student engagement and motivation. To promote acceptance and a judgment-free environment, student response systems were handled anonymously. Students had to complete the Vortex quiz activities using any name or ID number. The summer 2022 study was designed to examine gender differences in completing game-based tasks, and students were rewarded for completing activities, but no reward was offered for participating in the survey.

2.2. Study Design

This study is descriptive in nature and uses a survey research design to examine the status of transformation. The present study was conducted during the spring semester for sophomore students studying the "Electrical and Computer Engineering Sophomore Seminar" course toward a Bachelor of Electrical Engineering. This was borne out of the lecturer's (first author) desire to enhance the online lecture experience for engineering students with the overall goal of improving student engagement by providing active learning opportunities in the classroom. These activities can be referred to as competitive games as participants in competing games attempt to complete the task ahead of their opponents. These competition-based games are also called rousing games as they are used to energize students. Students can access these activities through the link provided on the course page on Moodle.

We based our study on the hypothesis that intrinsic motivation creates deeper engagement, which leads to deeper learning. Our focus was on motivating the students to engage with the learning material. Instrumental students pay more attention to the activities which can help them to improve their grades. In this context, students are less bothered to pay attention to such a course which does not help them in improving their GPA. It is a very challenging task to motivate the students to engage with the material in such a course, and this was the rationale behind the selection of this course for implementing game-based learning. This proposed weakness is actually the main strength of our study. If this instruction strategy proves successful in motivating and engaging students, then its success is guaranteed in a high-importance course.

2.3. Instruction Design

This study assesses the use of game-based and Moodle-based quiz activities (MBQAs) promoting active learning in the online setting of teaching. Game-based activities are created in accordance with Keller's [66] ARCS (attention, relevance, confidence, and satisfaction) model of motivation and self-determination theory (SDT) [67]. ARCS stresses that the teaching activities and materials must be matched with these four factors to improve the learning performance of the students and attain increased stimulation. Similarly, SDT is frequently used to comprehend human motivation in a variety of contexts, including games, employment, and education. According to SDT, people are most motivated when they feel in control of their conduct, when they are competent in what they do, and when they are linked to other people. Games that give players the chance to feel related, competent, and autonomous are more likely to be entertaining and increase player motivation. Individuals are less likely to be motivated when these requirements are not met, and they may also suffer from negative effects including stress, anxiety, and sadness. The GBQAs implemented in this study, shown in Table 1, are a relatively new experience for students which draws the attention of students' attention, piques their enthusiasm, and fosters a positive learning environment. These activities are related to the curriculum; they are played independently without intervention from the instructor, thus providing them with full control and resulting in confidence. Students feel satisfied when they answer a question correctly, finish an activity quickly, and see themselves performing better than their peers. The complexity of the topic, the timing, and the integration of an activity into a class were all taken into consideration when developing the activities. Each activity can be completed within one to three minutes, allowing it to incorporate more diverse activities without repetition and getting students bored.

A student's motivation is what propels them to act. The visible activity or proof of that motivation is engagement. Engagement requires motivation, yet successful engagement may also encourage students to remain motivated in the future. Meaningful engagement fosters deeper learning. These activities supplement the current instruction design, which is aligned with the course learning outcomes. Thus, completing these activities will help students in achieving the learning outcomes. In addition to being a goal in and of itself, student engagement in learning also serves as a vehicle for students to achieve successful academic outcomes [68]. We can also measure how helpful these activities were in achieving the learning outcome. We had data in the form of assessment grades as this course has six assessments covering one or two. These assessment grades could be an indication if the student achieved learning outcomes or not, but the literature does not recommend using assessment grades to assess the student's learning as a result of these activities. This issue can be addressed in future work.

Table 1. List of activities.

SR. #	Topic	Questions
A1	Plan of study	10
A2	Lab safety	25
A3	Cover letter writing	15
A4	Resume writing	12
A5	Professional ethics	21
A6	NSPE code	12
A7	EDP	20
A8	Making PowerPoint slides	17
A9	Learning strategies	12
A10	Writing report	20

means Serial Number in this Table.

2.4. Instrument

A short questionnaire comprising three parts was designed as a research instrument to collect data. The first part was designed to obtain demographic information from the participants. The second part used a five-point scale, ranging from strongly disagree (SD) to strongly agree (SA), to capture the opinions of the participants on 13 statements given in Table 2. The third part comprised open-ended questions to obtain the participants' unrestrained opinions. The first half of the questionnaire was focused on assessing engagement and motivation, and the second half was focused on the leaderboard. Q1 assessed the enjoyment imparted by the game. Q2, Q3, Q4, Q7, Q10, and Q11 assessed the perceived feeling of motivation, while Q3 and Q6 were a self-assessment of student learning. Q7–Q11 focused on assessing the impact of the leaderboard. Q12 and Q13 assessed students' engagement in and out of class. The reliability of the questionnaire calculated using Cronbach's alpha (CA) was found to be 0.835; thus, it was highly reliable.

Since this study explores the effectiveness of instruction design based on digital technology for engaging students, we considered both the technology acceptance model (TAM) [69] and the student engagement in schools' questionnaires [70] to gauge the degree to which students accepted the GBL and became engaged. The success of integrating game-based learning activities into the current teaching technique cannot be assured unless students accept it. According to the technology acceptance model (TAM), if students are prepared for the technology and it satisfies their expectations, it will be accepted. The simplicity of use and utility of technology are perceived using this paradigm, which might affect people's behavior toward embracing the technology. Candidate items 1, 8, 12, and 13 in the questionnaire indicated ease of use, while others were related to perceived usefulness. Similarly, SESQ is an instrument to measure engagement from a student perspective that is an outcome of the collaboration of researchers from 19 different countries. For the objectives of this study, only the items expressing engagement markers, such as affective (Q1, Q2, Q4, Q8, Q9) and behavioral (Q10–Q13) are considered.

Table 2. Survey questions.

Number	Description
Question 1	I had fun when playing the game.
Question 2	The game-based activities motivated me to complete the class activities.
Question 3	I believe that the games improved my understanding of the covered topics.
Question 4	The game-based activities motivated me to arrive at class on time.
Question 5	The game-based activities helped me to engage with the class material.
Question 6	The game-based activities were beneficial to my overall learning.
Question 7	I was more motivated to study the course material every week to do well on the leaderboard for the game-based activities.
Question 8	I saw my comparison with the class.
Question 9	It is important for me to see my position among my class fellows.
Question 10	My comparison with the class fellows motivated me to study more.
Question 11	Seeing my class fellow doing well made me study more.
Question 12	I prefer to play game live during class time.
Question 13	I also played this game outside lecture time just for fun.

There was only one open-ended question for knowing the opinion of the participant:

- Mention anything you liked or did not like about game-based activity or if you have any suggestions.

We omitted negatively phrased questions to keep the questionnaire short, as, on the basis of our experience, lengthy questionnaires may demotivate students and they might not keep the complete questionnaire, thus affecting the completion rate in a negative way. There is a long tradition of including items in questionnaires that are phrased both positively and negatively to minimize extreme response bias and acquiescent bias. Despite published concerns about acquiescence bias, there is little evidence that the common practice of including both positive and negatively worded items solves the problem. The research conducted by Sauro and Lewis [71] found little evidence for these biases and reported that response bias effects are at best small and outweighed by the real effects of miscoding and misinterpreting by users. Furthermore, we used a five-point scale, ranging from strongly disagree (SD) to strongly agree (SA), to capture the opinions of the participants on 13 statements given in Table 2. Therefore, the negative statements are reflected by the scale.

2.5. Research Procedure

In the first experiment investigating the students' engagement, interactivity, and the impact of the leaderboard, all participants were divided into five different groups with 30–50 students in each group as shown in Table 3. The groups either completed the Vortex game-based activities or the MBQAs which were not designed using games. Furthermore, we made use of a leaderboard for some groups. During the second phase of the experiment, both groups completed the game-based activities only as we wanted to investigate the gender differences in the game-based instructions.

An online Survey Monkey form was used for data collection, and the link was shared with participants through the Moodle page and Moodle messages. The participants' responses were recorded. The questionnaires provided to the participants were anonymous, ensuring that they did not carry any information that could help identify them. Analyses of the data, frequency, percentage, mean, standard deviation, and survey results are discussed in Section 3. A thematic analysis was used to analyze the open-ended questions, and three main themes were identified using an inductive approach. Similar conceptual categories were merged to create larger overarching themes relevant to teachers' perceptions.

Table 3. Experiment and control groups.

Control Group #	Semester	Mode	Leaderboard	Enrolled	Surveyed
TCG1	Spring 2022	GBQA/MBQA	No	51	24
TCG2	Spring 2022	GBQA	Yes	30	29
TCG3	Spring 2022	GBQA	No	32	13
TCG4	Spring 2022	MBQA	No	49	17
TCG5	Spring 2022	MBQA	Yes	38	18
TCG6	Summer 2022	GBQA	No	66	63
TCG7	Summer 2022	GBQA	No	60	44

means Control Group Number in this Table.

2.6. Research Ethics

The study was conducted by the Declaration of Helsinki and the protocol was approved by the Research Committee (RSV-004-03/08/2022). The survey was conducted online to ensure the anonymity of the participants. In addition, the participants were given an anonymous questionnaire with no data that could be used to identify the respondents.

3. Results

The collected data were analyzed using the R software version 4.0.3 [72]. First, we performed a univariate analysis including the descriptive statistics of the survey results. We then performed a bivariate analysis including the hypothesis tests for comparing the results of different groups in the activities. Regarding the range of studies attained, it can be seen that the vast majority of the participants belonged to the freshman year (47.5%), followed by the junior year (35.6%), and 6.9% belonged to the senior year. A breakdown of the participants is provided in Table A1 in Appendix A.

3.1. Activities Results

The activity completion rate for five different groups is shown in Figure 2. It can be seen that the completion rate of TCG1 was approximately 70% or higher for activities 2–5 which are game-based and dropped below 50% for subsequent activities which were Moodle-based. TCG2, assigned to game-based activities incorporating a leaderboard, initially had a completion rate of more than 60%, which dropped to as low as 30% later on. TCG3, game-based activities without a leaderboard, had an activity completion rate of approximately 70% or higher for the first six activities and then dropped below 40% for subsequent activities. Groups TCG4 and TCG5 (both groups assigned MBQA) had consistently low activity completion rates of approximately 20% or below. However, TCG5 had a higher activity completion rate than TCG4 did.

The average number of times that students completed activities is presented in Figure 3. It can be observed that the game-based groups had a higher access rate compared to the Moodle-based groups, indicating greater online engagement among students in the former. Furthermore, the access rate for TCG1 dropped to below 1.5 after switching from GBQAs to MBQAs after five activities. Additionally, TCG2 has a higher access rate compared to TCG3, suggesting that students in groups with a leaderboard tended to complete activities more frequently than those without a leaderboard.

Figure 4 presents the average scores of three groups, TCG1, TCG2, and TCG3, who completed game-based activities. The score recorded was the time taken to complete the activity, which serves as an indicator of performance, with lower scores indicating better performance. It can be observed that the group with the leaderboard (TCG2) outperformed the groups without a leaderboard, namely, TCG1 and TCG3, in nearly all activities, suggesting that the presence of a leaderboard may have positively impacted performance in these activities.

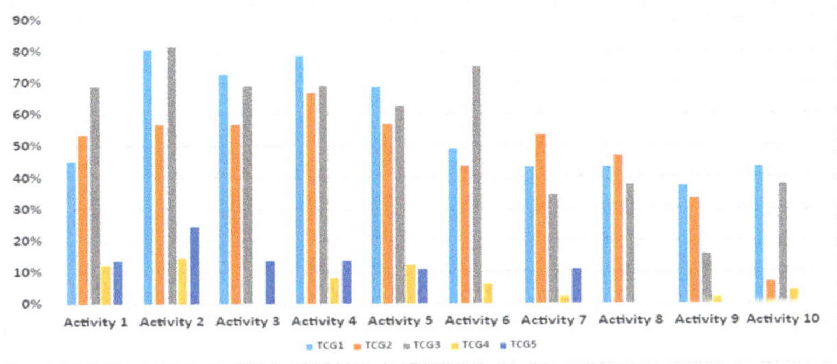

Figure 2. The activity completion rate for different groups during spring 2022.

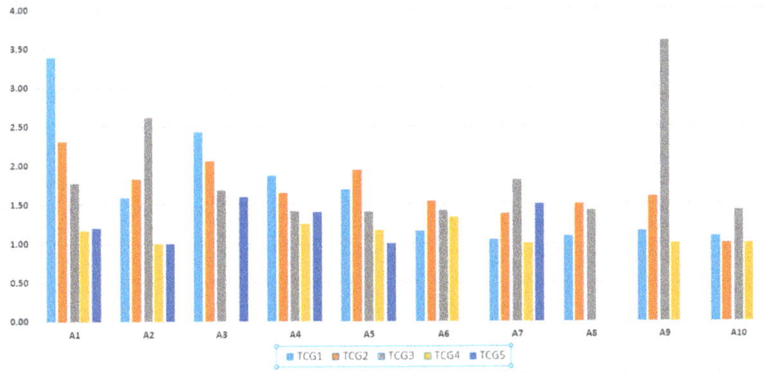

Figure 3. Number of times an activity was accessed by a student on average.

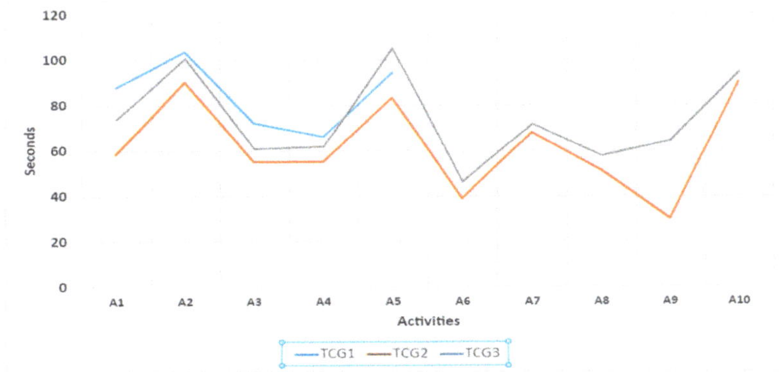

Figure 4. GBQA completion time comparison for different groups.

TCG2 completed the activities using Vortex with a leaderboard, while TCG3 (M3) completed the game-based activities without the leaderboard. It should be noted that a lower score for game-based activities is an indication of better performance. TCG3 performed slightly better than TCG2. We performed t-tests ($\alpha = 0.05$), and all p-values were greater than 0.05, indicating no statistically significant difference between the average activity scores for the groups with leaderboard and without leaderboard. The leaderboard created a competition among the students, and the parameter measuring the performance was the time taken to complete the activities. Competition motivates the students to do well and reduces the time to complete the activities. This is only possible if students grasp the concepts. Thus, a lower score means that the student was motivated to do better.

We also collected data for Moodle-based online quiz activities. Table 4 summarizes the average scores and standard deviations in TCG5 (with leaderboard) and TCG4 (without leaderboard). It should be noted that a higher score for MBQAs indicates higher performance. We can see that TCG5 performed better than TCG4 in three out of four cases, showing that the leaderboard had an impact on student performance. We can observe that all p-values were greater than 0.05, indicating that there was no statistically significant difference between the average activity scores of TCG5 and TCG4. Thus, using a leaderboard in Moodle to complete the various game activities had no particular impact.

Table 4. Comparison of scores between groups that completed MBQA with and without a leaderboard.

Activity	TCG5	TCG4	p-Value
A1	88.0 (8.37)	65.0 (30.2)	0.125
A2	92.8 (10.9)	83.6 (23.7)	0.368
A3	76.7 (22.4)	91.7 (9.62)	0.228
A5	75.0 (16.7)	63.9 (26.7)	0.441

The results provided in Table 5 represent a comparison of the activity completion times of the male and female groups. Activity completion times were higher for females than for males for every game activity, except for the first activity. Completing the activity related to lab safety was the most time-consuming for both genders. On the other hand, the activity related to making PowerPoint slides was completed in half the time required for lab safety activities. The p-values indicated a statistically significant difference between the average score for the activity regarding cover letter writing (p-value = 0.001), resume writing (p-value < 0.001), professional ethics (p-value = 0.004), and the engineering design process (p-value = 0.001) in the two groups. These results suggest that male users could complete these activities significantly faster than female users.

Table 5. Activity completion times for female and male participants.

Activity	TCG7 (Male)				TCG6 (Female)			
	Mean	SD	Min.	Max.	Mean	SD	Min.	Max.
A1	73.04	52.50	17	232	73.16	73.50	21	351
A2	103.72	46.76	45	204	110.87	59.38	45	321
A3	68.74	34.35	25	175	97.36	51.92	30	336
A4	48.04	23.55	22	141	84.27	57.96	33	438
A5	83.20	25.80	36	166	102.95	41.28	52	253
A7	78.90	21.75	46	138	105.14	47.01	42	314
A8	51.67	25.59	27	161	56.59	23.84	31	152

3.2. Survey Results

The distribution of the survey results is shown in Figures 5 and 6 for spring 2022 and summer 2022, respectively. A detailed breakdown of responses based on demographics is provided for spring 2022 and summer 2022 in Table A1 in Appendix A.

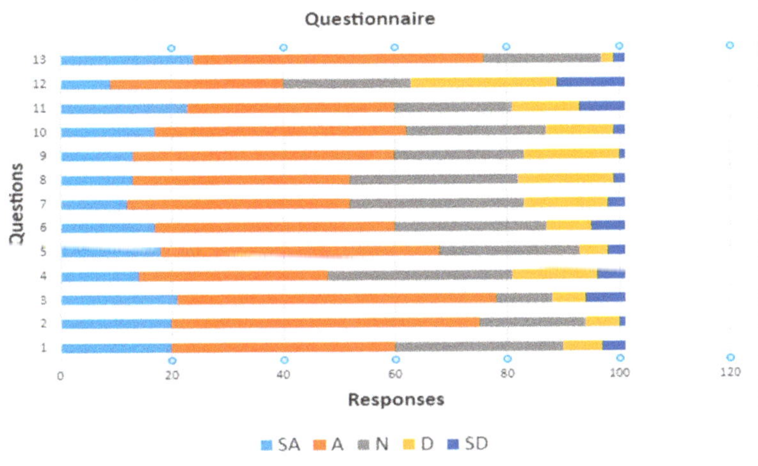

Figure 5. Responses to survey questions during spring 2022.

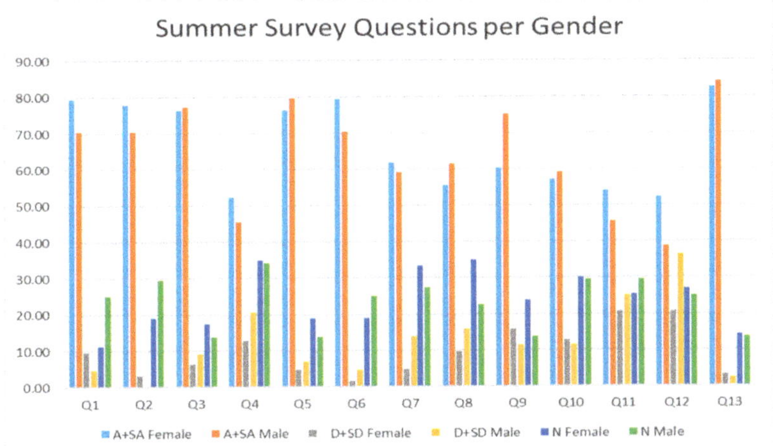

Figure 6. Comparison of questionnaire responses from different genders from summer 2022.

In response to question 1, only 59.94% of the participants (mean = 2.92; SD = 1.24) reported having fun while playing the game to complete the GBQAs, and 10.89% did not find it enjoyable at all. Interestingly, a higher percentage of females (83.3%) compared to males (54.2%) found it fun. In the summer, 58.59% of participants agreed that the game was enjoyable, with 74.9% of females responding positively compared to 79.4% of males. It is noteworthy that around 40% of the participants did not agree that they had fun, with 30% expressing a neutral stance. This finding is surprising, as games are generally believed to be enjoyable and memorable for most people, making them effective tools for learning. It can be speculated that students with high expertise levels may not have found the game challenging, which could have influenced their perception of fun. When asked about their motivation to complete the activities, the responses showed that 74.25% of participants in spring (mean = 2.92; SD = 1.22) and 74.76% in summer felt motivated. Interestingly, a higher percentage of females reported feeling motivated compared to male students, both in spring (88.9% vs. 71.1%) and in summer (77.8% vs. 70.5%).

Around 77% of the participants for both phases thought that these activities improved their understanding of the covered topic and, again, more females agreed to this point as compared to male counterparts for spring, 88.9%, and 74.7%, respectively. The ratio was the same for both genders in the summer. A very low number of participants, around 18% during spring and 49.5% during summer, agreed when asked if the activities motivated them to arrive in class on time. An equal percentage of both males and females had this opinion during spring and summer. The results related to the engagement with class material showed that only 67.73% of participants during spring and 77.5% during summer agreed that the game-based activities helped them to engage with the class material, while 24.75% disagreed, and the others were neutral. More males agreed than females in spring (68.7% vs. 79.5%) and summer (79.5% vs. 76.2%). For spring data, around 60% of participants thought that these activities were beneficial to their overall learning, while 13.86% disagreed and others were neutral. A slightly higher percentage of males agreed than females, 60.2% and 55.6%, respectively. For summer, around 75% of the participants thought that these activities were beneficial to their overall learning, while 21.49% were neutral. The percentage of males who agreed was lower than that of females, 70.5% and 79.4%, respectively. Only half (52%) of the participants during spring felt motivated to study the course material every week to do well on the leaderboard, and this number was 60.74% during summer. Female students were more determined to do well than males, with agreement rates of 72.2% and 47%, respectively. The gap narrowed during the summer, and the response was around 62% and 59% during the summer. More senior students agreed (71.4%) than the sophomore (50.9%) and junior (50%) students. Only slightly more than half (51.28% during spring and 57.94% during summer) of the participants confirmed that they saw their comparison with the class, and 30% were neutral for both spring and summer. A higher female proportion (61.1%) saw their comparison than males (49.4%) in spring, and this trend reversed in summer (55.6% females and 61.4% males).

Around ~60% during spring and 66.35% during summer agreed that it was important for them to see their position among the class, whereas around 18% during spring and 14% during summer disagreed, and the remainder were neutral. A higher number of sophomore students (66.7%) agreed than others. More than 60% of participants registered in spring agreed that their comparison with the class fellows motivated them to study more, while 14% disagreed, and others were neutral. The response was similar in the summer, where 57.94% agreed and 29.91% were neutral. The gender response was the same both in spring and summer. In response to the question of whether seeing their class fellows made them study more, around 60% of participants agreed, 20% disagreed, and others were neutral during spring. Overall, 50% of females and 61.4% of males responded positively. For the summer survey, 50.46% agreed and 22.42% disagreed. The percentage of female (54%) participants agreeing was more than males (45.5%).

Students did not like to play the game during lecture time as only 39.60% and 46.72% of participants said so for spring and summer surveys, respectively. More females said so during spring (50.4% females vs. 37.3% males) and during summer (52.4% females vs. 38.6% males), and this proportion was higher for females and sophomore students. The majority of the participants who took part in the survey during spring 2022 (around 75%) played this game outside the lecture hour, with 22% being neutral. There was no major discrepancy among the responses of participants belonging to different demographics.

There were two survey questions where the participants had the opportunity to state their preferences regarding the GBQAs or MBQAs.

Q14: Which of the activities did you enjoy more?

Q15: Which one would you recommend for future use?

More than half of the participants enjoyed game-based activities (68.32%), and they recommended it for future use (67.33%).

3.3. Analysis of Open-Ended Survey Responses

The opinions of the survey participants regarding game-based activities, including their suggestions, were assessed through open-ended questions. Open-ended questions do not restrict the participants to a set of predetermined answer options; therefore, they allow for gathering a wide range of sincere opinions from the survey subject, but they demand more time, consideration, and thought from the respondent. Therefore, some participants abstained from responding or responded limitedly, making the responses hard to analyze. The responses were imported to R, and thematic analyses, including text-mining processes, were carried out. Similar responses based on commonly used frequent keywords were grouped, forming three main categories.

Theme 1: Game-based activities are a good way to review the course material.

Thematic analysis revealed that the students found game-based activities useful because they helped them to provide an overview of the topics studied during the lectures.

"What I like is that it is a new way to understand and review the course material."

"What I liked about the game-based activity is that it is a fantastic method to review lecture material."

Theme 2: Game-based activities help students to become more engaged in the lectures.

The students felt more engaged when participating in game-based activities which helped them focus their attention on the lecture topics. This was also evident from the student responses given below.

"Great idea to engage the students in the class material."

"It is good to use live games where all students get engaged at the same time with the same question and to see who solves them faster and correctly."

Theme 3: Playing games was a fun and satisfying experience.

The thematic analysis revealed that playing the game-based activities created a positive atmosphere in the classroom, which could help students to perform better.

"I enjoyed playing the games; they helped to build a better connection between me and my class and professor. It was fun interacting with everyone when playing the game."

"Winning the game was so satisfying."

4. Discussion

RQ1: How are students' engagement and motivation affected by the usage of game-based activities?

The analysis of activity data and survey responses revealed that GBQAs were more effective in engaging students in the educational process compared to MBQAs. This is evident from the higher activity completion rate (Figure 2), the average activity access rate (Figure 3), and the responses to the survey questions. It is also clear from Table A1 that groups completing game-based elements said that they were more engaged and had slightly more fun than those completing Moodle-based games. The higher completion rate for GBQAs compared to Moodle-based learning suggests that game-based learning was more engaging for students. Additionally, the higher average completion rate indicates that students were more actively involved in the game, which aligns with the findings of previous studies (e.g., [20,29,62]). Furthermore, students accessed game-based activities more frequently than MBQAs, which could be for entertainment purposes or to improve their scores for self-satisfaction. This highlights another important aspect of game-based learning, as students who initially struggled may be motivated to improve and develop a growth mindset, as discussed in Dostal's study (2015) [73]. Consequently, students with a growth mindset are more likely to attempt new approaches multiple times until they succeed.

During the spring semester, over 60% of participants and, during the summer semester, 81% of participants expressed that they had fun while completing game-based activities, which can serve as an indicator of engagement. Fun is commonly recognized as a crucial element of in-game engagement, as it signifies that players are enjoying the gameplay and are emotionally invested in the experience. When players have fun, they are more likely to continue playing, explore the game world, and be motivated to achieve in-game goals [32]. The responses from Q5 demonstrate that a significant number of participants found the game-based activities engaging. This innovative approach of using gaming elements to present the material and challenge the students was successful in attracting their attention and engaging them with the learning material [33]. Similarly, a large number of participants during both phases were of the view that the games improved their understanding of the covered topics, revealing that students were engaged in meaningful ways through these game-based activities. When individuals have a clear understanding of a topic or concept, they are more likely to engage with it. Understanding provides a foundation for meaningful engagement, as it enables individuals to connect with the subject matter, ask questions, and participate in discussions or activities related to it. Students who understand the material being taught are more likely to actively participate in discussions, ask questions, and complete assignments, leading to higher levels of engagement. From the reciprocal perspective, meaningful engagement can deepen and reinforce understanding. When individuals are actively engaged in an activity, they are more likely to process and internalize the information, leading to a better understanding of the subject matter.

Analysis of Figure 2 revealed that the activity rate for groups completing GBQAs was much higher than that for MBQAs. This indicates that game-based activities are an effective strategy to motivate and engage students in learning, which is in line with the findings of [34,55,57,60]. This is also evident from the statistics of TCG1, which had a higher completion rate for the first half of GBQAs and a lower completion rate for MBQAs. The use of GBQAs introduces variety and novelty into the learning experience, which can help prevent monotony and increase students' motivation. The interactive and dynamic nature of the platform created a fresh and engaging learning environment, which may pique students' curiosity and motivation to explore and learn. It should be noted that this is a zero-credit hour course with a pass or fail as a possible outcome. This means that students had no extrinsic motivation to complete the activities; hence, we can safely claim that they were intrinsically motivated to complete these activities. It can be seen that the activity completion rate dropped in the latter half, which can be attributed to several reasons. First, some students might have become bored after completing a few activities because of simple game mechanics and considering the founding elements of educational video games include fantasy, curiosity, challenges, and power when designing games [74]. To sustain students' interest, it is important to introduce new information so that students feel challenged. However, designing such activities might overload the teacher, and the nature of courses does not allow for the luxury of spending huge time on gaming due to its disruptive nature. In addition, some teachers have no prior gaming experience, which makes it difficult for them to modify it for educational reasons [75]. Second, as these activities did not carry any significant weight toward the final mark, some students may have viewed them as unnecessary. Thirdly, the majority of students knew about the possible outcome of their results and did not pay much attention to this course as it would not have any impact on their grades, and they concentrated their efforts on other courses whose outcomes could improve their grade point average (GPA). It can also be noted that TCG5 had higher completion rates than TCG4, meaning that the leaderboard did motivate slightly. Furthermore, as mentioned earlier, students were engaged more through GBQAs, and such meaningful engagement promotes a sense of ownership and responsibility for the learning process. When individuals are actively involved, they are more motivated to take ownership of their learning and are more likely to be invested in the outcomes. This can result in increased intrinsic motivation and a deeper sense of commitment to the subject matter. This is also evident from the student response to question 13, where an overwhelming majority of the students declared that they played the games outside the lecture hour, which is an indication of intrinsic motivation. This also indicates that the activities created interest in the subject matter and students were willing to go beyond the required class hours to do well. Students can typically choose their own pace, select topics or levels of difficulty, and have the flexibility to revisit and review content as needed. This autonomy can foster a sense of ownership and control over their learning, which can positively impact their motivation. Another aspect of GBQAs is the immediate feedback, which allows students to quickly assess their progress and make improvements. This instant feedback can boost students' motivation by providing them with a clear understanding of their strengths and weaknesses and encouraging them to strive for better performance.

RQ2: What is the impact of the leaderboard on student motivation and behavior?

The analysis of the average completion time for the game-based activities for three different groups provided in Figure 4 reveals that the group with an additional gamification element as a leaderboard performed better, which may have resulted in higher task performance than those without a leaderboard. A similar trend can be observed from the data provided in Table 4, where TCG2 performed slightly better than TCG3. Furthermore, it can be seen in Table A1 that groups TCG2 and TCG5 has more fun playing and were more motivated than the groups not using the leaderboard. This means that the leaderboard can motivate individuals or teams to perform better and strive for higher rankings [53,54]. The visual representation of rankings and scores on a leaderboard can trigger a desire to improve one's position and achieve recognition, leading to increased effort and engagement with the task. The desire to be at the top of the leaderboard can create healthy competition and drive individuals to put in more effort. Knowing that their performance is being tracked and compared to others can encourage individuals to stay on track and perform to the best of their abilities. In some cases, leaderboards can foster a sense of achievement, provide a clear goal to strive for and create a positive feedback loop that encourages learners to perform better. Furthermore, the time to complete activities was higher for groups without leaderboards (i.e., TCG1 and TCG2), indicating that these students were not motivated to do well. The use of social features such as a leaderboard promotes social interaction and competition among students. This social element can create a sense of community, foster friendly competition, and increase motivation through social recognition and support.

However, the impact of the leaderboard is not the same for everyone and depends on multiple factors, including the specific context, design, and implementation of the leaderboard system, as well as individual learner characteristics. This is evident from the responses to Q7–Q11 as many students did not have a favorable opinion toward the use of the leaderboard. For example, in response to question 11, both groups with leaderboards, TCG2 and TCG5, did not agree that seeing others doing well motivated them. For some students, leaderboards may create a sense of pressure or anxiety, leading to a negative impact on their performance. It can also result in students focusing solely on achieving a high rank on the leaderboard, rather than engaging deeply with the learning content or developing a deep understanding of the material.

While leaderboards can be motivating for some individuals, they can also be demotivating for others. Individuals who are consistently ranked lower may become discouraged and give up, even if they are making progress and improving in other ways. Leaderboard can create a culture of winners and losers, which may not be conducive to a positive work environment. Students are less inclined to share knowledge or help each other, as they may perceive others as competitors on the leaderboard. This can negatively impact peer-to-peer learning, collaboration, and cooperation. This can be observed by the fact that a very small number of the students responded positively to questions Q10 and Q11, which were related to the leaderboard. It is also evident from the activity completion rate provided in Figure 2 that group TCG3 without a leaderboard had a higher activity completion rate compared to the group with the leaderboard. In this research, we used absolute/infinite leaderboards where all users and their scores are displayed on the Moodle page [19], giving players at the top a greater feeling of accomplishment than players at the bottom. This has a negative impact as it is not inclusive and poses a threat to introverted students as they feel that they are forced into the competition, which may impact their attitude negatively. Students who believe they will never reach the top are more likely to give up on their goals and might not take part in them at all, thus missing an opportunity to learn [76]. Students who do not perform well or who are consistently at the bottom of the leaderboard may experience decreased self-esteem or feelings of inadequacy, which can negatively impact their motivation to continue participating or learning.

RQ3: Do males or females have the same perception toward game-based activities?

In terms of motivation for completing game-based activities, 77.8% of the female gender answered affirmatively, compared to 70.5% of the male gender. In other words, a greater number of females were motivated than males. This finding corresponds with that of [77] implying that female players are considerably more motivated than male players in a digital game of a moderate genre. The results from the comparison of activity completion time for both genders, presented in Table 5 indicate that there was a difference in gameplay behavior between males and females. On average, male students were slightly faster in completing the activity compared to their female counterparts. This finding aligns with a study conducted by [78], which reported that female students consistently spent more time than male students on gameplay across different studies. Additionally, research by [79] suggested that female students tend to prioritize goal clarity and social interaction as more important factors in digital learning games, while male students tend to place more emphasis on the challenge, progress feedback, and visual appeal in such games. These findings highlight gender differences in gameplay behavior and preferences among students, which could have implications for designing effective digital learning games that cater to the diverse needs and preferences of learners of different genders.

When we analyzed the survey results of summer 2022, which contained a more balanced proportion of students of both genders than those of spring 2022, it was revealed that females enjoyed playing games more than males, and the same was evident from the spring 2022 outcomes. Although more males (58.5%) play video games than females (41.5%), as per the distribution of video game users in the United States in 2021, the enjoyment of digital games is ultimately a personal preference and cannot be generalized by gender. Males favor gameplay that involves strategy and clear directions from the system, in contrast to females, who favor games that encourage exploration. Moreover, males view digital games as a medium for socializing and skill development, whereas women prefer to adopt autonomous learning. Unfortunately, Vortex-based quizzes lack strategies but do have socialization features in the form of scores and leaderboards. All of the groups had explicit leaderboards, due to which male students had slightly less fun and motivation while playing games. This discovery concurs with that of Joiner et al. [80], whose findings showed that gender differences in digital game preferences have an impact on each group's degree of motivation.

The responses to Q9 indicate that male students were more inclined to the comparison with other students than females. In other words, male students were more inclined toward the social comparison in this particular context in order to assess their competence. The competitive nature of the leaderboard might have urged them to make more upward comparisons and try to improve themselves compared to females who liked to have more downward comparison. On the basis of the responses to Q12 of the summer 2022 survey, it appears that a higher number of males compared to females did not prefer to complete activities during class time. This could be attributed to various factors, such as gender stereotypes, perceived lack of challenge, technological limitations, compulsory nature of the activity, or personal learning preferences. Some male students may feel societal pressure to conform to traditional gender norms and stereotypes that view game-based activities as childish or not serious. They may worry about being perceived as immature or not conforming to traditional masculine expectations, thus choosing to avoid such activities to prevent potential social judgment. Additionally, some males may not have found the games challenging enough or may have faced limitations in accessing a stable internet connection, which could have impacted their engagement. Moreover, the game-based activities may not have aligned with the preferences or learning needs of some male students. Furthermore, if the game-based activities were conducted during class time, some students may have viewed them as compulsory without any perceived benefit or reward, which could have resulted in a lack of motivation to participate for instrumental students. However, some female students may have viewed in-class activities as an opportunity to demonstrate their abilities and engage in healthy competition with male students, potentially influencing their motivation to participate.

Limitations of Study

This study had several potential limitations. Firstly, all groups were not taught by the same teacher, which may have introduced inconsistency in the delivery of instruction and impacted the continuity and coherence of the study. This limitation was encountered in the subsequent phase where different groups were taught by different teachers. Additionally, some students considered playing games during class time as an alternative approach to roll call during spring 2022, despite being explained that it was optional activity and did not count for anything in terms of attendance and grades. These misconceptions may have influenced their engagement and opinion in the study. Moreover, the Vortex sorting game used in the study was chosen for its simplicity, but it may not have been challenging enough for engineering students, which could have affected their motivation and engagement. Lastly, the study was conducted in a single course at one university with a similar cultural background, and the findings may have limited generalizability. Conducting the study with participants from diverse cultures and backgrounds could enhance the meaningfulness of the results.

5. Conclusions

We utilized game-based quizzes implemented using the Vortex sorting game to assess the engagement and motivation of undergraduate students enrolled in a sophomore seminar course. The findings indicate that incorporating digital games into engineering education can effectively motivate students and sustain their interest in the course material. Analysis of anonymous feedback surveys revealed positive responses from students toward the game-based activities. Although not statistically significant, the gamified Vortex activities were found to have a more positive impact on student engagement and motivation. However, the use of a leaderboard as a gaming element was observed to have both positive and negative effects, improving the performance of some students while demotivating others. The favorable response from students toward game-based activities suggests that integrating games into undergraduate general engineering lectures can be an enjoyable and engaging experience. We also observed some differences in perception of game-based activities between genders, with female students showing slightly higher levels of engagement and motivation compared to their male counterparts, but not preferring to compare themselves with other students. In summary, the instructional approach and design of game-based activities need careful consideration and support from academia, with a focus on creating games that offer appropriate challenge levels, provide clear instructions, relevant content, and meaningful feedback, and align with the preferences and learning needs of male students in particular. Additional training and resources may be needed to ensure the effective implementation of game-based activities in engineering education.

Author Contributions: Conceptualization, M.N.; methodology, M.N. and W.F.; software, M.O.; validation, M.N. and W.F.; formal analysis, M.N., M.O. and W.F.; investigation, M.N. and M.O.; resources, M.N.; data curation, M.N.; writing—original draft, M.N. and M.O.; writing—review & editing, W.F.; visualization, M.N.; supervision, M.N.; project administration, M.N.; All authors have read and agreed to the published version of the manuscript.

Funding: This research received no external funding.

Data Availability Statement: Not applicable.

Conflicts of Interest: The authors declare no conflict of interest.

Appendix A

Table A1. Breakdown of responses for spring and summer 2022 surveys.

Q.#	Resp.	Spring 2002							Summer 2022	
		Female	Male	TCG1	TCG2	TCG3	TCG4	TCG5	TCG6	TCG7
Q1	SA + A	15 (83.3%)	45 (54.2%)	14 (58.34%)	19 (65.52%)	8 (61.54%)	9 (52.94%	11 (61.11%)	50 (79.4%)	31 (70.5%)
	D + SD	2 (11.10%)	9 (10.8%)	5 (20.83%)	8 (27.59%)	4 (30.77%)	6 (35.29%)	5 (27.68%)	6 (9.5%)	2 (4.5%)
	N	1 (5.6%)	29 (34.9%)	5 (20.83%)	2 (6.89%)	1 (7.69%)	2 (11.77%)	2 (11.11%)	7 (11.1%)	11 (25.0%)
Q2	SA + A	16 (88.9%)	59 (71.1%)	14 (58.33%)	24 (82.76%)	9 (69.23%)	12 (70.59%)	16 (88.89%)	49 (77.8%)	31 (70.5%)
	D + SD	1 (5.56%)	6 (7.23%)	5 (20.83%)	5 (17.24%)	3 (23.08%)	5 (29.11%)	1 (5.56%)	2 (3.2%)	0 (0.0%)
	N	1 (5.56%)	18 (21.7%)	5 (20.83%)	0 (0.00%)	1 (7.69%)	0 (0.00%)	1 (5.56%)	12 (19.0%)	13 (29.5%)
Q3	SA + A	16 (88.9%)	62 (74.7%)	20 (83.33%)	23 (79.31%)	9 (69.23%)	12 (64.70%)	14 (77.78%)	48 (76.2%)	34 (77.3%)
	D + SD	1 (05.6%)	12 (14.0%)	0 (0.00%)	3 (10.34%)	3 (28.08%)	2 (17.65%)	2 (11.11%)	4 (6.3%)	4 (9.09%)
	N	1 (05.6%)	9 (10.8%)	4 (16.67%)	3 (10.34%)	1 (7.69%)	3 (17.65%)	2 (11.11%)	11 (17.5%)	6 (13.6%)
Q4	SA + A	9 (50.0%)	9 (47.00%)	15 (62.50%)	10 (34.48%)	4 (30.77%)	10 (58.82%)	9 (50.00%)	33 (52.4%)	20 (45.5%)
	D + SD	3 (16.7%)	17 (20.5%)	5 (20.83%)	11 (37.93%)	7 (53.85%)	4 (23.53%)	6 (33.33%)	8 (12.7%)	9 (20.4%)
	N	6 (33.3%)	27 (32.5%)	4 (16.67%)	8 (27.59%)	2 (15.38%)	3 (17.65%)	3 (16.67%)	22 (34.9%)	15 (34.1%)
Q5	SA + A	11 (61.1%)	57 (68.7%)	18 (65.00%)	21 (72.41%)	10 (61.54%)	10 (58.82%)	11 (55.55%)	48 (76.2%)	35 (79.5%)
	D + SD	1 (05.6%)	7 (8.4%)	4 (16.67%)	6 (20.69%)	3 (23.08%)	4 (23.53%)	6 (33.33%)	3 (4.8%)	3 (6.8%)
	N	6 (33.30%)	19 (22.9%)	2 (8.33%)	2 (6.90%)	2 (15.38%)	3 (17.65%)	1 (5.56%)	12 (19.0%)	6 (13.6%)
Q6	SA + A	10 (55.6%)	50 (60.2%)	15 (62.50%)	17 (58.62%)	7 (53.85%)	11 (64.71%)	10 (55.56%)	50 (79.4%)	31 (70.5%)
	D + SD	2 (11.1%)	12 (14.50%)	4 (16.67%)	9 (31.03%)	4 (30.77%)	4 (23.53%)	6 (33.33%)	1 (1.59%)	2 (4.55%)
	N	(33.3%)	21 (25.3%)	5 (20.83%)	3 (10.34%)	2 (15.38%)	2 (11.76%)	2 (11.11%)	12 (19.0%)	11 (25.0%)
Q7	SA + A	39 (47.0%)	0 (0.0%)	13 (54.17%)	11 (37.93%)	5 (38.46%)	10 (58.82%)	13 (72.22%)	39 (61.9%)	26 (59.1%)
	D + SD	16 (19.3%)	0 (00.0%)	6 (25.00%)	13 (44.83%)	4 (30.77%)	5 (29.41%)	3 (16.67%)	3 (4.76%)	6 (13.6%)
	N	3 (16.70%)	28 (33.7%)	5 (20.83%)	5 (17.24%)	4 (30.77%)	2 (11.76%)	2 (11.11%)	21 (33.3%)	12 (27.3%)
Q8	SA + A	11 (61.1%)	41 (49.4%)	15 (62.50%)	10 (34.48%)	6 (46.15%)	10 (58.82%)	11 (61.11%)	35 (55.6%)	27 (61.4%)
	D + SD	15 (18.1%)	0 (0.0%)	5 (20.83%)	11 (37.93%)	5 (38.46%)	6 (35.29%)	3 (16.67%)	6 (9.52%)	7 (15.9%)
	N	3 (16.7%)	27 (32.5%)	4 (16.67%)	8 (27.59%)	2 (15.38%)	1 (5.88%)	4 (22.22%)	22 (34.9%)	10 (22.7%)
Q9	SA + A	11 (61.1%)	49 (59.0%)	15 (62.50%)	16 (55.17%)	7 (53.85%)	11 (64.71%)	11 (61.11%)	38 (60.3%)	33 (75.0%)
	D + SD	3 (16.7%)	15 (18.1%)	4 (16.67%)	7 (24.14%)	5 (38.46%)	3 (17.65%)	4 (22.22%)	10 (15.9%)	5 (11.4%)
	N	4 (22.20%)	19 (22.90%)	5 (20.83%)	6 (20.69%)	1 (15.38%)	3 (17.65%)	3 (16.67%)	15 (23.8%)	6 (13.6%)
Q10	SA + A	11 (61.1%)	51 (61.4%)	14 (58.33%)	18 (62.07%)	7 (53.85%)	12 (70.59%)	11 (61.11%)	36 (57.1%)	26 (59.1%)
	D + SD	1 (5.56%)	13 (15.7%)	4 (16.67%)	8 (27.59%)	4 (30.77%)	3 (17.65%)	6 (33.33%)	8 (12.7%)	5 (11.4%)
	N	6 (33.3%)	19 (22.9%)	6 (25.00%)	3 (10.34%)	2 (15.38%)	2 (11.76%)	1 (5.56%)	19 (30.2%)	13 (29.5%)
Q11	SA + A	9 (50.0%)	51 (61.4%)	16 (66.67%)	14 (48.28%)	9 (69.23%)	12 (70.59%)	9 (50.00%)	34 (54.0%)	20 (45.5%)
	D + SD	5 (27.8%)	15 (18.1%)	4 (16.67%)	7 (24.14%)	3 (23.08%)	3 (17.65%)	4 (22.22%)	13 (20.6%)	11 (25.0%)
	N	4 (22.2%)	17 (20.5%)	4 (16.67%)	8 (48.28%)	1 (7.69%)	2 (11.76%)	5 (27.78%)	16 (25.4%)	13 (29.5%)
Q12	SA + A	9 (50.0%)	31 (37.3%)	10 (41.67%)	9 (31.03%)	2 (15.38%)	10 (58.82%)	9 (50.00%)	33 (52.4%)	17 (38.6%)
	D + SD	4 (22.2%)	34 (41.0%)	5 (20.83%)	6 (20.69%)	5 (38.46%)	2 (11.76%)	5 (27.78%)	13 (20.6%)	16 (36.4%)
	N	5 (27.8%)	18 (21.7%)	9 (37.50%)	14 (48.28%)	6 (46.15%)	5 (29.41%)	4 (22.22%)	17 (27.0%)	11 (25.0%)
Q13	SA + A	14 (77.8%)	62 (74.7%)	17 (70.83%)	22 (75.86%)	9 (69.23%)	14 (82.35%)	14 (77.78%)	52 (82.5%)	37 (84.1%)
	D + SD	1 (5.56%)	3 (03.6%)	6 (25.00%)	5 (17.24%)	4 (30.77%)	3 (17.65%)	3 (16.67%)	2 (3.2%)	1 (2.3%)
	N	3 (16.7%)	18 (21.7%)	1 (4.17%)	2 (6.90%)	0 (0.00%)	0 (0.00%)	1 (5.56%)	9 (14.3%)	6 (13.6%)

means the number of the question in the Table.

References

1. UNICEF. *The State of the Global Education Crisis: A Path to Recovery: A Joint UNESCO, UNICEF, and World Bank Report*; UNICEF: New York, NY, USA, 2021.
2. Hoffman, A. Reflections: Academia's Emerging Crisis of Relevance and the Consequent Role of the Engaged Scholar. *J. Chang. Manag.* **2016**, *16*, 77–96. [CrossRef]
3. Nadeem, M.; Blumenstein, M. Embedding online activities during lecture time: Roll call or enhancement of student participation? *J. Univ. Teach. Learn. Pract.* **2021**, *18*, 11–23. [CrossRef]

4. Akhtar, S.; Nadeem, M.; Rashdan, M.; Hussain, B.; Ansari, E.; Aslam, M. Online Mode of Teaching and Learning Process in Engineering Discipline: Teacher Perspective on Challenges Faced and Recommendations. *Educ. Sci.* **2023**, *13*, 200. [CrossRef]
5. Tsegay, S.; Ashraf, M.; Perveen, S.; Zegergish, M. Online teaching during COVID-19 pandemic: Teachers' experiences from a Chinese university. *Sustainability* **2022**, *14*, 568. [CrossRef]
6. Ahshan, R. A Framework of Implementing Strategies for Active Student Engagement in Remote/Online Teaching and Learning during the COVID-19 Pandemic. *Educ. Sci.* **2021**, *11*, 483. [CrossRef]
7. Hernández-de-Menéndez, M.G.A.V.; Martínez, J.C.T.; Alcántara, D.H.; Morales-Menendez, R. Active learning in engineering education. A review of fundamentals, best practices and experiences. *Int. J. Interact. Des. Manuf.* **2019**, *13*, 909–922. [CrossRef]
8. Nadeem, M.; Blumenstein, M.; Biglari-Abhari, M. Exploring the Impact of in Class Writing Exercises in an Engineering Course. In Proceedings of the 2018 IEEE International Conference on Teaching, Assessment, and Learning for Engineering, Wollongong, NSW, Australia, 4–7 December 2018.
9. Fahimirad, M.; Kotamjani, S.S. A review on application of artificial intelligence in teaching and learning in educational contexts. *Int. J. Learn. Dev.* **2018**, *8*, 106–118. [CrossRef]
10. Adamopoulou, E.; Moussiades, L. Chatbots: History, technology, and applications. *Mach. Learn. Appl.* **2020**, *2*, 100006. [CrossRef]
11. Campbell, G. Podcasting in education. *Educause* **2005**, *5*, 33–44.
12. Nadeem, M.; Chandra, A.; Livirya, A.; Beryozkina, S. AR-LabOr: Design and Assessment of an Augmented Reality Application for Lab Orientation. *Educ. Sci.* **2020**, *10*, 316. [CrossRef]
13. Nadeem, M.; Lal, M.; Cen, J.; Sharsheer, M. AR4FSM: Mobile Augmented Reality Application in Engineering Education for Finite-State Machine Understanding. *Educ. Sci.* **2022**, *12*, 555. [CrossRef]
14. Hamari, J.; Xi, N.; Legaki, Z.; Morschheuser, B. Gamification. In Proceedings of the 56th Hawaii International Conference on System Sciences, Maui, HI, USA, 3–6 January 2023.
15. Serrano, K. *The Effect of Digital Game-Based Learning on Student Learning: A Literature Review*; Graduate Research Papers; University of Northern Iowa: Cedar Falls, IA, USA, 2019; p. 943.
16. Jordan, T.; Dhamala, M. Video game players have improved decision-making abilities and enhanced brain activities. *Neuroimage Rep.* **2022**, *2*, 100112. [CrossRef]
17. de Carvalho, C.V.; Escudeiro, P.; Coelho, A. Serious games, interaction and simulation. In Proceedings of the 6th International Conference, SGAMES 2016, Porto, Portugal, 16–17 June 2016.
18. Bai, S.; Hew, K.F.; Huang, B. Does gamification improve student learning outcome? Evidence from a meta-analysis and synthesis of qualitative data in educational contexts. *Educ. Res. Rev.* **2020**, *30*, 100322. [CrossRef]
19. Ortiz-Rojas, M.; Chiluiza, K.; Valcke, M. Gamification through leaderboards: An empirical study in engineering education. *Comput. Appl. Eng. Educ.* **2019**, *27*, 777–788. [CrossRef]
20. Bai, S.; Hew, K.F.; Sailer, M.; Jia, C. From top to bottom: How positions on different types of leaderboard may affect fully online student learning performance, intrinsic motivation, and course engagement. *Comput. Educ.* **2021**, *173*, 104297. [CrossRef]
21. Huang, B.; Hew, K.F. Implementing a theory-driven gamification model in higher education flipped courses: Effects on out-of-class activity completion and quality of artifacts. *Comput. Educ.* **2018**, *125*, 254–272. [CrossRef]
22. Toda, A.; Palomino, P.; Oliveira, W.; Rodrigues, L.; Klock, A.; Gasparini, I.; Cristea, A.; Isotani, S. How to gamify learning systems? An experience report using the design sprint method and a taxonomy for gamification elements in education. *J. Educ. Technol. Soc.* **2019**, *22*, 2019.
23. Kalygua, M.; Mantai, L.; Maronne, M. Efficient Vocabulary Learning Through Online Activities. *Procedia Soc. Behav. Sci.* **2013**, *83*, 35–38. [CrossRef]
24. ISFE. Key Facts 2020. In *The Year We Played Together*; European Games Developer Federation: Stockholm, Sweden, 2021.
25. Statistical Office of the European Union. *Key Figures on Europe: Statistics Illustrated—2019 Edition*; Publications Office of the European Union: Luxembourg, 2019.
26. Fosnot, C.T. *Constructivism: Theory, Perspectives, and Practice*; Teachers College Press: New York, NY, USA, 2013.
27. Kolb, A.Y.; Kolb, D.A. Experiential learning theory as a guide for experiential educators in higher education. *Exp. Learn. Teach. High. Educ.* **2017**, *1*, 7–44. [CrossRef]
28. Umirziyaev, U.; Abdurakhmonov, V. Flow Theory. *Eurasian J. Soc. Sci. Philos. Cult.* **2022**, *12*, 261–264.
29. Zahra, I. Online Game-Based Learning to Enhance Student Engagement, Motivation and 21st-Century Skills. *Learning* **2023**, *4*, 192.
30. Barata, G.; Gama, S.; Jorge, J.; Gonçalves, D. Studying student differentiation in gamified education: A long-term study. *Comput. Hum. Behav.* **2017**, *71*, 550–585. [CrossRef]
31. Giang, V. Gamification techniques increase your employees' ability to learn by 40%. *Bus. Insid.* **2013**, *18*, 37.
32. Hew, K.F.; Huang, B.; Chu, K.W.S.; Chiu, D.K. Engaging Asian students through game mechanics: Findings from two experiment studies. *Comput. Educ.* **2016**, *92*, 221–236. [CrossRef]
33. Çakıroğlu, Ü.; Başıbüyük, B.; Güler, M.; Atabay, M.; Memiş, B.Y. Gamifying an ICT course: Influences on engagement and academic performance. *Comput. Hum. Behav.* **2017**, *69*, 98–107. [CrossRef]
34. Koivisto, J.; Hamari, J. The rise of motivational information systems: A review of gamification research. *Int. J. Inf. Manag.* **2019**, *45*, 191–210. [CrossRef]
35. Ekici, M. A systematic review of the use of gamification in flipped learning. *Educ. Inf. Technol.* **2021**, *26*, 3327–3346. [CrossRef]

36. Legaki, N.Z.; Xi, N.; Hamari, J.; Karpouzis, K.; Assimakopoulos, V. The effect of challenge-based gamification on learning: An experiment in the context of statistics education. *Int. J. Hum. Comput. Stud.* **2020**, *144*, 102496. [CrossRef]
37. Dervan, P. Increasing in-class student engagement using socrative (an online student response system). *All Irel. J. Teach. Learn. High. Educ.* **2014**, *6*, 1801–18013.
38. Malone, T.W. Toward a theory of intrinsically motivating instruction. *Cogn. Sci.* **1981**, *5*, 333–369. [CrossRef]
39. Sweetser, P.; Wyeth, P. GameFlow: A model for evaluating player enjoyment in games. *Comput. Entertain.* **2005**, *3*, 3. [CrossRef]
40. Asa'd, R.; Gunn, C. Improving problem solving skills in introductory physics using Kahoot! *Phys. Educ.* **2018**, *53*, 053001. [CrossRef]
41. Prieto, M.C.; Palma, L.O.; Tobías, P.J.B.; León, F.J.M. Student Assessment of the Use of Kahoot in the Learning Process of Science and Mathematics. *Educ. Sci.* **2019**, *9*, 55. [CrossRef]
42. Jones, S.M.; Katyal, P.; Xie, X.; Nicolas, M.P.; Leung, E.M.; Noland, D.M.; Montclare, J.K.A. 'KAHOOT!' Approach: The Effectiveness of Game-Based Learning for an Advanced Placement Biology Class. *Simul. Gaming* **2019**, *50*, 832–847. [CrossRef]
43. Yabuno, K.; Luong, E.; Shaffer, J. Comparison of Traditional and Gamified Student Response Systems in an Undergraduate Human Anatomy Course. *J. Hum. Anat. Physiol. Soc.* **2019**, *23*, 29–36. [CrossRef]
44. Rahim, A.S.A.; Ziden, A.A.; Yap, B.K. Gamified Online Quizzes: Pharmacy Student Perceptions of Learning in an Undergraduate Medicinal Chemistry Course. *Malays. J. Pharm.* **2020**, *6*, 6–12. [CrossRef]
45. Wang, A.I.; Tahir, R. The effect of using Kahoot! for learning—A literature review. *Comput. Educ.* **2020**, *149*, 103818. [CrossRef]
46. Murciano-Calles, J. Use of Kahoot for Assessment in Chemistry Education: A Comparative Study. *J. Chem. Educ.* **2020**, *97*, 4209–4213. [CrossRef]
47. Youssef, M. Assessing the Use of Kahoot! in an Undergraduate General Chemistry Classroom. *J. Chem. Educ.* **2021**, *99*, 1118–1124. [CrossRef]
48. Bohuslavická, Z. From Practising Vocabulary through Games to Using It in Context. Ph.D. Thesis, Masarykova Univerzita, Pedagogická Fakulta, Brno, Czechia, 2021.
49. Buckley, P.; Doyle, E.; Doyle, S. Game on! Students' perceptions of gamified learning. *J. Educ. Technol. Soc.* **2017**, *20*, 1–10.
50. Richter, G.; Raban, D.R.; Rafaeli, S. Studying gamification: The effect of rewards and incentives on motivation. In *Gamification in Education and Business*; Springer International Publishing: Cham, Switzerland, 2015; pp. 21–46.
51. Barata, G.; Gama, S.; Jorge, J.; Gonçalves, D. Engaging engineering students with gamification. In Proceedings of the 2013 5th International Conference on Games and Virtual Worlds for Serious Applications (VS-GAMES), Poole, UK, 11–13 September 2013.
52. Rapp, A.; Hopfgartner, F.; Hamari, J.; Linehan, C.; Cena, F. Strengthening gamification studies: Current trends and future opportunities of gamification research. *Int. J. Hum. Comput. Stud.* **2019**, *127*, 1–6. [CrossRef]
53. Aldemir, T.; Celik, B.; Kaplan, G. A qualitative investigation of student perceptions of game elements in a gamified course. *Comput. Hum. Behav.* **2019**, *78*, 235–254. [CrossRef]
54. Landers, R.N.; Collmus, A.B.; Williams, H. The greatest battle is within ourselves: An experiment on the effects of competition alone on task performance. *Int. J. Hum. Comput. Stud.* **2019**, *127*, 51–61. [CrossRef]
55. Mekler, E.D.; Brühlmann, F.; Touch, A.N.; Opwis, K. Towards understanding the effects of individual gamification elements on intrinsic motivation and performance. *Comput. Hum. Behav.* **2017**, *71*, 525–534. [CrossRef]
56. Philpott, A. *Students' Reactions to the Use of Leaderboards in an EFL Class: A Gamification-Related Pilot Study*; Kwansei Gakuin University: Nishinomiya, Japan, 2015.
57. Morales, M.; Amado-Salvatierra, H.R.; Hern, R.; Pirker, J.; Gütl, C. A practical experience on the use of gamification in MOOC courses as a strategy to increase motivation. In *International Workshop on Learning Technology for Education Challenges*; Springer: Berlin/Heidelberg, Germany, 2016.
58. Attig, C.; Franke, T. I track; therefore, I walk—Exploring the motivational costs of wearing activity trackers in actual users. *Int. J. Hum. Comput. Stud.* **2019**, *127*, 211–224. [CrossRef]
59. Diefenbach, S.; Müssig, A. Counterproductive effects of gamification: An analysis on the example of the gamified task manager Habitica. *Int. J. Hum. Comput. Stud.* **2019**, *127*, 190–210. [CrossRef]
60. Philpott, A.; Son, J.-B. Leaderboards in an EFL course: Student performance and motivation. *Comput. Educ.* **2022**, *190*, 104605. [CrossRef]
61. De Andrade, B.; Poplin, A.; de Sena, I.S. Minecraft as a Tool for Engaging Children in Urban Planning: A Case Study in Tirol Town, Brazil. *ISPRS Int. J. Geo Inf.* **2020**, *9*, 170. [CrossRef]
62. Smiderle, R.; Rigo, S.J.; Marques, L.B.; de Miranda Coelho, J.A.P.; Jaques, P.A. The impact of gamification on students' learning, engagement and behavior based on their personality traits. *Smart Learn. Environ.* **2020**, *7*, 3. [CrossRef]
63. Matthews, J.S.; Ponitz, C.C.; Morrison, F.J. Early gender differences in self-regulation and academic achievement. *J. Educ. Psychol.* **2009**, *101*, 689. [CrossRef]
64. Denden, M.; Tlili, A.; Essalmi, F.; Jemni, M.; Chen, N.S.; Burgos, D. Effects of gender and personality differences on students' perception of game design elements in educational gamification. *Int. J. Hum. Comput. Stud.* **2021**, *15*, 102674. [CrossRef]
65. Schwabe, G.; Göth, C. Mobile learning with a mobile game: Design and motivational effects. *J. Comput. Assist. Learn.* **2005**, *21*, 214–216. [CrossRef]
66. Keller, J. Development and use of the ARCS model of instructional design. *J. Instr. Dev.* **1987**, *10*, 2–10. [CrossRef]

67. Ryan, R.M.; Rigby, C.S.; Przybylski, A. The motivational pull of video games: A self-determination theory approach. *Motiv. Emot.* **2006**, *30*, 344–360. [CrossRef]
68. Saeed, S.; Zyngier, D. How motivation influences student engagement: A qualitative case study. *J. Educ. Learn.* **2012**, *1*, 252–267. [CrossRef]
69. Maruping, L.; Bala, H.; Venkatesh, V.; Brown, S. Going beyond intention: Integrating behavioral expectation into the unified theory of acceptance and use of technology. *J. Assoc. Inf. Sci. Technol.* **2017**, *68*, 623–637. [CrossRef]
70. Lam, S.; Jimerson, S. Exploring Student Engagement in Schools Internationally. The International School Psychology Survey: Data from Austria, Romania, China, Portugal, and Canada. In Proceedings of the XXX ISPA Conference: School Psychology in a Changing Society, Utrecht, The Netherlands, 8–13 July 2008.
71. Sauro, J.; Lewis, J.R. When designing usability questionnaires, does it hurt to be positive? In Proceedings of the SIGCHI conference on human factors in computing systems, Vancouver, BC, Canada, 7–12 May 2011.
72. Team R Core. *R: A Language and Environment for Statistical Computing*; R Foundation for Statistical Computing: Vienna, Austria, 2013.
73. Dostál, J. Theory of problem-solving. *Procedia Soc. Behav. Sci.* **2015**, *174*, 2798–2805. [CrossRef]
74. Hwang, G.J.; Wu, P.H.; Chen, C.C.; Tu, N.T. Effects of an augmented reality-based, educational game on students' learning achievements and attitudes in real-world observations. *Interact. Learn. Environ.* **2016**, *24*, 1895–1906. [CrossRef]
75. Zhou, S.; Li, C.; Galloway, N.; Rennie, R. Attitudes towards Digital Game-Based Learning of Chinese Primary School English Teachers. In Proceedings of the Innovation in Language Learning International Conference, Florence, Italy, 8–9 November 2018.
76. Callan, R.; Bauer, K.; Landers, R. How to avoid the dark side of gamification: Ten business scenarios and their unintended consequences. In *Gamification in Education and Business*; Springer: Berlin/Heidelberg, Germany, 2015; pp. 553–568.
77. Chung, L.Y.; Chang, R.C. The effect of gender on motivation and student achievement in digital game-based learning: A case study of a contented-based classroom. *Eurasia J. Math. Sci. Technol. Educ.* **2017**, *13*, 2309–2327. [CrossRef]
78. Nguyen, H.; Hou, X.; Richey, J. The impact of gender in learning with games: A consistent effect in a math learning game. *Int. J. Game-Based Learn.* **2022**, *12*, 1–29. [CrossRef]
79. Dele-Ajayi, O.; Strachan, R.; Pickard, A.; Sanderson, J. Designing for All: Exploring Gender Diversity and Engagement with Digital Educational Games by Young People. In Proceedings of the 2018 IEEE Frontiers in Education Conference (FIE), San Jose, CA, USA, 3–6 October 2018.
80. Joiner, R.; Iacovides, J.; Owen, M.; Gavin, C.; Clibbery, S.; Darling, J.; Drew, B. Digital games, gender and learning in engineering: Do females benefit as much as males? *J. Sci. Educ. Technol.* **2011**, *20*, 178–185. [CrossRef]

computers

MDPI

Article

Developing a Sustainable Online Platform for Language Learning across Europe

Alexander Mikroyannidis [1,*], Maria Perifanou [2] and Anastasios A. Economides [2]

[1] Knowledge Media Institute, The Open University, Walton Hall, Milton Keynes MK7 6AA, UK
[2] Smart and Mobile Learning Environments (SMILE) Lab, University of Macedonia, Egnatia 156, 546 36 Thessaloniki, Greece; maria.perifanou@uom.edu.gr (M.P.); economid@uom.gr (A.A.E.)
* Correspondence: alexander.mikroyannidis@open.ac.uk

Abstract: In this paper, we present a sustainable approach for addressing the language skills gap among EU citizens, which significantly hinders their mobility across the EU and their participation in education, in training, as well as in youth programmes. Our approach is based on the sustainable design of the OpenLang Network platform, which provides an open and collaborative online learning environment for language learners and teachers across Europe, and addresses the limitations of existing computer-assisted language learning approaches. The OpenLang Network platform is bringing together educators and Erasmus+ mobility participants to improve their language skills and cultural knowledge. To this end, the OpenLang Network platform offers a collection of multilingual Open Educational Resources and language learning services. The paper presents the results from the user evaluation of the platform, which has been conducted with members of its community of language teachers and learners. A mixed methods approach has been adopted in order to collect and analyse both qualitative and quantitative data from users about the sustainable design of the OpenLang Network platform, as well as to measure the user satisfaction levels of the platform's language learning services. According to the user evaluation results, the platform offers a sustainable online environment and a positive user experience for language learning. The user evaluation has also helped us identify a set of best practices and challenges associated with the long-term sustainability of an online language learning community.

Keywords: computer-assisted language learning; sustainable design; open educational resources; language learning services; OpenLang Network platform; Europe

1. Introduction

One of the fundamental principles of the European society is the freedom of movement for people within the European Union (EU) member states [1]. The Erasmus+ programme was launched in 1987 and since then, it has had over 12 million mobility participants [2]. Erasmus+ provides exclusive chances for students and staff in higher education and in schools, as well as for trainees, adult learners, young people, youth workers and sport staff, to study, train, work, or volunteer across the EU. Nevertheless, insufficient language skills continue to hinder people's participation in education, training and youth programmes within the EU. As communication through language plays a vital role in mutual understanding and comprehension, promoting and supporting sustainable language learning for Erasmus+ mobility participants is critical.

In this paper, we present the development of a sustainable online language learning platform. The motivation behind this work is to address the language skills gap across the EU, which comprises an essential step towards facilitating mobility and knowledge exchange between participants from all EU member states. The overall research objective of this work is to explore the use of sustainable design towards providing language learning services to different groups of stakeholders. In particular, we investigate the impact of the sustainable design principles of openness, customisation, interoperability, mobility, community support, monitoring, storytelling, interactivity and gamification on the development of an online language learning environment and the resulting user experience. Our methodology is based on understanding the shortcomings of existing computer-assisted language learning approaches, followed by the sustainable design and development of an online platform that addresses these shortcomings. Additionally, our methodology includes the evaluation of the online platform that we have developed, using mixed methods to measure the satisfaction levels of end users from using the platform's language learning services, as well as to collect and analyse their views on the sustainability of the platform.

This work has been conducted in the context of the OpenLang Network, which is a research project supported by Erasmus+, aiming to address the language skills and cultural awareness requirements of Erasmus+ mobility participants and the training requirements of language teachers [3]. Specifically, the project aims to focus on the following groups of stakeholders:

- **Erasmus+ KA1 mobility participants,** such as Higher Education students and staff, vocational education and training participants, adult and school education staff, youth learners, youth workers and youth entrepreneurs, who require the enhancement of their language skills and cultural awareness.
- **Volunteer language teachers,** who assist Erasmus+ KA1 mobility participants by sharing their professional experience while receiving professional certified training on how to create, share and use language open educational resources (OERs) [4].

In the context of the OpenLang Network project, we have developed the OpenLang Network platform, the design of which has been based on a set of sustainable design principles. The OpenLang Network platform provides language learners and teachers with a range of services, such as a personal dashboard, a tandem language learning matching service, an interactive forum, a database of high-quality language OERs, as well as a responsive design that is accessible on various devices. The platform is a core output of the OpenLang Network project, aiming to establish a European language learning community [5]. In this paper, we present the sustainable principles that have driven the design of the platform, the language learning services that the platform offers to EU citizens, as well as the results from the user evaluation conducted with a representative user sample of the platform.

The remainder of this paper is organised as follows. Firstly, we discuss existing approaches and the latest developments in the research area of computer-assisted language learning. We then introduce the principles that have driven the sustainable design of the OpenLang Network platform. Subsequently, we present the language learning services that the platform offers to its community of language teachers and learners. We then present the results of the user evaluation of the platform and the feedback obtained from members of the platform's community. Finally, we distil the user feedback into a set of best practices and challenges associated with the continued sustainability of an online language learning community.

2. Related Work

The research area of computer-assisted language learning (CALL) is defined as "the search for a study of applications of the computer in language teaching and learning" [6]. This research area has undergone significant changes in the wake of recent technological developments related to the emergence of e-learning platforms and mobile apps. However, there are still certain shortcomings in the sustainability and effectiveness of the educational technologies used in the area of CALL [7]. Relevant systematic literature reviews reveal the need for technology-enhanced collaborative language learning [8] and gamified language learning [9], as well as for flexibility, continuity, timely feedback, personalisation, socialisation, self-evaluation, active participation and peer coaching in language learning [10].

A specific type of massive open online courses (MOOCs) called language MOOCs (LMOOCs) has emerged as "dedicated web-based online courses for second languages with unrestricted access and potentially unlimited participation" [11]. Although LMOOCs are quite popular with language learners and teachers, they are often designed with a prescribed learning sequence in mind, without addressing the needs and preferences of individual learners [12]. Additionally, LMOOCs often lack interactivity between instructors and learners and between learners, as well as learner-centred formative assessments [12]. Mobile-assisted language learning (MALL) is also quite popular presently, with mobile apps such as Duolingo preferred by learners for their flexibility and their gamification elements [13–15]. However, these apps are often focused on English-speaking learners and do not offer sufficient learning materials in less popular languages [16,17].

In order to address the language skills gap of EU citizens, the EU is offering linguistic support to selected participants for studying, carrying out a traineeship, or volunteering abroad in the framework of long-term mobility activities through online linguistic support (OLS) [18]. OLS participants have the opportunity to assess their language competence and they may then follow an online language course to improve their language skills. However, this approach suffers from significant limitations, most notably a lack of openness, a lack of multilingual language learning resources, as well as a lack of opportunities for collaborative language learning.

3. Sustainable Design

The design of the OpenLang Network platform has been driven by a set of sustainable design principles, which address the limitations of existing CALL approaches as discussed in the previous section. Additionally, the sustainable design of the OpenLang Network platform has been informed by a series of surveys and interviews, which have been previously conducted with Erasmus+ KA1 mobility participants in order to capture their language learning needs [19]. The resulting sustainable design principles of the OpenLang Network platform are the following:

- **Openness**: Offer an open-source code and free access to the platform's language learning materials and services.
- **Customisation**: Provide users with the ability to customise their language learning experience by allowing them to create their own learning paths or integrate third-party tools.
- **Interoperability**: Ensure that the platform can easily exchange data with other learning management systems or educational tools.
- **Mobility**: Create a mobile-responsive design or offer a dedicated mobile application for learning on-the-go.
- **Community support**: Build a community of users who can provide continuous feedback, support and opportunities for collaborative language learning.
- **Monitoring**: Provide language learners with a dashboard that allows them to track their progress and performance while studying a course and that offers teachers detailed reports on the progress of their students.
- **Storytelling**: Enable the creation of interactive and engaging language learning materials, such as simulations, games, or videos, that can help learners engage with language learning through storytelling.
- **Interactivity**: Offer a variety of tools that facilitate interactive and collaborative language learning, such as discussion forums, private messaging, live chats and more.
- **Gamification**: Incorporate gamification techniques, such as badges, in order to increase student motivation and engagement.

A key factor contributing to the sustainable design of the OpenLang Network platform has been the selection of a suitable learning management system (LMS), which provides the technological foundation for the creation, management and delivery of online learning materials [20]. The LMS comprises an integral part of the online learning experience, by enabling educators to design and deliver a wide range of pedagogical activities and by allowing learners to perform these activities either collaboratively or individually and to monitor the progress of their learning. There is currently a plethora of LMSs available to use for online learning, including both free and paid options. We have selected Moodle, an open-source LMS that has gained a remarkable level of adoption by the global education community, with more than 160,000 Moodle sites offering over 40,000,000 courses to more than 350,000,000 users worldwide, making Moodle the world's most widely used LMS [21].

Moodle fulfils all the above principles for the sustainable design of the OpenLang Network platform. As an open-source software, Moodle is completely free and can be easily modified with custom plugins to extend its codebase. It also supports interoperability with other educational platforms and systems. With its mobile application and responsive interface, Moodle offers a flexible and accessible learning experience for students. Moodle has a large and active community of developers, who continuously provide support and publish new releases. Through its tools for course authoring and third-party plugins, Moodle supports storytelling, interactivity and gamification, while also offering communication tools such as forums, messaging and live chats. Teachers can use Moodle to monitor students' progress and obtain detailed reports.

4. Language Learning Services

Based on the sustainable design principles described in the previous section, the following language learning services have been developed and are offered by the OpenLang Network platform to its community of language learners and teachers.

4.1. Language Placement Tests

As discussed in Section 2, a limitation of existing CALL approaches is the lack of multilingual language learning resources, as well as the lack of self-evaluation opportunities available to language learners. In order to address both of these limitations, the OpenLang Network platform provides 24 language placement tests for all European languages to help users self-assess their proficiency level in a specific language. Each test is accessible through a link and a PDF file, allowing users to take the test online or offline by downloading the PDF file.

The language placement tests that are available via the platform follow the language proficiency levels defined by the Common European Framework of Reference for Languages (CEFR) [22]. According to CEFR, language proficiency is recognised in six levels, A1 to C2, which can be further regrouped into three broader categories: Basic User, Independent User and Proficient User. The language placement tests service of the OpenLang Network platform allows users to self-assess their CEFR level and record it in the platform, so that they can find potential tandem language learning partners, as described in the next section.

4.2. Tandem Language Learning

In order to address the need for peer coaching in language learning, as discussed in Section 2, the OpenLang Network platform provides a matching service that enables platform members to connect with one another and engage in collaborative language learning. This service enables users to locate other members with whom they can communicate both synchronously and asynchronously for the purpose of learning a language together. Furthermore, platform members can find other members with specific language proficiency levels and review their profiles to establish connections and begin studying a language collaboratively.

Figure 1 shows the search interface of the OpenLang Network platform for finding tandem language learning partners, by selecting their preferred language, language proficiency level and time zone.

Figure 1. Finding language learning partners on the OpenLang Network platform.

4.3. *Recommended Language OERs*

The OpenLang Network platform addresses the need for multilingual language learning resources, as discussed in Section 2, by providing a language learning service that recommends high-quality language OERs from reputable educational institutions for learning European languages. The recommended language OERs available via the platform cover a wide range of languages, language proficiency levels, learning activities, as well as language learning skills. The platform users can find these language OERs via a faceted search interface, which allows them to customise their searches by using a range of filters, such as language, target language, level, resource type and more. The search interface for finding recommended language OERs on the OpenLang Network platform, and the set of search filters that enable search customisation, are shown in Figure 2.

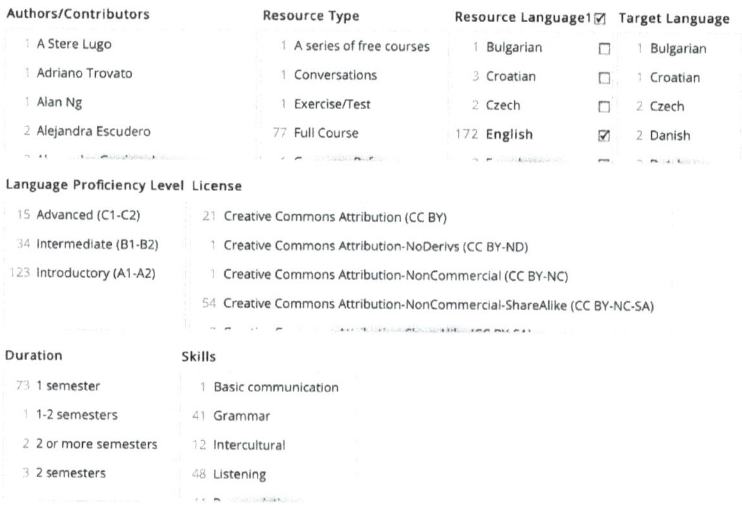

Figure 2. Search filters for finding recommended language OERs on the OpenLang Network platform.

4.4. *Shared Language OERs*

This language learning service of the OpenLang Network platform enables its users to share language OERs within the community of language learners and teachers. Users can also search for shared language OERs, and they can customise their searches by applying the same set of search filters as the ones available in the recommended language OERs service (see Figure 2 above). A gamification element has been introduced to encourage and motivate the sharing of language OERs on the platform, via the awarding of badges to the uploaders of language OERs. More specifically, users that share language OERs reach the following statuses on the platform and are awarded the corresponding badges:

- **Junior Uploader**: The user has uploaded their first language OER.
- **Senior Uploader**: The user has uploaded 5 language OERs.
- **Super Uploader**: The user has uploaded 10 language OERs.

4.5. Community Discussions

This language learning service offers a forum dedicated for collaborative language learning and discussions between all users of the platform. Through this forum, users can ask questions, search for answers, exchange experiences, seek advice, etc. Users of the platform can also subscribe to the whole forum or certain discussion threads that interest them, so that they receive notifications when a new message is posted in the forum.

4.6. OpenLang MOOC

The OpenLang Network project has developed the massive open online course (MOOC) entitled: *"Exploring how to (re)use Language Open Educational Resources (OERs)"*. The primary audience of the MOOC is language teachers and learners that want to explore the lifecycle of language OERs. The MOOC consists of 4 weeks, with each week comprising a set of modules and a quiz. After studying the learning materials of each week and passing the quiz, learners are awarded a badge. Upon completion of the whole MOOC, learners are awarded a digital certificate of participation.

Additionally, the MOOC features an Announcements forum and a Discussion forum, where announcements about the MOOC are made and discussions about the MOOC take place between learners. It should be noted that several learning activities within the modules of the MOOC invite the learners to post in the Discussion forum in order to share their views and reflections with other learners. Figure 3 shows a snapshot from the introductory materials of the MOOC, featuring a promotional video, a short description of the MOOC, as well as links to the forums of the MOOC.

Figure 3. Snapshot from the introductory materials of the OpenLang MOOC.

4.7. Personal Dashboard

The OpenLang Network platform addresses the need for personalisation in language learning, as discussed in Section 2, by offering a personal dashboard to its registered members. This dashboard displays the personal data of members that have been recorded on the platform, such as the courses they have enrolled in, the messages they have sent and received, their network of contacts, the badges they have earned and a list of other users who are currently online. The personal dashboard serves as a convenient jumping point into the personal learning journey of users on the platform, allowing them to quickly resume their learning activities on the platform from where they left off previously.

Figure 4 shows a snapshot from the personal dashboard of a user of the platform featuring, among other elements, the badges earned by the user upon completing the 4 weeks of the OpenLang MOOC, as well as the badges earned for sharing more than 10 language OERs on the platform.

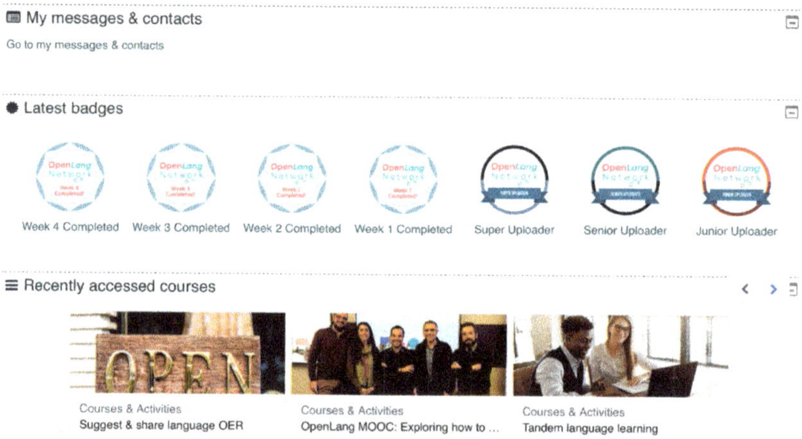

Figure 4. Snapshot from the personal dashboard available on the OpenLang Network platform.

5. User Evaluation

5.1. Methodology

The purpose of this user evaluation is to investigate the views of end users about the sustainable design of the OpenLang Network platform and measure the satisfaction levels of end users from using the language learning services of the platform. Additionally, this user evaluation intends to collect the views of end users about the continuous sustainability of the platform beyond the lifetime of the OpenLang Network project.

The user evaluation of the OpenLang Network platform has been conducted via an online survey administered via email to members of its community of language learners and teachers. The survey was administered in the English language, as this is the most widely spoken language in this community. The sampling method employed was judgment/purposive sampling, according to which participants are selected for a specific quality relevant to the study in question [23].

The survey sample of platform members was selected based on their level of engagement with the platform. More specifically, community members were selected based on the number of language learning services that they have used on the platform, as well as the amount of time that they have spent using these services. We have therefore included in this user evaluation community members that could provide informed feedback based on their high level of knowledge of the platform's language learning services.

Based on the judgment/purposive sampling method, 112 members of the platform were selected and invited via email to respond to the online survey. A total of 61 community members (Females = 38, Males = 22, N/A = 1) responded to the online survey (54% response rate). Their average age was 36–45 years. Most of them (36) had a medium level of digital skills, 19 stated a high level and 6 perceived their level of digital skills to be low.

Additional feedback was collected from members of the OpenLang community of language learners and teachers via an online consultation workshop. During this workshop, the outcomes of the OpenLang Network project were presented, and discussions were held about the sustainability of the OpenLang Network platform beyond the end of the project. The workshop was attended by 56 participants (Females = 29, Males = 27) with an average age of 36–45 years. Most of the participants (33) were language teachers and the rest were language learners (9) and academics/researchers (14).

The sample of this user evaluation has been deemed sufficient for the analysis of the collected data, based on several factors. Firstly, the research objectives and scope of the study were considered, focusing on specific themes or patterns within the collected responses. Secondly, the concept of saturation was taken into account, ensuring that new information or insights were no longer emerging from additional participants. Moreover, the research context, including the diversity of the population, was considered to determine the adequacy of the sample size. Finally, practical constraints, such as time and resources, were considered when determining the sample size.

We adopted a mixed methods approach by collecting and analysing both qualitative and quantitative data from the users of the platform. In this way, we acquired more thorough user feedback than from a standalone qualitative or quantitative evaluation. More specifically, qualitative data were collected via open-ended questions in the administered survey, as well as by recording the discussion sessions with participants during the online consultation workshop. Quantitative data were collected via Likert scale questions in the administered survey. Subsequently, content analysis was performed for the analysis of the qualitative data collected via the survey and the workshop. For the analysis of the quantitative data collected via the survey, descriptive statistics methods were used. The results from this analysis are presented and discussed in the following sections.

5.2. Results

Table 1 shows the results of the Likert scale questions of the administered survey regarding user experience with the OpenLang Network platform. As depicted in Table 1, all survey items were rated above 4.00 out of 5.00, indicating a positive experience with the platform and its language learning services.

Table 1. Descriptive statistics of the survey results regarding user experience with the OpenLang Network platform.

Question	Min	Max	Mean	Std. Deviation
The platform is easy to use.	3	5	4.42	0.752
The speed of the platform is sufficient not causing any access delays.	3	5	4.21	0.631
The platform can be accessed using any device (desktop, laptop, smartphone, etc.) and any operating system (Windows, MacOS, iOS, Android, Linux, etc.).	3	5	4.28	0.705
The platform functions well all the time.	3	5	4.11	0.790
The technical support of the platform solved any technical problems that I encountered.	3	5	4.37	0.694

A set of open-ended questions in the administered survey captured the views of respondents about the positive and negative aspects of the platform, suggestions for potential improvements of the platform's language learning services, as well as how the teaching and learning practices of respondents have been affected as a result of using the platform's language learning services. Some indicative responses were the following:

> *"I especially came to understand the existence and potential of reaching, using and sharing OERs in my own teaching setting."*

> *"I am planning to develop a Reading course based solely on the use, revision and adaptation of OERs by applying the knowledge and skills I gained from the [OpenLang] MOOC."*
>
> *"[The platform is] easy to navigate. The material is clearly presented and easy to follow."*
>
> *"[The platform offers] self-paced learning and networking opportunities."*
>
> *"[The platform offers] useful suggestions to OER directories, platforms, repositories."*
>
> *"Just one thing I can suggest is that there should have been a clear and tangible demonstration of a working example of an adapted and real OER in the form of a running course."*
>
> *"I would like a hands-on workshop to consolidate knowledge acquired."*

5.3. Discussion

The results of the user evaluation indicate that users had a positive experience with the platform and its language learning services. More specifically, they found the platform to be easy to navigate and to use, to be sufficiently responsive, to be easily accessed from various devices, as well as to provide sufficient technical support. The platform had a positive impact on the teaching and learning practices of teachers and learners, specifically regarding the use, adaptation and sharing of language OERs.

During the discussion sessions of the online consultation workshop, participants indicated that continued technical and end-user support is critical for the sustainability of the OpenLang Network platform. Another sustainability factor that emerged from the workshop discussions was the need for community events (online, face-to-face, or hybrid) that will bring together members of the community to discuss and share their views on common language learning and teaching issues, as well as to share their best practices on language learning and teaching.

All these factors will be taken into consideration by the consortium of the OpenLang Network project, in order to ensure the sustainability of the OpenLang Network platform and the growth of its community of language learners and teachers beyond the lifetime of the project. Additionally, the analysis of the qualitative feedback collected via the survey and via the workshop led to the identification of a set of best practices and challenges, which are presented in the following section.

6. Best Practices and Associated Challenges

Building and sustaining an online community of language learners and teachers requires the careful consideration of strategies that can help ensure the long-term viability of such an initiative. Based on the analysis of the user feedback received from the community of the OpenLang Network platform, we identified the following set of best practices and challenges associated with ensuring the sustainability of such a community:

1. **Fostering community engagement**: Encouraging users to participate actively in the community by promoting a friendly and inclusive online environment, encouraging open communication and collaboration and providing opportunities for users to interact with each other can foster engagement and interaction among members, thus creating a sense of community.
2. **Providing high-quality resources**: Providing high-quality resources, such as language learning OERs and other interactive language learning services, can attract members and create value for them. However, it can be challenging to provide relevant and up-to-date resources that meet the diverse needs of community members.
3. **Promoting user-generated content**: Encouraging users to create and share their own language learning resources, such as OERs, can help to build a more diverse and comprehensive set of resources, as well as increase user engagement. However, ensuring the quality and accuracy of user-generated content can be challenging,

especially when dealing with a large number of contributors. This challenge can be partially overcome by allowing users to rate user-generated content.

4. **Ensuring effective communication**: Ensuring effective communication among members of the community can facilitate collaboration, knowledge sharing, as well as the exchange of language learning strategies. However, it can be challenging to ensure effective communication due to language barriers, different time zones, as well as technical issues.
5. **Providing continuous support and feedback**: Providing users with access to support resources, such as FAQs and help forums, as well as regularly soliciting feedback from users to identify areas for improvement and address user concerns is an important sustainability factor. Nevertheless, it can be challenging to provide effective support and feedback when dealing with a large and diverse user base. Additionally, addressing user concerns can be time-consuming and resource intensive.
6. **Maintaining up-to-date technology**: Keeping the community platform and the associated technology up-to-date to ensure compatibility, security and accessibility can help to ensure the sustainability of the community in the long term. Nevertheless, maintaining up-to-date technology can be quite challenging, especially when dealing with limited resources or technological barriers.

The above best practices can potentially offer opportunities to language learners and teachers by creating an inclusive and collaborative online environment for learning, teaching and sharing language learning resources. Members can benefit from high-quality language learning resources and services, gain access to a network of peers and experts and improve their language skills and cultural knowledge. However, each of the above best practices presents unique challenges that must be addressed in order to ensure the long-term sustainability of an online language learning community.

7. Conclusions

The goal of the OpenLang Network platform is to address the EU language skills gap by offering a sustainable online environment to language teachers, language learners and Erasmus+ mobility participants who desire to enhance their language abilities and cultural knowledge. The contribution of this work is primarily in the field of computer-assisted language learning and, specifically, in addressing the limitations of existing CALL approaches, including the lack of openness, the lack of multilingual language learning resources, the lack of self-evaluation opportunities available to language learners, the lack of peer coaching, as well as the lack of opportunities for collaborative language learning. In order to address these limitations, we have employed a set of sustainable design principles and we have developed a wide range of language learning services. The design of the OpenLang Network platform has been based on the sustainable design principles of openness, customisation, interoperability, mobility, community support, monitoring, storytelling, interactivity and gamification. The OpenLang Network platform is an inclusive and collaborative online environment that offers a wide range of language learning services, notably language placement tests, tandem language learning, as well as a vast array of language OERs. We have adopted a mixed methods approach in order to collect and analyse user feedback about the platform. The feedback collected from this user evaluation has been distilled into a set of best practices towards ensuring the sustainability of an online language learning community.

A limitation of the present study has been the limited number of participants in the user evaluation of the platform. This limitation is attributed to the relatively small number of participants that have been actively using the platform during its early stages of development. The authors plan to address this limitation in subsequent user evaluation studies that will enable larger numbers of platform members to participate, as the community of language learners and teachers that are actively using the platform is growing over time. Another direction for future work is further investigating and monitoring the continued sustainability of the platform by organising additional consultation workshops with more members of the platform's community. Additionally, the authors will continue improving the platform's language learning services as a means to further sustain the platform. Such improvement plans include enhancing the accessibility of the platform by ensuring compliance with accessibility standards and providing tools to assist learners with disabilities.

Author Contributions: Platform design and implementation: A.M.; evaluation design and reporting of results: A.M., M.P. and A.A.E. All authors have read and agreed to the published version of the manuscript.

Funding: This research has received funding from the European Union's Erasmus+ programme under grant agreement 2018-1-EL01-KA203-047967 (OpenLang Network).

Informed Consent Statement: Informed consent was obtained from all subjects involved in the study.

Data Availability Statement: All data were presented in the main text.

Conflicts of Interest: The authors declare no conflict of interest.

References

1. Ritzen, J.; Haas, J.; Kahanec, M. *EU Mobility*; IZA Institute of Labor Economics: Bonn, Germany, 2017.
2. European Commission. *Erasmus+ Annual Report*; European Commission: Brussels, Belgium, 2021.
3. Perifanou, M.; Economides, A.A. The OPENLang Network pedagogical framework: Designing an open and collaborative language learning environment for Erasmus+ KA1 mobility participants. In Proceedings of the Learning and Collaboration Technologies: New Challenges and Learning Experiences: 8th International Conference, LCT 2021, Held as Part of the 23rd HCI International Conference, HCII 2021, Virtual Event, 24–29 July 2021; Part I. pp. 140–160.
4. Atkins, D.E.; Brown, J.S.; Hammond, A.L. *A Review of the Open Educational Resources (OER) Movement: Achievements, Challenges, and New Opportunities*; The William and Flora Hewlett Foundation: Menlo Park, CA, USA, 2007.
5. Mikroyannidis, A.; Perifanou, M.; Economides, A.; Giordano, A. The OpenLang Network Platform: Building a European Community of Language Learners and Teachers. In Proceedings of the 23rd International Conference on Interactive Collaborative Learning (ICL 2020), Tallinn, Estonia, 23–25 September 2020.
6. Levy, M. *Computer-Assisted Language Learning: Context and Conceptualization*; Oxford University Press: Singapore, 1997.
7. Zhang, R.; Zou, D. Types, purposes, and effectiveness of state-of-the-art technologies for second and foreign language learning. *Comput. Assist. Lang. Learn.* **2022**, *35*, 696–742. [CrossRef]
8. Su, F.; Zou, D. Technology-enhanced collaborative language learning: Theoretical foundations, technologies, and implications. *Comput. Assist. Lang. Learn.* **2022**, *35*, 1754–1788. [CrossRef]
9. Dehghanzadeh, H.; Fardanesh, H.; Hatami, J.; Talaee, E.; Noroozi, O. Using gamification to support learning English as a second language: A systematic review. *Comput. Assist. Lang. Learn.* **2021**, *34*, 934–957. [CrossRef]
10. Kukulska-Hulme, A.; Viberg, O. Mobile collaborative language learning: State of the art. *Br. J. Educ. Technol.* **2018**, *49*, 207–218. [CrossRef]
11. Bárcena, E.; Martín-Monje, E. Introduction. LMOOCs: An emerging field. *LMOOCs Provid. Learn. Transcending Boundaries* **2014**, 1–15. [CrossRef]
12. Chong, S.W.; Khan, M.A.; Reinders, H. A critical review of design features of LMOOCs. *Comput. Assist. Lang. Learn.* **2022**, 1–21. [CrossRef]
13. Shortt, M.; Tilak, S.; Kuznetcova, I.; Martens, B.; Akinkuolie, B. Gamification in mobile-assisted language learning: A systematic review of Duolingo literature from public release of 2012 to early 2020. *Comput. Assist. Lang. Learn.* **2021**, *36*, 517–554. [CrossRef]
14. García Botero, G.; Questier, F.; Zhu, C. Self-directed language learning in a mobile-assisted, out-of-class context: Do students walk the talk? *Comput. Assist. Lang. Learn.* **2019**, *32*, 71–97. [CrossRef]
15. Kukulska-Hulme, A. Reflections on research questions in mobile assisted language learning. *J. China Comput.-Assist. Lang. Learn.* **2021**, *1*, 28–46. [CrossRef]
16. Loewen, S.; Crowther, D.; Isbell, D.R.; Kim, K.M.; Maloney, J.; Miller, Z.F.; Rawal, H. Mobile-assisted language learning: A Duolingo case study. *ReCALL* **2019**, *31*, 293–311. [CrossRef]
17. Shadiev, R.; Liu, T.; Hwang, W.Y. Review of research on mobile-assisted language learning in familiar, authentic environments. *Br. J. Educ. Technol.* **2020**, *51*, 709–720. [CrossRef]
18. Online Language Support. Available online: https://erasmus-plus.ec.europa.eu/resources-and-tools/online-language-support (accessed on 23 June 2023).
19. Kosmas, P.; Parmaxi, A.; Perifanou, M.; Economides, A.A.; Zaphiris, P. Creating the Profile of Participants in Mobility Activities in the Context of Erasmus+: Motivations, Perceptions, and Linguistic Needs. In Proceedings of the International Conference on Human-Computer Interaction, Copenhagen, Denmark, 19–24 July 2020; pp. 499–511.

20. Turnbull, D.; Chugh, R.; Luck, J. Learning Management Systems, An Overview. *Encycl. Educ. Inf. Technol.* **2020**, *44*, 1052–1058. [CrossRef]
21. Moodle Statistics. Available online: https://stats.moodle.org (accessed on 23 June 2023).
22. Common European Framework of Reference for Languages (CEFR). Available online: https://www.coe.int/en/web/common-european-framework-reference-languages/home (accessed on 23 June 2023).
23. Chaudhuri, A.; Stenger, H. *Survey Sampling: Theory and Methods*; CRC Press: Boca Raton, FL, USA, 2005.

computers

MDPI

Review

Design Recommendations for Immersive Virtual Reality Application for English Learning: A Systematic Review

Jessica Rodrigues Esteves [1,*], Jorge C. S. Cardoso [2,*] and Berenice Santos Gonçalves [1]

[1] Department of Design, Federal University of Santa Catarina, Florianópolis 88040-900, Brazil; berenice@cce.ufsc.br

[2] Department of Informatics Engineering, Centre for Informatics and Systems of the University of Coimbra, 3030-790 Coimbra, Portugal

* Correspondence: jessica.rodrigues.esteves@gmail.com (J.R.E.); jorgecardoso@dei.uc.pt (J.C.S.C.)

Abstract: The growing popularity of immersive virtual reality (iVR) technologies has opened up new possibilities for learning English. In the literature, it is possible to find several studies focused on the design, development, and evaluation of immersive virtual reality applications. However, there are no studies that systematize design recommendations for immersive virtual reality applications for English learning. To fill this gap, we present a systematic review that aims to identify design recommendations for immersive virtual reality English learning applications. We searched the ACM Digital Library, ERIC, IEEE Xplore, Scopus, and Web of Science (1 January 2010 to April 2023) and found that 24 out of 847 articles met the inclusion criteria. We identified 18 categories of design considerations related to design and learning and a design process used to create iVR applications. We also identified existing trends related to universities, publications, devices, human senses, and development platforms. Finally, we addressed study limitations and future directions for designing iVR applications for English learning.

Keywords: immersive virtual reality; English learning; education; learning

1. Introduction

Technological development has given rise to various interface typologies that facilitate the use of immersive technologies, including augmented and virtual reality, tangible elements, wearable computing, etc. [1]. This expansion of interaction modes has enabled the design of digital interfaces to enhance user experiences, whether through immersive technologies or human senses. In this context, Virtual Reality (VR) has gained popularity and found application in diverse fields.

Traditionally, VR is defined as an interactive virtual environment composed of digital objects. In general, VR entails a three-dimensional computer-generated environment that users can interact with using a VR headset. Two key concepts in understanding immersive VR applications are immersion and presence. Slater [2] defines immersion as the objective level of sensory fidelity a VR system offers, while presence refers to a user's subjective psychological response to a VR system. Immersion is measurable and objective, whereas presence is an individual and context-dependent user response connected to the feeling of "being there" [2].

Immersive Virtual Reality (iVR) provides the highest level of immersion, where users engage fully with computer-generated simulations, exploring sensory experiences in a virtual world. iVR applications induce a sense of presence or "being there" in the user's perception [3]. In this way, iVR environments allow human and virtual agents to co-exist, which creates a mixed reality environment of the physical and virtual worlds [4].

In recent years, consumer Virtual Reality (VR) devices have become more affordable, introducing a consistent number of users to this technology [5]. Accordingly, VR has been applied to training and learning in many fields, as well as industrial processes [6,7], cultural heritage [8,9], military training [7], surgery [10], and geography [11], physics [12] and language learning [13–24].

In educational settings, VR and head-mounted displays (HMDs) can provide learners with exposure to demanding or instructional scenarios, enabling them to repeatedly hone new skills in an environment conducive to making corrections and experiencing non-harmful mistakes [10]. Within the context of language education, educators confront a formidable challenge: seamlessly integrating a range of technologies into their teaching methods, all the while catering to the diverse learning needs of their students. In this way, virtual reality can provide an innovative avenue for engaging learners in the educational process [25].

Virtual Reality (VR) has captured considerable interest within the realm of English language education, since it provides an immersive and interactive environment that enhances and enriches the language learning experience [15,17,21,23,24,26–28]. According to Pinto et al. [29], VR enhances language learning by boosting motivation and engagement, increasing student interest, and introducing gamified elements into the learning process. Additionally, VR technologies can support second language acquisition, and their integration with traditional learning methods is crucial for advancing knowledge and facilitating adaptation to various interaction methods and contexts, particularly in foreign language learning.

Huang et al. [30] reported that Augmented Reality (AR) and VR technologies enhance language learning by promoting immersive experiences, motivation, interaction, and reducing learning anxiety. However, the authors highlighted challenges such as student distraction caused by virtual content, which might divert their attention from the learning material. Moreover, the effectiveness of AR and VR in promoting language learning may hinge on factors like technology quality, activity design, and individual learner differences.

Peixoto et al. [31] concluded that the relationship between iVR and foreign language learning is largely positive, especially compared with conventional pedagogical methods. They noted that iVR was more enjoyable and significantly more effective than traditional teaching methods for language learning. Notably, participants who used VR exhibited significantly better vocabulary retention than those using traditional methods. Additionally, the kinesthetic aspect of VR played a substantial role in vocabulary retention.

In a systematic review encompassing 32 peer-reviewed studies published between 2015 and 2020, Dhimolea, Kaplan-Rakowski, & Lin [32] found that multiple exposures to VR are effective for learning. In addition, VR was advantageous for contextual vocabulary learning, and perceptions of VR-based language learning were positive.

Parmaxi [33] discovered that VR has the potential to offer dynamic learning experiences and enhance language learning performance, motivation, critical thinking, and higher-order cognitive skills. The use of VR in language education also led to increased student learning and the development of twenty-first century skills, such as communication and problem-solving. Furthermore, VR provides access to environments and situations that are challenging to replicate in traditional classrooms, facilitating the adoption of various instructional strategies.

Bahari [34] observed a research trend favoring the application of VR tools and affordances for improving listening and speaking skills in language learning compared with reading and writing skills. The VR environment provides affordances that foster language skill development through strategies like contextualized learning, immersive experiences, increased engagement, interactive learning, collaboration, and scaffolding. While listening and speaking skills have received more attention in VR-based research, reading and writing skills are less compatible with virtual environments.

The aforementioned articles collectively highlight the potential of VR for English language learning, addressing topics such as gamification [29], benefits of AR and VR for learning outcomes [32], features and educational methods [33], as well as affordances and challenges [34]. VR-assisted language learning has expanded in recent years, and proven to be beneficial in both the cognitive and affective aspects [30,33,35,36]. There were not found, however, studies that address guidelines or considerations to design iVR applications for English learning. To address this gap, we present a systematic review with the following objectives:

- Identify design recommendations for immersive Virtual Reality (iVR) applications focused on English language learning.
- Examine the process of developing iVR applications for English language learning.
- Analyze the utilization of human senses in iVR applications for English language learning.
- Provide directions for future research.

To achieve these objectives, this systematic review will address the following research questions:

RQ1: "Which human senses are most frequently employed in iVR applications for English language learning?"

RQ2: "Which iVR platforms are most commonly used for developing English language learning applications?"

RQ3: "What characterizes the design processes employed to create iVR applications tailored for English language learning?"

RQ4: "What design recommendations guide the design and development of iVR applications for English language learning?"

2. Method

A systematic evaluation of existing literature was conducted using a well-defined and methodical search approach, including criteria for inclusion and exclusion. In this process, the researchers have adhered to the guidance provided by the PRISMA Statement [37].

2.1. Eligibility Criteria

The inclusion and exclusion criteria were established to ensure that the selected studies were relevant and met the objectives of the review (Table 1). These criteria were applied independently by two reviewers to ensure objectivity and to minimize bias in the selection of studies. It was decided to limit the search to articles published from the year 2010 onwards, as this was the year in which relevant VR headsets were released.

Table 1. Inclusion and exclusion criteria.

	Inclusion Criteria	Exclusion Criteria
Publication period:	Published between January 2010 to May 2023.	Published before January 2010 or after May 2023.
Type of document:	Scientific article published in peer-reviewed journal or conference.	Not an article published in a peer-reviewed journal or conference.
Availability:	Accessible with Coimbra University's credentials	Behind a paywall
Type of study:	Applied research.	Other research (review, surveys, systematic literature review...).
Language:	English.	Not English.
Theme:	English learning.	Not English learning.
Research topic:	Immersive virtual reality.	Not immersive.
Number of pages:	Paper with 5 pages or more.	Paper with 4 pages or less.

2.2. Search Strategy

The ACM Digital Library, ERIC, IEEE Xplore, Scopus, and Web of Science were the databases chosen for this study. These databases are acknowledged as substantial and dependable sources of high-quality publications within the fields of Computer Science and

Engineering. In their initial search, the researchers employed a basic string to encapsulate the primary components of this systematic literature review (SLR): "Virtual reality" AND "English learning". In order to ensure a more all-encompassing exploration, synonyms and adjacent terms were incorporated. As a result, the ensuing search query was formulated as shown in Table 2.

Table 2. Search string.

Topic	Search Terms
Immersive virtual reality	("virtual reality" OR "immersive virtual reality" OR "immersive VR" OR "virtual environment" OR "immersive environment")
English learning	("English teaching" OR "English learning" OR "English teaching" OR "English as a second language" OR "English as a foreign language" OR "English as an additional language" OR "English training")

The search string was used to search these six global educational databases, specifically in the title, abstract, and/or keywords sections. The search was carried out in May 2023, resulting in the initial detection of 847 records.

As mentioned in the eligibility criteria subsection, the year 2010 was established as a limit due to the release of important VR headsets. These headsets played a crucial role in laying the groundwork for the subsequent surge in interest and development in VR technology. The gathered papers were brought into Mendeley using the BibTeX format, with the intention of removing duplicate papers, making necessary adjustments, and subsequently exporting them to a spreadsheet.

2.3. *Study Selection*

For each paper that was gathered, the title, abstract, and keywords were cross-referenced against the eligibility criteria. This stage involved both researchers independently and systematically reviewing the abstracts of the collected papers in an unbiased manner. When agreement was not reached, the articles were preserved for a more meticulous examination during the full-text analysis phase.

2.4. *Data Collection Process*

A data extraction form was generated to streamline the data collection process. This form was devised in accordance with the objectives of the systematic review, guaranteeing the comprehensive retrieval of pertinent information. Initially, the collected variables encompassed article data, including particulars such as publication type, year, keywords, abstract, journal name, and the country of the affiliated university. Also, it was registered with what type of VR headset the study was conducted, article main findings, and human senses used for the VR application. Regarding the design recommendations and process of developing iVR applications, it was registered in the sheets based on a text analysis.

The data were organized in spreadsheets for initial data processing. Subsequently, this document was imported into ATLAS.ti (Version 23.3.0) for content analysis.

Content analysis refers to a set of techniques for analyzing communications in order to obtain, through systematic and objective procedures for describing message content, indicators that allow for the inference of knowledge related to the conditions of these messages [38].

The process of content analysis is divided into four phases: (I) pre-analysis; (II) codification; (III) categorization, and (IV) analysis. The goal is to present the content and meaning of patterns in the data, which will give rise to codes. These codes, in turn, are identified by the researchers before, during, and after the analysis.

2.5. Quality Assessment

The full texts included for analysis were assessed for a quality assessment, based on three criteria:

- Criteria 1: Reports design or use of an application for teaching English; AND
- Criteria 2: Provides design considerations or guidelines; OR
- Criteria 3: Explain how VR applications are developed.

If the article matches the criteria 1 and one of the criteria 2 or 3, it was included in the review. Two researchers conducted a quality assessment of the full texts selected for analysis, using three criteria. The evaluation was performed to ensure that the chosen articles aligned with the review's objectives. Specifically, criterion 1 was obligatory, while criteria 2 and 3 were considered as optional. To clarify, for an article to be included in the review, it needed to meet criterion 1 and at least one of the other criteria. For instance, if an article satisfied criterion 1 and either criterion 2 or 3, it was deemed eligible for inclusion in the review.

3. Results

A total of 847 records were identified in the first phase of the study. Figure 1 offers a visual representation of the article identification, screening, and inclusion process, providing specific information about the criteria used.

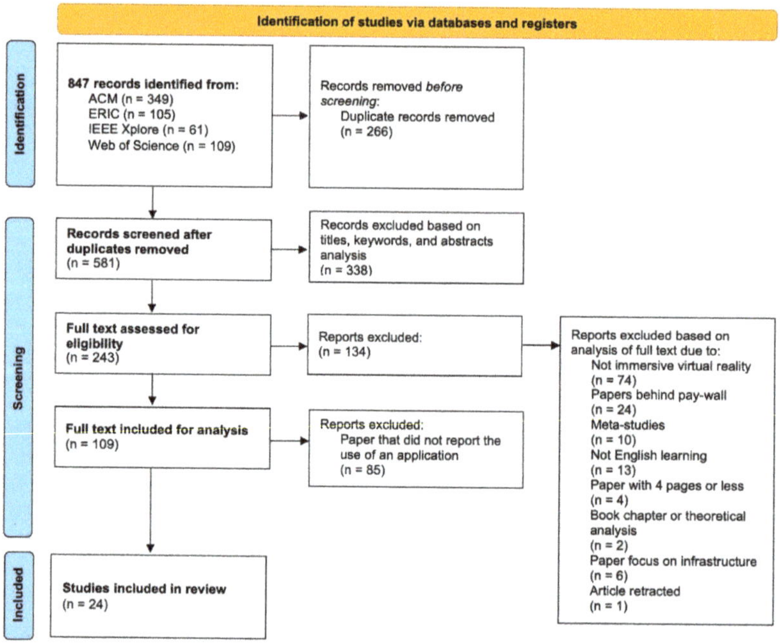

Figure 1. PRISMA flow diagram of the systematic literature review carried on. The diagram is divided three phase: identification, screening, and included.

After removing duplicate articles (n = 266), 581 papers were analyzed in the screening phase. In the second phase, 338 records were rejected based on titles, keywords, and abstract analysis. It is worth noting that a significant number of articles (n = 338) identified during the screening phase were excluded because they did not meet the inclusion criteria. Many of these studies focused on the use of virtual environments, such as online virtual worlds and three-dimensional virtual environments, rather than immersive virtual reality environments. Therefore, the exclusion of these studies does not affect the outcome of the conducted systematic review.

For a full-text assessment of eligibility, 243 papers were analyzed. Later, 134 reports were excluded based on eligibility criteria, and 85 were excluded because they did not report the use of an application. Lastly, 24 were included in the review.

3.1. Overview Analysis

The findings of the SLR revealed an observation: although we initially used the year 2010 as a research filter, the studies encompassed in the review were actually published from 2018 onwards, as indicated in Figure 2. Notably, the bulk of these studies emerged in 2021 (n = 9), followed by 2020 (n = 6). Since this SLR was conducted in May 2023, the researchers anticipate that more studies will likely be published by the end of the year.

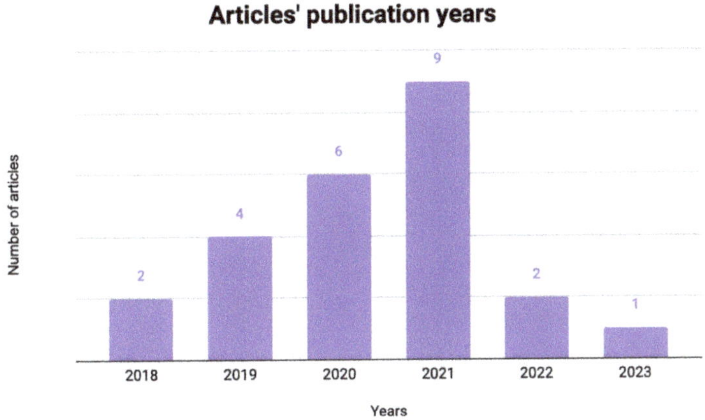

Figure 2. Graph of articles' publication years.

In terms of articles categorized by the affiliating university's country of the authors, Figure 3 shows China as the predominant contributor with the highest number of articles (n = 10). This was trailed by Taiwan (n = 6).

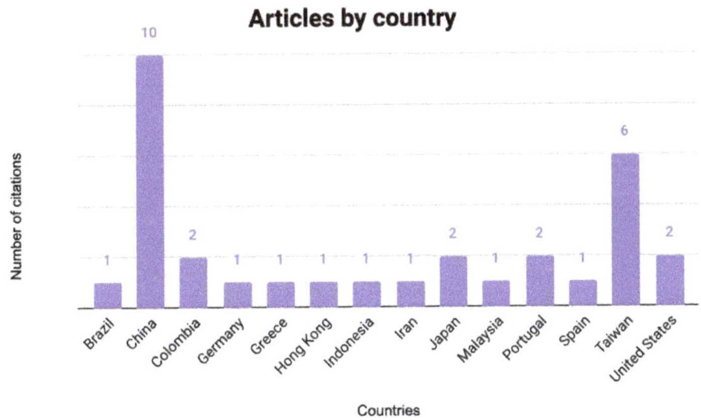

Figure 3. Graph of articles by country.

In order to represent the most used keywords, a word cloud was designed. Figure 4 reveals that the common keywords related with iVR and English learning are education, language, virtual, learning, reality, English, and environments.

Figure 4. Word cloud of most used keywords.

In relation to typical journals or conference proceedings, it was not possible to identify a pattern. However, an observation was made: half of the articles were published in conference proceedings, while the other half were published in journals (Figure 5).

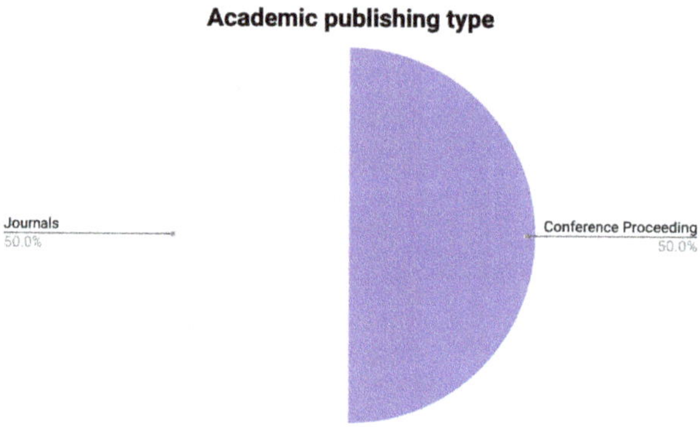

Figure 5. Graph of academic publishing type.

Figure 6 shows that the HTC Vive is the most common VR headset used in the analyzed articles; however, 8 papers did not report which VR headset was used in their studies. It is also important to highlight that many studies used low-cost VR headsets, such as Google Cardboard ($n = 3$), Samsung Gear VR ($n = 2$), and VR Box ($n = 1$).

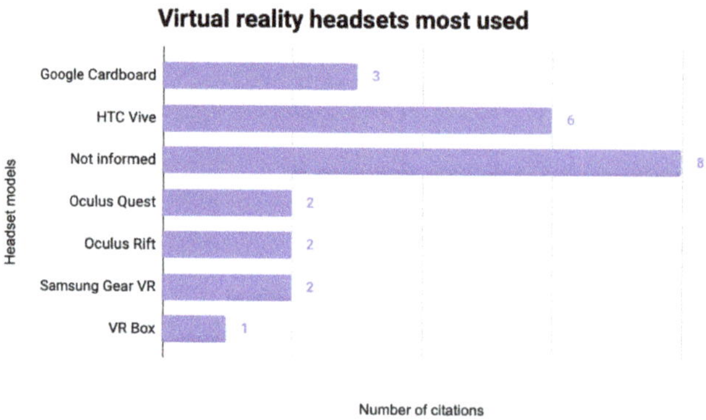

Figure 6. Graph of virtual reality headsets most used.

Visual and auditory stimulation are the most explored senses in the analyzed iVR applications (Figure 7). Touch was also mentioned (n = 3), and proprioception (n = 1) was noted as well. Unity was the most used platform to develop iVR applications (Figure 8).

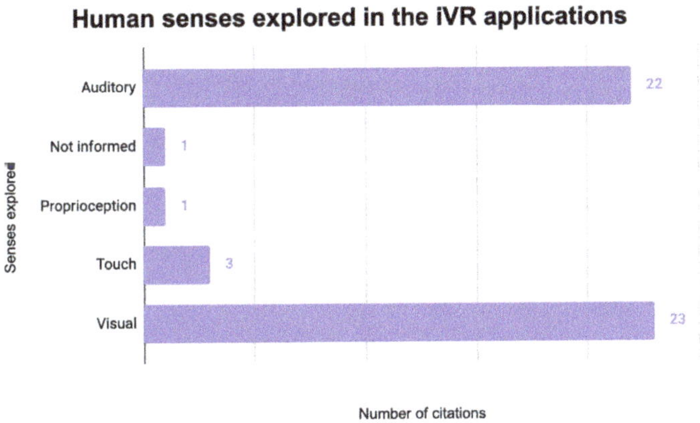

Figure 7. Graph of human senses explored in the iVR applications.

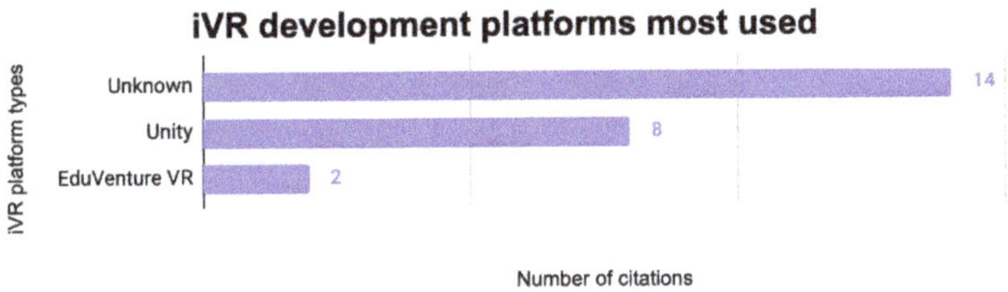

Figure 8. Graph of iVR development platforms most used.

To examine the approach employed in creating iVR applications, the researchers analyzed whether the article detailed the design of a novel application for English learning or reported the utilization of pre-existing ones. Figure 9 shows that most studies used a novel iVR app developed by themselves (n = 9). It is also important to notice that some studies used a pre-existing iVR app (n = 8) and pre-existing 360-degree video (n = 3). Additionally, some studies created a novel iVR app using EduVenture VR, a web-based authoring tool (n = 2).

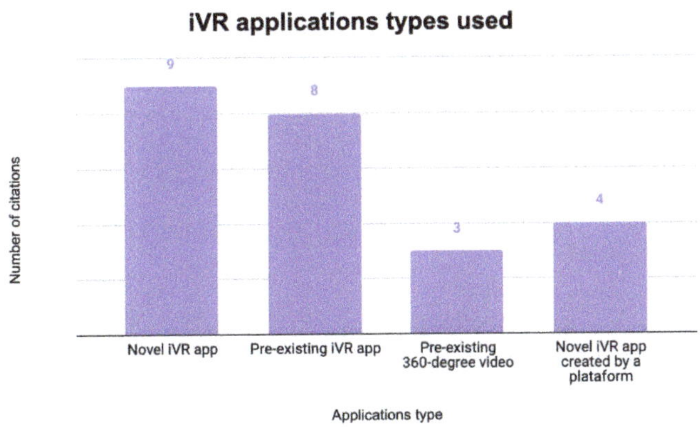

Figure 9. Graph of iVR applications types used.

3.2. Content Analysis

3.2.1. Design Process to Develop iVR Applications

Although most of the articles (Figure 9) propose novel iVR applications ($n = 9$), it was not possible to identify a clear and descriptive design process to develop iVR applications. Nevertheless, by analyzing articles that delve into iVR application development, we were able to distill common design process patterns. From this analysis, ten articles emerged that provide insights into the design of iVR applications. Based on similar terms and expressions, we identified patterns and group them into categories. Figure 10 shows a Sankey diagram illustrating the relationship between authors and categories identified in the content analysis. The Sankey diagram was generated by ATLAS.ti (Version 23.3.0).

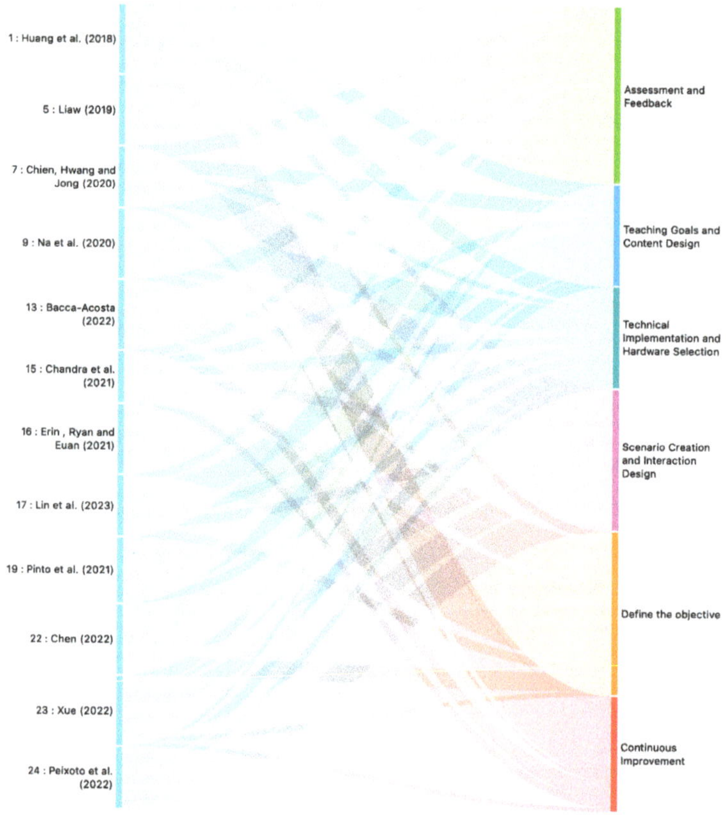

Figure 10. Sankey diagram depicting categories of the design process identified based on authors [15–19,21,23,24,26,27,39,40]. The left column presents references to articles extracted from the SLR, while the right column displays the identified categories. The connecting lines within the diagram illustrate the relationships between authors and categories. The width of these lines directly quantifies the volume of encoded text, with wider lines denoting greater content and narrower lines indicating smaller amounts of content.

The Sankey Diagram serves as a technique for visualizing the interrelation of data elements, showcasing data flows and connections across diverse fields. The line widths within Figure 10's diagram directly reflect the extent of content marked during the coding process. Consequently, categories featuring broader lines signify a greater volume of text, whereas narrower lines denote smaller amounts of coded content. In this way, all the connections to the left are directly related to right side.

Huang et al. [24] developed a VR English learning game based on the Assessment, Pedagogy, and Technology (APT) model. The design process emphasizes alignment with pedagogical goals, student engagement, real-time feedback, and collaboration between technology and education experts. The iterative nature of testing and refinement ensures that the final product effectively supports language learning while leveraging the potential of VR technology.

Chien, Hwang, and Jong [16] presented a VR application based on spherical video. To develop the application, the design process involved selecting the development environment, structuring the spherical video-based virtual reality (SVVR) system, creating authentic learning contexts, scripting interactions, integrating tags for guidance, and incorporating learning tasks. The design aimed to provide students with immersive experiences, allowing them to engage in authentic conversations and practice their English-speaking skills within a virtual environment.

Na et al. [26] developed a VR application that aims to leverage the immersive capabilities of VR technology. Regarding the design process, it encompasses various elements such as VR environment setup, practice scenarios, result assessment, and integration of speech recognition technology.

In Bacca-Acosta's [21] work, the design process involved collaborating with educators, adapting theoretical frameworks, designing scaffolds, implementing an experimental setup, and employing eye-tracking technology to evaluate the effectiveness of the designed scaffolds within the IVR learning environments. The specific topic chosen for the applications aimed to address a challenging area in English language learning and capitalize on the interactive nature of IVR technology.

Chandra et al. [15] utilized the Scrum methodology, involving stages such as requirement gathering, backlog creation, and sprint development. Four sprints were executed sequentially: the first encompassed storyboarding and asset preparation; the second focused on GUI design and data collection; the third involved game level development and testing; and the fourth centered on programming and testing using the C# language. Stakeholder evaluation and acceptance occurred after each sprint, with continuous improvement and risk management.

For Lin et al. [18], the design process involved selecting a pedagogical framework, defining learning goals, composing content and activities, creating interactive elements, and utilizing the EduVenture VR platform to develop an immersive and engaging language learning experience focused on English for Tourism Purposes.

Pinto et al. [29] developed an application featuring seven scenarios, using the Unity game engine. The initial tutorial introduced game mechanics, while subsequent scenarios presented context-based evaluation exercises in tourism-related contexts. Players' progression depended on correct answers, facilitated by interaction with a virtual TV that provided feedback through videos and indicators. In Chen's [23] study, the design process entails meticulous deliberation of gameplay mechanics, educational objectives, technical implementation, and user experience, resulting in the development of a mobile VR English learning game enriched with captivating and interactive features.

Xue [27] designed a realistic simulation, offering flexibility and immediate feedback. It offers a multi-modal learning experience with sound, 3D images, animations, and videos. Cartoon-style scenes and situational dialogues create an engaging atmosphere. Students can personalize their learning, fostering creativity and innovative thinking. The application includes functional modules for exercise guidance, International English Language Testing System (IELTS) training, stage tests, and online interaction. A training evaluation system records progress and provides feedback. Peixoto et al.'s [40] process involved script creation, audio recording, VE creation, avatar placement, user interaction design, and hardware setup, resulting in an iVR experiment for English learning assessment.

As mentioned in the studies outlined, the creation of iVR applications for English learning involves distinct steps, as can be observed in Table 3. After defining the objective, it is necessary to establish teaching goals and content design, which need to be in alignment.

Defining the technology and hardware is important to specify the application's particularities and limitations, which in turn will impact the creation of scenarios and interaction design. During this phase, the type of scenario to be created and the interaction metaphors of the platform will be determined. Assessment and feedback emphasizes the need to implement feedback mechanisms and integrated exercises to motivate student learning. Finally, in continuous improvement, it is emphasized that applications need to undergo constant development.

Table 3. iVR design process based on RSL.

Steps	Authors	Description
Define the objective:	[15,17,21,23,24,26–28]	Identify the application's purpose, target audience, collect data, understand business processes, roles, and user requirements for the application.
Teaching goals and content design:	[15,16,18,24,27,29,40]	Define teaching objectives such as learning topic, activities, and storyline.
Technology	[15,16,24,26,27,29,31]	Describe the technology to be used in the application and specify the device for development.
Scenario creation and interaction design:	[15,16,18,23,24,26,27,40]	Illustrative scenarios should incorporate contextual objects that enhance user interaction. Avatars and dialogue scripts can be employed to foster an immersive experience.
Assessment and feedback:	[15,16,18,21,23,24,26,27,29,31]	Implement feedback mechanisms, integrate assessments, and display motivating feedback for learners.
Continuous improvement:	[15,16,21,24,27,39]	Create iVR environment that promotes continuous improvement, ensuring it remains engaging and effective for learners. Continuously update and revise based on users' feedback and changing technology.

3.2.2. Design Recommendations for iVR

Based on content analysis, it was possible to divide the design recommendations for iVR applications for English learning into two main categories: design and learning, as explained below.

Design

Fifteen papers offer design recommendations for iVR applications aimed at English learning. Figure 11 presents these recommendations in a Sankey diagram, illustrating the contributions of each paper regarding each aspect. Among the aspects, interaction design and realism and learning context garnered a substantial number of citations per article.

In cognitive experience, it was categorized recommendations that cover aspects such as cognitive load [18,21,41], diversity of cognitive styles [14], and potential of cognitive experiences in iVR environments [27]. iVR applications should offer fresh cognitive experiences for effective content acquisition within iVR environments [27]. While immersive experiences enhance engagement, designers should be cautious about overwhelming learners' working memory with excessive immersive elements, as it may hinder cognitive processing [18,21,41]. To reduce cognitive load, designers can implement scaffolds that gradually provide information [21] and incorporate verbatim on-screen text to enhance comprehension by reducing cognitive load during listening exercises [18].

Comfort plays a crucial role in the design of iVR language learning applications. Designing an effective iVR language learning environment involves ensuring a safe and supportive atmosphere that minimizes anxiety and encourages active participation [39]. By incorporating avatar-based interactions and anonymity, learners can feel more comfortable practicing and making mistakes in the virtual space [39]. To further reduce anxiety and enhance confidence, the iVR application should provide opportunities for learners to interact with characters, receive feedback, and create a non-threatening learning environment [22]. This involves designing the platform to boost students' self-esteem, risk-taking abilities, and motivation, especially beneficial for those who may feel uneasy speaking in front of others [13]. Additionally, iVR can be leveraged to build students' confidence in expressing themselves in English and foster an error-tolerant environment where learners can practice and improve without fear of judgment [13].

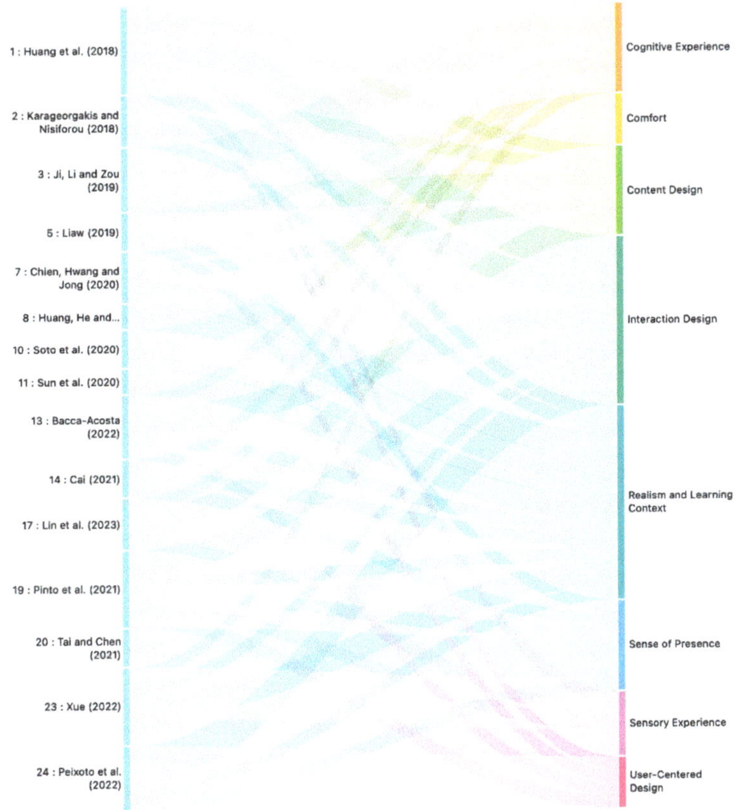

Figure 11. Sankey diagram depicting categories of the design process identified based on authors [13,14,16,18,21,22,24,27,29,39–44]. The left column presents references to articles extracted from the SLR, while the right column displays the identified categories. The connecting lines within the diagram illustrate the relationships between authors and categories. The width of these lines directly quantifies the volume of encoded text, with wider lines denoting greater content and narrower lines indicating smaller amounts of content.

A well-planned content design can ensure effective language learning within iVR applications that is easily comprehensible by users [24]. Immersive experiences can simplify the visualization of abstract and complex concepts [42]. Striking a balance between engagement and learning outcomes, designers should consider a combination of adapted and selected authentic materials, carefully choosing and modifying them as needed [41]. Furthermore, promoting comprehensive language learning requires incorporating a diverse range of content, spanning different topics, vocabulary, and language structures [22]. The validity of content design is paramount, aligning VR content with the intended language use and context [18].

In interaction design, recommendations were incorporated to address user flow [30], interactivity [42], visual and textual cues [21,40], as well as strategies to reduce distractions and prevent cybersickness. Related to user flow, it is crucial to prioritize clear, well-structured learning content while ensuring a seamless flow and logical organization of activities within the application [30]. Interactivity allows users to modify objects, manipulate elements, and have personal experiences within virtual worlds [42]. Other recommendations include emphasizing intuitive user interactions, offering clear tutorials for users unfamiliar with VR, and minimizing distractions caused by novelty in interaction design [29,40]. Employing a variety of cues, including text, images, and on-site indicators, such as scaffolds, and providing multiple representations of information to accommodate different learning preferences ultimately enhances engagement and improving learning performance [21,40]

Finally, it is crucial to address potential cybersickness issues, especially for VR newcomers. This involves minimizing dynamic content that can induce cybersickness symptoms and ensuring a comfortable, nausea-free VR environment, as these directly impact the quality of the learning experience [29]. Additionally, it is important to consider the potential impact of cybersickness on user preferences and learning outcomes, and proactively design interventions to reduce the risk of cybersickness and its influence on user attitudes [40].

Creating environments based on realism and applying 3D visualization can form effective language learning, increase engagement, and facilitate the collaborative learning process [13,29,30,43]. Furthermore, iVR applications should facilitate experiential learning through practical scenarios [21] while ensuring cultural relevance and relatability [27]. Additionally, interactions should be intuitive and meaningful, avoiding unrealistic actions to foster an effective learning process [40]. Finally, achieving a high degree of immersion through advanced technologies is crucial for enhancing learning experiences [42].

The sense of presence is a crucial characteristic to design iVR applications. Designers should focus on creating immersive and engaging virtual environments that facilitate both physical and social affordances, allowing users to feel fully present in the virtual space and fostering co-presence among participants [39]. Encouraging learners to interact with the virtual environment from a first-person perspective enhances their engagement and participation [14]. Maintaining a strong sense of presence within the application, considering factors like audio quality, is essential for user immersion and engagement [29]. Leveraging the mobility and interactivity features of iVR promotes active participation and a sense of "being there" [44]. Designers should strike a balance between creating presence and avoiding cognitive overload to prevent distractions [44]. Prioritizing fidelity of representation and interactivity contributes to immersion and user satisfaction [44], enhancing comprehension and language learning outcomes [40].

The synergy between sensory experiences and the sense of presence and immersion has the potential to significantly enhance user engagement, resulting in improved language learning outcomes [27]. For the optimization of iVR applications in the context of language learning, designers should incorporate audio elements, including character voices and captivating sound effects [30]. Additionally, the incorporation of multimodal inputs, encompassing audio, visual, and textual elements integrated within the VR environment can further enhance the language learning experience by exposing users to diverse sensory modalities [18]. Finally, to ensure a positive sensory experience for users, it is essential to align aspects such as sound design, scenario composition, and interactivity [29].

Regarding user-centered design, designers should prioritize user-friendly interactions, ensuring that the application is intuitive, easy to understand, and responsive to users' actions [30,39]. Collaborating with educators or subject matter experts to create a user-centered design that considers learners' needs, preferences, and cognitive styles is essential [21]. Furthermore, a focus on user satisfaction by developing captivating scenarios, interactions, and visual/audio elements contributes to the application's effectiveness and appeal [29].

Learning

In total, 16 papers describe general recommendation related to learning aspects of iVR applications for English purposed. Figure 12 visually conveys these recommendations, delineating the contributions of each paper in relation to each aspect. Adaptive learning and feedback emerge as focal points, garnering a substantial number of citations per article.

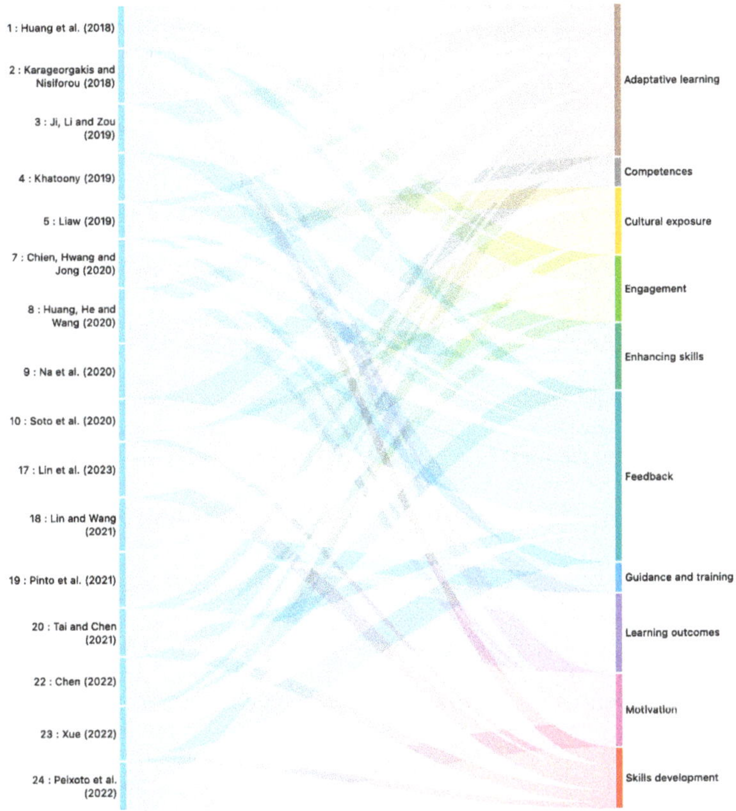

Figure 12. Sankey diagram depicting categories of the design process identified based on authors [13,16,18,20,23,24,26–29,39–44]. The left column presents references to articles extracted from the SLR, while the right column displays the identified categories. The connecting lines within the diagram illustrate the relationships between authors and categories. The width of these lines directly quantifies the volume of encoded text, with wider lines denoting greater content and narrower lines indicating smaller amounts of content.

Most of the papers ($n = 9$) report that it is necessary to guarantee that iVR applications are highly adaptable, and responsive to individual differences, enabling effective and inclusive learning experiences for a wide range of users with varying needs and preferences [13,23,24,28,39,41–44]. In the context of learning evaluation, emphasizing the promotion of language competence is crucial [18]. This involves crafting scenarios that nurture fluency, comprehension, and formulaic competence, motivating students to articulate ideas cohesively, comprehend spoken language, and recall fundamental language elements to facilitate effective communication.

Several papers ($n = 5$) underscore the significance of engagement in iVR applications, highlighting its role in capturing users' attention and sustaining their interest during the learning process [13,24,28,42,44]. Furthermore, these papers emphasize that engagement not only enhances comprehension and motivation [44], but also underscores the need to design language learning activities capable of creating authentic contexts that fully immerse learners [28,42].

In the context of enhancing language skills, three papers emphasize the importance of incorporating specific elements into iVR applications. These elements include facilitating interactions with native speakers [20], promoting collaborative strategies and effective verbal communication [20,43], and creating immersive learning environments that replicate real-world business scenarios [23]. Researchers also emphasize the significance of learning outcomes [29,41], contending that the design of iVR applications should prioritize the attainment of positive learning outcomes, substantiating their educational value through pre- and post-game assessments, and proficiently aiding language learning objectives.

Incorporating feedback mechanisms within the iVR application is essential to enhance user engagement and learning. These mechanisms encompass various aspects, such as allowing users to express their opinions and feelings [30], providing real-time feedback on user performance [30], utilizing automatic speech recognition for pronunciation feedback [20], enabling reflective feedback processes [39], implementing peer evaluation features [22], and gathering user perceptions through questionnaires [26] and interviews [44]. Detailed feedback, including pronunciation and grammar errors, fosters autonomous learning [27], and an evaluation system that tracks progress objectively is crucial [27]. Regularly collecting feedback from users helps identify strengths and weaknesses [27], and a comprehensive evaluation system should assess sensory, interactive, and cognitive experiences [27]. These feedback mechanisms collectively contribute to an effective iVR language learning environment.

To enhance the effectiveness of iVR language learning, it is crucial to integrate guidance and training [22]. Teachers can contribute by designing scenarios, offering initial feedback, and steering students toward effective language learning strategies. Additionally, the successful implementation of innovative technologies like VR in the classroom necessitates proper training [28]. Diverse teaching approaches, comprehensive guidance, and adequate training are essential to bolster students' self-efficacy across various dimensions of language learning.

When designing iVR applications for language learning, it is imperative to prioritize learning outcomes [41]. The focus should be on evaluating whether increased engagement and immersive experiences translate into positive learning outcomes and improved language skills. To achieve this, designers must ensure that the iVR application substantially contributes to users' learning outcomes and effectively supports language learning goals, as validated through pre- and post-game assessments [29]. The application should demonstrate a significant enhancement in learning outcomes to justify its educational value.

Incorporating motivation is essential for designing effective iVR-based language learning experiences [13,22,24,28,39,40,42]. Creating enjoyable activities and challenges not only makes the learning process engaging and memorable but also encourages active participation. Motivational factors play a crucial role in iVR language learning, with the immersive nature of VR applications enhancing learner motivation and fostering a positive attitude toward learning [22,24,28,39]. Emphasizing the convenience of VR, the novelty of avatars, and global interactions can make language practice enjoyable and motivating [39]. Overcoming initial skepticism by ensuring positive and enjoyable experiences within the virtual environment is vital for dispelling doubts [39]. Incorporating interactive and engaging activities within the VR environment can further boost learning motivation [22]. Fostering a positive and constructive learning atmosphere, where students support each other and collaborate in language improvement, contributes to motivation and enjoyment [22]. Finally, enhancing creative self-efficacy can reduce anxiety and enhance intrinsic motivation, particularly in projects using VR technology for learning [28].

Recommendations about skills development were also noticed by researchers. iVR technology holds significant promise for language learning, as noted by researchers [42]. Its built-in translation capabilities can enhance students' comprehension and expedite educational progress. Moreover, a well-designed iVR platform has the potential to foster not only speaking skills, but also reading proficiency and vocabulary acquisition through immersive, self-paced, and engaging learning experiences [13]. Lin et al. [18] highlighted the immersive nature of VR for improving language accuracy and knowledge retention, while fluency and pronunciation may require additional explicit instruction and practice. Additionally, Tai and Chen [44] stressed the importance of contextual interpretation within iVR experiences to enhance learners' comprehension of spoken content by leveraging the "here and-now" orientation. Finally, Xue [27] advised a balanced approach to foreign language skill development, encompassing listening, speaking, reading, and writing, combining teaching with practical exercises to enhance overall language proficiency.

4. Discussion

In this systematic literature review, we identified 18 categories of iVR design recommendations for English learning and a design process used to create iVR applications. Additionally, we investigated existing trends related to universities, publications, devices, human senses, and development platforms. In this section, we reflect on our findings and discuss the study limitations. The first section provides an overview analysis to address RQ1 and RQ2, followed by a section on the design process to tackle RQ3, and finally a section on design recommendations to address RQ4.

In general, overview analysis provides information about the current state of iVR applications for English learning. Regarding usual VR headsets, we highlighted that although the HTC Vive is the most common device, most articles reported the use of low-cost VR headsets (Google Cardboard, Samsung Gear, and VR Box), which demonstrates a preference for cost-effective solutions in the development of English learning applications in the iVR domain. In terms of human senses, the findings indicate that visual and auditory perception predominates, underscoring their fundamental importance in engaging users within iVR applications for English language learning.

In the realm of designing innovative iVR applications, we identified that nine articles delved into the intricacies of creating entirely new applications, while another eight papers zeroed in on the utilization of pre-existing applications (Figure 9). Furthermore, other articles featured the incorporation of pre-existing 360-degree videos ($n = 3$) or the utilization of novel iVR applications generated through a platform ($n = 4$). This analysis highlights the fact that the majority of articles did not engage in the development of entirely new iVR applications, a trend evident in Figure 8. Given the inherent complexity and cost associated with crafting iVR applications, it is conceivable that researchers may choose a more accessible and cost-effective path by harnessing pre-existing applications or platforms. Table 4 shows the platforms used to design iVR applications.

Table 4. iVR platform used to design applications.

iVR Platform Used	Articles
EduVenture VR	[16,18,28]
Experience Colorblindness	[45]
Google Expedition	[42]
Google Tour Creator	[28]
ImmerMe	[13]
MindShow	[14,22]
Mondly	[44]
Pre-existing 360-degree video	[27,30,41,43]
Tilt Brush	[17]
vTime	[39]

Regarding the design process, it was possible to identify six stages: define the objective, teaching goals, content design, technology, scenario, interaction design, assessment and feedback, and continuous improvement. This process elucidates the need for applications to include assessment and feedback components and concerns related to scenario and interaction design. The importance of implementing exercises and automatic feedback, allowing students to test and measure their learning in real-time, becomes evident. Additionally, the significance of the aesthetic quality of virtual simulations is emphasized, as they should incorporate contextual interactions to ensure a seamless navigation experience.

Issues related to technology, such as technical implementations and hardware definition, also received significant attention in terms of the number of mentions. Given that the development of immersive reality applications demands substantial investments, it becomes essential to predefine the technical aspects to be incorporated into the platform and specify the hardware for which it will be developed. The definition of the device is crucial for addressing interaction-related issues.

Design recommendations for iVR applications in English learning serve as an initial guiding framework, assisting designers and developers in carefully considering crucial factors prior to initiating a project. These recommendations have been derived from a systematic literature review and organized into two categories: design and learning. The design category encompasses topics such as cognitive experience, comfort, content design, interaction design, realism, and learning context, as well as the sense of presence, sensory experience, and user-centered design. These topics integrate subjects aimed at improving the user experience in iVR environments. The learning category includes recommendations related to adaptive learning, competences, cultural exposure, engagement, skill enhancement, feedback, guidance and training, learning outcomes, motivation, and skills development. In this way, the learning category encompasses aspects related to improving the user's learning experience. We purposefully omit language teaching/learning strategies as these would fall outside the scope of this work, and have been well-addressed by other works [22,30,33,35,36,46]

Under the design category, we integrated user experience design recommendations that will exert a substantial influence on the application's development. Notably, interaction design and realism in learning content emerged as prominent themes by their substantial citation count in the literature, highlighting their significance in the referenced papers. The identification of eight themes underscores the intricate nature of designing iVR applications for English learning, encompassing various aspects and challenges.

The design of iVR applications for language learning is a multifaceted endeavor, with several critical considerations. Managing cognitive load while offering fresh cognitive experiences is essential to ensure learners can engage effectively without feeling overwhelmed. Moreover, fostering user confidence and reducing anxiety through features like avatar-based interactions and anonymity plays a pivotal role in creating a safe and supportive learning atmosphere. Content design must balance realism, 3D visualization, and cultural relevance to enhance engagement and comprehension. Interaction design recommendations, including user flow, interactivity, and the use of cues, are vital for improving user engagement and performance. Additionally, addressing cybersickness challenges and finding ways to mitigate its impact on user attitudes is crucial for a positive learning experience. Achieving a high degree of immersion through advanced technologies and striking the right balance between engagement and learning outcomes are overarching goals. These discussions offer insights into the intricate world of iVR language learning applications, where technology, psychology, and pedagogy converge to create immersive and effective learning experiences.

5. Conclusions

This article had as objective to identify design recommendations for iVR English learning applications. Our research was motivated by the existing gap in the research literature, which led us to seek guidelines or considerations for designing iVR applications for English learning. To fulfil this objective, we considered four research questions: RQ1: "Which human senses are most frequently employed in iVR applications for English language learning?"; RQ2: "Which iVR platforms are most commonly used for developing English language learning applications?"; RQ3: "What characterizes the design processes employed to create iVR applications tailored for English language learning?"; and RQ4: "What design recommendations guide the design and development of iVR applications for English language learning?". With the obtained results of the investigation, we were able to answer each one of them.

Visual and auditory are the most used senses in iVR applications for English language learning, answering the research question (RQ1). Some papers also reported the use of proprioception [17] and touch [14,23,27].

The design process to design iVR applications can be characterized by six steps: (1) define the objective, (2) teaching goals and content design, (3) technology and hardware selection, (4) scenario creation and interaction design, (5) assessment and feedback, and (6) continuous improvement. Regarding design recommendations, we identified two main categories, design and learning, that bring together 18 recommendations.

These diverse approaches in VR-based English language learning offer valuable insights into the evolving landscape of technology-assisted education. Discussing the design processes and pedagogical considerations can help educators, researchers, and developers explore new avenues for enhancing language learning through VR technology.

The results of this research are based on systematic literature review. Future studies will delve deeper into recommendations based on interviews with virtual reality experts. Based on the interviews, the recommendations will be evaluated and subsequently reissued.

Author Contributions: Conceptualization, J.R.E. and J.C.S.C.; methodology, J.R.E., J.C.S.C. and B.S.G.; formal analysis, J.R.E. and J.C.S.C.; investigation, J.R.E. and J.C.S.C.; resources, J.C.S.C. and B.S.G.; writing—original draft preparation, J.R.E.; writing—review and editing, J.C.S.C. and B.S.G.; visualization, J.R.E.; supervision, J.C.S.C. and B.S.G. All authors have read and agreed to the published version of the manuscript.

Funding: This work was funded by national funds through the FCT—Foundation for Science and Technology, I.P., within the scope of the project CISUC—UID/CEC/00326/2020 and by European Social Fund, through the Regional Operational Program Centro 2020. Funding support for Jessica Rodrigues Esteves' Ph.D. scholarship is provided by the Coordination for the Improvement of Higher Education Personnel (Coordenação de Aperfeiçoamento de Pessoal de Nível Superior—Brasil, CAPES), under Finance Code 001.

Conflicts of Interest: The authors declare no conflict of interest.

References

1. Helen, S.; Jenny, P.; Yvonne, R. *Interaction Design: Beyond Human-Computer Interaction*; Wiley: Hoboken, NJ, USA, 2019.
2. Slater, M. A note on presence terminology. *Presence Connect.* **2003**, *3*, 1–5.
3. Bowman, D.A.; McMahan, R.P. Virtual reality: How much immersion is enough? *Computer* **2007**, *40*, 36–43.
4. Zhang, Z. Building Symmetrical Reality Systems for Cooperative Manipulation. In Proceedings of the 2023 IEEE Conference on Virtual Reality and 3D User Interfaces Abstracts and Workshops (VRW), Shanghai, China, 25–29 March 2023.
5. Avola, D.; Cinque, L.; Foresti, G.L.; Marini, M.R. A novel low cybersickness dynamic rotation gain enhancer based on spatial position and orientation in virtual environments. *Virtual Real.* **2023**, *27*, 1–19. [CrossRef]
6. Lv, Z.; Chen, D.; Lou, R.; Song, H. Industrial Security Solution for Virtual Reality. *IEEE Internet Things J.* **2020**, *8*, 6273–6281. [CrossRef]
7. Manca, D.; Brambilla, S.; Colombo, S. Bridging between Virtual Reality and accident simulation for training of process-industry operators. *Adv. Eng. Softw.* **2012**, *55*, 1–9. [CrossRef]
8. Bekele, M.K.; Pierdicca, R.; Frontoni, E.; Malinverni, E.S.; Gain, J. A Survey of Augmented, Virtual, and Mixed Reality for Cultural Heritage. *J. Comput. Cult. Herit.* **2018**, *11*, 1–36. [CrossRef]
9. Taipina, D.; Cardoso, J.C.S. Spectare: Re-Designing a Stereoscope for a Cultural Heritage XR Experience. *Electronics* **2022**, *11*, 620. [CrossRef]
10. Jensen, L.; Konradsen, F. A review of the use of virtual reality head-mounted displays in education and training. *Educ. Inf. Technol.* **2018**, *23*, 1515–1529. [CrossRef]

11. Lv, Z.; Li, X.; Li, W. Virtual reality geographical interactive scene semantics research for immersive geography learning. *Neurocomputing* **2017**, *254*, 71–78. [CrossRef]
12. Stella, E.; Agosti, I.; Di Blas, N.; Finazzi, M.; Lanzi, P.L.; Loiacono, D. A virtual reality classroom to teach and explore crystal solid state structures. *Multimedia Tools Appl.* **2022**, *82*, 6993–7016. [CrossRef]
13. Soto, J.H.B.; Ocampo, D.C.T.; Colon, L.D.C.B.; Oropesa, A.V. Perceptions of ImmerseMe Virtual Reality Platform to Improve English Communicative Skills in Higher Education. *Int. J. Interact. Mob. Technol. (iJIM)* **2020**, *14*, 4–19. [CrossRef]
14. Cai, J.-Y.; Wang, R.-F.; Wang, C.-Y.; Ye, X.-D.; Li, X.-Z. The Influence of Learners' Cognitive Style and Testing Environment Supported by Virtual Reality on English-Speaking Learning Achievement. *Sustainability* **2021**, *13*, 11751. [CrossRef]
15. Chandra, A.Y.; Prasetyaningrum, P.T.; Suria, O.; Santosa, P.I.; Nugroho, L.E. Virtual Reality Mobile Application Development with Scrum Framework as a New Media in Learning English. *Int. J. Interact. Mob. Technol. (iJIM)* **2021**, *15*, 31–49. [CrossRef]
16. Chien, S.-Y.; Hwang, G.-J.; Jong, M.S.-Y. Effects of peer assessment within the context of spherical video-based virtual reality on EFL students' English-Speaking performance and learning perceptions. *Comput. Educ.* **2019**, *146*, 103751. [CrossRef]
17. Frazier, E.; Lege, R.; Bonner, E. Making virtual reality accessible for language learning: Applying the VR application analysis framework. *Teach. Engl. Technol.* **2021**, *21*, 131–143.
18. Lin, V.; Barrett, N.E.; Liu, G.-Z.; Chen, N.-S.; Jong, M.S.-Y. Supporting dyadic learning of English for tourism purposes with scenery-based virtual reality. *Comput. Assist. Lang. Learn.* **2021**, *36*, 906–942. [CrossRef]
19. Pinto, R.D.; Monteiro, P.; Melo, M.; Cabral, L.; Bessa, M. Does gamification in virtual reality improve second language learning? In Proceedings of the 2021 International Conference on Graphics and Interaction (ICGI), Porto, Portugal, 4–5 November 2021; pp. 1–8. [CrossRef]
20. Khatoony, S. An Innovative Teaching with Serious Games through Virtual Reality Assisted Language Learning. In Proceedings of the 2019 International Serious Games Symposium (ISGS), Tehran, Iran, 26 December 2019; pp. 100–108. [CrossRef]
21. Bacca-Acosta, J.; Tejada, J.; Fabregat, R.; Kinshuk; Guevara, J. Scaffolding in immersive virtual reality environments for learning English: An eye tracking study. *Educ. Technol. Res. Dev.* **2021**, *70*, 339–362. [CrossRef]
22. Sun, C.; Yao, Y.; Wang, R.; Ye, X. A Study on the Influence of Scene Reality of VR Environment on English Learners' Learning Engagement and Learning Effectiveness. In Proceedings of the 2020 IEEE 2nd International Conference on Computer Science and Educational Informatization (CSEI), Xinxiang, China, 12–14 June 2020; pp. 181–185. [CrossRef]
23. Chen, H. Research and Application of English Learning Games Based on VR technology. In Proceedings of the 2022 International Conference on Education, Network and Information Technology (ICENIT), Liverpool, UK, 2–3 September 2022; pp. 93–97.
24. Huang, X.; Han, G.; He, J.; Du, J.; Liang, Y. Design and Application of a VR English Learning Game Based on the APT Model. In Proceedings of the 2018 Seventh International Conference of Educational Innovation through Technology (EITT), Auckland, New Zealand, 12–14 December 2018; pp. 68–72. [CrossRef]
25. Klimova, B.; Pikhart, M.; Polakova, P.; Cerna, M.; Yayilgan, S.Y.; Shaikh, S. A Systematic Review on the Use of Emerging Technologies in Teaching English as an Applied Language at the University Level. *Systems* **2023**, *11*, 42. [CrossRef]
26. Na, K.S.; Mohamed, F.; Isham, M.I.M.; Siang, C.V.; Tasir, Z.; Abas, M.A. Virtual Reality Application Integrated with Learning Analytics for Enhancing English Pronunciation: A Conceptual Framework. In Proceedings of the 2020 IEEE Conference on e-Learning, e-Management and e-Services (IC3e), Kota Kinabalu, Malaysia, 17–19 November 2020; pp. 82–87. [CrossRef]
27. Xue, Y. Research on the Application of Virtual Reality Technology in IELTS Teaching Under the COVID-19. In Proceedings of the 2022 4th International Conference on Inventive Research in Computing Applications (ICIRCA), Coimbatore, India, 21–23 September 2022; pp. 1323–1328.
28. Lin, Y.-J.; Wang, H.-C. Using virtual reality to facilitate learners' creative self-efficacy and intrinsic motivation in an EFL classroom. *Educ. Inf. Technol.* **2021**, *26*, 4487–4505. [CrossRef]
29. Pinto, R.D.; Peixoto, B.; Melo, M.; Cabral, L.; Bessa, M. Foreign Language Learning Gamification Using Virtual Reality—A Systematic Review of Empirical Research. *Educ. Sci.* **2021**, *11*, 222. [CrossRef]
30. Huang, X.; Zou, D.; Cheng, G.; Xie, H. A Systematic Review of AR and VR Enhanced Language Learning. *Sustainability* **2021**, *13*, 4639. [CrossRef]
31. Peixoto, B.; Pinto, R.; Melo, M.; Cabral, L.; Bessa, M. Immersive Virtual Reality for Foreign Language Education: A PRISMA Systematic Review. *IEEE Access* **2021**, *9*, 48952–48962. [CrossRef]
32. Dhimolea, T.K.; Kaplan-Rakowski, R.; Lin, L. A systematic review of research on high-immersion virtual reality for language learning. *TechTrends* **2022**, *66*, 810–824. [CrossRef]
33. Parmaxi, A. Virtual reality in language learning: A systematic review and implications for research and practice. *Interact. Learn. Environ.* **2020**, *31*, 172–184. [CrossRef]
34. Bahari, A. Affordances and challenges of teaching language skills by virtual reality: A systematic review (2010–2020). *E-Learn. Digit. Media* **2021**, *19*, 163–188. [CrossRef]
35. Hua, C.; Wang, J. Virtual reality-assisted language learning: A follow-up review (2018–2022). *Front. Psychol.* **2023**, *14*, 1153642. [CrossRef] [PubMed]
36. Legault, J.; Zhao, J.; Chi, Y.-A.; Chen, W.; Klippel, A.; Li, P. Immersive Virtual Reality as an Effective Tool for Second Language Vocabulary Learning. *Languages* **2019**, *4*, 13. [CrossRef]

37. Page, M.J.; McKenzie, J.E.; Bossuyt, P.M.; Boutron, I.; Hoffmann, T.C.; Mulrow, C.D.; Shamseer, L.; Tetzlaff, J.M.; Akl, E.A.; Brennan, S.E.; et al. The PRISMA 2020 statement: An updated guideline for reporting systematic reviews. *Syst. Rev.* **2021**, *10*, 89. [CrossRef]
38. Bardin, L. Análise de conteúdo. *São Paulo Edições* **2016**, *70*, 288.
39. Liaw, M.-L. EFL learners' intercultural communication in an open social virtual environment. *J. Educ. Technol. Soc.* **2019**, *22*, 38–55.
40. Peixoto, B.; Bessa, L.C.P.; Gonçalves, G.; Bessa, M.; Melo, M. Teaching EFL With Immersive Virtual Reality Technologies: A Comparison With the Conventional Listening Method. *IEEE Access* **2023**, *11*, 21498–21507. [CrossRef]
41. Ji, S.; Li, K.; Zou, L. The Effect of 360-Degree Video Authentic Materials on EFL Learners' Listening Comprehension. In Proceedings of the 2019 International Joint Conference on Information, Media and Engineering (IJCIME), Osaka, Japan, 17–19 December 2019; pp. 288–293. [CrossRef]
42. Karageorgakis, T.; Nisiforou, E.A. Virtual reality in the EFL classroom: Educational affordances and students' perceptions in Cyprus. *Cyprus Rev.* **2018**, *30*, 381–396.
43. Huang, X.; He, J.; Wang, H. A Case Study: Students' Perception of a Collaborative Game-Based Virtual Learning Environment. In Proceedings of the 2020 6th International Conference of the Immersive Learning Research Network (iLRN), Obispo, CA, USA, 21–25 June 2020; pp. 46–53. [CrossRef]
44. Tai, T.-Y.; Chen, H.H.-J. The impact of immersive virtual reality on EFL learners' listening comprehension. *J. Educ. Comput. Res.* **2021**, *59*, 1272–1293. [CrossRef]
45. Urueta, S.H.; Ogi, T. Web-Portal-Based Repurposing of VR Scenarios for TEFL Applications. In Proceedings of the 2020 3rd International Conference on Image and Graphics Processing, Singapore, 8–10 February 2020. [CrossRef]
46. Yudintseva, A. Virtual reality affordances for oral communication in English as a second language classroom: A literature review. *Comput. Educ. X Real.* **2023**, *2*, 100018. [CrossRef]

computers

MDPI

Review

Impact of the Implementation of ChatGPT in Education: A Systematic Review

Marta Montenegro-Rueda [1], José Fernández-Cerero [1], José María Fernández-Batanero [1] and Eloy López-Meneses [2,*]

[1] Department of Teaching and Educational Organization, University of Sevilla, 41013 Sevilla, Spain; mmontenegro1@us.es (M.M.-R.); jfcerero@us.es (J.F.-C.); batanero@us.es (J.M.F.-B.)

[2] Department of Education and Social Psychology, Pablo de Olavide University, 41013 Sevilla, Spain

* Correspondence: elopmen@upo.es

Abstract: The aim of this study is to present, based on a systematic review of the literature, an analysis of the impact of the application of the ChatGPT tool in education. The data were obtained by reviewing the results of studies published since the launch of this application (November 2022) in three leading scientific databases in the world of education (Web of Science, Scopus and Google Scholar). The sample consisted of 12 studies. Using a descriptive and quantitative methodology, the most significant data are presented. The results show that the implementation of ChatGPT in the educational environment has a positive impact on the teaching–learning process, however, the results also highlight the importance of teachers being trained to use the tool properly. Although ChatGPT can enhance the educational experience, its successful implementation requires teachers to be familiar with its operation. These findings provide a solid basis for future research and decision-making regarding the use of ChatGPT in the educational context.

Keywords: ChatGPT; artificial intelligence; education; impact; systematic review

1. Introduction

Over the past decades, artificial intelligence (AI) has experienced rapid growth and has transformed many areas of society. AI has positioned itself at the forefront of research fields ranging from medicine and robotics to education and autonomous driving. Broadly speaking, artificial intelligence refers to the ability of a computer system to mimic the behaviour of the human brain. This involves receiving information in the form of external data, learning through training and based on that learning, achieving the goals for which it was designed [1].

The implementation of artificial intelligence in education has had a significant impact, evidenced by improvements in the efficiency of the educational process, the promotion of global learning, the personalisation of learning, the creation of more intelligent content and the optimisation of educational management in terms of effectiveness and efficiency [2]. Nowadays, new technologies play a fundamental role in optimising the teaching–learning process. Education is not limited to being a mere product but is a process in which learning goes beyond the simple acquisition of knowledge. In this sense, artificial intelligence (AI) emerges as a new technology with great potential in the field of education, as AI-based systems could foster personalised learning, adapting to the needs and interests of each student [3].

Within education, it is critical to recognise that the implementation of AI raises significant challenges and ethical considerations. Issues such as data privacy, equity of access to education and the impact on the role of the educator require careful attention. It is essential to address these aspects in a responsible manner to ensure that AI is used in a beneficial and equitable way for all learners [4]. In this regard, it is critical to find a balance between technology and the essential role of educators to ensure that the focus remains on the holistic development of students and their preparation for an ever-changing world. Due to the short time between the launch of ChatGPT (end of November 2022), no systematic reviews addressing its impact on education have been found [5]. Therefore, the main objective of this systematic review is to analyse the existing literature on the use of ChatGPT in education in order to identify its impact, benefits, challenges and areas of application in teaching and learning. In this regard, the following research questions are addressed:

1. What is the general state of scientific research on the use of ChatGPT in education?
2. What are the benefits and challenges of implementing ChatGPT in the classroom?
3. What are the future trends and emerging research areas in the use of ChatGPT in education?

2. Use of ChatGPT in Education

The use of ChatGPT in education has generated considerable interest due to its potential to enrich the learning experience of students. By providing quick and personalised responses, this system has the ability to address individual student needs, offer immediate feedback and facilitate the understanding of complex concepts. In this way, it becomes a promising tool that promotes a student's active participation and cognitive advancement by adapting to their learning pace and offering continuous support in their knowledge acquisition process [6].

Following this line, it has proven to be a valuable tool to promote the development of writing skills in students. By interacting with the system, students can receive grammatical corrections, suggestions for improvement and detailed feedback on their writing, which gives them the opportunity to improve their written communication and achieve greater effectiveness in their written expression [7]. Thus, this application presents itself as an invaluable assistance tool for scientific writing; however, it is essential to understand that it should not be considered as a complete solution for scientific content creation. Writers must exercise their knowledge and experience to validate and complement the information provided by the tool. However, it also excels in its ability to facilitate group discussions and promote collaborative student participation in projects and assignments. This fosters a sense of community among learners by allowing interaction and an exchange of ideas [8].

Several studies have tried to explore the potential impact of artificial intelligence, especially with the famous ChatGPT tool for students in education. Various applications of artificial intelligence in education were studied, such as personalised learning experiences, adaptive testing, predictive analytics and chatbots. As a result, it shows an incredible potential to improve learning efficiency and provide personalised educational support to both students and teachers. However, it is essential to consider the risks and limitations associated with these technologies, such as data privacy, cultural differences, language proficiency and associated ethical implications [9].

Its influence over the last year has sparked a growing interest in education. This innovative tool has positioned itself as a disruptive technology that is revolutionising the way students are taught, promoted, and supported in academic environments. In this sense, educational centres are rethinking how to incorporate this technology into their didactic models in order to improve the teaching and learning process of educational agents [10]. Therefore, teachers must approach this tool in the classroom and present it as an additional resource that complements the learning process. However, it is crucial to highlight that this tool does not replace the cognitive processes necessary in learning or other sources of information such as books, articles or interactions with others.

3. Method

Following an explicit and systematic search strategy, with inclusion and exclusion criteria, a systematic review of the literature will be carried out. For this, the researchers have followed the recommendations of the PRISMA Statement [11].

3.1. Search Strategy

The selected databases were Web of Science, Scopus, and Google Scholar. The search string (Table 1) was applied in the three international databases in the field of education, in the fields of title, abstract and/or keywords. The literature search was conducted between May and June 2023, with an initial identification of 154 records.

Table 1. Search strategy.

Topic	Search Terms
Artificial Intelligence	"ChatGPT" OR "Chatbot" OR "Artificial Intelligence"
Context	"Education" OR "Educational Institution"

3.2. Inclusion and Exclusion Criteria

After eliminating duplicate studies (n = 73), the inclusion and exclusion criteria were established to ensure that the selected studies were relevant and met the objectives of the review (Table 2). These criteria were applied independently by two reviewers to ensure objectivity and to minimise bias in the selection of studies. It was decided to limit the search to articles published from the year 2022 onwards, as this was the year in which this artificial intelligence chatbot developed by OpenIA was launched.

Table 2. Inclusion and exclusion criteria.

	Inclusion Criteria	Exclusion Criteria
Publication period	Published between 2022—present (June 2023)	Published before 2022
Type of document	Scientific article published in peer-reviewed journal	Not an article published in a peer-reviewed journal
Type of study	Theoretical and empirical research	Other research (review, opinions, letters to the editor...)
Language	English or Spanish	Neither in English nor in Spanish
Population	Education	No focus on education
Research topic	Use of ChatGPT in education	Does not use ChatGPT

3.3. Methodological Quality Assessment

The Johanna Briggs Checklist (JBI) is a tool used to assess the methodological quality of research studies. It consists of a set of criteria used to determine the rigour and validity of a study. When applying the JBI checklist, aspects such as study design, participant selection, data collection and analysis, among others, are analysed. The 14 identified articles were assessed for their methodological quality. The included studies were examined through a critical and independent review using an eleven-point checklist developed by Aromataris and Munn [12].

To ensure an unbiased assessment, a masked review of the checklist was conducted by two independent researchers, unrelated to the study. This measure was implemented to avoid any assessment bias on the part of the study authors themselves. The selected studies had to meet at least four of the checklist criteria. The checklist used covered the following assessment criteria:

- Is the purpose of the research clearly specified?
- Does it address the use and impact of ChatGPT in education?
- Are the data extraction instruments appropriate?
- Are the results obtained useful to the research community?
- Are the authors' conclusions supported by the data analysed?
- Are recommendations made for future research?

Two studies [7,13] were excluded based on the quality issues raised in the checklist, as they did not meet at least four of the criteria provided above.

3.4. Selection of Studies

A total of 154 records were identified in the three electronic databases analysed. After removing duplicate records ($n = 73$), studies were reviewed by title and abstracts to assess eligibility ($n = 81$). A total of 67 studies were excluded as they did not meet the established inclusion and exclusion criteria. Subsequently, the remaining 14 studies were assessed for methodological quality, eliminating 2 studies. Finally, a total of 12 studies were eligible for inclusion in the review. Figure 1 shows the flow chart of the record selection process based on the Preferred Reporting Items for Systematic Reviews and Meta-Analyses (PRISMA) guidelines [11].

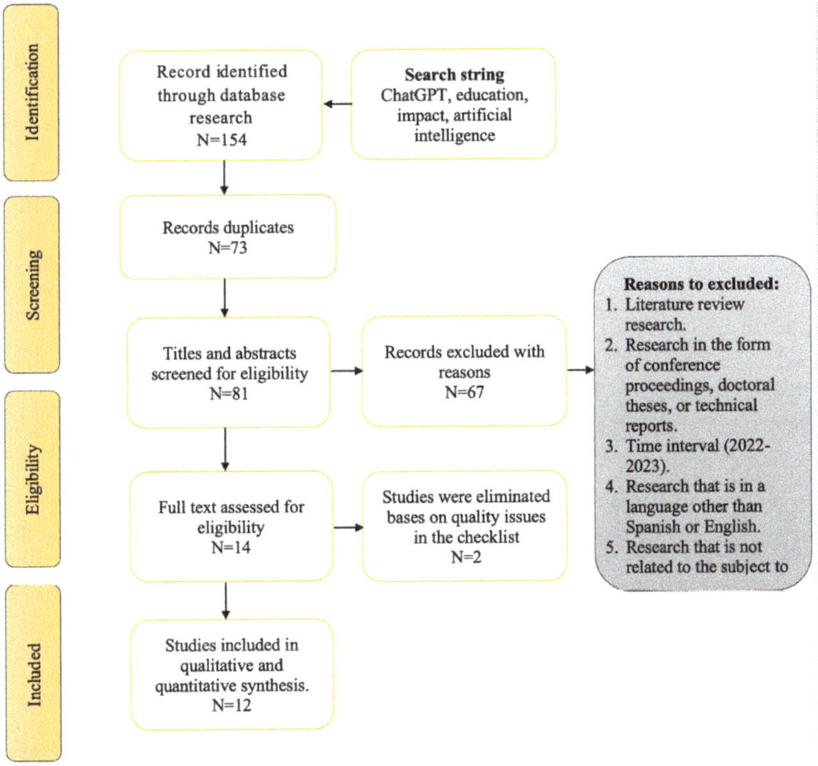

Figure 1. Flow chart of the study selection process.

3.5. Data Extraction and Analysis

In order to address the research questions posed previously, we carried out a content analysis combining qualitative and quantitative approaches to the 12 research studies obtained. The quantitative analysis allowed us to visualise and understand general aspects of the topic through descriptive graphs. For the qualitative analysis, we used the VOSviewer 1.6.15. tool to identify the main trends and scientific impact of the research field [14,15]. Each of these clusters has a different number of elements, colour, and size. The size is determined by the frequency of occurrence. The larger the circle, the more frequently that keyword is used in the studies [16]. The main characteristics of the studies included in the review related to ChatGPT in education are provided in Table 3.

Table 3. Characteristics of the studies included in the review.

Authors/Year	Methodology	Country/Continent	Findings	
			Advantages	Disadvantages
Diego Olite et al. (2023) [17]	Theoretical	Cuba, America	• Strategy that will bring about changes in the way of thinking and educating (educational process).	• Lack of training.
García Peñalvo (2023) [10]	Theoretical	Spain, Europe	• Promotes the development of critical thinking.	• Provides training for both teachers and students to encourage appropriate and ethical use.
Sánchez García (2023) [6]	Theoretical	Mexico, America		• Educational institutions should take into account the concerns expressed by students when using artificial intelligence.
Halaweh (2023) [18]	Theoretical	United Arab Emirates, Asia	• It offers numerous opportunities for teachers and lecturers to develop ideas.	• Provides teacher training on the functions of artificial intelligence tools, as well as how to evaluate and use it correctly.
Rahman and Watanobe (2023) [19]	Quantitative	Bangladesh, Asia	• Very useful as a support for educational work.	• Lack of training. • Lack of common sense in its use. • Difficulties in complex reasoning.
Ausat et al. (2023) [20]	Quantitative	Malaysia, Asia	• Offers improvements in learning.	• It does not completely replace the role of the teacher. Therefore, a teacher's digital competence is necessary to integrate it effectively and appropriately.
Rincón Castillo et al. (2023) [21]	Qualitative	Indonesia, Asia	• ChatGPT significantly impacts the teaching–learning process.	• Many students use ChatGPT to manage and deliver their work without learning anything.
Javaid et al. (2023) [22]	Theoretical	Mexico, America	• Both students and faculty can benefit from this tool. • Faculty can save time on numerous tasks by using these technologies. • Students can use it as a support tool.	• Lack of training.

Table 3. *Cont.*

Authors/Year	Methodology	Country/Continent	Findings	
			Advantages	Disadvantages
Qadir (2023) [8]	Theoretical	India, Asia	• It offers numerous benefits in the teaching–learning process.	• It is important to use these tools with caution, as they can be misleading. • Provides equitable access to advanced technology, especially for marginalised communities, so as not to exacerbate existing inequalities.
Firat (2023) [23]	Qualitative	Qatar, Asia	• This tool can increase student engagement and satisfaction. • It can enhance learning experiences and transform the role of educators.	• Need to improve the training of teachers and students.
Fauzi (2023) [24]	Qualitative	Turkey, Asia	• It offers learners the chance to improve their language skills. • Facilitates collaboration. • Increases time efficiency and effectiveness. • Provides support and motivation.	• Lack of training.
Strzelecki (2023) [25]	Quantitative	Indonesia, Asia	• Tool accepted by university students. • Increases students' performances. • Increases students' motivation.	• Lack of training.

4. Results

Once the studies related to the impact of ChatGPT application in education were collected, a total of 12 relevant articles were selected for this systematic review. When observing the distribution of the collected research according to the year of publication, it is evident that all the articles found belong to the year 2023. This is due to the fact that the implementation of ChatGPT in education was implemented at the end of 2022, which did not allow enough time for studies to be conducted and articles on its impact to be published until the following year. Looking at the distribution of the studies according to the place of publication, research from the Asian continent predominates with 66.67% of the research collected, coming from countries such as the United Arab Emirates, Qatar, Indonesia, Turkey, India and Bangladesh. However, we also found research from the Americas (25%) and Europe (8.33%) to a lesser extent. Some of these countries are Spain, Mexico, Poland and Cuba. No articles were found from the African or Oceanic continent (Figure 2).

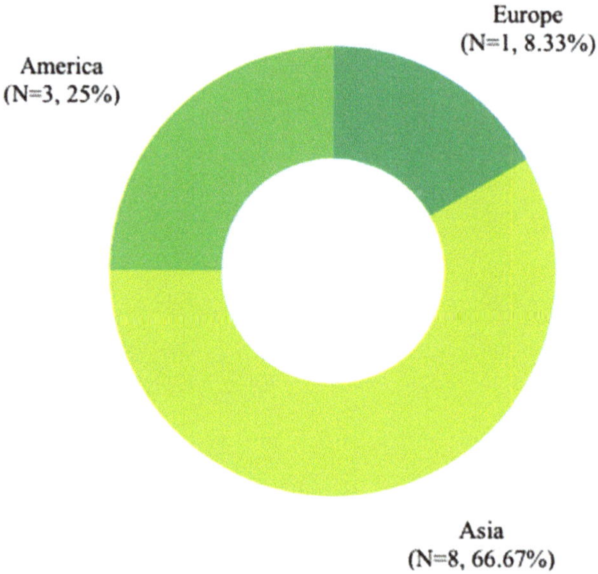

Figure 2. Distribution of studies by population location.

Regarding the methodology used in the selected articles, it is worth noting that most of the research published on the impact of ChatGPT in the educational field has been carried out through a theoretical approach (50%), with the aim of understanding the potential and challenges of this tool. To a lesser extent, there are other studies that have chosen to approach the study from both a qualitative and quantitative methodology (25%) (Figure 3).

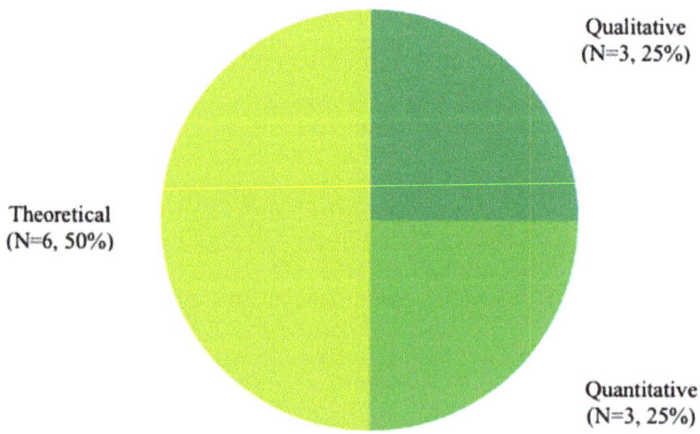

Figure 3. Distribution of studies by methodology used.

Considering the main findings that were found after reading the selected articles, Figure 4 shows that the main result obtained was that the use of ChatGPT in education is a great educational support in the teaching and learning process for both students and teachers (82%). This is closely linked to the improvement of performance, motivation, organization and efficient time management, as well as the promotion of a more effective and collaborative learning environment. At the same time, there is a lack of teacher training regarding the use of ChatGPT for its subsequent application and use in educational classrooms (58%), as many teachers do not have the necessary skills to apply it efficiently. However, it is necessary that all educational agents know how to use this tool in a responsible way, following ethical guidelines, since inappropriate use could be an obstacle in the learning process of students (52%). On the other hand, and closely related to the previous finding, a large part of the research collected in their articles shows the great changes at the educational level that the use of ChatGPT can create by generating a strong impact on the way of teaching and carrying out tasks (46%). Lastly, the articles reflect a concern for the clear need for student training (32%) and the possible problems in the educational system that can be generated after prolonged use of this application (28%).

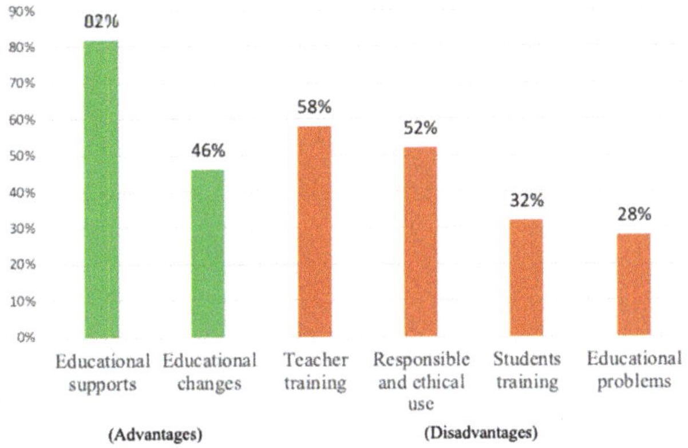

Figure 4. Main findings of the analysed studies.

Finally, to find out the lines of research in this field, three clusters were obtained from the mapping of VOSviewer. The three clusters obtained are (Figure 5):

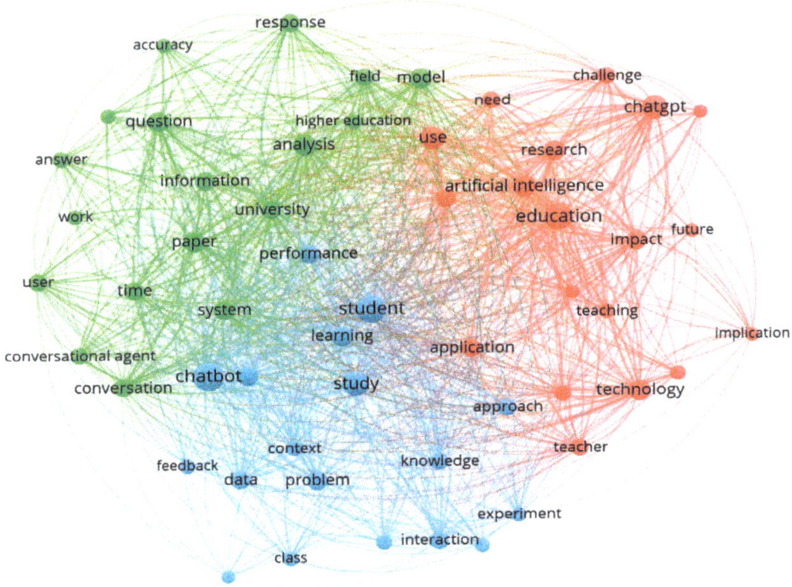

Figure 5. Labelled bibliometric map.

- Cluster 1 (red). The cluster marked in red has 19 items, including application, artificial intelligence, challenge, ChatGPT, critical thinking, education, future, impact, implication, limitation, need, opportunity, research, strategy, teacher, teaching, technology, tool and use. This cluster is therefore linked to research on the role of the teacher in an educational environment driven by artificial intelligence, including their training, the impact of using artificial intelligence tools and their adaptation to changes in their pedagogical practice.
- Cluster 2 (blue). The cluster marked in blue has 18 items, including approach, chatbot, chatbot technology, class, context, data, development, experiment, feedback, interaction, knowledge, learning, participant, performance, problem, skills, student and study. This cluster is related to the line of research on the use of chatbots in education, including their impact on students.
- Cluster 3 (green). The cluster marked in green has 18 items, including accuracy, analysis, answer, conversation, conversational agent, field, higher education, information, model, order, paper, question, response, system, time, university, user and work. This cluster is related to research on the impact of the chatbot on teaching and learning processes, including factors such as the socioeconomic, cultural, institutional and technological environment in which it is developed.

5. Discussion

To address the research questions posed in the study, the findings obtained through the qualitative and quantitative content analysis conducted in the 12 selected research will be explored.

Q1: What is the general state of scientific research on the use of ChatGPT in education?

The general state of scientific research on the use of ChatGPT in education is limited due to the recent implementation of this application in the educational setting, being still in its initial stages. A total of 12 relevant articles were collected for a systematic review, all published in the year 2023. This is because the use of ChatGPT in the educational setting is a relatively new practice, since its launch occurred at the end of 2022, so there has not been enough time to conduct long-term studies and collect meaningful data on the impact on education until the first months of the following year [26].

In terms of geographic focus, a greater representation of studies belonging to the Asian continent was observed. The predominance of research from Asian countries may be related to the early adoption of technology in these regions and their focus on educational research. Other factors such as the availability of research funds and collaboration between university institutions may also influence these data. It should also be noted that in different countries, the use of this tool has been banned in educational centres [25].

In relation to the methodology used in the selected articles on the impact of ChatGPT in education, a high predominance of theoretical articles stands out, as opposed to qualitative and/or quantitative studies. This may be possible because the development and implementation of artificial intelligence technologies in education, such as ChatGPT, are still at a relatively early stage, so the exploration of the possibilities and challenges presents a mainly theoretical approach before conducting empirical research [10].

Q2: What are the benefits and challenges of implementing ChatGPT in the classroom?

In an ever-changing society, technological advancement has taken on a fundamental role in our existence and, naturally, it has left its mark on the field of education. OpenAI's innovative creation, known as ChatGPT, is revolutionising the way educators and students approach the learning process in the classroom. The implementation of ChatGPT in schools brings a number of benefits and challenges that educational agents need to be aware of in order to improve the quality of education in the classroom.

Its use in the classroom is offered as a promising tool that offers multiple benefits for learning. This tool allows content and activities to be customised to the specific needs of each student, improving the effectiveness of teaching and learning. In other words, it allows students to adapt to their learning pace and provides constant support in their knowledge acquisition process.

All of this results in having more individualised and personalised learning, which leads to an improvement in motivation and commitment on the part of students, being considered as a fundamental educational support for the improvement of the teaching and learning process [6]. At the same time, ChatGPT promotes collaboration by allowing students to work together to research topics and develop communication and teamwork skills, leveraging this tool to support the educational process. ChatGPT is also an easy-to-use and accessible tool for teachers and students, allowing for quick integration into the classroom. Finally, by providing support in the generation of content and activities, ChatGPT allows teachers to focus on more important aspects of teaching, such as personalised interaction and feedback.

However, for an effective implementation of this tool, the importance of providing training appropriate to the current context is highlighted. Teachers must be provided with the necessary technological knowledge to be able to use this tool effectively in the educational environment, preventing teachers themselves from being an obstacle in the implementation of this tool. In this sense, teachers must not only learn how to use the technology itself but also understand its possibilities and limitations, as well as address the associated ethical and pedagogical challenges [10]. Along these lines, the implementation of this tool should be approached in a reflective manner to ensure a responsible classroom environment. Its use in the education system must be carefully evaluated to ensure that it is not used to that it is not used to replace these important skills [26]. However, there is a need to consider the academic misuse of ChatGPT that may be implied by using text generation technology for dishonest or unethical purposes in academia [19]. In addition, ChatGPT's knowledge is still limited and has not yet been updated with information beyond 2021 [27]. Therefore, its answers may not always be accurate or reliable, especially on specialised topics and recent events. In addition, ChatGPT may generate incorrect or even inaccurate information [28]. This situation can pose a challenge for students who rely on ChatGPT for information during their learning process. In this context, one of these specific limitations is the phenomenon known as "hallucinations". In the context of chatbots such as ChatGPT, hallucinations refer to responses that sound plausible but are incorrect or nonsensical. That is, the chatbot may generate responses that appear to be well-written and coherent but are actually erroneous or unsubstantiated information. This phenomenon can be problematic in the educational context since students could receive incorrect or confusing information, which would negatively affect their learning and understanding of the topics. This is why it is important to take these limitations into account and carefully evaluate the accuracy and reliability of the chatbot before using it as an educational tool [29].

Q3: What are the future trends and emerging research areas in the use of ChatGPT in education?

After conducting an analysis using the VOSviewer software, a bibliometric analysis was performed to visualise research trends in relation to the use of ChatGPT in education. This analysis revealed three clusters grouping the keywords present in the titles and abstracts of the studies found in the databases, allowing us to identify three main emerging research areas and the directions that the research in this field is taking.

The first is focused entirely on the role of the teacher in the educational setting driven by the use of artificial intelligence. The role of the teacher in the context of the use of artificial intelligence is crucial for improving educational practice and fostering new teaching methodologies [23]. ChatGPT is a valuable tool for trainers, providing them with a starting point for designing curricula, teaching materials and assessment activities [30].

The second line of research in the field of education focuses on the impact and use of artificial intelligence (AI) in the classroom, which has aroused great interest among educators and pedagogical experts. The incorporation of artificial intelligence as a complementary tool in the teaching–learning process has shown promise and has generated a variety of research [20]. In this context, artificial intelligence, and in particular ChatGPT, has been highlighted for its ability to improve a student's academic performance and foster the development of critical thinking. By providing quick and accurate answers to specific questions, ChatGPT facilitates access to relevant and up-to-date information, which can be particularly beneficial for students in their process of inquiry and understanding of different topics [22]. In addition, artificial intelligence adapts to each student's individual learning pace, allowing them to progress at their own pace and receive personalised support based on their needs. This not only improves student motivation and engagement but also frees up time for educators to focus on more interactive and creative tasks, such as one-to-one tutoring and constructive feedback [21]. However, it is also important to bear in mind some challenges and ethical considerations when incorporating artificial intelligence in the classroom. For example, it is essential to ensure the privacy and security of student data, as well as to assess the accuracy and reliability of the answers provided by AI to avoid the spread of erroneous or biased information [20].

The last line is closely related to the impact of artificial intelligence on teaching and learning processes, including factors such as the socioeconomic, cultural, institutional and technological environment [19]. In summary, AI technologies such as ChatGPT can help educational institutions achieve intelligent management and allocation of learning resources, improve the utilisation and effectiveness of educational resources, greatly change the shape of education quality and efficiency, provide better learning services to students and help them to better adapt to the development needs of future society.

6. Conclusions

The systematic literature review has shown that scientific research on the use of the ChatGPT tool in education is still scarce, as it turns out to be a novel tool launched in late 2022. The use of ChatGPT in education has emerged as an innovative and promising tool that seeks to enhance the learning experience and foster greater interaction between students and teachers. As its possibilities are investigated and understood, the use of ChatGPT in education reveals a significant potential to transform teaching and learning methods. In this sense, this artificial intelligence tool proves to be a motivating tool for students, by having to apply Information and Communication Technologies, and significantly improves students' academic performances, if it is used appropriately. However, it is essential to bear in mind that its use presents a series of challenges, which teachers must be aware of to avoid incorrect use. Along these lines, proper training of teachers and students can be effective to know how to use the application and avoid its misuse in the academic environment. With ethical implementation and proper supervision, this technology can open new educational possibilities and enrich the teaching and learning process.

In this sense, although artificial intelligence is not something new, the emergence of ChatGPT has generated debate in education, questioning aspects such as traditional tasks, methodology and evaluation. Therefore, it is important to continue researching the potential of these tools and their impact, considering didactic and scientific aspects, and promoting an ethical and responsible integration of artificial intelligence in education.

The main limitation of this review lies in the limited amount of literature included in the analysis. This is because, so far, not enough studies that address the specific use of ChatGPT in higher education institutions have been conducted. Educational technology, such as ChatGPT, is a constantly developing and evolving field, and its implementation in higher education may be relatively new and therefore less researched compared to other levels of education. Despite this limitation, the review provides an overview of how ChatGPT has influenced the university level. As more research is conducted and knowledge about the use of ChatGPT in higher education expands, it will be useful to expand the study to gain a more complete understanding of its impact and benefits at this specific educational level. In future studies, other databases such as ERIC or Dialnet, among others, could be included to ensure an exhaustive and comprehensive search for relevant studies.

Author Contributions: Conceptualization, M.M.-R., J.F.-C., J.M.F.-B. and E.L.-M.; data curation, M.M.-R., J.F.-C., J.M.F.-B. and E.L.-M.; formal analysis, M.M.-R., J.F.-C., J.M.F.-B. and E.L.-M.; investigation, M.M.-R., J.F.-C., J.M.F.-B. and E.L.-M.; methodology, M.M.-R., J.F.-C., J.M.F.-B. and E.L.-M.; supervision, M.M.-R., J.F.-C., J.M.F.-B. and E.L.-M.; writing—original draft, M.M.-R., J.F.-C., J.M.F.-B. and E.L.-M.; writing—review and editing, M.M.-R., J.F.-C., J.M.F.-B. and E.L.-M. All authors have read and agreed to the published version of the manuscript.

Funding: This research is part of the R&D&I project, PID2019-108230RB-I00, funded by MCIN/AEI/10.13039/501100011033.

Data Availability Statement: Not applicable.

Conflicts of Interest: The authors declare no conflict of interest.

References

1. Brazdil, P.; Jorge, A. *Progress in Artificial Intelligence: Knowledge Extraction, Multi-Agent Systems, Logic Programming, and Constraint Solving*; Springer: Berlin/Heidelberg, Germany, 2021. [CrossRef]
2. Jara, I.; Ochoa, J.; Usos Y Efectos de la Inteligencia Artificial en la Educación. Sector Social División Educación. 2021. Available online: https://ie42003cgalbarracin.edu.pe/biblioteca/LIBR-NIV331012022134652.pdf (accessed on 3 June 2023).
3. García-Peña, V.R.; Mora-Marcillo, A.B.; Ávila-Ramírez, J.A. La inteligencia artificial en la educación. *Domino De Las Cienc.* **2020**, *6*, 648–666.
4. Incio Flores, F.A.; Capuñay Sánchez, D.L.; Estela Urbina, R.O.; Valles Coral, M.A.; Vergara Medrano, S.E.; Elera Gonzáles, D.G. Inteligencia artificial en educación: Una revisión de la literatura en revistas científicas internacionales. *Apunt. Univ.* **2021**, *12*, 353–372. [CrossRef]
5. Neuman, M.; Rauschenberger, M.; Schön, E.M. "We Need To Talk About ChatGPT": The Future of AI and Higher Education. *Hochschule Hannover* **2022**, *1*, 1–4. [CrossRef]
6. García Sánchez, O.V. Uso y Percepción de ChatGPT en la Educación Superior. *Rev. De Investig. En Tecnol. De La Inf.* **2023**, *11*, 98–107. [CrossRef]
7. Osorio, J.A.C. Explorando el potencial de ChatGPT en la escritura científica: Ventajas, desafíos y precauciones. *Sci. Et Tech.* **2023**, *28*, 3–5.
8. Qadir, J. Engineering Education in the Era of ChatGPT: Promises and Pitfalls of Generative AI for Education. *TechRxiv* **2022**, *1*, 1–10. [CrossRef]
9. Wang, T.; Lund, B.D.; Marengo, A.; Pagano, A.; Mannuru, N.R.; Teel, Z.A.; Pange, J. Exploring the Potential Impact of Artificial Intelligence (AI) on International Students in Higher Education: Generative AI, Chatbots, Analytics, and International Student Success. *Appl. Sci.* **2023**, *13*, 6716. [CrossRef]
10. García Peñalvo, F.J. La percepción de la Inteligencia Artificial en contextos educativos tras el lanzamiento de ChatGPT: Disrupción o pánico. *Educ. Knowl. Soc. (EKS)* **2023**, *24*, e31279. [CrossRef]
11. Page, M.J.; McKenzie, J.E.; Bossuyt, P.M.; Boutron, I.; Hoffmann, T.C.; Mulrow, C.D.; Shamseer, L.; Tetzlaff, J.M.; Akl, E.A.; Brennan, S.E.; et al. The PRISMA 2020 statement: An updated guideline for reporting systematic reviews. *J. Clin. Epidemiol.* **2021**, *134*, 178–189. [CrossRef]
12. Aromataris, E.; Munn, Z. *JBI Manual for Evidence Synthesis*; Joanna Briggs Institute: Adelaide, Australia, 2020.
13. Fuchs, K. Exploring the opportunities and challenges of NLP models in higher education: Is Chat GPT a blessing or a curse? *Front. Educ.* **2023**, *8*, 1166682. [CrossRef]
14. Sorensen, A.; Seary, A.; Riopelle, K. Alzheimer's Disease Research: A COIN Study Using Co-authorship Network Analytics. *Procedia Soc. Behav. Sci.* **2010**, *4*, 6582–6586. [CrossRef]
15. Nandiyanto, A.B.D.; Al Husaeni, D.F. A bibliometric analysis of materials research in Indonesian journal using VOSviewer. *J. Eng. Res.* **2021**, *9*, 1–16. [CrossRef]
16. Mulyawati, I.B.; Ramadhan, D.F. Bibliometric and visualized analysis of scientific publications on geotechnics fields. *ASEAN J. Sci. Eng. Educ.* **2021**, *1*, 37–46. [CrossRef]
17. Olite, F.M.D.; Suárez, I.D.R.M.; Ledo, M.J.V. Chat GPT: Origen, evolución, retos e impactos en la educación. *Educ. Médica Super.* **2023**, *37*, e3876.
18. Halaweh, M. ChatGPT in education: Strategies for responsible implementation. *Contemp. Educ. Technol.* **2023**, *15*, 421. [CrossRef]
19. Rahman, M.M.; Watanobe, Y. ChatGPT for education and research: Opportunities, threats, and strategies. *Appl. Sci.* **2023**, *13*, 5783. [CrossRef]
20. Ausat, A.; Massang, B.; Efendi, M.; Nofirman, N.; Riady, Y. Can Chat GPT Replace the Role of the Teacher in the Classroom: A Fundamental Analysis. *J. Educ.* **2023**, *5*, 16100–16106. [CrossRef]

21. Castillo, A.G.R.; Silva, G.J.S.; Arocutipa, J.P.F.; Berríos, H.Q.; Rodríguez, M.A.M.; Reyes, G.Y.; López, H.R.P.; Reves, R.M.V.; Rivera, H.V.H.; González, J.L.A. Effect of Chat GPT on the digitized learning process of university students. *J. Namib. Studies.* **2023**, *33*, 1–15.
22. Javaid, M.; Haleem, A.; Singh, R.P.; Kahn, S.; Khan, I.H. Unlocking the opportunities through ChatGPT Tool towards ameliorating the education system. *BenchCouncil Trans. Benchmarks Stand. Eval.* **2023**, *3*, 100–115. [CrossRef]
23. Firat, M. What ChatGPT means for universities: Perceptions of scholars and students. *J. Appl. Learn. Teach.* **2023**, *6*, 57–63.
24. Fauzi, F.; Tuhuteru, L.; Sampe, F.; Ausat, A.; Hatta, H. Analysing the Role of ChatGPT in Improving Student Productivity in Higher Education. *J. Educ.* **2023**, *5*, 14886–14891. [CrossRef]
25. Strzelecki, A. To use or not to use ChatGPT in higher education? A study of students' acceptance and use of technology. *Interact. Learn. Environ.* **2023**, 1–14. [CrossRef]
26. Alonso-Arévalo, J.; Quinde-Cordero, M. ChatGPT: La creación automática de textos académicos con Inteligencia artificial y su impacto en la comunicación académica y educativa. *Desiderata* **2023**, *6*, 136–142.
27. Gilson, A.; Safranek, C.W.; Huang, T.; Socrates, V.; Chi, L.; Taylor, R.A.; Chartash, D. How does CHATGPT Perform on the United States Medical Licensing Examination? *The Implications of Large Language Models for Medical Education and Knowledge Assessment. JMIR Med. Educ.* **2023**, *9*, e45312.
28. Megahed, F.M.; Chen, Y.J.; Ferris, J.A.; Knoth, S.; Jones-Farmer, L.A. How Generative AI Models such as ChatGPT Can be (Mis)Used in SPC Practice, Education, and Research? *An Exploratory Study. arXiv* **2023**, arXiv:2302.10916. [CrossRef]
29. Rudolph, J.; Tan, S.; Shannon, T. ChatGPT: Bullshit spewer or the end of traditional assessments in higher education? *J. Appl. Learn. Teach.* **2023**, *6*, 263–343.
30. Topsakal, O.; Topsakal, E. Framework for a Foreign Language Teaching Software for Children Utilizing AR, Voicebots and ChatGPT (Large Language Models). *J. Cogn. Syst.* **2022**, *7*, 33–38. [CrossRef]

MDPI AG
Grosspeteranlage 5
4052 Basel
Switzerland
Tel.: +41 61 683 77 34

Computers Editorial Office
E-mail: computers@mdpi.com
www.mdpi.com/journal/computers

www.ingramcontent.com/pod-product-compliance
Lightning Source LLC
Chambersburg PA
CBHW061438210926
51850CB00008B/1548